Democracy
and
Development
in Mali

Democracy and Development in Mali

edited by R. James Bingen,
David Robinson, and John M. Staatz

Michigan State University Press
East Lansing

∞ The paper used in this publication meets the minimum requirements of ANSI/NISO Z39.48–1992 (R 1997) (Permanence of Paper).

Michigan State University Press
East Lansing, Michigan 48823-5202

Printed and bound in the United States of America.

07 06 05 04 03 02 01 00   1 2 3 4 5 6 7 8

LIBRARY OF CONGRESS CATALOGING-IN-PUBLICATION DATA

Democracy and development in Mali / edited by R. James Bingen, David Robinson, John M. Staatz.
     p.   cm.
Includes bibliographical references.
ISBN 0–87013–560–0 (pbk. : alk. paper)
     1. Democracy—Mali—History—20th century. 2. Mali—Politics and government—20th century. 3. Mali—Economic conditions. 4. Mali—Social conditions. I. Bingen, R. James. II. Robinson, David, 1938–   . III. Staatz, John M.

JQ3389.A91 D45 2000
966.23 21

00-010415

Cover design by Nicolette Rose
Book design by Michael J. Brooks

Visit Michigan State University Press on the World Wide Web at:
www.msu.edu/unit/msupress

CONTENTS

Economic and Agricultural Policy Reform

Political Innovation

Epilogue

Acknowledgments

The idea for this volume originated during a series of discussions in late 1997 as the editors were planning how to host President Alpha Oumar Konaré and Mme. Adame Ba Konaré on the occasion of the awarding of an honorary Doctor of Humanities degree to President Konaré from Michigan State University in May 1998. Given the Konarés' contributions to intellectual life in Mali, we felt that a volume representing twenty years of scholarly work by MSU faculty and students in Mali appropriately complemented the conferral of the honorary degree.

The intimate link between the visit of President and Mme. Konaré to MSU and the preparation of this volume, however, has exponentially expanded the list of those to whom we are deeply indebted. Those who helped make the visit a success were as important to this volume as those who were so generous with their time, financial support, and encouragement in bringing this volume to publication.

The successful visit by a visiting head of state, an accompanying official delegation, and obligatory security personnel requires a special engagement and commitment from across the university. The leadership and personal attention given by MSU President M. Peter MacPherson and Provost Lou Anna K. Simon to all of the arrangements and their enthusiasm for the special occasion were clearly evident and indispensable at every stage from the initial planning through the farewells. Equally vital to assuring the success of the Konaré visit were the time and commitment of several other university executives and administrators: Robert Huggett, Vice President for Research and Graduate Studies; Charles Greenleaf, Vice President for Special Projects; John Hudzik, Dean of International Studies and Programs; Fred Poston, Dean, College of Agriculture and Natural Resources; and David Wiley, Director, African Studies Center.

Others at MSU, who brought their experience, skills, and knowledge, and devoted countless hours to ensuring attention to the myriad of details associated with the visit by a head of state, include Nancy Pogel, Executive Assistant to the President and Secretary of the Board of Trustees; Jim Jay, Office of Minority Affairs in the College of Agriculture and Natural Resources; Dawn Pysarchik, International Studies and Programs; Sharon Noall, Board of Trustees; Ginny Haas, Governmental Affairs; Betsy White, Office of the Provost; Janet Rohler, the Graduate School; Kristin Anderson, Media Communications; Sandi Bauer, Department of Agricultural Extension and Education; and Chris Penders, Department of Agricultural Economics. In addition, we would like to thank Jim Hradsky, USAID/Bamako, and Doral Watts, USAID/Washington, for helping to keep open the lines of communication between the U.S. and Mali, and Mahamane Touré of the Malian Embassy in Washington for helping arrange the logistics of the visit.

Business leaders whose excitement, interest, and financial support helped assure that a broader community also benefited from the opportunity to meet President and Mme. Konaré include David Miller and Nicole Lescarbeau, Corporate Council on Africa; Bella Marshall, Barden International; and Frank Fountain, Vice President for Governmental Relations, Chrysler Corporation.

Finally, Ambassadors David Rawson and Cheick Oumar Diarrah deserve our very special recognition for distinguishing the event with the prestige of their offices as well as their personal engagement, and the support of their staff in coordinating the hundreds of details that such an event entailed.

Publishing guidance, financial support, and editorial skill are critical to any publication, and this volume is no exception. We gratefully acknowledge the guidance, insights, and endorsement of Fred Bohm, Director, Michigan State University Press, for making this an MSU publication of MSU scholarship.

For their extremely generous financial support which helped to make the publication of this volume possible, we owe very special thanks to: Cynthia Fridgen, Chair, Department of Resource Development; Larry Hamm, Chair, Department of Agricultural Economics; and Wendy Wilkins, Dean, College of Arts and Letters.

Our greatest gratitude and appreciation goes to our editor, Nancy Gendell. Her keen eye, much-needed (and welcome) attention to every detail, and particularly her patience in pulling each of the separately formatted chapters into a common format truly made this volume a reality.

R. James Bingen
John Staatz
David Robinson

Foreword

The invitation by the editors to write the foreword for this volume, which highlights the long commitment by Michigan State University to research in Mali, provided me with the occasion to reflect upon my own twenty-year research career on arts and culture in Mali. My professional associations with African Studies were first nurtured at Michigan State University.

When I was a master's degree student in African art history at MSU, the faculty and graduate students at the African Studies Center provided a supportive and intellectually exciting environment within which to pursue my particular interests in West African arts. Later, for my doctoral research at Indiana University, I narrowed my focus to Malian arts and culture and concentrated on the Ségou region youth masquerade.

My initial two-year study of masquerades focused on the ways troupes explore their community's place in local, regional, and national histories. Using masques, song, and dance, performers create characters that speak to people's multiple social identities as men and women who are members of local communities, ethnic groups, and citizens of the nation state. The masquerade festivals began in pre-colonial times and are still one of the most important performance events in many Ségou communities. Many older masquerades celebrate the hunter/warrior heroes of past generations; these characters remain favorites in the theaters and join with newer, more topical masquerades. The topical masquerades speak to changes in the economy, the political landscape, and family and domestic life. With the establishment of a free press in the early 1990s and the increase in radio and television transmission throughout the country, the flow of information between urban and rural areas is now more comprehensive and more immediate. People in rural communities are talking about and debating the very same issues that urbanites do. Consequently, authors, popular songwriters and singers, and rural masqueraders are all responding to many of the same political, economic, and social issues. Recent masquerades, for example, focused on issues of poverty and economic development, marriage and divorce, and governance. In the guise of play, the masquerades illustrate allegorically the complex and thorny issues facing these communities today.

The awarding in May 1998 of an honorary doctorate by Michigan State University to Dr. Alpha Oumar Konaré, archeologist and museologist and President of Mali, reminded me that over the past two decades I have received support and encouragement for my research from many Malian colleagues among whom are Drs. Alpha Oumar Konaré and Adame Ba Konaré.

In 1977, I had the pleasure of meeting Dr. Alpha Konaré in Bloomington, Indiana, when he was on an official visit to the United States as Mali's minister of Youth, Sport, Arts, and Culture. It was Thanksgiving Day and the university campus was all but deserted. Dr. Konaré's official program had finished and he was due to leave the campus the next day. My apartment-mates and I always hosted a Thanksgiving dinner for African student friends in Bloomington and we invited Dr. Konaré to attend. He graciously accepted. More than thirty people crammed into our small flat, including guests from Mali, Senegal, Gambia, Ethiopia, Malawi, Zimbabwe, Ghana, and Nigeria. One of my most vivid memories of that occasion was how Alpha enthusiastically engaged with everyone in the room. Lively conversations in French and English covered everything from economic development and future aspirations for Africa, to philosophy, politics, and culture. That afternoon I had an opportunity to discuss with Alpha my own dissertation research project on masquerade arts in Mali. His openness and interest, and his encouragement and thoughtful responses to my questions about Malian heritage, history, and culture were inspiring.

In 1978, I arrived in Mali for two years of research. While I was not often in Bamako, I did return periodically to the city to renew my research visa and occasionally ran into Alpha at the Ministry of Culture. He always asked after my project, encouraged my efforts, and made welcome and helpful suggestions on the research. Since that first study, whenever I have returned to Mali to continue arts research, stopping to talk to Alpha is always a priority. One afternoon, I popped into the Jamana office (Jamana is the cultural organization founded by Dr. Konaré) to say hello. Because he was just off to check on the progress of a favorite project—the construction of neighborhood health clinics—he took me along and we talked about my ideas for future research on Mali's youth and arts festivals. On another occasion in the late 1980s when I was in Bamako, Dr. Adame Konaré, then on the faculty of the *Ecole Normale*

Supérieure, was planning a trip to the United States to visit university African Studies programs. I was invited to a luncheon hosted by the American ambassador where the trip itinerary was being discussed. I remember Alpha turning to Adame during the luncheon and saying enthusiastically, "When you finish your official day's program in Washington, grab a taxi and go to the Library of Congress to do research; it's open until midnight!"

These anecdotes are more than simply stories about two charismatic individuals. For me they underscore Alpha and Adame's deep commitment to Mali and to international scholarly exchange. The Konarés' openness and personal support of research by Malians and foreign scholars has sustained Malian scholarship through the best and worst of times. Their example over the past decades has in very concrete ways contributed to the openness and synergy in the current research climate in Mali.

Since 1978, I have also developed important personal and professional friendships with many of the faculty and students from Michigan State University, whose works are published in this volume. We have shared information and insights with one another about our different projects in the formal settings of conferences and symposia, through reports and published works, and more informally in conversations in Mali and in the United States. Through these interactions I have come to a better understanding of the ways in which our different fields of endeavor, knowledge, and experiences significantly overlap in the larger context of Malian studies. While our disciplines and research interests are varied and might seem from an outsider's perspective to be tangential or even completely unrelated to one another, our studies are all informed by an understanding, gained on the ground in Mali, of the importance of history in everyday Malian life. Most of us, I believe, would agree with Alpha and Adame that neither idealizing the past nor assigning a sentimental value to it should be the aim of any research effort. Rather, the aim should be to understand the ways in which Mali's different pasts specifically inform people's present experience and their expectations. An understanding and analysis of these histories serve as a critical resource for informed decisions now and for the future. What the chapters in this volume make clear is that the twenty-plus years of research by MSU faculty and students have contributed in real and important ways to international scholarly exchange and to building Mali's essential resource base.

Mary Jo Arnoldi
Smithsonian Institution

Preface

In May 1998, President Alpha Oumar Konaré of Mali was granted an honorary doctorate by Michigan State University in honor of his strong commitments to democracy and human rights, and to freedom of speech and scholarship during his career as a scholar and in his presidency of Mali. On that occasion, President Konaré and the first lady of Mali, Madame Adame Ba Konaré, were invited to participate in a one-day academic symposium as a celebration of their scholarship. They accepted the invitation, and a major *Symposium on Democracy and Development in Mali* was convened. Many of the papers presented at this academic symposium are published in this volume.

African Studies and the Scholarship of Mali

This symposium in 1998 appropriately connected the Malian and American communities devoted to the study of Africa, reminding participants that the field of African studies is not new in this century. Africanists from both countries need to remember that the study of Africa began more than 2,000 years ago as geographers, philosophers, historians, and social observers from Mediterranean countries and the Middle East focused on the continent. But the second source was from Mali when, at the beginning of the second millennium, African elders, griots, and scribes south of the Sahara were mounting their own scholarship of Africa, first in oral tradition and then, by the fourteenth to sixteenth centuries, in written records.

Mali offers to the West the probable beginnings of literate studies of Africa from south of the Sahara. Long before the Western colonial authors explored Africa's cultures and histories, the scholars of Jenne had begun recording information about Africa. In the fifteenth and sixteenth centuries, African scholars in both Jenne and Timbuktu, such as the Kati family of Jenne, were gathering oral traditions and genealogies, and recording chronicles and biographies of earlier African histories of the empire of Songhay. They relied primarily on their newly found tools of written Arabic and used the more global perspective of Islam as a paradigm for their conceptualizations. This tradition spread southward and westward from Timbuktu in the seventeenth and eighteenth centuries. Like African studies in North America, the first focus was on chronicling African history, clan genealogies, biographies, and religious texts and histories.[1]

By the nineteenth century, building on these Malian initiatives, there was a flowering of African scholarship in Hausa, Kanuri, Fulfulde, and other Sahelian languages with chronicles of great cities of the region. Western European studies of Africa emerged more slowly, starting first with the Portuguese geographers and the geography of the continent and only developing after the colonial expansions of the nineteenth and twentieth centuries. By that time, a broad array of African writings already existed—about Africa and its peoples and about the foreigners who were invading. In fact, scholarship about Africa among African-American and other Western scholars came very late in the field of African studies.

This symposium reminded us that not only have African scholars and their institutions been at the center of African studies, but also that African scholarship has been resurgent in recent years in spite of the economic and political trials of the Cold War and post-Independence periods. It also put us on notice that the writing of the history of Africa in the world should be a partnership, and that Western and African scholars need each other in this enterprise. In that partnership, scholars can draw on competing models as well as on global and local contexts to portray continuities and changes. With diverse perspectives, scholars can write and criticize the histories that have shaped the structures of society on this planet we share. Such an ecumenical enterprise can be mutually enriching and will be less governed by the individual perceptions, dominating theories and traditions, and national interests that so frequently have shaped the work of the scholars.

The Scholarly and Political Commitments of the
Presidential Family of Mali

Inviting President and Mme. Konaré to the seminar was especially appropriate because both are scholars of Malian history and culture and both have completed doctoral degrees. In the 1960s, President Konaré completed his undergraduate work at the *Ecole Normale Supérieure* in Bamako, a teacher-training institution that was then the sole institution of higher education in Mali. Konaré was an active leader of student protest and of a 1969 student strike against the authoritarian military regime of Lieutenant-General Moussa Traoré, who had seized power in 1968.

President Konaré taught in the middle and high schools in Mali before going abroad to pursue his doctorate in history and archaeology at the University of Warsaw. In 1975, he completed his Ph.D. and returned to Mali and served first in the Ministry of Sports, Youth, Arts and Culture under General Traoré's military regime and from 1978 to 1980 as the head of that ministry. His many responsibilities focused on research, archaeology, and Malian history, including his position as *Chargé de recherches, à L'Institut des Sciences Humaines du Mali,* where he met many Western scholars visiting Mali.

After resigning from the government in protest over the military regime, Konaré became a private scholar and wrote widely about Mali's astonishingly rich cultural heritage—both as a professional archaeologist and as a popular writer for newspapers and magazines. From this period came a rich production of scholarship and many publications. His most recent work, *Les Partis Politiques au Mali,* is scheduled for publication.

As a public figure in Mali who identified with democracy in African governance, Konaré became the principal leader of a major pro-democracy party, the *Alliance pour la Démocratie au Mali* (ADEMA). And it was no surprise when, after the overthrow of the Traoré regime in 1991 and the opening of the political stage in Mali, he was elected president of Mali in 1992 and re-elected in 1997.

Mali, under Konaré, has maintained and broadened its democratic tradition, brought new levels of sustained economic growth, and begun to address longstanding problems that were ignored under the military regimes. The needs of the country are massive; no more than one-third of the population is literate, its GDP is one of the lowest in Africa, there is malnutrition among young people under fifteen, and perhaps only half of the population has access to clean water. Since independence, in addition to critical development problems, the government continues to deal with the social turbulence of several outbreaks of conflict between the Tuareg pastoralists and the agriculturalists of the Niger River Valley near Timbuktu.

Moreover, across Mali, there has been a tragically large plunder of the vast archaeological heritage as the rural populations, caught in poverty and the Sahelian droughts, responded to foreign demand for the pottery, iron castings, burial jars, and other rare treasures of Mali's great civilizations in the Niger River region. The written record of Mali, too, is at risk, as insufficient storage facilities leave ancient manuscripts at the mercy of the elements and insects.

Consequently, while addressing the country's immense development problems, the Konaré government is also tackling the loss of its rich antiquities to collectors from the West. Under Konaré's leadership, the government has mounted an educational campaign in towns and villages to preserve Mali's antiquities heritage, legislated prison sentences for archaeological pillage, and is teaching its peoples to appreciate the great value of Mali's contributions to African history.

Recently, President Konaré reiterated the rationale for the cultural awareness campaign even while the country faces such pressing development needs. He commented, "In Mali our greatest riches are those which have been created by man. It is important that our people understand this, to know their history and culture, and respect it, understand its place in daily life. Only by this can we guarantee the possibility of enrichment. . . . These are the only real values. The rest are perishable."[2]

Mme. Adame Ba Konaré also received her doctorate from the University of Warsaw in 1975 and began teaching at the *Ecole Normale Supérieure*. She continued to teach and maintain a productive publication program there until her husband was elected to the presidency in 1992. Mme. Konaré's special interest in the precolonial history of Mali is reflected in her many publications.

Throughout the struggle for democracy in Mali, both Konarés kept their focus on their core values of celebrating Mali's long history and actively disseminating Mali's rich traditions while maintaining their long-held commitment to democracy. The fruits of their scholarship and their politics can be esteemed by all.

MSU's Historical and Development Links to Mali

Michigan State University has a special commitment to Mali, and the MSU involvement with Mali runs deep in graduate education, research, and service. Today, Malians trained at MSU hold key positions in Mali's agricultural research organization, food policy making institutions, and central bank, among others.

Several MSU faculty—in agricultural economics, history, and resource development—have long-standing research ties in Mali on which this partnership is built.

Prof. R. James Bingen (resource development) lived in Ségou with his family in 1975-76 and conducted his original research in Mali for his book on *Food Production and Rural Development in the Sahel: The Case of Opération Riz Ségou in Mali* (Boulder: Westview Press, 1985). He also assisted in a study of Mali's livestock requirements (1975) and an agricultural sector survey

(1976). In 1991 and 1992, Bingen helped to design the Mali SPARC Project and to assess the service delivery programs in the USAID-sponsored development project in the Haute Vallée region of the country. Since the early 1990s, he has worked closely with several Malian farmer groups in the cotton sector. Bingen has written extensively on Malian agriculture and the farmers' movement. He was also a consultant on a mission of the Africa Development Bank to develop a new university in Mali.

Prof. David Robinson (history) is one of the leading experts on Malian history and culture, having studied and written on it since the 1960s. Working in French, Pulaar/Fulfulde, and Arabic, he has conducted research on the history of West Africa in Mali and Senegal. Robinson has translated and annotated important late-nineteenth-century Arabic documents from Segu and Nioro and is the author of many books and articles on Malian history and culture. Robinson and his colleague, Louis Brenner, also undertook a project to inventory a seminal Arabic library that was taken from Mali in 1890 by the conquering French. Now published as *La bibliothèque Umarienne de Ségou*, the project was supported by President Konaré.

MSU's Department of Agricultural Economics has been involved continuously in food security research, outreach, and education (both in-service training and graduate training) since 1985. Prof. John Staatz has led this team effort of many faculty members, graduate students, and Malian colleagues. The work has focused on (a) analyzing the impact of economic reforms, such as market liberalization and currency devaluation on food security and real incomes, particularly among the poor; (b) improving the efficiency of the entire food system (from seed to table); and (c) strengthening agricultural research planning. Specific areas of research and outreach have included strengthening market information systems and policy analysis capacity in Mali, improving strategic planning of agricultural research, analyzing the impact of changing institutional and legal frameworks on food production and availability, examining the role of non-farm activities in promoting food security, promoting regional trade to foster income growth and more secure food supplies, and studies of food consumption/nutrition. Staatz has worked with Malians for more than a decade, especially with Dr. Josué Dioné and Dr. Niama Nango Dembélé. Since 1985 Staatz has directed a joint Malian-MSU research project on food security in Mali and has assisted in supervising a joint initiative of MSU with the *Institut du Sahel* on regional food security issues in the Sahel. He has written widely on the economics of Malian agriculture and food security.

A number of MSU graduate students have served in Mali as Peace Corps Volunteers, conducted pre-dissertation and dissertation research there, and studied Bambara (Bamanakan) and Fula (Pulaar), two major Malian languages offered at MSU. In addition, the MSU Sahel Project and *Sahel Bibliographic Bulletin*, edited by MSU Africana Librarian Dr. Joseph Lauer, has kept many links with, and served the development needs of, Mali.

Other agricultural economics faculty involved in this long-term effort, primarily through the *Institut d'Economie Rurale*, include Rick Bernsten, Eric Crawford, Niama Nango Dembélé, Josué Dioné, Valerie Kelly, Jean-Charles LeVallée, Thomas Reardon, Allan Schmid, James Shaffer, James Tefft, Michael Weber, and Mbaye Yade. The work has been carried out collaboratively with several Malian and regional organizations, including the National Agricultural Research Institute, the national cereals market information system, and the *Institut du Sahel*. The MSU Institute of International Agriculture currently coordinates graduate training of Malian researchers from Mali's National Agricultural Research Institute. In this broader program, more than a dozen Malians have completed graduate work or shorter-term programs at MSU in conjunction with this work, especially through the Sahel Masters Training Program in 1979–80.

This enduring commitment among U.S. Africanists at MSU and elsewhere to scholarship about, and the development of, Mali provided the foundation for this seminar. It offered one more occasion for dialogue and added this volume of essays to the scholarly canon about Mali. This effort also continues to build the relatively new partnerships between the North American scholars of Africa with the scholars of Mali, who continue their centuries-old tradition of studies of the continent.

David Wiley, Professor of Sociology and Director of the
African Studies Center, January 2000

Notes

1. See I. Hrbek, "Written sources from the fifteenth century onwards," in *General History of Africa, I: Methodology and African Prehistory*, edited by J. Ki-Zerbo (Paris: UNESCO, 1981), 129–30.

2. John Balzar, "Pillaging the Past in Mali," *Los Angeles Times*, electronic edition, 11 August 1995.

Introduction

R. JAMES BINGEN, DAVID ROBINSON, JOHN M. STAATZ

A Tradition of African Studies

Most observers would agree that Michigan State University President John Hannah's response to the invitation in 1960 from his personal friend and president of Nigeria, Nnamdi Azikiwe, to help build a new University of Nigeria at Nsukka represented the real beginning of African Studies at Michigan State University. MSU faculty had been active in higher education institution-building projects in Latin America since the 1950s, but none of these compared to the depth and breadth of MSU's initial involvement in Nigeria. From 1960 through 1969, more than 140 MSU faculty worked on long- and short-term assignments to establish faculties of agriculture, business administration, education, engineering, science, social studies, law, and human medicine at Nsukka. Then, drawing in part on a grant from the Ford Foundation to enhance international development programs at MSU, for over ten years this large and diverse "Nsukka group" was instrumental in putting MSU African Studies on the map. In doing so, this group played a key role in fashioning an internationally recognized, enduring, and distinctive MSU approach to research and development work in Africa.

Prior to expanding and strengthening MSU Africanist faculty in the humanities and social sciences, this approach was honed through a regular succession of projects funded primarily by the U.S. Agency for International Development from the mid-1960s to the present day.[1] Since Nsukka, this approach has consistently involved a package approach. This package included MSU faculty and graduate students—integrated into national agencies and units and working directly with or mentoring and learning from national colleagues—plus various types of long- and short-term degree and training programs. The training programs, or capacity-building, have always been a centerpiece of MSU's approach and a key reason for the continued vitality and MSU commitment to African development. Since the mid-1960s, over 1,000 African undergraduate and graduate students have received degrees from MSU. This type of contribution to African development is one of the key reasons why African Studies at Michigan State has become one of the most comprehensive and highly ranked programs in the United States.

Since the late 1970s, the number of Africanist faculty and students over the years has expanded well beyond economics and development fields and into the humanities and social sciences. Today African Studies counts approximately 100 faculty and graduate students who pursue active research, teaching, and outreach programs in agriculture, communications, education, health, the humanities, and social sciences in over twenty-five countries. Many of these programs take place through various linkage projects and exchange relationships with the University of Zimbabwe, Addis Ababa University, the Université Cheikh Anta Diop in Dakar, and a wide range of other research and education institutions. MSU faculty maintain collaborative academic and exchange relationships with colleagues at universities and colleges in Benin, Botswana, Burkina Faso, Burundi, Ethiopia, Ghana, Kenya, Lesotho, Mali, Malawi, Rwanda, South Africa, Sudan, Tanzania, and Zambia. Moreover, MSU undergraduates have the opportunity to study at the University of Zimbabwe, and MSU leads the national Consortium for Study in Africa in order to promote and expand study opportunities in Africa. Finally, the opportunity for on-campus instruction in at least one of approximately twenty-five African languages that are taught helps to renew the cohort of scholars and professionals committed to African Studies.

With significant funding from a diverse number of public and governmental agencies (National Institutes of Health, National Endowment for the Humanities, the World Bank, the Food and Agriculture Organization, the UN Environmental Program, the Social Science Research Council) and private foundations (Rockefeller, Ford, MacArthur, Kellogg), MSU Africanist faculty and students have distinguished themselves in many areas, including:

- Historical studies of Islam in Mali and Senegal, of Haile Selassie, and of the economic role of women in southern Africa.
- Economic assessments of small-scale industry and enterprises in rural Africa.
- Food security and economic development issues in west, east, and southern Africa.

- The role that beans and cowpeas can play in improving food production, farm incomes, and infant nutrition in Nigeria, Kenya, Malawi, and Zimbabwe.
- The discovery of an "African Stonehenge" calendrical system in east Africa.
- Public policy and socioeconomic change in Malawian fishing villages, as well as work on the ecological crises of east African lakes.
- Major studies of the causes and prevention of malaria, onchocerciasis, and schistosomiasis.
- Hypertension, diet, and maternal and child health in southern Africa.
- Path-breaking political research on political transitions in Africa, including major studies on democratization in Zambia, farmer unions and professional associations in Francophone Africa, and the political implications of structural adjustment policies.
- The construction of race in the African Diaspora.
- Geographical research on dryland farming strategies to cope with food insecurity.
- Pioneering methods to improve the instruction of African languages in the United States.
- History of Art research on the influence of interactions between sub-Saharan West Africa and the Islamic Middle East and the West.
- Teacher education in Africa, higher education management, science education, educational efficiency, and training of education faculty.
- Communications and development in Nigeria, Zimbabwe, and Mozambique, as well as health communications in Kenya.

Outreach in the U.S. and in Michigan represents the third part of the MSU Africanist approach. Established in 1977, the African Studies Outreach Program now involves about eighty elementary and secondary school teachers annually through institutes, thematic seminars, in-service workshops, and cross-cultural education on Africa. The program also involves active collaboration with more than sixty post-secondary institutions, several support programs for almost forty community colleges in Michigan, and a major media program to review films and videos on Africa.

Celebrating Collaboration

Home to perhaps the most comprehensive center for African Studies in the United States, Michigan State University sought to recognize its deep ties to Africa and African development with awards of honorary doctoral degrees to

Robert Mugabe, president of Zimbabwe, in 1986 and to Alpha Oumar Konaré, president of the Republic of Mali, in 1998. While the award to President Mugabe marked the beginning of a long-term program of support and faculty development at the University of Zimbabwe, President Konaré's award symbolized a long history of MSU scholarly interest and involvement in Mali since the mid-1970s, as well as MSU's key role in educating more than twenty Malian graduate students and in strengthening Malian research and educational institutions.

Given the keen interest of both President and Mme. Konaré in the contribution of applied scholarly research and education to national development, as noted by Mary Jo Arnoldi in the foreword to this volume, MSU arranged a special "Symposium on Democracy and Development in Mali" during the Konarés' 1998 visit to MSU.

Hosted by MSU President M. Peter McPherson, Provost Lou Anna K. Simon, Dean John Hudzik, and the U.S. ambassador to Mali, David Rawson, the symposium included major presentations by President Konaré and Mme. Adame Ba Konaré on topics of education, democracy, and development (see her chapter in this volume). Following these presentations, invited scholars of Malian history, society, economics, and politics from across the United States offered their perspectives on Malian history and culture, economic and agricultural policy reform, and political innovation.[2]

Democracy and Development in Mali

Over the past twenty-five years, the scholarly research and applied development work of MSU faculty and current and former students in Mali represent the most significant, combined, long-term, and continuing contribution of any group of university faculty in the United States and Europe to the study of Malian society, economy, and politics. The applied nature of this work has resulted in a significant number of working papers, reports, and conference presentations. Consequently, the acceptance by President Alpha Oumar Konaré of the award of an honorary doctor of philosophy in May 1998, and the "Symposium on Democracy and Development in Mali," offered an excellent incentive and opportunity to bring together this work by MSU-trained scholars in a volume published by the MSU Press.

We believe this volume should appeal to a broad range of Africanist scholars in several disciplines, including history, economics, and political science, as well as those in various professional areas such as education and communications. Moreover, we believe these collected essays—only a few of which have been previously published—should attract the attention of scholars and development specialists in the U.S., Europe, and Africa who have specific interests in political and economic development and reform, democratization, and agricultural policy.

Given the internationally recognized scholarly and development work of MSU faculty and students, the volume offers an excellent resource for research as well as for university courses in African politics and development, economic development, agricultural policy and development, and comparative politics, as well as contemporary African history. Moreover, development practitioners and specialists in governmental, non-governmental and international agencies should find this combination of essays to be an excellent source of background information on democracy and development in Mali, but a source with wider applicability in sub-Saharan Africa.

With the exception of the invited chapters by Mme. Konaré and Ambassadors David Rawson and Cheick Oumar Diarrah, all of the chapters in this volume are the result of scholarly research and development work by MSU faculty or current and former graduate students. This work is presented in three sections: Cultural and Historical Setting, Economic and Agricultural Policy Reform, and Political Innovation. The chapters in the first section are significantly revised and updated versions of previously published articles. All of the other chapters are adapted from unpublished working papers or conference presentations or were written specifically for this volume.

Notes

1. A selected list includes Consortium for the Study of Nigerian Rural Development (CSNRD): 1965–71; Rural Employment in Tropical Africa: 1971–7; Poor Rural Households: 1976–9; Sahel Master's Degree Training: 1976–85; Sahel Secretariat and Documentation Center: 1976–85; Alternative Rural Development Strategies: 1977–85; Eastern ORD-Integrated Rural Development (Burkina Faso): 1977–81; Off-Farm Employment: 1977–83; Senegal Agricultural Research and Planning Project: 1981–9; University of Zimbabwe Faculty Expansion & Zimbabwe Linkages Grant: 1983–9; Mali Strengthening Research Planning and Research on Commodities Project (SPARC): 1991–6; Food Security in Africa Cooperative Agreement: 1985–94; Food Security in Africa II Cooperative Agreement: 1994–present.

2. Presentations and presenters at the symposium included the following: *Perspectives on History and Culture*—David Robinson, MSU; David Conrad, SUNY-Oswego; Maria Grosz-Ngaté, University of Florida; John Hanson, University of Indiana; Cherif Kéita, Carleton College; and Rod McIntosh, Rice University; *Perspectives on Economic and Agricultural Policy Reform*—John Staatz, MSU; Josué Dioné, African Development Bank; and Niama Nango Dembélé, MSU; *Perspectives on Political Innovation*—James Bingen, MSU; Ambassador David Rawson; Barbara Lewis, Rutgers; Andrew Clark,

University of North Carolina-Wilmington; Kassim Koné, SUNY-Cortland; and Nancy Mezey, MSU.

Cultural and Historical Setting

Overview of the Section on Cultural and Historical Contributions

DAVID ROBINSON

Mali arguably has the richest cultural heritage of all of the nation states of West Africa. The explanation is both simple and complex. The simple reason is the state of Old Mali, based in the Niger River valley. Starting as a chiefdom, expanding to a kingdom, and becoming an empire under the leadership of Sunjata Kéita, Mali was the dominant force in much of the West African savanna from about 1200 to 1400 CE. It controlled a vast amount of territory, extending into today's Côte d'Ivoire and Guinea in the south, Burkina Faso and Niger in the east, and Senegambia and Mauritania in the west. Its reach extended even further, through the state-licensed traders who plied long-distance routes across the different ecological zones and through settlers who went far and wide into those same zones. They took their languages, Malinke and other Mande languages, and they took a social hierarchy in which key artisan skills—metal working, leather working, wood working, weaving and dyeing, music-making, and historical chronicle—were allocated and transmitted by endogamous groups.[1] These "castes," as they are often called, are found across a whole range of societies in the western portions of West Africa today. Many of the musical and dance traditions that are enacted by national troupes owe their inspiration to the Old Mali heartland, which corresponds to the demographic center of Mali today.

There are also older and more complex reasons for Mali's centrality that go back to the attraction of the same Niger River and especially its middle valley. Archeological excavations have taken the history of urban and proto-urban development in this zone back 2,000 years and more. Rod and Susan McIntosh have led these excavations, and their work around the city of Jenne has made this ancient heritage known. We can see that the rich flood plain, the wealth in fish and minerals, and other factors have been drawing people into this area for two millennia. These population concentrations help explain much of the later state and urban formation in the area—Old Ghana, the Sosso state destroyed by Sunjata, Songhay, and Old Mali, as well as Timbuktu, the famed city of scholars and merchants.

Much of this history remains to be explored, but the material and human resources for carrying it out are extremely limited. Since Mali's independence in 1960, Malian and expatriate scholars have worked together to search, gather, and write up the story. Faculty and students from the *Ecole Normale Supérieure* provided much of the momentum, often collaborating with foreign researchers affiliated with the *Institut des Sciences Humaines*. President Konaré, who served successively as the *directeur du Patrimoine National* and minister of Culture, Youth, Sports, and Arts, played a pivotal role in this collaboration. His wife, Adame Ba Konaré, a key faculty member at the *Ecole Normale*, wrote invaluable works on Songhay, Old Mali, and the more modern state of Segu, and inspired a generation of students. Her essay in this volume shows how inextricably entwined is the relation between present-day Malian politics and the heritage of many centuries.

In the 1990s this widespread interest in Mali and the cultural diffusion from the Niger River valley has spawned a very active association of teachers and scholars called MANSA: the Mande Studies Association. With membership in countries on four continents, MANSA has become arguably the most successful of the regional cultural associations of Africa. It has held meetings in Bamako, Banjul, Leiden, and other cities on an almost annual basis. MANSA quickly endorsed Michigan State University's move to confer the doctoral degree on President Konaré in 1998, and several of its key leaders—David Conrad, Rod McIntosh, and Cherif Kéita—came to East Lansing for the event.

Michigan State University has been an important center for studies on the culture and history of Mali. A number of Malian students have received degrees at MSU and provided language instruction in Bambara and Malinke to their American counterparts. Pulaar or Fulfulde has been an even more important language of instruction at the university, and some of it has involved the Masina dialect spoken in the Middle Niger. Recently Don Osborn, David Dwyer and Joseph Donohoe have published an important resource for the study of Masinanke Fulfulde—*A Fulfulde (Maasina)-English-French Lexicon: A Root-Based Compilation Drawn from Extant Sources Followed by English-Fulfulde and French-Fulfulde Listings* (East Lansing: Michigan State University Press, 1993).

MSU scholars have made important contributions to the study of Mali, especially those cultures stretching from the Middle Niger to the border with

Senegal. In this section we have featured several of these articles; each one is a revised version of an article or chapter already published.

The first and framing article in this section, "Perspectives on History and Culture," comes appropriately from Professor Adame Ba Konaré. In the presentation that she made at the MSU symposium on 9 May 1998, and subsequently revised for this publication, Professor Konaré reveals how the history of Mali, and especially of Old Mali, comes alive in the contemporary republic and in the public personas of its political leaders. She shows how history, whether presented by the "traditional" historians (*griots*), politicians, or the common people, is constantly reconstructed for "presentist" needs, and the ways in which the dramatis personae of the Sunjata story in particular are used to symbolize appropriate values for women and men in contemporary Malian society. She calls for a de-politicization of history, for forgetting as well as selectively remembering, and thereby for the forging of a new future for the country.

John Hanson's "generational conflict" features the region of Karta or northwestern Mali and is set in the late nineteenth century. Hanson prepared his dissertation under the direction of David Robinson, who at the time was preparing a long study of a Muslim holy war set in the mid-nineteenth century.[2] Al-Hajj Umar of Senegal, a scholar, pilgrim, and military leader, led a series of successful campaigns against societies of western Mali that he labeled as "pagan." Umar succeeded in most of his military endeavors and also in a project of settlement, which brought in many Senegalese Muslims to the newly conquered areas. The greatest number settled in Karta, the region that became the focus of Hanson's dissertation and his first monograph, *Migration, Jihad and Muslim Authority in West Africa: the Futanke Colonies in Karta* (Bloomington: Indiana University Press, 1996).

In the article in this volume, Hanson shows the Umarian contribution to the political economy of the region after the holy war. The early settlers participated in the gum trade centered on Medine, the uppermost port on the Senegal River reached by boats operating out of the French commercial and political center of St. Louis. At a slightly later date the Umarian settlers began to produce considerable quantities of grain—millet and sorghum—and to export the surplus to Medine. Much of the grain production depended upon the slaves acquired by these settlers in the Umarian military campaigns. This commercial and agricultural activity made the earlier settlers more "conservative" when confronted by a younger generation of migrants from Senegal. The new recruits of the 1880s were eager to wage war and make their own fortunes, while the settlers put their priority upon maintaining peace and stability in the Kartan political economy.

David Robinson has written on the role played by three Frenchmen in the creation of the modern day states of Senegal, Mali, and Mauritania. One of them, Colonel Louis Archinard, carved much of the core of the French Soudan out of the territories controlled by Al-Hajj Umar and his successors. Working out of a base in Senegal, Archinard manipulated the colonial troops, the new technologies, and the channels of information to gain a virtual free hand in the late 1880s and early 1890s. Almost single-handedly he made the Umarians into a great military threat and secured new supplies and reinforcements from France—over the objections of other local French authorities. In 1893, Archinard's duplicity and manipulation finally caught up with him and forced his transfer back to the métropole. His influence remained very strong in Mali, however, primarily in the form of his military subordinates who were active in the conquest of the rest of the region, which came to be known as French Soudan. Robinson's article testifies to the enduring role of human agency in history.

The next two articles fall squarely within the twentieth-century history of Mali, which is ordinarily divided into the colonial period—when the French called this area Soudan—and independence, which began in 1960 under the leadership of Modibo Kéita. Moussa Traoré overthrew the Kéita regime in 1968 and created a military dictatorship that survived until 1991. At that point some military officers, under Lt.-Colonel Amadou Toumani Touré, intervened, arrested Traoré, and oversaw the process of democratization, which resulted in the election of Alpha Oumar Konaré as president of a new democratic regime in the country.[3]

In "Unraveling a Neglected Report," Ghislaine Lydon, a graduate student writing up her dissertation on long-distance trade networks in northwestern Africa, has contributed significantly to understanding the forces operating in France and the French colonies during the short rule of the *Front Populaire* of Leon Blum (1936–8). This more progressive regime, concerned about the impact of the Depression and spurred on by women's groups and the Catholic Church, instituted a number of short-lived reforms in the Federation of French West Africa. Lydon deals with one initiative, the mission of Denise Moran Savineau to determine the conditions of women, children, and labor in the eight territories of the Federation. Moran, in more than 1,000 pages of careful reporting, documents the conditions under which women and children were working, living, and gaining access to Western courts, health care, and education. She was able to get beyond the colonial apparatus and gain access to African sources, women as well as men, and she does not flinch from showing the elements of force, approaching conditions of slavery, that were common in the colonial system. Moran was particularly critical of the *Office du Niger,* an area of the Middle Niger region that the French intended as the model of cotton and food production for the entire Soudan and even the Federation as a whole. Lydon brings this remarkable study of Moran to light and shows its importance for scholars assessing the shape of colonial rule and the situation of women and families.

In her article on labor migration, Maria Grosz-Ngaté develops her field work experiences of the 1980s in the village of Sana, not far from Ségou and Sansanding in the Middle Niger. Through interviews and comparative anthropological and historical studies, she is able to delineate the shifting patterns of labor migration for men and women. Over the colonial and independence periods, the migration of younger men, especially to the capital of Bamako, has become quite general among the households of Sana, but it has not necessarily weakened the ties between those who go and those who stay. Indeed, most migrants make significant contributions to family income and property, and their village identity remains important in the urban setting even when their migration becomes virtually permanent. The migration of younger women was a later and more problematic development, tolerated initially as a way to accumulate wedding goods; it was subjected to much greater constraints by elders, mothers, and the village itself, because it seemed to threaten—in the form of the greater autonomy of the migrant women themselves—the established constructions of relations between men and women. Through her nuanced analysis, Grosz-Ngaté is able to show not only the conflicts across gender and generational lines, and between individual and collective rights, but also the persistence of strong ties of common identity.

Notes

1. See Tal Tamari, *Les castes de l'Afrique occidentale: artisans et musiciens endogames* (Nanterre: Société d'ethnologie, 1997).

2. *The Holy War of Umar Tal: the Western Sudan in the Mid-Nineteenth Century* (Oxford: Clarendon, 1985).

3. See Andrew Clark's article in this volume.

Perspectives on History and Culture: The Case of Mali

ADAME BA KONARÉ

translated by *David Robinson*

*Presentation made to the "Symposium on Democracy and Development in Mali," orga-
nized on the occasion of the visit of President Alpha Oumar Konaré and Mme. Adame
Ba Konaré to Michigan State University, 9 May 1998*

Perspectives on history and culture: here is a subject which arouses vigorous debate among historians. This is because the relation between history
and culture is so vital to the life of human communities. To take the case of
Mali, it is said that the country is one of a great culture which draws its savor
from a glorious past, a rich and fecund history whose golden age is situated in
the time of the great medieval empires (eleventh to sixteenth centuries). To
hear Malians talk, you would think that this is their only point of reference.
How did we get to this point?

In fact, Malian culture is diverse and plural. Each ethnic group in Mali has
its own cultural identity. But it is also true that there is a common denominator to all of these cultures, a denominator strengthened by a long history of
cohabitation, conflict, and exchanges of all sorts—matrimonial, commercial,
or simply that of neighbors. This history has forged what we can call a veritable Malian identity of common characteristics and values that are internalized
and shared. Typical Malians are people who are proud of their past, who cultivate a sense of honor and dignity, and who derive many of their values from
their ancestors. They are also typically hospitable, warm, and generous. But
what is of interest in this reflection is the analysis of the process of development of an ideology that is both nationalist and progressive. In a way, it is a
matter of seeing how history is remembered by Malians today and how this
memory influences their culture.

Traditional Historiography and Culture

In the traditional conceptions of history, genealogy, and eulogy, history is neither a succession of dated facts nor an accumulation of chronological strata, but a site of integration of events that have marked the collective memory. Yesterday and today are blended together. This reductionist vision creates shortcuts and confluences in which the heroes of today and yesterday become one and the same person: heroes are personages frozen in time, they are timeless. Their names are recited for a present purpose, to permit their descendants to examine themselves and find their image embellished by the past. This history has thereby a distinctly utilitarian function. It is conceived in the first place to please the descendants. It is they, not the dead, who inspire the griots in their work. "Since the beginning of time one recites the names of the dead to dry the tears of the living; your ancestors are older than you but are not any more worthy than you," declaims the Malian genealogist Jeli Baba Sissoko in a typical recitation.

In this enterprise, the genealogist makes a selection, a "triage." What is forgotten and what is remembered is often deliberate. The narrative is elaborated in relation to the material environment surrounding the teller and the socio-cultural codes of the time, but it is also linked directly to political contingencies. It is not by accident that Sunjata has become the leading hero of independent Mali; he was associated with President Modibo Kéita, the father of Malian independence. Afterwards it was the turn of Tiramagan Traoré, who shares the same patronymic with President Moussa Traoré. Today we have come back to Sunjata. The Peul also have their place, because I, Adame Ba, am the wife of President Konaré; each time I appear, the songs of the Peul are recited loudly with the virtues that are supposed to be theirs—essentially modesty and bravery.

But one can say that these stories have a sub-text of contestation. Incompetent, cruel, and bloodthirsty types are deliberately forgotten. Facts about them are pushed aside so as not to obstruct the collective memory. But they remain present in the background; they are recited in the wings and, in case of need, can be brought to center stage to remind the living of the right course of action.

This dynamic and forceful conception of history is a great challenge to the practice of history as the science of a singular past that will not be reproduced. In fact, history is never over because the portraits of the heroes are never finished, their destinies are never definitive because they continue to play important roles and these roles are modified bit by bit in the changing context of the present. The exploits of the heroes are at one and the same time their own, those of those descendants, and those of their ethnic group, a continuous fluctuation between the past of some and the present and future of others, hence the anachronisms and telescoping in time. For example, Sunjata is himself, but his events and gestures are also those of his descendants or those who are supposed to be his descendants, such as Modibo Kéita, current-Prime Minister Ibrahim Boubakar Kéita, or President Alpha Oumar Konaré.

In the last analysis, if this conception involves a larger conception of history, it does not always encourage the establishment of historical truth. But it does broaden the domain of historical research. The event becomes less determinative than the way in which it is remembered and transmitted. This conception is very much in tune with the modern conception of Malian history.

Modern Malian History and the Birth of Nationalism

Malian historiography, indeed African historiography, cannot be understood outside of the colonial domination from which it came and in relation to which it is defined. French colonialism, in approaching the history of African people, had as its principal objective to transform the barbarous and bloody past of Africans to the current benevolence. The history of French penetration was depicted as beautiful and glorious and contrasted with the history of Africans, which was called only a story of vultures and grain-eating birds, a history driven by barbarous and bloodthirsty chiefs with a thirst for razzia and plunder, always ready to violate treaties.

In reaction to this ideology, the new leaders of Mali immediately after independence—in 1962—launched a program of pedagogical reform. The principal goal was to reverse the colonial hagiography and to rehabilitate our heroes and pre-colonial states. History was to be conceived as a "History Response." The political leadership knew the overwhelming importance of correcting history and entrusted the task to the historians. But these historians were formed in the old colonial school and had no sources other than the oral traditions of the griots and, to a lesser degree, the traditions of the marabouts. Moreover, the social and cultural commission charged with the history programs was directed not by a historian but by a political figure, Mamadou Madéra Kéita, then-Minister of the Interior. The politicians imposed their dictate on the historians, and the result was that history became a part of the overall nationalist project.

The ludicrous nationalism of the colonizer was now substituted by another nationalism. History became a narrative without objectivity, teleological and biased, mixed with civic education as it had been in the days of colonialism. Rapidly we fell into the excessive rehabilitation of our heroes, from Sunjata to Babemba—without forgetting Askia Mohamed, Biton Coulibaly, El Hadj Omar, and Firhoun—and into the exaltation of our pre-colonial states: Ghana, Mali, and Songhay. The historians offered grist for the mill of reminiscence of the political leadership and the society in general. Our ancestors could be compared to Alexander the Great or Napoleon. Their blemishes were transformed into positive qualities, provided they were located in that vast period before the colonial period, which in fact goes back to the beginning of time, and they were absolved of all sin. Their crimes and weaknesses mattered very little, as long as they lived in pre-colonial times; their conflicts with their subjects were secondary, forgotten or without interest, in comparison to the colonial shock.

We can thus say that historians fell into a trap. Perhaps the trap was inevitable, perhaps not. But this official history, directed from above and without nuance, became a true prison almost everywhere in Africa. It could not be corrected in public or even in private. When it came to the heroes, a critic ran the risk of offense, even blasphemy in relation to the warrior heroes of the past. The problem is even more complicated in Mali where it is difficult to develop an objective history when the descendants of the heroes are still alive, jealous of what they consider to be their family heritage, and sensitive to the honor due to their ancestors. Modern historians, prisoners of this trap of memory, have become extremely prudent.

The personalities who are stigmatized are those who are found at the frontier between myth and history. They have been frozen in time, they are no longer flesh and bone, even if historians discover that they really existed. This arrangement allows them to be manipulated, their mistakes to be castigated, their contestations with their subjects to be solved—contestations generally hushed up, and in general for a critique to be developed—in contrast to the heroes already cited. One of those stigmatized personalities seems to me to be Da Monzon Diarra of Segu.

The Rapport between Culture and History

The history of praise, recited by the genealogists, has a direct influence on behavior; it is alive, warm, and affecting. Mali is certainly a country with a rich history, but more than that history, it is memory that marks its culture. In fact, our ancestors invented everything, changed everything; they traced a path that their descendants had to follow. They incarnated noble virtues such as bravery, fearlessness, modesty, righteousness, generosity. It is culture that reconfigures history, which establishes the parameters by which history is read. The deeds of Sunjata furnish a marvelous example: more than lived history, these deeds are cultural ingredients defined for all time.

Let us take the actors involved these deeds. Everything coalesces around the cultural values dear to the Malinke and Bamana. The mother of Sunjata first: Sogolon reflects the image of the ideal woman for the Malinke. Made into a martyr by her co-wife, despised by her husband, she nonetheless remains a good person, submissive, devout, and especially enduring because, according to Malinke values, it is her capacity to accept social injustice and to endure the vicissitudes of marriage that forge the destiny of her son. For Malinke, the name comes from the father, but the blessing and mystical force come from the mother. This is the reason why the father of Sunjata is relatively unimportant in the story, he is only the progenitor.

The antithesis of Sogolon is her co-wife, Sassouma Bérété, stepmother of our hero: wicked, arrogant, full of intrigue, and manipulating the blood relations and links between her son Dankaran Touman and his unfortunate and infirm stepbrother, Sunjata. She pushes her son to despise Sunjata. Because of Sassouma Bérété's wickedness, Sunjata, his mother, brothers, and sisters are obliged to leave their country. Her behavior will also determine the destiny of her own son, who will pay for the wickedness of his mother; Dankaran Touman will experience the stereotyped destiny of children of "bad mothers" in Malinke society—downfall and decrepitude.

Sunjata's sister, Nana Triban, is another important figure in Malinke society. Tradition tells us that, after weaving a spell over Soumangourou Kanté, Nana Triban succeeds in extracting his magic secret, the spur of the rooster. It is only after this magical exploit that Sunjata can win the battle of Krina. We must understand that the Malinke believe that no victory can be won without supernatural intervention: overcoming the power of Soumangourou requires magical intervention. The intercession of a young woman at this point recalls Malinke values. It is believed that all great power comes to an end by the action of women. These are women who are young and beautiful, companions in pleasure, but who are also dangerous—they cannot be entrusted with secrets and must be carefully watched by those in positions of power. But Nana Triban is also the symbol of the triumph of blood ties so dear to the Malinke.

Finally there is Sunjata himself, terribly handicapped, who learns to walk after seven or seventeen years—depending on the sources, the period is unimportant. What is important is to prove that man must never despise his neighbor, even when he finds his neighbor in adversity, because no one can know the future that may be reserved for him. The handicapped of yesterday may be the blessed of tomorrow.

Sunjata also symbolizes the recompense accorded by nature to the child who is aware of the sacred character of blood relations, which he respects despite the wicked ways and obstacles erected by his unworthy brother, Dankaran Touman. Sunjata also represents the triumph of humility over the arrogance, self-conceit, and excess incarnated by Soumangourou Kanté.

The epic of Sunjata conforms to a strong Malinke logic of predestination. Sunjata is above all the accomplishment of a great destiny, that of *nankaman*, the predestined, the favorite protected by the gods, against whom no spell can succeed. His life has been framed and ordained by this determinism.

•If Sunjata had not been paralyzed, Soumangourou would have spared him;
•If his stepmother and older brother had protected the family unit, Sunjata would not have gone into exile;
•If he had not gone into exile, Sunjata might never have known the great destiny that became his.

In such a framework, it is useless to blame Sassouma and her son, since all was determined in advance. Without their behavior, never would the destiny of Sunjata, the predestined, have been accomplished. One could continue on and on. In summary, if all of the personages of the Sunjata story had not existed, it would have been necessary to create them. These are also the traumatic events that affect the collective memory to the greatest extent. There is a veritable fear of the past; every act that is inscribed in the framework or the re-awakening of these traumatisms is condemned along with its author. Excess, in deeds as well as language, is forbidden. Moussa Traoré, the former president of Mali, committed a fatal mistake when, on the day of celebration of the New Year, he publicly declared in the presence of all the distinguished people of the country that he would bring hell down on the head of his opponents.

The current president of Mali, a man of cultivation and former Minister of Culture, based his electoral campaign on a judicious exploitation of this culture. In particular, he made the electorate more keenly aware of the traditional key concepts: humility, tolerance, patience, solidarity, abnegation. He went so far as to implore the grace of God to give power to the one whom He believed the most apt to lead Mali in the interest of the prosperity of its citizens. The president reversed the traditional pattern of behavior of the powerful: he visited the villagers in their homes, ate by hand from the common dish, and honored the eminent citizens of the capital by visits and recognition of their roles as traditional chiefs. When his opponents insulted him and burned his house, he smiled, imperturbable, and said, adopting the local adage: "No one will tell me that, no one will do that to me, that one will not become our guide."

This discourse and behavior were innovative, indeed revolutionary. They contrasted with the comportment of all those who had held power until then. Finally, a chief did not worry, indeed, he reassured people. Finally, the men of yesterday—concerned about the prosperity of their people, humble, generous, and patient—find themselves reincarnated in their descendants. The president kept hidden his own princely origins. His mother is a direct descendant of the kings of Khasso, whose founding ancestor is greeted by the unflattering title of "king who tears the mouth and cuts off the ears of his opponents"; the president is from a lineage that is proud and combative. In summary, we can say that the relation of Malians with history is both active and emotional.

Malians and Historical Memory

Events are never entirely forgotten. Rather they are placed somewhere in memory and come to the surface in certain circumstances. They are not detached from the present and are never completely buried. One can pretend to forget but in fact one forgets nothing and wishes to forget nothing. The settlement of scores has always been present in history, which becomes a succession of struggles. History sharpens distrust. Recent political history in Mali gives some examples: when the electoral campaigns began with diatribe and invective, some saw there a re-emergence of the struggle that arrayed the leaders of the RDA against those of the PSP in the last hours of the colonial regime. When the descendants are anxious that their behavior is being judged in the light of old family atavisms of their ancestors, the fusion of present and past is quickly assumed and provides a pretext for distrust, and this is quickly exacerbated into distortion. The senses are alerted, the alarm is sounded. People go searching in history to find, even in the family genes, acts attributed to distant ancestors, the reasons for distrust and fear. The dead are more haunting than the living. People are quick to invoke the struggles that were poorly managed in the past.

The elders are so conscious of these mutations of the crimes of ancestors into blemishes of character in their descendants in the collective memory that they constantly urge, at every act, to pay attention to *ko kuma* (in Malinke and Bamana), that is, to the word that is spoken behind our back and after we have left.

Perspectives on History and Culture

One can say that the historical memory retained by Malians permits them to hold their heads high in front of other people, to give themselves the stature of a nation worthy of respect. History as it has been recorded for them has given them ammunition. From the matrimonial alliances of their ancestors and the rivalries that opposed them, Malians have developed a space of sociability and fraternity, often invoking the extraordinary system of *senankua*, the "joking relationship." After confrontation, after both sides judge the parties in presence and learn to respect each other, they become joking cousins who can say everything and tolerate everything of each other—a kind of Malian, indeed African, non-aggression pact. One can even negotiate with nature through the system of totems or taboos, whereby one is forbidden to kill or consume the meat of an animal that is judged to have performed a service for a certain family or clan at a moment of its history. All of these elements, internalized in the collective memory, are brought to the surface and invoked to protect Mali from ethnic conflict.

All the same, the perspectives on history and culture should tend to separate the present from the past and direct our regard to the future, to tackle the problems of our daily life. In a word, we have to come to terms with ourselves. Undoubtedly we must be interested in the past in order to draw lessons from it, especially the recent past when it is linked to tragic events whose victims and perpetrators are still alive. But it is in forgetting that one builds, not in fulminating and ruminating about the past. The perpetual agitation of the past and its heroes does not permit us to move forward; rather, it leads to the hardening of positions around values that are undoubtedly shared but which belong to another era. Too much remembering can become an obstacle.

These persistent values are not useful for mobilization because they are rooted in an undefined past, the period of the ancestors in which, conspicuously, the youth are not found. Indeed this kind of history hurts the younger generation by its peremptory and moralizing tone. The crisis of identity that we deplore can be explained by this failure. Is not the constant whipping up of the past a significant sign of weakness, of breakdown, or intellectual laziness? To say that our ancestors invented everything, is this not a confession of failure? What we need is a veritable social project, innovative, rigorously oriented toward the values that belong to our present and point toward our future. These values certainly include solidarity and sharing, justice, integrity, and tolerance. The struggle for us is a task of generating, but a task of generation which our capacity should permit us to bring about.

"French Africans"—Faidherbe, Archinard, and Coppolani: The "Creators" of Senegal, Soudan, and Mauritania

DAVID ROBINSON

In late 1944 French intellectuals began to think of the role that the "Empire" had played in the liberation of France and in the life of the nation generally. Robert Delavignette, a former colonial official and head of the colonial training school,[1] and Charles-André Julien, an emerging historian of Algeria, in *Les constructeurs de la France d'Outre-Mer*,[2] commemorated the debt to the colonies by publishing the main "action" texts written by the pioneers of the Second Empire.

The Second Empire began, it is usually assumed, with the conquest of the Algerian coast in 1830. Thomas Bugeaud, one of the *constructeurs*, played a leading role in the expansion of the French coastal enclave in the 1840s and put his mark on the character of colonial administration.[3] The next significant step in the story of the Second Empire was expansion into Senegal in the 1850s, where the chief architect was another *constructeur*, Leon Louis César Faidherbe. Faidherbe established the outlines of both the French territory of Senegal and crucial elements of what became French West Africa. He ran a forceful, sometimes brutal, administration, possessed a useful knowledge of indigenous societies and their weaknesses, and demonstrated a capacity for manipulating information to advantage for metropolitan consumption.

This paper deals with Faidherbe and two other Frenchmen who can be classified as *constructeurs* for West Africa: Louis Archinard and Xavier Coppolani. The three men were the architects, respectively, of Senegal, Soudan (Mali), and Mauritania. In imperial circles they were all *africains*. They had no intention of settling or retiring in Africa; they were "African" in the same way that they were "imperialists," part of a closed system whose members lived in cycles of going out to the colonies and returning to the metropole. Faidherbe was first an *algérien* and then a *sénégalais*; he was also a *mauritanien* and *soudanais* by vision, and he followed expansion to the

Niger in the 1880s with great interest. Archinard was the archetypical
soudanais and the leader of the clique that lobbied for *soudanais* interests in
Paris, when he was not on the ground in West Africa.[4] Coppolani was a
Corsican who became *algérien* in his formative years, used his Algerian
Islamic expertise to become a *soudanais*, and then became the *mauritanien*
who would "pacify" the last big block of French West Africa. His career was
cut short by assassination in 1905, but his imprint on "his" territory remained
every bit as great as Faidherbe's and Archinard's on theirs.

These men left their mark on the land, peoples, and institutions of West
Africa to a remarkable degree. In part this was due to French military superiority and the confidence borne of a sense of intellectual and cultural superiority over African societies. In part it was due to the extraordinary energy,
efficiency, and ambition of the individuals, and the fact that each operated on
the frontier of French expansion at a given moment. But they were also successful because the French regime did not pay careful attention to their arena
of activity. Where cabinets and citizens might watch closely over the
Mediterranean theater, they paid much less attention to what was going on in
West Africa. These activities fell under the less prestigious Ministry of the
Navy and Colonies,[5] and under the specific supervision of the even less prestigious *infanterie de marine*, *artillerie de marine*, and *troupes coloniales*.
Under these conditions ambitious men could create a legacy for themselves.

Faidherbe, Archinard, and Coppolani "constructed" their territories when
they were in the prime of life, in their thirties, and ambitious for further
achievement. None were distinguished students, but they distinguished themselves by their subsequent actions and, in the case of Faidherbe and Coppolani,
by their scholarly writings. Each knew well the requirements for metropolitan
support of a local agenda, and took advantage of that knowledge and of annual
furloughs to manipulate the understanding of key officials. Each had a trusted
team of collaborators who left their own mark on the territories and in many
cases stayed on after the *constructeur* had left.

The story of the three men and their "constructions" is ultimately about
the political culture of French colonialism. As African history has emerged as
a field of research and teaching over the last forty years, scholars and general-
ists have sought to remedy the weakness of the African perspective in the pre-
colonial and colonial histories of the continent. In the process, the distinctions
among European initiatives, the variations in time, the conflicts among depart-
ments, and the impact of individual personalities have been neglected. For
French rule in West Africa, this neglect has continued, with the exception of a
few scholars such as Sydney Kanya-Forstner and Yves Person.[6]

Faidherbe and the "Creation of Senegal"

Of the three men in question, Leon Louis César Faidherbe (1818–1889) is by far the most well known.[7] He is prominent because he stands at the beginning of the French empire in West Africa, remained an articulate and influential "republican" exponent of expansion for the rest of his life, and—in contrast to some of his fellow generals—played a respectable if not heroic role in the Franco-Prussian War.

Faidherbe got his training as engineer at the *École Polytechnique* and the Metz Engineering Corps. He spent six years in Algeria sandwiched around a period of service in Guadeloupe; his first assignment in Algeria corresponded to the tenure of Bugeaud. The Algerian experience gave him exposure to the Arabic language, Islamic societies, hard and harsh military campaigns, and the institution of *bureaux arabes*, all of which would play a large role in his approach to Senegal. His stay in Guadeloupe corresponded to the abolition of slavery in the empire (1848), and his declarations against slavery have become part of his image in French texts.[8]

In 1852 Faidherbe arrived in Saint-Louis, the capital of the network of French posts in Senegal, as the head of the Engineering Corps. He gained valuable experience over the next two years by traveling up the Senegal River and down the coast and directing public work projects. At some point during that time he developed a close relationship with the Bordeaux commercial houses that dominated French commerce around Senegal, and especially with Maurel and Prom. By the end of 1854, and partly through Bordeaux's intervention with the Ministry of the Navy and Colonies, he became governor and served in this position longer than any other person in the nineteenth century (1854–61, 1863–65).

Faidherbe was an Army man serving in a colonial outpost under the Navy. He began his service as governor as a *chef de bataillon* and was already a *général de brigade* by 1861. He chose his team carefully from Army, Navy, civilian, and indigenous groups. One key figure was Louis Alexandre Flize, who had been working for the government of Senegal since 1846. Flize became the head of the *Bureau des Affaires Extérieures*, the critical office for political and diplomatic action under the direct control of the governor. Another officer, with recent military experience in Algeria and knowledge of Arabic, took command of a key post on the river, while a graduate of the military school of Saint Cyr played a key role as a boat captain and expedition leader.[9] Two Navy men were important for Faidherbe's activities after 1859: Hyacinthe Aube and Aristide Vallon. Both became admirals in the Navy in the

1880s; Aube served as minister of the Navy and Vallon became the Senegal deputy to the French parliament.[10] Faidherbe also enlisted the support of two members of the moderate Catholic community of Saint-Louis: Frédéric Carrère, who served as judge of the Imperial Court, and Paul Holle, a mulatto officer who served in key posts along the river. And, not least, he gained the loyalty of the two most prominent Muslim notables of Saint-Louis: Hamat N'Diaye Anne, who became the head of the Muslim Tribunal that the governor established in 1857, and Bu El Mogdad, who worked in the External Affairs Bureau and accomplished many diplomatic missions with good effect.[11]

Faidherbe's reign is usually described in terms of campaigns against two principal enemies. The first, with respect to the time of encounter, was against Muhammad al-Habib, the emir of a loose confederation of Moors in Trarza, the southwestern corner of Mauritania. The Trarza Moors had dominated for some time the trade, political life, and even the land of the Wolof region of Walo, just east and north of Saint-Louis. The French had been paying tribute to them for the right to trade in gum arabic, the main export commodity produced along the river, and had thus contributed to the reinforcement of the emir's power. But Faidherbe and the Bordeaux houses saw that French dominance required a different relationship. By timing, quick strikes, and diplomacy, Faidherbe got the Trarza leaders to accept a French protectorate of the lower Senegal valley.[12]

Faidherbe's second enemy was more formidable and much more famous in imperial annals.[13] Al-Hajj Umar Tal was waging holy war in the Senegal River valley when Faidherbe took power. He designed his campaigns along a west-east axis, recruiting followers and weapons in the Senegambian zone, and using them to wage war against the Mandinka and Bambara states to the east, between the Upper Senegal and the Middle Niger River. His followers were Muslim, especially Fulbe like himself, and his opponents were non-Muslim, or at least lived under regimes that made no pretense to Islamic practice.

The conflict came when Faidherbe and Umar competed for the same space along the Senegal River. In 1855 Faidherbe established a fort to support commercial operations at Medine in the Upper Senegal under the command of Paul Holle, and its presence hampered the west-east campaigns of recruitment. In 1857, Umar laid siege to Medine at the height of the dry season. He was not able to use his advantage in numbers to storm the fort before Faidherbe, using the rising waters of the river to get his gunboats to the scene, raised the siege and dealt some terrible blows to the Muslim forces. The battle of Medine has gone down in French and Senegalese historiography as an epic confrontation of two resourceful, brilliant men, and has become part of the mythology of both.[14]

Umar responded to his defeat and large-scale desertions by conducting a massive recruitment campaign in his home area, the middle valley of the Senegal River, in 1858–59. What was remarkable about that year, when Umar secured perhaps 40,000 followers to carry the holy war to the Middle Niger, was the absence of any large-scale confrontation between the two sides; this is undoubtedly a tribute to the careful restraint of the ideologically opposed leaders. Faidherbe and Umar, once the main body of holy warriors had moved east, allowed their agents to begin negotiations about a division into geographical spheres of influence. The west, corresponding to Senegal, would be for the French, while the east, which would eventually become colonial Soudan, would be for the Umarians. Such an agreement was drafted and, though never ratified, served as a modus operandi for Franco–Umarian relations for the next two decades.[15]

The Umarian episodes reveal the style of Faidherbe. He was always well informed and clear about his objectives; he alternated between thrust and parry, attack and negotiation, stick and carrot, and military and commercial initiatives. Once Umar had moved his center of activity toward the Middle Niger, Faidherbe saw an opportunity for linkage with French commercial interests.[16]

Faidherbe's intervention in a third zone, the peanut basin—specifically Cayor, was even more important for the ultimate shape and character of Senegal.[17] By the 1850s it was clear that peanuts would eclipse gum as the major export commodity of the region. The governor, with the support of most of the Bordeaux merchants, moved to exacerbate divisions within the Cayor royal house and attract the support of some semi-autonomous Muslim communities in the northern reaches of the state. After a number of expeditions and false starts, and considerable loss of life, Faidherbe secured a dominant position in the area, a few treaties, several small posts, and a telegraph line. Cayor would constitute the core of the peanut basin for several decades, and Faidherbe helped ensure its subservience to French interests.

During these initiatives in Cayor, Faidherbe honed his skills as a manipulator of information for Paris[18] and dealt sharply with opposition from every quarter, even within the commercial establishment of Saint-Louis. In 1859 he replied to the managers of the Devès and Chaumet Company, which had close ties with commercial interests in Cayor, in harsh terms:

> In sending me a collective letter and protesting against my decisions, you arrogate to yourselves rights that you do not have. I will limit myself this time

to a simple warning and not call you before the Administrative Council, but you should know that in the future, using my powers under Articles 32 and 54 of the *Ordonnance Organique*, I will oppose any effort on your part that would tend to weaken the respect that is required by the Government.[19]

Faidherbe became a master at selective reporting to the Ministry of the Navy in Paris. He manufactured threats, made promises on which he could not deliver, and camouflaged his unauthorized initiatives. In the words of Yves Person, Faidherbe created the tradition of aggressive action in West Africa:

This obsession, which joined disdain for civilians to the pretension to be solely capable of judging local situations, prepared these [military] men for the systematic violation of instructions. An overly aggressive attitude ran the risk of irritating the Ministry, but Faidherbe found the solution by camouflaging aggressive actions as measures of security, and in stroking the old French chord of territorial sovereignty. He inaugurated a tradition of indiscipline and hypocrisy, which he held in check himself, but which became the custom of his successors.[20]

Faidherbe has often enjoyed a reputation as a fighter against slavery. He presided over the emancipation declaration of 1848 in Guadeloupe, and the "abolitionist" image has followed him ever since.[21] In fact, the record shows that he set down the policy of selective emancipation that the French followed consistently in West Africa. One of his successors, in explaining the practice of sending back refugee slaves who belonged to allies, said, "One must always follow the spirit of the confidential circular [of Faidherbe in 1857], that is, do nothing to displease the people with whom we are friends."[22] But Faidherbe went further: he was not above engaging in the slave trade when he felt it necessary. When his commander in Bakel took some 500 Umarian prisoners in campaigns in 1856 and then sold them into domestic slavery at the local market, Governor Faidherbe explained the incidents away and conveniently omitted them from his own works, the *Annales sénégalaises* and *Le Sénégal*, published in the 1880s.[23]

Faidherbe is unusual in the story of French expansion because of the long role that he played well after his retirement from active service.[24] From the mid-1870s he was increasingly paralyzed and confined to an apartment in Paris, but he used his reputation, his position as senator (from 1879), and his intelligence and keen interest in West Africa to stay abreast of events and to intervene selectively, but with great effect, on decisions in the 1880s. His former subordinate and brother-in-law, Hyacinthe Aube, became the Minister of the Navy during that period. Faidherbe was also in close contact with Joseph Gallieni, who served as *Commandant Supérieur* of the Soudan in 1886–88 and whose star was rising in the imperial firmament. As well, he supported Louis-Gustave Binger's plans to explore the Soudan and Ivory Coast. In fact, one can say that Faidherbe enlarged upon his earlier notions of expansion to formulate a kind of blueprint of the Soudan that was very influential in policy-making circles throughout the decade of the 1880s.[25]

Archinard and the "Creation of the Soudan"

Like Faidherbe, Louis Archinard (1850–1932) began his African command with a collection of posts from which to extend French influence. In his case, the posts were literally strung along a line of advance stretching from Kayes, on the Upper Senegal, to Bamako on the Niger. They were the product of the first wave of renewed expansion after the mid-nineteenth century. Beginning in 1878, under Governor Brière de l'Isle, the French became militarily active in the upper river valley. In 1880 the governor and the ministry agreed on a new structure, the *Commandement Supérieur du Haut Fleuve*, and appointed as head an aggressive and ambitious officer, Gustave Borgnis-Desbordes. Desbordes, following in the Faidherbean tradition, exceeded his orders constantly, but he persuaded the relevant officials in Paris to support him—over the opposition of successive governors in Saint-Louis, who were more inclined to conservative and commercial positions.[26] He completed the string of posts with the construction of the fort of Bamako in 1883.

Louis Archinard was one of Desbordes' principal assistants and an excellent apprentice in the school of expansion. Indeed, as Kanya-Forstner writes, Archinard put his mark permanently on the Soudan and the *soudanais*:

> With the appointment of Louis Archinard as *Commandant Supérieur* in 1888, the Sudanese Military came into their own. Under his leadership, they shrugged off the last restraints of metropolitan control, completed the conquest of the western portions of the Sudan, and created a military empire worthy of comparison with Algeria in the heyday of the *Armée d'Afrique*.[27]

Archinard served as *Commandant Supérieur*, rising to the rank of colonel, for four critical years: 1888–91 and 1892–93. During that time the Soudan became officially independent of the governor of Senegal, and many ambitious military officers came under the influence and training of the commandant.

Archinard was thirty-eight years old in 1888.[28] He grew up in a Reformed Protestant family, oriented himself very early toward a military career, and received his main military and engineering training, like Faidherbe, at the *École Polytechnique*. He graduated near the bottom of his class, and this helped determine his military service, in the *artillerie de marine*, where many of his future *soudanais* colleagues were also located. He received his first military experience in Indochina, before embarking for Senegal and the campaigns of Borgnis-Desbordes. The two men established a close bond during that time. Desbordes was based at the Ministry of Colonies while Archinard was in charge in the Soudan, and Desbordes' support, often over considerable opposition, was critical to Archinard's achievements.[29]

Like Faidherbe, Archinard saw his mission as expansion from a fragile collection of posts by waging war on two fronts. To the north and east lay the remnants of the Umarian state, under the nominal control of Ahmad al-Kabir, the eldest son of Al-Hajj Umar Tal.[30] Ahmad reigned principally from Segu, on the Middle Niger, but he tried to maintain his authority over Nioro and the western garrisons as well. By the time Archinard assumed command, Ahmad had left his son in charge in Segu, moved to Nioro, and put down a brother who had revolted against him. Ahmad sought to maintain the arrangement that had been endorsed by Faidherbe, but by 1888 it was clear to him and most observers that the French were determined to eliminate him.[31]

It was critical for Archinard's plan to portray Ahmad al-Kabir as a powerful threat to French expansion and civilization: for example, the "Tokolor Empire," as he and his contemporaries were wont to call it, was made up of fanatics and would never truly negotiate a settlement or coexist with the French; and Ahmad was coordinating an anti-French league bonded in Tokolor ethnicity and a Tijaniyya Muslim identity.[32] The strategy worked; the Ministry provided the funds, men, matériel, and authorization to destroy the last garrisons of the Umarian state. In April 1890 Archinard took Segu; in the process he captured the large group of women attached to the royal family and distributed them to the indigenous allies of the French.[33] In January 1891 he took Nioro, and in May 1893, during his final campaign, he expelled Ahmad from the last Umarian center, Bandiagara, and put Ahmad's brother Agibu in his place.

The second enemy was a much greater military threat. Samori Ture, working from the savanna and woodland settings of the Mandinka of the Upper Niger, constructed a powerful and relatively well integrated state by the 1880s. He posed a serious challenge to expansion into the areas that became Guinea and Ivory Coast, as well as the Soudan, and caused extensive damage to several

French contingents over a decade. He was finally captured in 1898—by *soudanais*, some of whom had seen their first service under Archinard.[34]

Archinard gathered a much larger team than Faidherbe, a team that had enormous impact on the French empire. The three most famous members were Charles Mangin, who became a general and the architect of African recruitment for French military service; J. P. Marchand, explorer and conqueror in Central Africa and leader of the Fashoda expedition; and William Ponty, later the governor of Soudan and governor-general of French West Africa.[35] He had African allies as well, most conspicuously Agibu Tall, whom he placed at Bandiagara as the "king" of Masina, and Mademba Sy, a Saint-Louisian telegraph operator, intelligence source, and jack-of-all-trades, who became the Fama or "king" of Sansanding. But Archinard did not have the intelligence operation or the patience to choose leaders who might exercise some real influence over his new subjects. Instead, he left in place an authoritarian military network that quickly frustrated the effort to establish civilian rule in the Soudan in 1894.

Archinard engaged in the fabrication and manipulation of information on a much larger scale than Faidherbe. He learned this from his predecessors, and especially from Borgnis-Desbordes and Gallieni. On the eve of Archinard's departure for the Soudan in 1888, Gallieni wrote him a letter of advice:

> If you follow my example, you won't pay any more attention to the missives of M. Billecoq and Co [the Colonial Department] than you think necessary. The *Commandant Supérieur* . . . can alone decide what measures have to be taken, especially on matters affecting the political situation. Everything I accomplished during these two campaigns [of 1886–87 and 1887–88] was done in spite of the Ministry which was always afraid to commit itself, to say nothing of Saint-Louis which panicked at the hint of any action. . . . Everything was done on my own initiative, despite the objections of Saint-Louis and the criticisms of everybody. And I advise you to do the same.[36]

The *soudanais* team, by their consistently aggressive and unauthorized actions, produced a growing chorus of critics. The cost and cost overruns mounted, and there was no strategy for tapping into commerce or investing in development— in short, no way of providing revenue. Gallieni, who had played a critical role in Archinard's appointment, became increasingly disenchanted, and with him most influential policy makers in and around the Ministry. By the time Archinard ended his term as *Commandant Supérieur* in 1893 and returned to Paris, his support had dwindled to a few military people such as Desbordes, and the pressure to turn the Soudan over to a civilian administration was irresistible.

But even then, even as Governor Albert Grodet sought to transform the command structure in 1894, Archinard was writing instructions to *soudanais* in the field about what to do during the campaign of 1893–94, when he was no longer in charge. This was carrying the Faidherbean tradition of indiscipline to new extremes. One result of the military momentum that Archinard created was the ill-fated Bonnier expedition to Timbuktu, in which a whole French column was annihilated.[37]

Archinard did not have the same impact outside of military circles as Faidherbe. He had no "humanitarian" reputation and made no pretense about supporting the end of slavery in the Soudan; indeed, he did not consider that he was required to respond to anyone but his military superiors. He is sometimes remembered for giving his blessing to the establishment of Spiritan and White Father missionaries in the areas that were demarcated "non-Muslim"; that is, certain areas of the Mandinka along the line of posts and societies such as the Bambara. The missionaries had positive memories of him.[38] He did not have the same intellectual impact as Faidherbe, but he did leave his name upon the Umarian library of Segu, which he sent back to Paris in 1890 and which became the *Fonds Archinard* at the *Bibliothèque Nationale*.[39]

Despite the opposition that he aroused, Archinard continued to enjoy the protection of powerful allies in military circles, and he moved up the hierarchical ladder of achievement. He became a general and advanced through the ranks of the *Légion d'Honneur*. He did not play a major role in World War I, because of age, but he did preside over a number of military and colonial activities.[40]

Coppolani and the "Creation of Mauritania"

Xavier Coppolani (1866–1905) followed a very different trajectory into his West African service. He was born in Corsica, not France, and to very humble beginnings.[41] His family moved to Algeria to seek new opportunity during his childhood, and it was there that he acquired his *lycée* education, his familiarity with Arabic, and his knowledge of Islam. He was not a military man; indeed, from a civilian post he moved into scholarly pursuits and acquired his first visibility as co-author of the enormous compendium on Muslim Sufi orders in Algeria.[42] With its publication Coppolani became an "expert," part of the Algerian School of Islamic Studies (*École algérienne d'Islamologie*) and its foremost young exponent. He stressed Islam's brotherhood—its lodges and networks—as the keys to understanding and controlling Muslim societies.

But Coppolani worked for an administration with a strong military orientation. He did not see an easy path to an administrative or scholarly career in

Algeria, at least not one commensurate with his talent, vision, and ambition. He did see opportunities in the desert, where the French were expanding from two directions: the Algerian administration of Governor-General Jules Cambon and the Soudan administration of Governor de Trentinian, who had taken over from the *soudanais* and the failed civilian regime. Coppolani cast himself as a Saharan expert and accepted an invitation from Trentinian in 1898 for a mission among the nomads of the Soudan.[43]

Unlike his predecessors, Coppolani did not work within any single bureaucratic structure. He came from Algeria, an area governed by a governor-general and the War Ministry. He was "loaned" to the governor of the Soudan, which was part of the French West African Federation and was administered by the now-separate Ministry of Colonies. A few years later he would need the support of the Ministry of Foreign Affairs to bring pressure to bear upon the Ministry of Colonies to authorize his work in Mauritania. But he did demonstrate the same ability to impress and persuade at each point where his vision and mission were threatened. And it is likely that, had he been in a conventional military chain of command, at this late point in French expansion and with the memories of the excesses of the *soudanais* still fresh, he would never have been allowed to pursue the "pacification" of Mauritania. Much more than his predecessors, he was a man of the "frontier"—the bureaucratic frontier, the frontiers of French expansion, and the constantly changing frontiers of nomadic societies; he relied, perhaps excessively, on his charm and power of persuasion.

The mission in 1898 was to study the frontier and gain the submission of nomads—the Moors and Tuaregs who lived in the northern confines where Algeria and the Soudan were now drawing their boundaries. These nomads lived in the Saharan and Sahelian zones; in the French ethnographic paradigm they were "natural Islamic races" who might respond favorably to an *algérien* who was scholar and administrator, fluent in Arabic, and familiar with Islam. Coppolani was their man; at least, Coppolani portrayed his expedition, in company with his *algérien* colleague, Robert Arnaud, as a great success. His widely circulated report ended with a trenchant suggestion: to establish French control of the far western Sahara, under the name of Mauritania, through a policy of peaceful extension or "pacification."

Coppolani spent 1900 and some of 1901 in France working for his Mauritanian proposal. He secured the support of the minister of Foreign Affairs, the president of the Republic, and Ernest Roume, the new governor-general of French West Africa, who was of a more "imperial" frame of mind than his Senegal-oriented predecessors.[44] The factor that probably worked most in Coppolani's favor was Morocco. The northwestern corner of Africa

fell within the sphere that the French expected to control, yet it was still independent, in close contact with the British, Germans, and Spanish, and had
"designs" on the Sahara.[45] The Moroccan unknown, and the expansion of the
colonial regime of Algeria to the south, gave new value to the "empty" desert.

At the same time, Coppolani launched a new journal, the *Revue Franco-
Musulmane et Saharienne*, with a patronage committee that included the leading lights of the French imperial and diplomatic world. In the publication he
and his collaborators articulated their view of France's greatness as a nation
with a special "vocation" for ruling over Muslim societies, assuring them of its
benevolence, and even creating a kind of paid Muslim clergy.[46] The journal
and Coppolani's articles gave him as much scholarly visibility as Faidherbe
had enjoyed when governor of Senegal; they marked him as probably the leading French exponent of "Islamic" policy at the time.

In 1901 Coppolani began to prepare his Mauritanian program in Saint-
Louis, which would be the capital of the territory of Mauritania as well as
Senegal. He solidified his rapport with Ernest Roume, who became the governor-general early in 1902. He built his team: some were *algériens* such as
Arnaud, others were *soudanais*; some were civilian; and some had military
backgrounds. He made great use of Bu El Mogdad Seck II, the son of the interpreter and diplomat who worked with Faidherbe.[47] The team gradually
expanded as the French domain in Mauritania expanded, and many stayed on
after Coppolani's death.

The first year of the campaign, 1902–3, was devoted to Trarza, the southwestern corner just north and east of Saint-Louis. The second year, 1903–4,
was devoted to Brakna and adjacent zones, to the north of Podor. The third
year, 1904–5, was to be devoted to the Tagant, the zone east of Brakna. But in
May 1905, at the edge of the desert and a considerable distance from the
Senegal River and any French reinforcements, Coppolani was assassinated by
Moors who slipped into his camp at night. It would take four additional years
before the French, under Colonel Henri Gouraud, the *soudanais* who captured
Samori, could take the center of resistance, the Adrar.[48]

Coppolani's approach depended upon working with the *marabouts* or
zwaya, the division of Moorish or *baydan* society that concerned itself with
religious and commercial matters. The *zwaya*, whom he had encountered in the
Soudan exploration a few years before, were organized in networks of traders,
scholars, and religious specialists over large areas, and they provided a sem-
blance of order in an otherwise chaotic zone. In the case of Mauritania,
Coppolani could not have asked for two more influential and cooperative
marabouts than two men he met in his travels in Trarza in 1901–2, and he

relied much more heavily on them than Faidherbe and Archinard had depended on their African allies.

Sa'ad Bu (c. 1848–1917) had been a close ally of the French for thirty years.[49] After the death of his father he moved, in about 1870, from Hodh to Trarza. From that point on he developed a significant following in Saint-Louis and began a pattern of annual visits. Saint-Louis masons built his residence in Touizit and some 100 pupils from the town were studying in his school in the 1880s. By the mid-1880s he was brokering colonial interests in Salum and establishing the pattern of collection tours to sustain his camp in the Trarza desert. In the 1890s he assisted a number of missions of exploration in the desert. In the early 1900s he became important as a counterweight to his brother, Ma-El-'Ainin, who was the galvanizing rod for *baydan* resistance to Coppolani's "pacification" and the subsequent conquest.[50]

An even more indispensable ally for Coppolani was Sidiyya Baba (c.1862–1924). He was the grandson of Sidiyya al-Kabir, who had kept his distance from the colonial authorities in the mid-nineteenth century. Sidiyya Baba broke this pattern in 1898 when he made his first trip to the colonial capital.[51] From that point on he became a frequent visitor and visible friend of French Islamicists and other officials, and especially Coppolani. He came to Saint-Louis in November 1902 to support the "pacification" program, over the opposition of many merchants as well as *baydan*, and wrote a eulogy after his friend's assassination.[52] Coppolani and his successors consulted Sidiyya Baba constantly about the campaign against Ma-El-'Ainin.[53]

Coppolani followed a pattern similar to Faidherbe with respect to slavery, emancipation, and the existing social hierarchy. He complained at some length about the continuing *baydan* raids into Senegal to seize animals, women and children and the complicity of Saint-Louisian traders in such a system. But he could not afford to alienate his main indigenous allies, who were large slave owners themselves, and he gave no indication that he intended any significant attack on *baydan* slavery. To use the language of Faidherbe, he would "do nothing to displease the people with whom we are friends." In terms of manipulation of evidence, he was no less adept at presentation and packaging than his predecessors. He realized that Governor-General Roume provided the essential cover for his mission and that the limitations that he imposed must be obeyed. At no time, then, did Coppolani move deliberately against his orders, in the pattern of Archinard. He did, however, keep "pushing the envelope" of possibility, and it is likely that had he survived and continued to enjoy some success, he would have implicated the French in a "pacification" of the Adrar in 1905–6. As it was, his death made the French engagement in Mauritania irreversible.

Conclusion

The three *africains* and *constructeurs* of Senegal, Soudan, and Mauritania offer significant contrasts. Archinard operated in the most narrow frame of reference, the *infanterie* and *artillerie de marine* within the Navy, and he reflected least about the institutions of government in "his" African territory. His team was entirely military, while his African allies brought little legitimacy to their tasks. Faidherbe had a broader base. He was an engineer by training, located within the Army but seconded to the Navy, and he knew how to cross bureaucratic boundaries. He chose his subordinates and allies carefully, and left a significant institutional heritage for his successors in Senegal and French West Africa. Coppolani had to forge his own path and knew how to secure critical support from key European and African collaborators. He was a civilian who relied on small elite military units for protection and selective raiding. He was sensitive to the need to use and create institutions, but never got the opportunity to fashion his own, and we cannot see the results of what he would have created in Mauritania.

At the same time, all three men show similar ability to "carve out" territory and create traditions and institutions. They were ambitious, opportunistic, and authoritarian; they were men of strong personality, presence, and persuasive ability; they knew how to divide the opposition, of whatever kind, in order to dominate it. They learned from their predecessors and a tradition of West African service, invention, and manipulation. Coppolani learned from the schools of the *soudanais* and Faidherbe, while Archinard absorbed the lessons of the aggressive Senegalese administration of Faidherbe. All three men operated at the frontiers of French interest and thus at the frontiers of French control. They were able to manufacture and manipulate information, pursue their missions, and "create" their territories without serious reprimand or recall. Or, in the case of Archinard, the recall came too late to change the course of events in the Soudan and did not seriously impede his military advancement.

What ultimately matters about this essay is what it says about Africa or about European ideas of Africa. For a certain period, in a certain social and psychological space, it was possible for ambitious men to establish agendas, boundaries, and institutions. Since these men and their French contemporaries did not face, or did not think that they faced, any African civilizations worthy of consideration, they could become *africain*, that is, fashion their own African identities. Through the institutions that backed them and sometimes questioned their knowledge and truthfulness, through the teams and traditions that they left behind, they have bequeathed an enduring legacy to West Africa.

Notes

1. The *École Coloniale* became the *École Nationale de la France d'Outre-Mer* in 1937 under Delavignette's leadership. He had served in French West Africa and was one of the leading intellectuals of the empire. See William Cohen, *Rulers of Empire. The French Colonial Service in Africa* (Stanford: Hoover Institution Press, 1971), 99–104, 143–48.

2. The work appears in a series edited by Charles Braibant entitled *Les Grandes Professions Françaises: Collection d'Anthologies* (Paris: Corrêa, 1946) and is dedicated to Felix Eboué, the first black governor-general who had recently passed away.

3. For a recent treatment of French expansion in the Second Empire, see Denise Bouche, *Histoire de la colonisation française: Flux et reflux (1815–1962)*, vol. 2 (Paris: Fayard, 1991).

4. By the time of Archinard and Coppolani, *sénégalais* had come to mean a conservative no longer interested in imperial expansion.

5. A separate Ministry of Colonies was created in 1894, so was operative when Coppolani was in West Africa. For this and the whole story of expansion in West Africa, see Sydney Kanya-Forstner, *The Conquest of the Western Sudan. A Study in French Military Imperialism* (Cambridge: Cambridge University Press, 1969).

6. Kanya-Forstner, *Conquest*; Yves Person, *Samori: une révolution dyula*, 3 vols. (Dakar: IFAN, 1968–75). A recent example of the francophone historiography that I am criticizing is Catherine Coquery-Vidrovitch, ed., *L'Afrique occidentale au temp des français. Colonisateurs et colonises, c. 1860–1960* (Paris: Editions la découverte, 1992).

7. One of the most recent biographies is Alain Coursier, *Faidherbe 1818–1880. Du Sénégal à l'Armée du Nord* (Paris: Tallandier, 1989). For two very thorough studies of his administration in Senegal, see Leland Barrows, "General Faidherbe, the Maurel & Prom Company, and French expansion in Senegal" (Ph.D. thesis, UCLA, 1974), and Yves-Jean Saint-Martin, *Le Sénégal sous le second Empire* (Paris: Karthala, 1989). For a listing of other biographies and short accounts, see David Robinson, *Chiefs and Clerics. The History of Abdul Bokar Kan and Futa Toro 1853-1891* (Oxford: Clarendon Press, 1975).

8. See Delavignette and Julien, *Constructeurs*, 232ff; Georges Hardy, *Faidherbe*, 11–17.

9. Pascal de Negroni and Paul Brossard de Corbigny, respectively. For Faidherbe's collaborators, see Saint-Martin, *Le Sénégal sous le Second Empire*, 257ff.

10. Saint-Martin, *Second Empire*, 271.

11. On the contributions of these two men to the French image in Senegal, see David Robinson, *The Holy War of Umar Tal. The Western Sudan in the Mid-Nineteenth Century* (Oxford: Clarendon Press, 1985), 2llff.

12. One detailed account is Boubacar Barry, *Le royaume du Waalo* (Paris: Karthala, 1972, 1985).

13. See Robinson, *Holy War*.

14. One might say that Senegalese identity is positioned between Umar, its native son who fought against "paganism" and European intrusion, and Faidherbe, the architect who designed the institutions, understood Islam, and forced Muslims to accept European

override. See Robinson, *Holy War*, 370–75.

15. See Robinson, *Holy War*, chapter 6.

16. Ibid., chapter 5.

17. The best source is Mamadou Diouf, *Le Kajoor au XIXe siècle. Pouvoir ceddo et conquête coloniale* (Paris: Karthala, 1990).

18. The manipulation of information for the métropole and for Senegalese is well documented in Oumar Ba, *La pénétration française au Cayor: 16 décembre 1854–28 mai 1861* (Dakar: l'Auteur, 1976). The dates correspond to Faidherbe's first term as governor.

19. See *Archives Nationales du Sénégal*, 3B74, letter of 14 November 1859, of Governor Faidherbe to Devès and Chaumet. Cited in Ba, *Pénétration*, 202–3.

20. Person, *Samori*, 1:364.

21. Faidberbe dedicated his most important work, *Le Sénégal et la France dans l'Afrique Occidentale* (Paris: Hachette, 1888), to Victor Schoelcher, the best-known French abolitionist, and evoked his memories of the slave trade to the Antilles.

22. In an 1869 letter of the governor to the commandant of Saldé, contained in ANS 13G 148, no 81. Also cited in Robinson, *Chiefs and Clerics*, 113.

23. For a summary description of these episodes, see Robinson, *Holy War*, 171–72. See also Barrows, "General Faidherbe," 485–93. Faidherbe's works were published in 1885 and 1889, respectively.

24. See, for example, AOM, SENEGAL VII 21.

25. For Faidherbe's later influence, see Leland Barrows, "L'oeuvre, la carrière du général Faidherbe et les débuts de l'Afrique Noire Française: une analyse critique contemporaine," *Le Mois en Afrique* No. 235–36 (1985): 120–50, No. 237–38 (1985): 130–56, No. 239–40 (1985–6): 120–50; Faidherbe, *Le Sénégal*, passim; Person, *Samori*, I: 369, II: 704. Parfait Louis Monteil, the explorer and rising star of the imperial world, visited Faidherbe often in the mid-1880s in his apartment in Paris. See Henri Labouret, *Monteil. Explorateur et soldat* (Paris, 1937), chapter 5.

26. The best account of the expansion into Soudan is Kanya-Forstner, *Conquest*, 55ff. The *Commandant Supérieur* was ostensibly subordinate to the Governor in Saint-Louis, but the military men who assumed this position consistently circumvented his authority, and the new territory and its officials were officially declared independent of Senegal in 1894.

27. Kanya-Forstner, *Conquest*, 174. The "heyday" in Algeria corresponded to the period of Bugeaud.

28. For a brief biography of Archinard, see Kanya-Forstner, *Conquest*, 174. For an extensive hagiography, see Jacques Méniaud, *Les Pionniers du Soudan avant, avec, et après Archinard (1879-1894)* (Paris, 1931). Méniaud was also a Navy officer, and his military orientation marks the organization, style, and tone of his volumes.

29. Kanya-Forstner, *Conquest*, passim.

30. The most recent source is John Hanson and David Robinson, *After the Jihad: The Reign of Ahmad al-Kabir in the Western Sudan*, (East Lansing: Michigan State University Press, 1991).

31. Kanya-Forstner, *Conquest*, 176ff.

32. For the tortuous construction which Archinard and the Governor of Senegal made, see Kanya-Forstner, *Conquest*, 181–82, and Robinson, *Chiefs and Clerics*, 149–50 and especially 150n. For the important role of the "Tokolor Empire" in the justification for the conquest of the Soudan, see John Hanson, "Generational conflict in the Umarian movement after the *jihad*: perspectives from the Futanke grain trade at Medine," *Journal of African History* 31 (1990) and "Umarian migrations in the late nineteenth century Senegal valley," *Journal of African History* 35 (1994).

33. The Umarians probably resented the distribution of the women from the Segu harem more than any other single act of their long history of relations with the French. Those who accepted the "gift" of Segu women were marked as collaborators with the colonial authorities; among their number were Mademba and Agibu. Agibu asked for and received a large share of the women for safe-keeping. See ANS 15G 75, 15G 76, 15G 78, and 1D 121.

34. The definitive work on Samori, with extensive treatment of the French who engaged him, is Person, *Samori*. His relations with the French are also extensively treated in Kanya-Forstner, *Conquest*.

35. For their roles under Archinard, see Kanya-Forstner, *Conquest*, passim.

36. Gallieni to Archinard, 25–9–88, quoted in Kanya-Forstner, *Conquest*, 175.

37. See Kanya-Forstner, *Conquest*, 215ff. On the attitudes of the *soudanais* military to Grodet's civilian administration, see, for example, Général Henri Gouraud, *Souvenirs d'un africain. Au Soudan* (Paris: Editions Pierre Tisne, 1939), and Henri Labouret, *Monteil*.

38. Joseph-Roger de Benoist, *Eglise et pouvoir colonial au Soudan français. Administrateurs et missionaires dans la Boucle du Niger (1885-1945)* (Paris: Karthala, 1987).

39. See Noureddine Ghali et al., *Bibliothèque Umarienne de Ségou* (Paris: CNRS, 1985). This catalog of the *Fonds Archinard*, renamed the Umarian library, contains a short introduction on the history of this collection brought from Segu by Archinard.

40. See Méniaud, *Pionniers*, 2:515ff.

41. To the best of my knowledge, the only published biography of Coppolani is the one done by his friend and collaborator, Robert Arnaud (Randau), *Un Corse d'Algérie*, (Alger: A. Imbert, 1939). See also Cécile Frébourg, "Le Corse en Mauritanie. Xavier Coppolani (1866–1905). L'Islam au Service de la France, mémoire de maîtrise d'histoire," (Paris:Université de Paris VII, 1990).

42. Xavier Coppolani and Octave Depont, *Les confréries réligieuses musulmanes* (Paris: A. Jourdan, 1897). For the *École algérienne*, see Jean-Louis Triaud, "Les relations entre la France et la Sanusiyya (1840–1930). Histoire d'une mythologies coloniale. Découverte d'une confrérie saharienne," *Doctorates Lettres* (Paris: Université de Paris VII, 1991), chapter XXI.

43. De Trentinian organized a number of explorations and expeditions during the last two years of his term as governor of the territory. AOM, *Série géographique*, SOUDAN III 4, *Exploration et missions, 1894–1904.*

44. For Roume's role see Frébourg, "Coppolani," and AOM, *Missions* 115, Coppolani.

45. See, for example, Lieutenant d'Otton Loyewski, "Coppolani et la Mauritanie," *Revue d'Histoire des Colonies* 26 (1938): 1–7.

46. The purpose of the journal was expressed in the first number of the first volume, 1.1, 5–5–1902, ". . . to study the Muslim world in its political and religious organization . . . and seek the means to make our Muslim subjects evolve in the direction of progress . . . and to demonstrate our deep interest in making use of religious leaders who have been won over to our cause." The patronage committee was filled by prominent exponents of French expansion, including Eugène Etienne, Rene Basset, Louis-Gustave Binger, Joseph Chailley-Bert, André Chautemps, François Deloncle, Charles Dupuy, Gabriel Hanotaux, and Henri Poincaré. The journal apparently discontinued publication at the end of 1903.

47. The best source on Coppolani's team is Commandant Gillier, *La pénétration en Mauritanie. Découverte – Explorations – Conquête – La police du désert et la pacification définitive* (Paris: Geuthner, 1926).

48. Ironically, Mauritania in the wake of Coppolani's assassination got a military administration that resembled that of the Soudan in the 1880s and 1890s in many ways; several of its colonels, who commanded the territory under the title of *Haut Commissaire* under the governor-general, were old *soudanais*: Gouraud, Patey, and Gaden, for example. See Pierre Bonte, "L'émir et les colonels, pouvoir colonial et pouvoir émiral en Adrar mauritanien," in Pierre Boilley et al., eds., *Nomades et commandants. Administration et sociétés nomades dans l'ancienne AOF* (Paris: Karthala, 1993).

49. For Sa'ad Bu and Sidiyya Baba, see Paul Marty's treatments, "Cheikh Sidia et sa voie" and "Les Fadélia," in *Revue du Monde Musulman* 31 (1915–16). For French views of Sa'ad Bu in 1897, see SEN IV 128, letter of 3 June 1897, gouverneur général au Ministère des Colonies. See also Robinson, *Chiefs and Clerics*, 105, and my interview with Serigne Moustapha Ndiaye and Ousmane Dieye at Saint-Louis, 11 June 1985.

50. On Ma-El-'Ainin and the Moroccan efforts to mobilize resistance to the French in the Sahara, see Edmund Burke III, *Prelude to the Protectorate in Morocco. Precolonial Protest and Resistance, 1860-1912* (Chicago: University of Chicago Press, 1976), passim.

51. Bu El Mogdad wrote a report on his journey which can be found in the Archives of Mauritania. Sidiyya stayed at the Bu El Mogdad residence, and he received an important contribution from the Devès family to construct his library. See my interview with Amadou Diagne Yaya, son of Gaspard Devès' maternal brother, on 19 March 1985.

52. Frébourg, "Coppolani," 109.

53. Coppolani, in his report to the Governor-General on 1 July 1904, gave great credit to the role of Sidiyya (AOM, MAURITANIE IV 1 1902–4).

Generational Conflict in the Umarian Movement after the *Jihad:* Perspectives from the Futanke Grain Trade at Medine

JOHN H. HANSON

A l-Hajj Umar Tal's call to *jihad* enticed tens of thousands of Futanke[1] to fight in his mid-nineteenth-century conquest of the Western Sudan.[2] Expansion came to a halt with Umar's death in 1864, but his sons continued waging war in the region until the French ended Umarian rule with their late-nineteenth-century conquests.[3] The military campaigns of Umar's sons prompted another several thousand young Futanke to leave the Senegal valley in hope of accumulating wealth in booty. In Karta, the Umarian state that received the largest influx of young recruits, criticism of the wars emerged among earlier Futanke colonists who had fought in Al-Hajj Umar's armies and then settled in Karta. Many of these settlers had acquired land and slaves, managed agricultural enterprises that produced surplus grain for regional markets, and sought to protect trade in Karta from the disruptions of war.

Most discussions of the Umarian era in the Western Sudan overlook the emergence of agricultural interests among the Futanke settlers of Karta and emphasize the wars and raids conducted by Umar's sons and their followers.[4] This emphasis reflects and reinforces the image of Futanke militancy expressed in the extant sources. Most Umarian oral accounts stress the victories of the *jihad* which, combined with accounts of social dislocation and devastation in the traditions of the conquered populations, foster an impression of continuing Umarian warfare.[5] French travelers, military personnel, and colonial officials also emphasize the wars of the Umarian Futanke; they refer to them as "fanatic Muslims," whose exuberance for warfare distinguished them from "productive" African populations whom the French moved "to protect" through their conquest of the Western Sudan.[6] While most practicing historians reject French colonial assumptions of distinct African ethnic "types," received images of the militant Futanke still influence the reconstruction of the past.

Claude Meillassoux offers a nuanced argument regarding the historical relations between military and commercial elites in the Western Sudan, but his discussion of the Umarian Futanke focuses merely on their role as a "Muslim warrior aristocracy" whose wars redistributed populations in the region.[7] Richard Roberts further clarifies the relations between these two elites for the eighteenth and nineteenth centuries, but he also argues that the Umarian Futanke were warriors who depended upon military campaigns for their social reproduction.[8] Neither author recognizes the emerging contradictions within the Umarian movement: Futanke settlers who had reaped the benefits of military conquest tried to protect their new positions by eliminating warfare in areas crucial to commercial activity. While the French advance ended Umarian rule without a conclusive resolution to this internal process, the conflict nevertheless points to the need to understand more fully the material bases of generational conflict within conquest states.[9]

Yves Saint-Martin, in his study of Franco-Umarian relations, notes that an elderly group of Futanke in Karta had become "bourgeois" and lost their desire for the "brutal exploits of old."[10] Although he points to generational cleavages, Saint-Martin does not discuss the "old men" as a social group. Nor does he mention agricultural or any other economic interests that might explain their disinterest in warfare. This essay uses Saint-Martin as a point of departure to document the emergence of agricultural interests among the earliest Futanke settlers as a first step toward reconstructing the social formation established in Umarian Karta. I have selected for discussion the case of Umarian Jomboxo, the southwestern part of Karta. Data from the nearby French post at Medine reveal the emergence of agricultural interests among the Futanke settlers. While previous studies conclude that little grain entered the market at Medine, these records show an extensive grain trade generated by the Jomboxo Futanke.[11] Since the grain trade at Medine was only one aspect of the political economy of Umarian Karta, I begin the essay with a summary of Umarian interventions in the regional economy.

The Political Economy of Umarian Karta

Karta is a Sahelian region of the Western Sudan that borders the Saharan desert-edge to the north and the upper reaches of the Senegal River valley to the west and south.[12] To the east, Karta's territory gives way to the frontiers of Segu and Masina, social formations based in the middle Niger River valley. The Massassi, a Bambara royal lineage from Segu, fled a civil war in the late seventeenth century and settled in Karta, where they used a combination of force and strategic alliances with local commercial and military families to gain control over heterogeneous communities of herders and farmers.[13] When Umarian armies invaded Karta and defeated the main Massassi army in 1855, local communities of Soninke and Fulbe submitted to Umar without a struggle. Umar's soldiers occupied garrisons abandoned by the Massassi and defended against rebellions led by the Massassi and their allies. The Umarians also had to contend with desert-side groups such as the Awlad Mbark, a powerful warrior confederation that organized a major offensive against the Futanke in the mid-1860s.[14] Once the Awlad Mbark challenge was defeated, the Umarians could turn to consolidating their hold over Karta.

Futanke colonists who had settled in the region after the *jihad* influenced the terms of Umarian consolidation in Karta.[15] In western Karta near the Umarian garrison at Konyakary, Umar gave several military leaders land and slaves immediately after the conquest in exchange for their agreement not to confiscate property from populations who had submitted to him. Umar also encouraged soldiers to settle in villages around Nioro, the largest garrison in northern Karta, creating a line of defense against attack. After a major recruitment campaign in the Senegal valley, when thousands of Futanke joined the ranks of the Umarian movement, soldiers who did not want to leave the region sought to settle near Nioro as well. By the time Umar left Karta to continue the effort against Segu in 1859, several thousand Futanke resided in rural areas surrounding Nioro and Konyakary. As the political consolidation of Karta gained momentum and freed the Futanke from constant vigil against attack, many soldiers began to use the slaves and land which they had received as conquerors of Karta. They soon produced surplus grain and sought access to regional markets where they could exchange their grain for other goods.

Umarian military leaders supported the economic activities of the Futanke colonists by pursuing a commercial policy which linked Karta with markets in the upper Senegal valley. This policy reversed Umar's embargo against trade at French-controlled posts; the desire for European-manufactured firearms and stable relations with the French moved Umar's appointees to alter course on this question.[16] Gum arabic, an exudate of the acacia tree that grows along the southern Sahara desert-side, was the primary commodity desired by the merchants who had access to French firearms.[17] Since the Massassi never had established effective control over desert-side gum caravans passing to the upper Senegal, Umarian leaders had to negotiate with desert-side commercial groups and Senegal Valley merchants to open trade routes in Karta and claim some of the profits in the gum trade as tolls and customs taxes.[18] The result of these negotiations was the creation of a new gum market at Medine, a French post established 1855.[19] Beginning in the mid-1860s, the Umarian army escorted caravans through Karta and collected tolls from desert-side caravans and customs from Medine gum merchants.

Desert-side gum caravans traveled across Umarian Karta in increasing numbers throughout the late nineteenth century, propelling Medine's transformation from a small village of a few hundred in the 1850s into a commercial center with close to 4,000 permanent residents in the 1880s.[20] The meteoric expansion of the gum trade is illustrated in table 1, which juxtaposes Medine's rise with the trade at Bakel, the other major gum entrepôt in the upper Senegal valley.[21] Medine's expansion came in part at the expense of Bakel; the

Table 1. **Volume of upper Senegal Valley gum purchases (in kilograms) during the rise of Medine, 1860–1879***

Year	Medine (kilograms)	Bakel (kilograms)
1860	0	221,780
1861	0	300,175
1862	0	n.f.
1863	0	265,727
1864	0	295,000
1865	0	306,807
1866	30,000	301,387
1867	42,000	105,316
1868	176,875	121,464
1869	211,459	511,825
1870	n.f.	n.f.
1871	n.f.	362,611
1872	483,300	438,755
1873	85,000	416,553
1874	580,545	368,671
1875	575,000	375,483
1876	363,672	414,667
1877	576,069	405,962
1878	360,758	522,508
1879	523,533	471,176

n.f. = no figures reported
*See note 21

Umarians claimed a portion of the gum arabic revenues previously controlled by the Idaw Aish, a warrior confederation north of Bakel.[22] While the gum boom at Medine ultimately depended upon the efforts of desert-side commercial groups and Medine's merchants, the initiative of Umarian leaders played a critical role in the establishment of a market at Medine. The expansion of the gum trade in turn influenced the political economy of Karta by providing the Umarian army with firearms and the Futanke colonists with a market for surplus grain.[23]

Mirroring the Umarian initiative toward Medine was the creation of Nioro as a regional market for Ijil salt.[24] Umar Tal used his ties to the Tijaniyya Sufi brotherhood to forge relations with the Tishiti families who organized the lucrative Ijil salt trade. As Tishiti merchants established a base in Nioro, the Umarian state responded by encouraging social groups to provide a consistent supply of grain and slaves for desert-side consumers.[25] Soninke families with regional commercial contacts moved into Nioro, where they sold prisoners captured by Umarian armies as well as slaves captured in the southern savanna.[26] Other communities in Karta expanded production of grain for exchange and invested in slaves to increase their productive capacities.[27]

The Umarian state favored Futanke grain producers over indigenous producers. Initially Umarian officials collected taxes on all communities in Karta, claiming up to a tenth to support the military apparatus. Futanke colonists who had settled near Nioro and Konyakary successfully threw off the obligation to pay Umarian taxes and claimed unrestricted access to sell surplus grain at markets in Umarian centers.[28] This two-tier system of taxation led to resentment of the Futanke among indigenous groups. Umarian leaders tried to mediate tensions through the elevation of a Soninke clerical family to a position as court councilor at Nioro.[29] Many indigenous groups expressed their discontent in the 1880s by supporting Mamadu Lamine, a Muslim reformer who attempted to form an autonomous state in sections of the Xoolimbinne valley.[30]

The capture of slaves was another dimension of the Umarian political economy in Karta. The wars of consolidation in the 1850s and 1860s provided captives to help launch commercial exchanges in Karta. As Futanke settlers retired from military service, several sons of Al-Hajj Umar assumed command at various Umarian garrisons and recruited Futanke soldiers in the Senegal valley to serve in their armies.[31] The arrival of new recruits put pressure on the sons of Umar to conduct military campaigns, as the young men usually arrived without many material possessions and saw warfare as their means to accumulate wealth. In response to the commercial interests of Futanke settlers, desert-side merchants, and regional slave-traders, Umar's sons directed their campaigns toward the southern regions of Karta, that is, toward areas removed from Medine, Nioro, and the trade routes leading to these commercial centers.[32]

Umarian Karta's consolidation occurred within the broader context of Umarian rule in the Western Sudan. Amadu Sheku, Umar's oldest son and successor as the commander of the Faithful, consolidated control at Segu in the middle Niger valley and then asserted his interest in controlling the commercial traffic in Karta beginning in the late 1860s.[33] The economic dislocation which the Umarian wars caused in the middle Niger valley and which Amadu could not resolve help to explain his interest in a productive and expanding political economy in Karta.[34] Access to French firearms was a major concern. During the 1870s, after a brief residence in Nioro, Amadu usurped control over Umarian customs taxes on the gum trade at Medine. During his return to Segu, he established an administrative system to supervise trade between Nioro and Segu, centered on the post of Guigné. By the early 1880s, however, Bambara attacks closed the Nioro-Segu road for months at a time, and Umarian leaders in Karta ignored Amadu's requests to direct their armies to open the Nioro-Segu route. Umarian leaders in Karta also succeeded in reclaiming local control over a portion of Umarian customs taxes collected at Medine. Umarian Karta, therefore, was a partially autonomous state, and its regional economy remained shielded from influences from the middle Niger economy.[35]

Beginning in the 1880s, the French altered the context in which the Umarians in Karta waged war by creating a series of posts between the upper Senegal and upper Niger valleys. Umarian wars and raids in the southern marches of Karta now brought Futanke soldiers into close proximity to the new French posts. The French initially hoped to forge an alliance with the Umarians in Karta as they moved against the state in Segu, but the military leaders at Nioro and Konyakary adopted a hostile policy toward the French.[36] As a result of increasing Franco-Umarian tensions, the French occasionally ordered embargoes on trade at Medine in order to express their dissatisfaction with Umarian actions. The French advance accentuated contradictions inherent in the Karta social formation; settlers with interests in regional exchanges opposed the politics of confrontation which adversely influenced their access to Medine and other regional markets.[37]

The growing division among Futanke settlers and soldiers is evident in the history of the Futanke grain trade at Medine. Futanke involvement in grain production began in the 1860s and continued until the eve of the French conquest of Karta in the 1890s. After the French victory, military officials expelled thousands of Futanke from Jomboxo and sent them to the Senegal valley.[38] This action destroyed the production complex and removed social groups who might have perpetuated oral memory of the grain trade in family reminis-cences.[39] Fortunately, archives from the post at Medine provide ample evi-dence for the reconstruction of the Futanke grain trade at Medine.

Futanke Grain at the Market in Medine

African traders (known as *traitants* in the French terminology) throughout the Senegal valley concerned themselves with the grain trade because desert-side commercial groups demanded grain in exchange for their loads of gum.[40] In the lower Senegal valley, for example, desert-side demand for grain far out-stripped the supply, forcing traders to search upstream for additional millet.[41] At the inception of the gum trade at Medine, the *traitants* necessarily involved themselves in the grain trade in order to meet the demands of their major gum suppliers.[42] Medine's *traitants* were not brokers but grain wholesalers, which allowed them to negotiate more freely the terms of their exchanges with the gum traders.[43]

The primary suppliers of grain to Medine were Futanke based in Konyakary and its hinterland, the province of Jomboxo. The first reference to Futanke involvement in the grain trade appears in a French report from Medine in 1872, which states unambiguously that "millet [is] brought almost exclu-sively by Futanke."[44] Corroborating evidence includes French descriptions of Medine's population that refer to a large seasonal influx of Futanke at a time when references to grain caravans also increased.[45] Subsequent French reports on the number of caravans arriving monthly in Medine assert that Futanke from Jomboxo supplied most of the grain arriving at the market.[46] While Futanke sold grain elsewhere, most notably in Konyakary where salt mer-chants accepted grain for Ijil salt, demand for grain at Medine probably drove prices high, luring suppliers to send most of their harvest to the *traitants*. Medine's market clearly functioned as an entrepôt for Jomboxo grain.

Jomboxo's status as a source of grain reflected the favorable conditions for production in the region and its proximity to Medine. Annual rains created a flood plain along the Xoolimbinne valley, where dry season cultivation allowed farmers to produce a second harvest. Mungo Park, who passed through Jomboxo in the late eighteenth century, noted that both the extent and productivity of the cultivated region around Konyakary surpassed everything that he had observed during his travels in Africa.[47] The communities of Jomboxo were between one to two days travel time from Medine, which kept transportation costs low for producers. The Futanke never had to establish exchange relationships with local herders from the desert-side, as did other

producers in the region, because they monopolized grain exchanges at
Medine.[48]

The volume of the Futanke grain trade with Medine is difficult to calcu-
late with precision and certainty. French reports only provide figures for the
grain trade that interested them; that is, millet sent to the colonial capital at
Saint-Louis (see table 2). For the period of the late 1870s and early 1880s, the
French reported annual figures of between 275 and 400 metric tons of grain
leaving Bakel.[49] Thus, the volume of Medine's grain trade reported by the
French quickly met and then exceeded the quantities for Bakel in the same
period.

Table 2. **Volume of *traitant* grain purchases at Medine, 1860–1890[50]**

Purchasing year(s)[51]	Kilograms of grain[52]
1860–71	n.f.
1871–72	65,000
1872–73	n.f.
1873–74	127,000
1874–77	n.f.
1877–78	400,000*
1878–81	n.f.
1881–82	355,282*[53]
1882–83	500,000*
1883–84	n.f.
1884–85	500,000*
1884–90	n.f.

n.f. = no figures reported
*Total does not reflect purchases for the entire marketing year

Medine's grain market also provided grain for the consumption needs of the
French army as their personnel increased with their military advances into the
Western Sudan during the 1880s. While the French planned initially to supply
their African troops with grain obtained through taxation and purchase at the
posts in the interior, their inability to tap these local sources forced them to buy
grain in the upper Senegal valley and transport the supplies over land to the
army.[54] Grain shortfalls frequently threatened the French position in the interior, and French officials turned increasingly to the market at Medine, which
was less than 15 kilometers away from their headquarters at Kayes.[55]

Desert-side commercial groups claimed most of the grain passing through the market at Medine. No figures exist upon which to estimate the volume of these exchanges at Medine, but François Manchuelle provides an indication of its quantity in his analysis of the grain trade at Bakel.[56] He argues convincingly that close to a thousand metric tons of grain left Bakel to supply desert-side demand for grain in the lower Senegal valley gum market during the early decades of the nineteenth century. The tapping of upper valley grain harvests, despite the transportation costs of moving the grain by boat, points to the importance of grain in the context of the gum trade. The expansion of the gum trade at Medine depended upon the annual arrival of hundreds if not thousands of metric tons of grain unreported in French documents. Whatever the precise volume of grain, the French sources are unambiguously clear that Futanke from Jomboxo brought most of the grain in the market at Medine.

Political Economy of the Grain Trade in Umarian Jomboxo

The fact that the Futanke monopolized the grain trade between Jomboxo and Medine is not surprising, given Umarian involvement in the establishment of Medine as a gum market and the tight control exercised over commerce in all the Umarian territories of the western Sudan.[57] Restricted participation in commercial life reflected the Umarian ideology which divided society into two classes: the followers of Al-Hajj Umar and subordinate groups of the state.[58] In the context of the grain trade at Medine, limited access to the market ensured that only those with privileged social positions were allowed to reap exchange values from the grain surpluses of the region. Futanke settlers were the main beneficiaries of restricted access to Medine.

Military leaders at Konyakary inaugurated the grain trade at Medine and controlled it during the initial years of the exchange. In 1863, Cerno Musa, a Futanke military leader at Konyakary, opened commercial relations with the French by sending grain to their post at Medine.[59] Grain exchanges continued at Medine throughout the mid-1860s, with Umarian agents exchanging grain for *guinée* cloth, European luxury goods, and weapons.[60] The French bought so much that one official boasted of being able to provision all the French posts of the Senegal valley with Umarian grain.[61] Once Medine emerged as a gum market, Umarian leaders from Konyakary sent larger quantities of grain to Medine. *Traitants* willingly exchanged weapons for grain to accommodate the needs of military leaders at Konyakary.

The Umarian state obtained the grain for exchange at Medine from direct taxation of Jomboxo's agricultural output. Umar Tal initially instituted a tax on the harvests of Jomboxo to stop the widespread grain confiscation by the army which was threatening to erode local support for Umarian rule.[62] The tax became known as the *jakka*, in conscious reference to the *zakat* (the alms tax in Islamic law). Authority for its assessment and collection fell on the military leaders of Konyakary, initially Cerno Jibi, the first Umarian governor of Konyakary, and eventually Bassiru Tal, Umar's son who resided in Konyakary from 1874. Most of the grain collected as *jakka* was stored at Konyakary, where the leaders used it to provision the standing army residing at the capital and to celebrate the major Muslim holidays. When the surpluses were high, state officials freely traded a portion at Medine.[63] State exchanges stopped, however, when military campaigns or official visitors placed demands on the use of surplus grain in the treasury.[64]

Umarian leaders assigned important lieutenants the task of collecting the tax in outlying areas, and these agents also participated in the grain trade at Medine.[65] Agents traditionally retained a portion of the tax for their own support, sometimes keeping up to one-half of the *jakka* for themselves. The emergence of the grain market at Medine encouraged agents to take their full share of the taxes, since grain now had both exchange and consumption value. As a result, tax collectors in Jomboxo usually met or exceeded the recommended tenth of the harvest in contrast to agents in other Kartan provinces.[66] The ability of Jomboxo's agents to exchange grain at Medine was circumscribed, however, by the fact that the military leader at Konyakary could revoke the right to collect taxes if he thought that the agent was abusing the privilege.

In addition to Umarian military leaders and their agents, Futanke settlers also participated in the grain trade at Medine. Suleyman Eliman, a Futanke who fought in the holy war and settled at Konyakary, described his involvement in the grain trade to Paul Soleillet, whom he accompanied on his trip to Segu in the late 1870s.[67] Suleyman told Soleillet how, during a diplomatic mission to Bakel, he exchanged several donkey loads of grain for *guinée* cloth, the primary currency in the gum markets.[68] Once back in Jomboxo, Suleyman traded the *guinée* cloth for Ijil salt bars from desert-side merchants who resided at Konyakary. Suleyman completed his transactions by exchanging the salt bars for gold at Buré, a gold-producing region southeast of Karta. These exchanges show the options available to transform surplus grain into gold or other goods.

Suleyman's description points to extensive Futanke participation in the grain trade. His travels, for example, reflect a desire to maximize a return on each exchange: grain fetched a higher price at the upper valley markets than in Konyakary, while the value of salt bars increased as one moved to the south, and gold prices were lowest near the source of production at Buré. By his actions, one can reasonably conclude that Suleyman was not an occasional participant in commercial dealings, but an experienced trader. Moreover, he probably recounted his exchanges to inform Soleillet of the commercial strategies of his social strata. Soleillet articulated his idea that French commercial expansion would greatly benefit the inhabitants of the western Sudan, and Suleyman responded by arguing for the virtues of restricted access to markets that benefited Futanke officials and settlers in Karta.

Suleyman Eliman was representative of Futanke settlers who had fought in the *jihad*, received numerous slaves as booty from the campaigns, and put them to work in Jomboxo. Many settlers owned slaves who worked on land in the outskirts of Konyakary or in agricultural settlements along the Xoolimbinne valley.[69] Many of these initial settlers had been state agents who collected taxes in the 1860s and subsequently retired from state service. Their official involvement in the grain trade gave them connections with the *traitants* and knowledge of the economic potential of increasing grain production. As prominent members of the Umarian community, they also had the social standing to ensure continued access to the market at Medine. The grain trade thus provided this older group of Futanke with the means to consolidate their hold over the agricultural sector of Jomboxo.

These same Futanke settlers invested in slave labor to expand production in Jomboxo. These investments in turn put pressure on the Konyakary slave market: in the 1880s, slave prices reportedly were twice as high in Konyakary as prices in the middle Senegal valley, thereby allowing migrants who arrived with slaves to obtain funds to send for additional family members.[70] These migrants also supported the production complex by joining Umarian armies, capturing slaves in the southern campaigns, and exchanging them in Konyakary. Futanke demand for labor seems to have increased prices for slaves in Jomboxo at a time when prices in other regions were declining.[71] Futanke purchases of additional slaves indicate that the grain trade at Medine was sufficiently profitable to merit investment in additional labor inputs in spite of the costs.

As Futanke settlers turned to production, the contradictions in the Umarian social formation came to the fore. By the 1870s, many settlers refused to join military campaigns, expressing their resistance in terms of their pressing involvement in agricultural production.[72] These settlers did not share the enthusiasm for military conquests of Bassiru, Umar's son who served as the military leader of Jomboxo after 1874. Bassiru's campaigns diverted labor and managerial talents from production and often caused a halt in the caravan traffic from

Jomboxo to Medine.[73] The settlers' resistence proved so successful that Bassiru began sending recruiters to Futa Toro in order to find enough soldiers to field an army.[74] Thousands of new recruits arrived in Jomboxo during the late 1870s and 1880s, creating tensions between the initial settlers and a new generation of Futanke soldiers led by Umar's sons.

Invitations to migrate to Umarian Karta were well received among the Fulbe communities of the lower valley, who began to migrate eastward in large numbers beginning in the late 1870s.[75] Many of these Fulbe were young men who left their families back in the Senegal valley with promises to send for their relatives when they had accumulated sufficient wealth to establish a household.[76] These migrants saw the army as the best vehicle for such accumulation, and joined it without hesitation. Not surprisingly, the French noted that the armies under the command of Bassiru and Muntaga consisted of young soldiers.[77]

Bassiru settled his recruits at Segala, the former Massassi garrison along the Xoolimbinne River. Soleillet passed through Segala in the late 1870s and observed that it actually was two settlements.[78] One village, which was surrounded by well-attended fields, was the residence of settlers who occupied the village immediately after the conquest.[79] The other village was a garrison for the Fulbe migrants of the late 1870s; it continued to receive Fulbe migrants well into the 1880s.[80] The two settlements of Segala reflected the larger conflicts emerging within the Umarian community in Jomboxo: the initial group of settlers controlled the productive land whereas subsequent migrants lived in garrisons and looked to military service for their material support. Their conflict expressed the social contradictions inherent in the creation of a state society after a conquest.

The initial settlers, whose military conquests had brought Karta under Umarian control, claimed that the holy war was over and felt that Bassiru's campaigns were unnecessary.[81] They felt that the state should support their efforts to exploit the agricultural potential of Jomboxo.[82] Their social status as Umar's disciples meant that Bassiru could not dismiss their opinions. At the same time, however, Bassiru had to respond to the demands of his recruits, who probably felt that the obligation of *jihad* fell upon all Muslims regardless of the past accomplishments.[83] They saw warfare as the primary occupation of the Umarian state. The conflict led Futanke settlers to challenge Bassiru's leadership during the mid-1880s. Amadu Moktar and Suleyman Eliman, Futanke leaders from Konyakary, led a Futanke delegation which met with Amadu Sheku, Umar's son and successor as Commander of the Faithful, during his second residence in Nioro.[84] They won his support for the replacement of

Bassiru with Amadu Moktar as the leader at Konyakary. The settlers' political victory was short-lived, however; after Amadu Moktar died in late 1885, the growing threat of French invasion forced Amadu Sheku to reappoint Bassiru to the leadership of Jomboxo.[85]

The social contradictions in Jomboxo remained evident during Amadu Sheku's brief reign in Karta. He spent his years in Karta suppressing rebellions—inspired by the Muslim reformer Mamadu Lamine—in the northern Xoolimbinne valley. Amadu also confronted the French and consequently tried to stop the flow of Jomboxo grain to Medine, but many Futanke settlers refused to comply with Amadu's order.[86] It should be noted that Futanke settlers in Jomboxo separated their economic interests in the grain trade from political affiliation: they never attempted to ally with the French. But Amadu was not able to coordinate a unified Umarian military strategy against the French because of the social divisions in Karta. His strongest base of support was among recent Senegal valley recruits, who enthusiastically joined his military campaigns against the French in the late 1880s.

Conclusion

Few have appreciated the importance of Karta in the context of the Umarian consolidation of power in the western Sudan. The tendency is to view the region as a periphery of an imperial Umarian state and focus on developments in Umarian Segu, the "center" of the state.[87] In Karta, the *jihad* overthrew an elite who had not established intimate relations with many subordinate communities. Umarian leaders pursued policies which linked Karta with regional commercial activity and initially benefited many groups in the region. In time, however, the large Futanke community of settlers came to influence state policy as they retired from the army, secured exemption from taxation, and gained economic benefits from the land and slaves obtained during the conquest. Their interests brought them into conflict with local producers and the Umarian military apparatus.

The emergence of the Futanke grain trade at Medine illustrates one aspect of the Umarian consolidation in Karta. State policy assisted in the rise of a gum market at Medine, where growing demand for grain provided Futanke settlers with an opportunity to reap benefits from their control over land and slaves in Jomboxo. The settlers used their social status to eliminate taxes on their harvests and gain access to the market at Medine, while Umar's sons and a new generation of Futanke recruits replaced them in the military apparatus. As long as the military campaigns did not disrupt commercial exchanges, the settlers tolerated continued warfare. Once the French advance altered the economic context of campaigns in the south, the settlers became more vocal in their opposition. Differences in material interests exacerbated generational cleavages related to the Umarian movement in Karta.

Notes

1. Futanke are residents of Futa Toro in the middle Senegal River valley, Tukolor and Toucouleur are synonyms for Futanke.

2. For a recent analysis of the Umarian *jihad*, see David Robinson, *The Holy War of Umar Tal* (Oxford: Clarendon Press, 1985).

3. S. Kanya-Forstner, *The Conquest of the Western Sudan* (London: Cambridge, 1969).

4. Yves Saint-Martin, *L'Empire toucouleur* (Paris: Livre africain, 1970); B. O. Oloruntimehin, *The Segu Tukulor Empire* (London: Longman, 1972); Richard Roberts, *Warriors, Merchants and Slaves* (Stanford: Stanford University Press, 1987).

5. See John H. Hanson, "Umarian Karta (Mali, West Africa) in the late nineteenth century: dissent and revolt among the Futanke after Umar Tal's holy war" (Ph.D. thesis, Michigan State University, 1989); hereafter referred to as "Umarian Karta."

6. Joseph Gallieni, *Voyage au Soudan français* (Paris, Hachette et cie, 1885); Paul Soleillet, *Voyage à Ségou (1878–79)* (Paris: Challamel, 1887); Henry Frey, *Campagne dans le Haut-Sénégal et dans le Haut-Niger* (Paris: Plon, 1888); Jacques Méniaud, *Les Pionniers du Soudan*, 2 volumes (Paris: Société des publications modernes, 1931).

7. C. Meillassoux, "The role of slavery in economic and social history of Sahelio-Sudanic Africa," in J. Inikori, ed., *Forced Migration* (London: Hutchinson, 1982).

8. Roberts' work initially focused on the middle Niger River valley, but he subsequently extended the scope of his analysis to include Karta. Compare Roberts, "Production and reproduction of warrior states: the Segu Bambara and Segu Tukolor," *International Journal of African Historical Studies* 13 (1980), with *Warriors, Merchants and Slaves*, 100–6.

9. Jean Bazin touches briefly on similar patterns in his analysis of the Bambara state of Segu: "Guerre et servitude à Ségou," in Claude Meillassoux, ed., *L'Esclavage en Afrique précoloniale* (Paris: F. Maspero, 1975).

10. Y. Saint-Martin, *L'Empire toucouleur et la France*, 183–84.

11. Sékéné-Mody Cissoko, "Contribution à l'histoire politique des royaumes du Khasso dans le Haut Sénégal des origines à la conquête française," 2 volumes, (thèse de Doctorat d'état, University of Paris, 1979), 640–44. François Manchuelle notes that the data for the grain trade at Medine are "almost non-existent" but he assumes that a considerable quantity flowed through the market; see Manchuelle, "Background to Black African emigration to France: The labor migrations of the Soninke, 1848–1987" (Ph.D. thesis, University of California, Santa Barbara, 1987), 182.

12. Charles Monteil, *Les Bambara de Ségou et du Kaarta* (Paris: G. P. Maisonneuvre & LaRose, 1924), 4–5.

13. The Massassi state in Karta, in contrast to its neighbor in Segu, is not blessed with extensive historical literature. Sékéné-Mody Cissoko provides a very useful overview in *Contribution à l'histoire politique du Khasso dans le Haut-Sénégal des origines à 1854* (Paris: Harmattan, 1986).

14. For an Arabic document discussing the defeat of the Awlad Mbark, see *Bibliothèque Nationale de Paris, Manuscrits Orientaux, Fonds Arabes* (hereafter BNP, MO, FA) vol. 5631, fos. 10–11.

15. This paragraph summarizes my argument in chapter 2 of "Umarian Karta."

16. Saint-Martin describes informal negotiations between Umarian leaders at Konyakary and the French in *L'Empire toucouleur et la France,* chapter 4.

17. James Webb, Jr., "The trade in gum arabic: prelude to the French conquest in Senegal," *Journal of African History* 26 (1985).

18. A. Raffenel, *Nouveau voyage dans le pays des Nègres,* vol. 1 (Paris, 1856), 386–87.

19. French officials report on the negotiations which occurred at Medine in their correspondence in the *Archives Nationales du Sénégal* (hereafter ANS) 13G210–213 and 15G108–109.

20. *Archives Nationales du Mali* (hereafter ANM) 1D48: "Monographie de Médine."

21. ANS Q23.

22. Pierre Amilhat (ed. and trans.), "Petite chronique des Id ou Aich, hériteurs guerriers des Almoravides sahariens," *Revue des études islamiques* II (1937): 41–130.

23. Very few data exist in the archives regarding the firearms trade; a reference for 1871 puts Umarian purchases at 1,500–1,800 guns for the year. ANS 13G171: Bakel, 28 February 1871, Ct. Bakel to the governor.

24. The Ijil salt trade is discussed in E. Ann McDougall, "The Ijil salt industry: Its role in the precolonial economy of the Western Sudan" (Ph.D. thesis, Birmingham University, 1980).

25. Paul Marty, *Etudes sur l'Islam et les tribus du Soudan,* vol. 4 (Paris: E. Leroux, 1921), 215–16.

26. See my taped oral interviews of 26 January 1986 with Amadou Ba and 6 February 1986 with Yilé Sibey at *Nioro-du-Sahel,* Mali.

27. Eric Pollet and Grace Winter, *La Société soninké* (Brussels:Éditions de Institute de sociologie, Université libre de Bruxelles, 1971).

28. ANM 1D51: "Notice historique sur la région du Sahel par Ct. de Lartigues;" ANS 1G310: "Renseignements historiques, géographiques et économiques sur le Cercle de Kayes par Administrateur Roux," Kayes, 30 March 1904.

29. Tiébilé Dramé, "Alfa Umar Kaba Jakite, fondateur de Kabala, marabout et conseiller de Siixumaru Tal (Al-Hajj Umar)," *Islam et sociétés au sud de Sahara* 2 (1988): 114–21. Alfa Umar's sons and grandsons continued to play a role in Umarian affairs.

30. B. O. Oloruntimehin, "Muhammad Lamine in Franco-Tukulor relations, 1885–87," *Journal of the Historical Society of Nigeria* 4 (1968); Daniel Nyambarza, "Le Marabout El Hadj Mamadou Lamine d'aprés les archives françaises," *Cahiers d'Etudes Africaines* 9 (1969); Abdoulaye Bathily, "Mahmadou Lamine Dramé et la résistance anti-impérialiste dans le Haut-Sénégal (1885–87)," *Notes Africaines* 125 (1970).

31. *Archives Nationales de la France, Section Outre-Mer* (hereafter ANF.SOM) SEN.I 61c: Saint-Louis, 5 June 1878, governor to the minister.

32. Emile Blanc, a French colonial official, published some oral traditions regarding the raids in "Contribution à l'étude des populations et de l'histoire du Sahel soudanais," *Bulletin du Comité d'Etudes Historiques et Scientifiques de l'Afrique Occidentale Française* 7 (1924).

33. During this era, Amadu Sheku obtained recognition as the commander of the Faithful from desert-side groups north of Karta. BNP, MO, FA., vols. 5640, fos. 25–38; 5713, fos. 46, 59, 182.

34. Roberts documents the economic dislocation and the rise of new regional commercial centers, such as Banamba, at the expense of previous commercial centers, such as Sinsani, in *Warriors, Merchants and Slaves*, especially on pages 107–12.

35. Local cloth served as the currency in Karta. During the late nineteenth century, *guinée* cloth expanded into Karta and functioned as a currency. Cowrie shells, however, never penetrated the Kartan economy, indicating that the middle Niger region did not pull Karta into its sphere; see Soleillet, *Voyage à Ségou*, 168. Karta's economic autonomy also is reflected in its ability to receive Ijil salt even when quantities were scarce in Segu. ANF.SOM SEN.I 58a: Saint-Louis, 21 July 1874, governor to the minister of Colonies.

36. Ct. Sup. Borgnis-Desbordes, who led the French advance in the early 1880s, felt that Muntaga, the Umarian leader at Nioro, would accept an alliance with the French in order to ensure Kartan access to French markets, but Muntaga refused all initiatives. ANS 1D68: Bamako, 11 and 14 February 1883, Ct. Sup. to the governor; ANS 15G144, no. 110: Nioro, n.d., Muntaga to Ct. Sup. (in Arabic).

37. Muntaga informed the French that their advance divided his followers into two groups: supporters and opponents of military confrontation. Ct. Sup. Borgnis-Desbordes summarizes Muntaga's letter in ANS 1D69: "Rapport sur la campagne, 1882–83."

38. Méniaud, *Pionniers*, 2:336–38; ANM 1D51: "Notice historique sur la région du Sahel."

39. Few current residents of western Mali remember the production complex in any detail. I discuss the issue in chapter 5 of "Umarian Karta."

40. *Guinée* cloth also was an item of exchange in the markets of the Senegal River valley. Abdoulaye Bathily notes a similar integration of the slave and grain trades for an earlier period in "La traite atlantique des esclaves et ses effets économiques et sociaux en Afrique: la cas du Galam," *J. Afr. Hist.* 27 (1986): 269–93.

41. Manchuelle discusses the activities of these traders, referred to by the French as *marigotiers*, for the Bakel area during the early nineteenth century: "Background to Black emigration," 94–99.

42. The first reference to the integration of the gum and grain trades at Medine appears in 1872, but the *traitants* surely were involved in the grain trade prior to that date. ANS 15G109: Medine, 1 August 1872, Ct. Medine to the governor.

43. This conclusion reflects assertions in French reports that the *traitants* brought grain at 'favourable' prices.

44. ANS 15G109: Medine, 6 January 1872, Ct. Medine to the governor.

45. ANS 15G113: "Recensement de la population de Médine—1882."

46. ANS 15G111: Medine, June 1877, [and] February, March, April, November 1879, "Registre journal"; ANM 1Q70: Medine, 26 July 1884, "Rapport commercial"; ANM 1Q70: Medine, 18 October 1885, "Rapport sur l'accroissement du commerce."

47. Mungo Park, *Travels in the Interior of Africa* (New York: D. P. Dutton, 1907). Similar assessments from subsequent eras appear in Major W. Gray and Staff Surgeon Dochard, *Travels in Western Africa* (London: J. Murray, 1825), 299, and ANS 1D117: n.p., n.d., "Lignes d'étapes de Konyakary à Dionkolané."

48. Local groups in the upper Xoolimbinne valley north of Jomboxo exchanged much of their surplus grain with desert-side herders for milk, hides, cattle, and small quantities of salt.

49. The French officials never distinguished between millet *(petit mil)* and sorghum *(gros mil)*. The quantitative estimates appear in: ANF.SOM SEN.I 56b: Saint-Louis, 14 September 1872, governor to the minister; ANS 12G109: Medine, July 1874 and April 1878, "Bulletin agricole, commercial et politique"; ANS 15G111: Medine, April 1882, "Bulletin agricole, commercial et politique"; ANM 1E54: Medine, May 1883, "Bulletin agricole, commercial et politique"; ANS 2B75: Saint-Louis, 12 September and 12 November 1885, governor to the minister.

50. The "purchasing year" began in October with the harvest of grains and ran until the end of the subsequent rainy season. Most of the grain trade occurred between January and June.

51. The *traitants* estimated the grain trade in terms of *barriques*, the largest unit of measurement used in the Senegal valley. I use a 20:1 ratio in my calculations for this table. French estimates of the *barrique* appear in ANM 1Q70: Medine, 1 April 1886, "Rapport commercial"; ANM 1E207: Medine, 13 May 1886, Ct. Medine to the Ct. des Cercles; ANS 2B75: Saint-Louis, 12 August 1885, governor to the minister.

52. Umarian leaders imposed an embargo on trade with Medine for several months in 1881–82, or the figure would have been higher.

53. ANS 13G184: Bakel, 1 October 1884, "Rapport trimestriel."

54. Richard Roberts, "The emergence of a grain market in Bamako, 1883–1908," *Canadian Journal of African Studies* 14 (1980).

55. ANS 1D62: Kita, 14 February 1881, Ct. Sup. to governor; ANS 3B98: Saint-Louis, 3 August 1883, governor to Ct. Sup.

56. Manchuelle, "Background to Black migration," 94–99.

57. Roberts, *Warriors, Merchants and Slaves*, 100–6.

58. Marty, *Etudes sur l'Islam*, 4:237–38.

59. ANS 13G168: Medine, 7 October 1863, Ct. Medine to Ct. Bakel.

60. ANS 13G210: Medine, 16 October 1865, Ct. Medine to Ct. Bakel; ANS 15G108: Medine, 27 March 1866, Ct. Medine to Ct. Bakel.

61. ANS 13G210: Medine, 27 July 1864, Ct. Medine to Ct. Bakel.

62. Information drawn from the Arabic chronicle composed by Cerno Yahya Tal of Konyakary. He presents information from extensive oral interviews conducted by Demba Sadio Diallo, a local oral historian. Cerno Yahya allowed me to tape his oral recitation of the chronicle.

63. ANS 15G108: Medine, 27 March 1866, Ct. Medine to Ct. Bakel.

64. ANS 15G109: Medine, 6 January 1872; ANM 1E54: Medine, June 1887, "Rapport politique."

65. A few local elites obtained the authorization to collect *jakka*, but most agents were Futanke immigrants; see Cissoko, "Contribution à l'histoire."

66. Compare, for example, the comments in ANM 1D51: "Notice historique," drawn from information from the Nioro region, and ANS 1G310: "Renseignements historiques," drawn from informants from the Konyakary region.

67. Soleillet, *Voyage à Ségou*, 222–23.

68. When Medine was closed, Futanke settlers sometimes took their grain to Bakel. ANS 13G173: Bakel, 21 February 1876, Ct. Bakel to the governor.

69. Soleillet describes Futanke slavery in *Voyage à Ségou*, 162ff.

70. ANS 13G187: Bakel 23 February 1887, Ct. Bakel to Ct. Kaves.

71. Calculations of slave prices in the aftermath of the trans-Atlantic slave trade are based on very limited data. Martin Klein offers numerous insights in his corpus of works on slavery. See, for example, M. Klein, "The demography of slavery in the Western Sudan," in J. Gregory and D. Cordell, eds., *African Population and Capitalism. Historical Perspectives* (Boulder: Westview Press, 1987). Other useful works in a growing literature include Paul Lovejoy, *Transformations in Slavery* (Cambridge: Cambridge University Press, 1983) and the contributions in Meillassoux, ed., *L'Esclavage en Afrique précoloniale*.

72. ANS 15G109: Medine, 1 May 1874, "Registre journal"; 15G110: Medine, 7 September 1876, Ct. Medine to the governor; 15G111: Medine, 3O June 1877, "Régistre journal"; Medine, June 1877, and March and April 1879, "Bulletin agricole, commercial et politique."

73. Between 1874 and 1885, the French report no less than ten instances of commercial stoppage, of one week to several months, due to wars or embargoes in Umarian Karta.

74. ANF.SOM SEN.I. 61c: Saint-Louis, 5 June 1878, governor to the minister.

75. See an analysis of the movement in chapter 3 of "Umarian Karta."

76. ANS 13G127: Podor, 14 March 1878, Ct. Podor to Ct. Bakel.

77. ANS 1D73: Kayes, 31 October 1883, Ct. Sup. to the governor; ANS 15G126: Kita, 29 April 1884, Ct. Kita to Ct. Sup.

78. Soleillet, *Voyage à Ségou*, 158–61.

79. "Rapport de M. Perraud sur un voyage à Nioro," *Le Moniteur du Sénégal et Dépendances* 488 (1865).

80. ANS 1D105: "Rapport militaire, 1889–90," 63.

81. Futanke settlers from Konyakary communicated these sentiments to the French *commandant* at Medine. ANS 15G110: Medine, 7 September 1876, Ct. Medine to the governor.

82. After the French conquest, Futanke settlers tried to convince French officials that they should be allowed to return to Jomboxo because they had expanded agricultural production in the region. ANM 1D74: "Rapport du Cpt. Mazillier sur le Jomboxo, le Séro et les Maures d'Askeur."

83. Taped interview of 25 September 1977 with Mamadou Alpha Diallo at Gavinané, Mali, by Abdoul Aziz Diallo. Diallo kindly shared his oral evidence with me.

84. The visit occurred in the context of Amadu's struggle with his brother Muntaga. I discuss the conflict in "Umarian Karta" chapters 8 and 9. French sources for the period include: ANM 1E207: Medine, 19 January, 6 March, 5, 13, and 28 April, 8 and 18 May 1885, Ct. Medine to Ct. Sup; ANM 1E54: Medine, 15 April 1885, "Rapport politique"; ANS 15G127: Kita, 15 May 1885, Ct. Kita to Ct. Sup.

85. The appeal to Amadu Sheku points to the broader Umarian context and the diversity of interests in Karta. Although Umar delegated power over Kartan affairs to local Umarian leaders when he left Nioro in 1859, Amadu Sheku claimed authority over the region by virtue of his subsequent appointment as commander of the Faithful. Other sons of Umar also tried to seize power in Nioro and Konyakary, leading to a confrontation among various claimants beginning in the late 1860s. Amadu Sheku marched to Nioro and defeated his main rivals, but not without the support of several brothers, whom he later appointed as military leaders in Karta. These appointees subsequently asserted their autonomy from Amadu, forcing him to march to Karta for a second time in 1885. He once again defeated the challenge and remained at Nioro until the French invasion of northern Karta in 1891. Several written sources point to the delegation of power, including an Arabic chronicle composed by members of the Kaba Jakite family and translated by French officials. See M. G. Adam, *Légendes historiques du pays de Nioro (Sahel)* (Paris: A Challamel, 1904); Maurice Delafosse, "Traditions historiques et légendaires du Soudan Occidental," *Bulletin du Comité d'Afrique Française, Renseignements Coloniaux* 8–10 (1913).

86. Only a poor harvest in 1889 brought the grain trade to a halt. ANM 1E54: Medine, June 1887, "Rapport politique"; ANM 1Q70: Medine, 31 July 1880, Ct. Medine to Ct. Sup.; ANS 15G76/3: Kayes, 1 November 1889.

87. Saint-Martin, *L'Empire toucouleur*; Oloruntimehin, *Segu Tukolor Empire*; Roberts, *Warriors, Merchants and Slaves.* Roberts's occasional references to autonomous garrisons and political 'zones' are obscured by his statements regarding an "Umarian state" which encompasses the entire Western Sudan.

The Fulbright-Hays Doctoral Dissertation Research Abroad Fellowship provided support for the field and archive research upon which I base this article. I would like to express my appreciation to David Robinson for his comments on this article at various stages of its preparation and to Joseph Miller for his comments on the penultimate draft.

Women in Francophone West Africa in the 1930s: Unraveling a Neglected Report

GHISLAINE LYDON

On 7 October 1937, Marcel Jules de Coppet, the governor-general of French West Africa (AOF),[1] delegated an important assignment to a *conseillère technique de l'enseignement*, Denise Moran Savineau. She was to head a *mission d'enquête*[2] in AOF on "la condition de la femme et de la famille, dans les écoles, l'emploi, etc."[3] That French administrators felt it necessary to finance a special inquiry for the sole purpose of gathering data on African women in the colonies was rather *avant-garde*. Furthermore, this project seems to have assumed a high-priority nature judging from the correspondence exchanged prior to and during Denise Moran's eight-month-long fieldwork. M. de Coppet took this project seriously and, in a circular addressed to all governors in AOF, he said:

> Madame Savineau . . . devra jouir d'une grande liberté de mouvement. . . .
> J'attache une grande importance aux conclusions de cette enquête, qui devra
> être minutieuse, et je vous serais reconnaissant d'assurer à Madame Savineau
> le concours le plus large de la part des commandants de postes, du personnel
> enseignant et médical, des magistrats, des indigènes qualifiés et notamment
> des interprètes, qui devront être soigneusement choisis.[4]

Yet what incentives drove the governor-general to sponsor such noteworthy research? Possible explanations can be inferred by placing this event in its historical context.

West Africa in the Great Depression

Throughout the 1930s, the Great Depression had detrimental repercussions in Africa. The period was characterized by an overall reduction in colonial economic activity linked to a drop in cash-crop prices and exports which led to increased unemployment and underemployment.[5] Although colonial enterprises were first hit, the Depression quickly precipitated local economies into decline. For Africans, an extreme scarcity of resources and cash was all the more debilitating with colonial taxation. In fact, taxes continued to rise in Francophone Africa throughout the 1930s, even in the worst years. As Catherine Coquery-Vidrovitch explains, "En Afrique noire, le contraste est frappant de la compensation budgétaire effectuée grâce à l'imposition indigène, qui continua de progresser en pleine crise, et dont le plafond coïncide précisément au moment où les cours, au plus bas, entraînaient la rémunération paysanne la plus faible, c'est-à-dire au moment où le producteur était le moins à même d'affronter la charge."[6] According to Patrick Manning's calculations, 1934 export prices fell to 20 percent of their 1927 level, yet government revenues were only cut in half "which meant that effective tax rates more than doubled."[7]

During the 1930s, poverty reached unsurpassed levels and people resorted to multifarious means of acquiring cash in order to meet tax duties as well as basic needs. As usual, money lenders provided their services, and to pay back loans many people reverted to pawning or pledging family members as securities for loans. Pawning of women and girls in particular was still practiced in the late 1930s when Moran was compiling her reports. That the colonial administration was concerned about the increased activity of pawning and such practices could perhaps account for the decision to launch a large-scale study of the condition of women and families in French West Africa.

European Concern for African Women

Colonial officials were familiar with the concerns of missionaries who adopted women's tribulations as a strategic theme. Evidence from the early 1930s indicates that French missionaries of the *Compagnie du Saint-Esprit* were actively embracing the cause of African women.[8] For the archbishop, Monseigneur A. Le Roy, the condition of indigenous women became a cardinal preoccupation. Family matters—namely, betrothal, polygamy, and inheritance rights—were among the prime targets. In May 1936, Monseigneur Le Roy produced a ten-page booklet entitled *Pour le relèvement social de la femme en Afrique française* in which the inferior status of African women was discussed and measures to redress it were stipulated.[9] Such preoccupations gave missionaries a perfectly humanitarian excuse to proselytize among African women, who were identified as vehicles for transmitting Christian beliefs and behavior.

In 1933, the vicar of Ouagadougou wrote to the governor-general of AOF to report his concerns about the incidence of female slavery and marriage transactions.[10] Missionaries' efforts to "relieve women" of oppressive indigenous practices probably influenced colonial matters. In fact, when placed against the conclusions of a recent study that links the Catholic Church to the Popular Front movement in France, these speculations carry further weight.[11] It is also likely that women's political and religious associations put pressure on the French government. Indeed, since the late 1920s, women's groups, often with close ties to the French Catholic Church, began turning their attention to the fate of women in African colonies.[12] It was during these times that French women were actively demonstrating for suffrage and emancipation.

Francophone women voiced their concern about the plight of African women at the 1931 *Exposition coloniale* held in Paris. They organized, under an umbrella movement, the *États généraux du féminisme*, to pay homage to women in the colonies (both the colonizers and the colonized) and foster deliberation on ways to improve the situation of indigenous women.[13] Such political considerations in France presumably inspired officials in the colonies, especially since the main organizers of this movement were the wives of prominent colonial administrators. These issues gained large audiences during the rise of the Popular Front movement in France and the short-lived government led by Léon Blum in 1936.

The Popular Front Government and Its Colonial Agenda

When examining the political climate in France during the mid-1930s, there are clear indications that the social situation in the colonies was a concern. In the years leading up to the socialist victory of May 1936, Popular Front slogans exalted the aim of socialism as the defense of "all the oppressed without distinction of race." Promises to "make the colonial system more humane" by placing an emphasis on public education and "granting political liberties" were also articulated during election campaigns.[14]

For Marius Moutet, nominated to head the colonial office, France's mission was unquestionably "d'amener les fruits de la civilisation française aux colonies."[15] As the first socialist Minister of Colonies, Moutet delegated posts to sympathizers. In so doing, he caused dramatic shuffles in colonial appointments in which eleven of the sixteen governorships in Africa changed hands.[16] This is how Marcel Jules de Coppet came to be appointed governor-general of French West Africa. In fact, Moutet personally installed his friend de Coppet in August 1936 during his first official tour of West Africa.

De Coppet was a socialist with a decidedly liberal reputation and a long-standing career in Africa. He served for over thirty years in Madagascar,

Senegal, Guinea, Chad, Dahomey (present-day Benin), Djibouti (Somalia), and Mauritania.[17] A close friend of André Gide, de Coppet was once suspected of supplying Gide with data that appeared in *Voyage au Congo* (1927), one of the first popular works to report on French abuses in Equatorial Africa. As governor-general, de Coppet's policies and actions reflected his progressive political drive and a seemingly genuine resolve to end exploitation and instill social justice in the colonies. Although de Coppet's style spurred sharp criticisms in and out of the colonial office, his approach was nonetheless a welcome move away from French authoritarianism. An examination of his political agenda is very telling with respect to Denise Moran Savineau's assignment.

In a note on Marius Moutet's colonial agenda, Robert Delavignette explains that it sought to address two broad issues. The first was the "improvement of the fate of the masses" with a focus on preventing famines and enacting protective labor legislation. Labor policies prohibited the employment of women and children on night shifts, shortened the working day, and reduced forced labor duty from fifteen to ten days. The second component of the colonial program was entitled "the road toward political emancipation" and it addressed the dismantling of the system of *indigénat* and the installment of a council of representatives to encourage the colonized to participate in local politics.

With these directives and the guidelines of the SFIO (*Section française de l'Internationale ouvrière*), de Coppet set to work in August 1936. He was the first governor-general to invite African students for a luncheon at the colonial palace. He also inaugurated a number of exceptional colonial reforms. He was the first to observe Muslim holidays (*'id al fitr* and *'id al-adha*), and ordered all colonial administrators in AOF to do the same.[18] De Coppet enacted labor legislation passed much earlier in France yet never applied to the colonies. A decree was activated regarding work-related accidents and compensations, another liberalized syndicalism.[19] This albeit limited political liberalization provoked a swell in trade unions and labor associations which led to a number of strikes starting in 1937. An interesting piece of legislation concerned the protection of women and children. The ordinance of 18 September 1936 contained five clauses on child, family, and female labor.[20] These determined the conditions under which child labor was considered permissible. One clause pertained to regulations of child labor in both public and private establishments. Moreover, so-called 'family labor' was defined, exempting women more than seven months pregnant from strenuous work. De Coppet's reforms modeled the political and social commitment of the Popular Front government which claimed to follow the guidelines of the SFIO, the Human Rights League, and the International Labor Office.[21]

The decision to finance an inquiry on the condition of women in AOF, however contextual, was not entirely of de Coppet's making. When they came to power, neither Léon Blum nor his ministers had a coherent colonial policy.[22] After much electoral rhetoric about reform overseas, the Popular Front government focused mainly on domestic issues. Yet, as discussed above, important social reforms applied in AOF set remarkable precedents.

In August 1936, the French parliament, acting on a proposal by the Minister of the Colonies, Marius Moutet, approved the launching of a wide-scale inquiry on the social conditions in the colonies.[23] The commission was to investigate "the needs and legitimate aspirations of the populations living in the colonies, protectorates, and mandates."[24] This bureaucratic commission of inquiry, which took six months to convene, was headed by Henri Guernut (former minister and Human Rights League delegate) and included among its members such personalities as Robert Delavignette, Hubert Deschamps, Lucien Lévy-Bruhl, and André Gide.[25] According to William Cohen, "instead of making on-the-spot investigations, the commission worked through questionnaires [and] in the end the commission did not carry out its assignment."[26] The project remained for the most part inoperative and eventually failed along with the Popular Front government. However, de Coppet was among the few colonial administrators to take the assignment seriously. Upon receiving the news of the Ministry of the Colonies' agenda, Governor-General de Coppet immediately set to work recruiting French officials to undertake inquiries in AOF, and Denise Moran Savineau was evidently a perfect candidate.

Denise Moran Savineau: An Elusive Biography

Little biographical information is available on Denise Moran Savineau although she was officially appointed to carry out an exceptional assignment. She has no personal file either in the French archives or in the *Archives nationales du Sénégal*. Furthermore, her name is repeatedly misspelled in correspondence exchanged between Moran Savineau and the colonial office; instead of "Moran" one finds "Maran," although she is most often referred to by her married name, "Madame Savineau."

The correct spelling of her family name is confirmed in her only publication, *Tchad*, in which she calls herself Denise Moran (and is hereafter referred to as such). *Tchad* is dedicated to her late husband Edmond Savineau who died in Chad "au service des noirs." In writing this testimony of nearly four years in Chad, she goes well beyond André Gide's *Voyage au Congo*, which was based on a nine-month trip to the area. Like Gide, Moran pays close attention to French concessionary companies and the incidence of forced labor in Equatorial Africa. She reports on the corrupt practices of colonial officials and private companies, and common abuses committed by *tirailleurs sénégalais* or colonial riflemen. Jean Suret-Canale quotes extensively from Moran's account in his seminal history of West Africa.[27] He rightfully ranks Moran's contribution alongside that of Gide as important attempts to publicize human rights violations linked to European presence in Africa.

Tchad reads like a travelogue, rich in dialogues and lengthy citations from local archives. Moran deliberately changed the names of people and places so as to avoid a "scandal." What is more, she is typically elusive about her personal life. For instance, she is never explicit about E. Savineau's post, although he is once referred to as "commandant." Perhaps he was a *commandant de cercle* or a military officer, which would explain why he was in charge of labor recruitment. As for Moran, she did not just play the traditional role of the colonial officer's wife engaged part-time as an educator and a nurse. She worked on several occasions for the administration, and managed "par intérim—le Bureau des affaires politiques et économiques" and explored the archives.[28] It is important to note that both Monsieur and Madame Savineau were to some degree fluent in Arabic, a skill that adds depth to their experiences.

Although she disclosed very little personal information in her writing, it is clear from both *Tchad* and Moran's reports that she was well-traveled. For instance, she compared the *Office du Niger* enterprise to harsh conditions in the Soviet Union where she visited.[29] She had obviously traveled extensively throughout Equatorial Africa, and was very eager to repeat the experience under Marcel de Coppet's governorship in 1937. There is also evidence in her publication that Moran and her husband were close friends with the de Coppets, a friendship that helped, no doubt, in securing her position as head of a mission of inquiry.

When applying for a position in the commission of inquiry, Moran was in Dakar (Senegal) serving as the *conseillère technique de l'enseignement en AOF*.[30] She volunteered to participate in the commission which was to conduct investigations throughout the French colonies in both West and Equatorial Africa.[31] Although she was obviously highly qualified, there seemed to be an initial reluctance on the part of the colonial ministry in France to enlist Moran. But after much deliberation, and de Coppet's support, her application was successful.

As stipulated by decision no 2811, on 21 October 1937, Moran embarked on an expedition accompanied by a *domestique voyageant en 6ᵉ catégorie* and 300 kilograms of luggage.[32] She traveled from Dakar to Bamako in present-day

Mali, then headed to Ségou, Mopti, Timbuktu, down to Gao, and over to Niamey (Niger). From there, she continued eastward to Dogondoutchi, and then turned south to Porto-Novo (present-day Benin), Cotonou, and Lomé (Togo), stopping in various towns along the way. Later, she headed north across Gold Coast (present-day Ghana) to Ouagadougou (in present-day Burkina Faso), before turning west to Bobo-Dioulasso, and then Guinea, slowly making her way back to Senegal in May 1938. It was the responsibility of each colonial territory to secure Moran's passage to the next location. Moran produced a total of eighteen typewritten reports: a *Rapport d'ensemble* (232 pages) and seventeen regional reports averaging forty-five pages each. The entire dossier, entitled *La famille en AOF: condition de la femme*, is approximately 1,000 pages long. Several themes from this report are discussed below.

Women's Roles in Production

Moran's remarkable awareness of economic affairs makes her observations particularly valuable for the study of economic history. She was acutely aware of the fact that colonial encroachment was disrupting patterns of African economic development. Moran expresses this throughout the study: "l'occupation française bouleversé profondément l'Afrique noire . . . nous avons bouleversé l'économie des noirs, et si violemment. . . ."[33] Moran studied a wide range of women entrepreneurs, producing anything from arts and crafts to subsistence commodities such as salt (she explains the varying boiling techniques in several areas) and palm oil (sometimes the labor was gendered, men provided the nuts and women did all the rest). In the late 1930s as today, women were involved in all levels of production, so much so that when attempting to list the commodities produced by women in Conakry, Moran exclaimed, "Les femmes font tout!"[34]

Wherever she visited, Moran inquired about women's activities in the sphere of production or what she termed *industries féminines*. She offered meticulous descriptions and calculated assessments of female occupations from artisans to producers of goods and services. Pottery production was one of the crafts that Moran studied carefully. Her comprehensive cost-evaluations in Niger, Ivory Coast, Mali, and Burkina Faso led her to conclude that over time women experienced a loss in productivity because of the time they spent walking to obtain raw materials. Moran also paid close attention to professional dyers, normally a woman's profession. In Guinea, she examined the various stages of production and estimated women's profits (in French francs).[35]

She calculated that, in Conakry, the average difference between the sale price and the production cost for one *pagne*[36] was Fr 12.25, and Conakry dyers earned about Fr 2.50 a day.

Given these low returns, Moran believed women were wasting their time. Indeed, she declared: "Les femmes ne savent ni établir un prix de revient, ni mesurer leur peine."[37] While it is clear that she did not always appreciate such factors as time and expended energy, which have different realities in the African versus European contexts, Moran apparently accounted for different variables, and such statistics represent a rare attempt to quantify the profits of women entrepreneurs.

Moran's research is not only rich in information on women's crafts and manufacturing activities, but also on the production and distribution of commodities such as foodstuffs. A typical example is the manufacture of shea butter in the Gaoua region of present-day Burkina Faso.[38] The production of shea butter (*beurre de karité*), from picking and carrying nuts to the lengthy cooking and processing, is carefully described. Five kilograms of shea nuts worth Fr 1.50 on the market produced one kilogram of butter worth Fr 1.[39] In other words, the women's work decreased the value of the product. It is likely, however, that the time/labor involved in transporting shea butter to the market was far less than that of carrying five times the weight in bulk nuts.

The reports also contain several other cases where women's production inputs, such as processing raw materials, were not compensated by a higher sales price of the end product. From these cases, Moran observed that seemingly unproductive processing of edible commodities to conserve them actually reduced their value: "Plus la matière est travaillée, moins la vendeuse gagne."[40]

Long-distance Traders

Aside from the rich descriptions of *industries féminines* Moran compiled data on commerce and long-distance female traders. In one detailed account from western Guinea in the Malinke town of Kankan, Moran explained how women bought cloth and then traveled to the towns of Beyla (approximately 400 kilometers to the south, near Liberia) or Kissidougou (about 200 km at the border with Sierra Leone), where they would sell the cloth and purchase rice, palm oil, and soap. They would then return to Kankan and make substantial profits selling these imported commodities on the market.[41] Other women, who did not engage in long-distance trade, would intercept the returning traders on the road before they entered the village. From them they purchased rice at the rate of Fr 3 for seven *mesures* (units of account), which they would later resell at

Fr 1 per *mesure* on the market.[42] Although Moran did not specify traders' regular mode of transportation, it is likely that long distances were sometimes covered in motorized vehicles.

Moran's most revealing case study is about a successful long-distance trader. Hounyo, thirty-two years old in 1938, lived in a town approximately 50 kilometers west of Porto Novo, the capital city of present-day Benin.[43] After refusing to marry the man chosen by her father, Hounyo established a large-scale commercial network. Traveling by railroad and truck, Hounyo purchased cassava directly from the producers in the town of Savalou (about 220 km north in a mountainous area) and beans in Djougou (550 km north of Allada) with the profits realized from her sales of imported goods (mainly cloth, buckets, and bowls). Moran drew a table detailing Hounyo's costs, including wholesale and retail purchases/sales. Her tri-monthly freight costs were the most burdensome. Hounyo spent the greater part of her earnings supporting her parents and paying for her younger brothers' education. In another report on the Ivory Coast, Moran assessed the activities of male kola nut traders who traveled from Man to Bamako in present-day Mali.[44] Still other descriptions of long-distance trade can be gleaned from this informative dossier.

Forced Labor

During the 1930s, in response to the Great Depression, large-scale agricultural plantations developed in AOF.[45] Moran studied both French and African plantations, reporting how women were compelled to increase their productivity in order to sustain and feed their families, including their wage-earning husbands. Her report is an invaluable source for future research on the subject of agricultural business and labor in colonial Francophone Africa.

Through an interpreter, Moran interviewed an elder Gouro woman who compared "the before and the after" in the Dabou region of the Ivory Coast:

> La vie des femmes autrefois était plus douce parce qu'on cultivait moins et on ne se 'promenait' pas beaucoup. Avec le coton, l'arachide, le riz, elles sont fatiguées trop. Il y a beaucoup de champs à sarcler, beaucoup de produits à récolter, beaucoup de promenade, c'est-à-dire de portage. Mais puisqu'on ne peut pas faire autrement. . . . Les enfants aussi travaillent plus qu'autrefois, aux champs et aussi sur la route, car il faut toujours des prestataires.[46]

The changes addressed by this woman were undoubtedly linked to both the development of colonial cash-crop economies and the repercussions of the

1930's Depression. In order to obtain female cotton laborers, for example, every village appointed a female chief whose responsibility it was to round up women for work. The example of cotton production in the Zuénoula region of the Ivory Coast clearly illustrates the relationship between economic depression and colonial reversion to coercion. Moran spoke with the subdivision chief of Zuénoula, Mr. Van Kampen, who was not ashamed to admit how he brutally forced African laborers to increase cotton production. Moreover, when farmers responded to a drop in prices by not sifting the cotton, Van Kampen burned down 1,200 houses to motivate his workers![47]

The coercive measures of French colonial enterprises are very much denounced, both overtly and indirectly, throughout the dossier. Moran's remarks will suffice to convey the extent of her indignation: "Certes, tous les planteurs ne sont pas des tortionnnaires, mais il ne paraît pas exagéré de dire que les travailleurs sont au moins giflés un peu partout (surtout en Côte d'Ivoire) et que les patrons vraiment humains sont rares."[48] She cites the testimony of a worker recruited as forced labor in Man (Ivory Coast): "Même malades on nous battait pour nous forcer à travailler. Ceux qui portaient plainte, le patron les remettait à l'administrateur, en disant qu'ils avaient voulu se sauver, et on les mettait en prison."[49] The remarks of another elderly woman in Ivory Coast equally describe the difficult times: "Autrefois, on avait beaucoup de riz et on mangeait bien. Maintenant on cultive beaucoup plus et on manque de nourriture parce qu'il faut fournir l'administration qui ravitaille les manœuvres des planteurs européens."[50]

An Early Critique of the *Office du Niger*

Moran's critique of French colonialism is an important facet of her research, and nowhere is this more apparent than in her report on the *Office du Niger*.[51] In the early 1930s, this development scheme was launched with the aim of yielding colossal outputs in cotton and other crops through the large-scale irrigation of the Niger River basin. This expensive enterprise, which included rather extensive flooding in the river basin, was an embarrassing fiasco for all European parties involved, starting with the French. Too ashamed to reveal the catastrophes generated by the *Office*, administrators concealed the facts from European audiences well into the 1960s.[52]

Moran spent two weeks studying the Niger River project, talking with families displaced as a result of the flooding. Her report is all the more significant since she visited the *Office du Niger* shortly after the project was fully operative; the majority of the *villages de colonisation* were founded in the early 1930s.[53]

Moran did a thorough investigation informed by official documentation, namely, the *Note sur les méthodes de colonisation de l'O.N.* by E. L. Bélime, the project's engineer and director.[54] She expressed her low opinion of Bélime in her final report: "Comme d'autres dictateurs de plus grande envergure, le Directeur de l'Office du Niger donne volontiers à cette politique les couleurs du socialisme. En réalité, il reconstitue l'esclavage."[55]

Moran transcribed her conversations with colonial officers and people whose lives had been disrupted by the *Office du Niger*. She first arrived in Baguineda and was welcomed by the *contrôleur du projet* who provided a car and chauffeur, as well as a young student from Bamako acting as a translator. They first visited the village of Kogni where Moran interviewed women and men residing in a camp founded in 1934 who volunteered seemingly rehearsed answers of contentment. She then inspected the main *villages de colonisation.* Moran obtained confidential information from an auxiliary doctor who described the sanitation problems and the most prevalent diseases exacerbated by the flooding of the Niger River. These included dysentery caused by contaminated water and especially malaria. He also provided statistics of mortality rates related to sickness and respiratory problems.[56] Moran deliberately avoided dealing with French officials and their agents because she sensed their inherent biases.[57] But she explained that the 'official visit' was not uninteresting insofar as it highlighted the attitude of 'colonizers' towards the *colons* (settlers).[58] In the camp named Dar Salath where she was escorted by *Office* agents, Moran reported, "Les femmes ont de jolis boubous que les maris leur ont achetés *avant* de quitter le pays. M. Grelat (instructeur) essaie vainement de leur faire dire *après*."[59]

The most intriguing incident occurred in the district of Kokry when she was approached one night by three *informateurs officieux* who disclosed confidential information. They revealed that the settlers were reluctant to voice their grievances even in the absence of a project agent because "ils ont peur."[60] They explained that no one could remain in the village from dawn to dusk or circulate without authorization, and punishments were inflicted upon those who did not work hard enough. It is interesting to note that women were not punished directly, but their husbands were instructed to execute the punishment.

The *Office*, which claimed to be a social *œuvre*, was in fact exploitation on a massive scale reminiscent of slavery.[61] Moran was most outraged by the indirect practice of forced labor which fell upon women and children. This unrecorded "free labor" was thus largely taken for granted. The more wives a man had, the wealthier he was likely to be because, as the chief of the village of Massakoni explained, snickering, "elles doivent s'y rendre [aux champs] c'est obligatoire."[62] Three young men in a peanut field explained in an interview: "il faut avoir beaucoup de femmes pour gagner une bicyclette."[63] Moran accused the *Office du Niger* of violating the labor laws drafted by the International Labor Office and enacted in August 1937 throughout AOF. From her own calculations based on estimates of female and child labor, she concluded that the *Office* not only used forced labor, but it also manipulated accounts and statistical records to make them reflect favorably on the project.[64]

> La collaboration de la femme et de l'enfant, on la qualifie de 'petits travaux,' l'homme seul 'cultivant,' c'est-à-dire usant de la houe ou de la charrue (ce qui d'ailleurs est faux). En réalité, des *heures* de travail sont fournies par les hommes, les femmes et les enfants. Que tous n'aient pas la même valeur, soit, mais dans le calcul des profits, il faut tenir compte de tous. C'est ce que l'O.N. ne fait pas.[65]

Persistence of Other Forms of Slavery

The *Office du Niger* is not the only institution discussed in Moran's dossier that exploited the labor of women and children. In Guinea, the industry of orange extract (*essence d'orange*) used for the manufacture of European perfumes relied entirely on this type of "free labor."[66] Extracting oils from orange peels was a remarkably painful task, for it involved scraping the surface of individual oranges with a spoon. According to Moran, the schoolmaster in Mamou literally forced his pupils to scrape oranges for a good part of the day. Another Frenchman explained to her: "C'est pas difficile . . . ils [les femmes et les enfants] font le travail en bavardant."[67] What is more, she describes the shady business practices of Lebanese (*Libano-syriens*) traders who purchased orange extract acting as commercial brokers between producers and export companies.

Whether in reference to forced labor or pawning, Moran examined various forms of slavery prevailing throughout AOF. This may well be an indication that her assignment was prompted by a concern with the incidence of pawning in the aftermath of the 1930's Depression. Henri Ortoli, an administrator for the French colonial office, defined pawning in 1939 as "une convention orale par laquelle un débiteur remet à son créancier, pour garantir le paiement d'une dette, une ou plusieurs personnes de sa famille ou s'engage lui-même."[68] The pawn was therefore a guarantee for the creditor, and the pawn's labor was comparable to the interest on a loan.

Ortoli asserts that the incidence of pawning was not a serious issue in the late 1930s. Yet it has been demonstrated elsewhere that French colonial officials were taking the matter rather seriously since pawning actually increased during the Depression. The governor-general of AOF in 1936 and 1937, Marcel de Coppet, was sufficiently concerned to issue "two circulars which addressed the linked problems of pawning and forced marriages."[69] As Toyin Falola and Paul Lovejoy explain in their recent study devoted to this neglected subject, pawnship was a "common mechanism for mobilizing labor and guaranteeing credit,"[70] and women and children were prime targets. Most of Moran's regional reports contain cases of girls and women forced into slavery as pawns. For instance, in Ouagadougou early in 1938, a man volunteered his daughter to someone who had given him a loan. The girl was entirely at the disposal of the creditor, and was in turn loaned to his brother.[71] In another case which took place in the courthouse of Pita, a town in Guinea, an owner sued to obtain possession of the child of a slave he had pawned. This, as well as similar examples, caused Moran to declare that "ni l'esclavage ni la mise en gage n'ont entièrement disparu du Fouta comme certains commandants et chefs le prétendent."[72]

Although the distinction between slavery and marital status is at times ambiguous, Moran was very much aware of the situations she encountered. She perceived as slaves what missionaries called wives.[73] However, she was not duped into believing that women and children did not mind transporting cash-crops because they enjoyed going to the market, as some French men argued.[74] The subject of porterage has too often been overlooked by scholars of West Africa, just as it was taken for granted by the colonial administrations.[75] Throughout AOF, Moran noticed the amount of women and children carrying heavy loads of one type of commodity or another, literally forming human trains alongside expanding roads. The testimony of the elder Gouro woman she interviewed who complained about porterage is an indication that the incidence had increased in recent years.

Women and the Colonial Justice System

Describing colonial court records, Richard Roberts and Kristin Mann argue that Europeans perceived African customary law as one homogeneous and "immutable tradition."[76] This opinion was shared by Moran who was aware of European stereotypes about African legal systems. She formulated her thoughts on this issue at the beginning of her final report: "Les Européens font souvent allusion à la 'vraie coutume indigène' comme à un édifice construit dans son entier par quelques sages des temps préhistoriques et qui aurait dès lors fixé les mœurs. Tout apport étranger, ils l'appellent 'altération.' Il n'y a pas de 'vraie'

coutume, mais, témoin de mœurs changeantes, un ensemble d'usages en inces-
sant devenir."[77] Moran's attempt to debunk commonly held beliefs that
Africans were locked-up in a static tradition is indeed remarkable. She realized
that African laws were constantly changing as a result of internal and external
factors, including European influence.

Courts are particularly fertile grounds for gleaning information on women
who often brought their grievances to the colonial justice system. Moran carefully examined women's relationship with the law and often includes in the
regional reports a section under the heading "la femme et la justice." She studied the reasons behind women's recourse to French justice, recording the number of women in prisons and ascertaining causes of incarceration. She reported
where legal practice was biased in favor of men, providing invaluable data on
the multifarious brands of justice carried out in the colonies.[78] She focused
mainly on women and on the types of cases men brought to colonial courts
concerning women.[79] One of her most interesting findings, applicable to a
majority of cases, is neatly captured in words of the president of the court in
the village of Diezon (Ivory Coast) who said, "Sans les femmes, on pourrait
fermer le Tribunal!"[80]

Evidence suggests that women more than men sought to obtain divorces
in colonial courts. In Kindia (Guinea) for example, half of the civil cases in
1937 were introduced by women seeking divorces.[81] These facts should be
considered against the backdrop of Muslim law prevailing in many parts of
West Africa which rules that only men can divorce without the mediation of a
Muslim judge.

In her final report, Moran lists in priority order the motives for divorces,
or at least those vocalized in court since she was aware that many agreements
settled in or out of court were verbal and therefore left no records. These
include sterility, impotence, leprosy, syphilis, and adultery.[82] In the hinterland
areas of Niger, northern Ivory Coast, and northern Benin, women often cited
abandonment by husbands who had migrated to the coast as justification for
seeking a divorce. Women of rank in the coastal towns sometimes demanded
a divorce to avoid following their husbands who were assigned positions in the
interior.[83] Other reasons included assault and battery, betrothal, and neglect.
Moran differentiated between motives and pretexts given by women to successfully obtain divorces. She also noted the areas where women rarely
appeared before colonial tribunals and assessed why this was so.[84] She found
that men rarely sought divorces unless their wives left them, in which case husbands tried to recover the bridewealth from their wives' families.[85] Arguments
about the reimbursement of bridewealth varied between colonies as well as

within regions. Data on legislative decisions regarding child allocation and divorce settlements also feature in her reports.

This manuscript is a rich source on the complex interactions of African men and women with the colonial judicial system. Although Moran clearly perceived the implementation of French justice in Africa as a beneficial recourse for Africans, especially for women,[86] she was aware of gender inequities in legal practice. It is clear from Moran's account that colonial justice was actuated by African and French male officers who regulated and controlled the institution of marriage and interpreted the law to women's disadvantage. According to Moran, the local judge tended to take justice in his hands. The concerted effort of legal officers "[pour] préserver l'unité de la famille" by turning down women's appeals for divorces is a key indicator. As she explained in the case of Bamako, "les juges, de leur aveu, s'efforcent avant tout de renvoyer la femme à son mari."[87] In Moran's final report, she seriously questioned this policy in feminist terms:

> L'on peut se demander jusqu'à quel point il est moral et utile à la famille de maintenir unis des êtres qui ne parviennent pas à former une famille, de maintenir auprès de ses enfants une femme qui les quitterait sans regret. À moins de considérer (ce que l'ethnologie dément) que l'homme est le maître *naturel* de la femme, une telle politique n'est pas défendable, actuellement en Afrique noire.[88]

An examination of legal records sheds much light on myriad episodes shaping the lives of men, women, and children. Collected by a French official who was one of the rare women to serve in the colonial office, these data inform about the variation in legal practice in AOF as each local context shaped enforcement. This is an important recognition in order to move beyond some of the generalizations which characterize scholarship on the law in colonial Africa. In a pioneering historical examination on women and the law in Africa, edited by Margaret Jean Hay and Marcia Wright, studies of West Africa were sorely lacking.[89] Scholars will find in Moran's reports an invaluable resource for future research on the social and legal history of Francophone West Africa.

Health and Educational Facilities

As part of her assignment, Moran studied colonial services focusing on schools and health care facilities. Indeed, she provided an ideal source for studies of health practices and colonial medicine in West Africa as her seventeen reports contain information on prominent diseases, medical facilities, and staff in every region. She examined cases of social misfits and people with disabilities who were often associated with, or even confined within, prisons. In the town of Bouaflé (Ivory Coast) she reported a curiously high incidence of suicides, including conjugal suicides.[90] Moran also recorded many instances of infanticide, as well as abortions (which were sometimes performed by mothers on their daughters), child abandonment, and other such practices.

Health care facilities and medical schools, such as the leprosy center in Bamako, are described in detail. Moran also examined nurses' attempts to lure women into their sphere of control,[91] as well as the "cultural obstacles" they encountered in attracting women to maternities and health dispensaries.[92] When commenting on the training program for nurses in Senegal, one of AOF's rare medical schools, she noted with humor: "les infirmières-visiteuses européennes parviennent, à Dakar, à donner aux femmes l'idée du *microbe*, de la "petite bête" qui communique le tétanos à l'enfant."[93]

Wherever possible, Moran gathered data on the increasing incidence of African births in maternity wards, illustrating the headway western medical practice was making in AOF. In Bamako, she noted that hospitalized births had increased over 1,000 percent in a decade, from 500 in 1927 to 6,100 in 1937.[94] In her report on eastern Guinea, Moran describes the health care center in the town of Nzerekore where women came voluntarily usually one month before they were due, and wove mats which they sold in the market as they waited.[95] It is important to recall colonial legislation, passed under de Coppet's administration, which prohibited forcing women over seven months pregnant to undertake strenuous 'family labor.'[96] If this law had actually been advertised to the interested parties, women could have been released from family and work obligations two months prior to giving birth, a luxury which no doubt few could afford. It would be optimistic, however, to directly link the increase in hospitalized births recorded by Moran to legal innovations in the capital of AOF. Besides, these statistics, which must in no way be viewed as absolute, appear negligible when compared to the total population.[97] In general, Moran noticed that African women were reluctant to visit colonial medical facilities, choosing to rely on their own health practices. When women did come to the dispensaries they explained that they did so for their children.[98]

Moran appears to have attached great significance to France's role in the colonies. For her, the French colonial mission was above all one motivated by educational prerogatives. As an education administrator, Moran believed in the *mission civilisatrice* but she obviously disagreed with the way most colonial representatives carried out their duty. Moreover, she argued that Europeans had much to learn from Africans, including in the field of education. Moran was therefore particularly interested in the various establishments of education. Although she investigated all levels of schooling, she paid close attention to rural schools which provided vocational as well as classical educational training. Official statistics of schooling in AOF inform that there was one classroom for every 14,350 people, and one student per 650 inhabitants in 1937.[99] Moran's information details both male and female students. On female education, she believed that the role of French education was to bring forward what she called 'cultural evolution,' and that schooling was especially important as the only opportunity available for girls to improve their status in society.[100] Yet, she appreciated African educational systems and cultures, namely, the transmission of oral history and the practice of learning by demonstration, games, mimes, dances, and songs.

From her remarks about missionary schools, it is clear that Moran favored secular institutions of education. In her final report, she wrote a detailed account on missionary schools describing the tasks they generally assigned to pupils. She denounced the misconduct of some missionaries and was highly critical of the instruction delivered by certain priests.[101] Missionary schools rarely accepted female students and in the few sisters' schools in AOF, the emphasis was on the teaching of domesticity which, according to Moran, was a disguised form of free labor.[102] Moran complained that the purpose of schooling in Protestant missions was to produce catechists and catechists' wives who participated in the economy of the mission. Moran also visited other schools, including Quranic and private African schools.

Moran's mission of inquiry must be understood within the context of Marcel de Coppet's social agenda and the priority placed on education by the Popular Front government.[103] Moreover, the French colonial administration then began extending education to girls, although in 1930 there had been an initial concern about the implications of girls' schooling, for "si elle [la fillette noire] allait à l'école, qui donc irait à la fontaine, au marché, aux champs et promènerait le petit fils cramponné à son dos?"[104]

Conclusion

The themes chosen for discussion here cannot be viewed as inclusive. The dossier compiled by Moran is an extremely rich mine of facts, figures, and insights on Francophone West Africa in the 1930s. This is not to say that equally relevant information cannot be found in other sources, but women and families being Moran's main focus makes her research unique. Despite its originality, the manuscript contains certain limitations alluded to throughout the present study. Unquestionably, her analysis is somewhat undermined by a conservative notion that France's role in the colonies was to bring 'civiliza- tion' and 'cultural evolution' to Africa. Yet, she was obviously open-minded and believed that Africans also had lessons to teach to Europeans. When her assumptions on what constitutes economic rationality seem to distort her analysis, scholars must as always remain critical. One apparent shortcoming is that she often derived her data from European and African men linked to the colonial administration. However, she was able to overcome this by inter- viewing a wide range of women, men, and children.

Moran's opinions about French colonial rule are original. The caustic rep- rimand of the *Office du Niger* is a case in point, when one considers that the failure of this massive enterprise was concealed for many decades. Her candid outlook on colonial atrocities committed in the name of "French progress" makes the data she provides all the more valuable. Without doubt, one of the reasons why Moran's work has been stored away and her research largely ignored was because it raised many controversial issues which were easily dis- regarded by the colonial office.

In a recent history of women and French colonialism in Africa which reviewed the available sources written by women, Moran's seminal report escaped attention.[105] In light of what has been discussed here, and in recalling the exploits of Odette du Puigaudeau, the assertion that sources written by women in the colonial period never bear official seals must be corrected. Clearly, Denise Moran Savineau was an exception to the typical French offi- cial hired by the colonial administration, and therefore it is altogether surpris- ing that she has been forgotten. The answer to this puzzle would seem to lie in the fact that the Popular Front government which hired her was not nearly as popular by the time it was ousted. In fact, it bore such a bad reputation that the work undertaken in those two years (1936–38) was simply swept under the carpet. As Nicole Bernard-Duquenet explains, the legacy of the Popular Front movement in AOF was systematically destroyed and written sources of the period are therefore rare.[106] Surely de Coppet's liberal governance in particu- lar stirred much resentment in and out of AOF, and ultimately caused his pre- mature discharge. Moreover, Léon Blum's grandiose commission of inquiry into the situation in the colonies was essentially a failure. So Moran's efforts were bound to be disregarded, though this does not explain why her document has been overlooked by researchers until now. Whatever the reasons may be, historians must take it upon themselves to find such exceptional sources that have been similarly neglected and await an unraveling on a dusty shelf of an archive.

Notes

1. By French West Africa is meant *Afrique occidentale française*; hereafter AOF.

2. *Mission d'enquête*, or mission of inquiry, was the appellation given to data-collecting projects undertaken by the French colonial administration (discussed below).

3. These were Governor-General de Coppet's instructions as described in a circular he addressed to the governors of AOF ("Circulaire du Gouveneur-Général aux Gouveneurs de l'AOF, 21 octobre 1937," in *Voyages et Missions*, lettres S à Z, ANS, 17G/217/104; hereafter V and M).

4 Ibid.

5. Coquery-Vidrovitch 1977, 131. For a statistical assessment of the 1930s crisis in Senegal, see Bernard-Duquenet 1985, 15–20.

6. Coquery-Vidrovitch 1977, 129.

7. Manning 1988, 51.

8. Goyau 1934.

9. ANS, 17G/160/28, "Situation de la femme en AOF, 1934–1938." This booklet contains seven propositions on how to ameliorate women's prerogatives, especially vis-à-vis customary and Muslim laws and issues such as the legal age of marriage, the rights of widows, and polygamy.

10. Klein and Roberts 1994, 307.

11. Murphy 1989.

12. Rabaut 1978, 283.

13. An account of this conference indicates that ambiguous conclusions were reached. But French women were unanimously in favor of both the abolition of polygamy and the education of girls, which had hitherto been neglected by the *Bureau de l'enseignement colonial*, see Knibiehler and Goutalier, 1987, 16–36.

14. Cohen 1972, 373–74.

15. Julien 1981, 376.

16. Delavignette 1981, 392.

17. The most accurate biographical information published to date on Marcel de Coppet is contained in Bernard-Duquenet 1985, 81–90. Bernard-Duquenet explains that de Coppet studied law and also took courses at the *École des langues orientales* before entering the colonial office. He spent five years in Madagascar before transferring to AOF. He served seven years in various regions of Senegal where he got the reputation of a 'negrophile.' In 1918, he was sent to Guinea, and was later governor of Chad until 1933. He subsequently was governor of Dahomey, Somalia, and Mauritania before his long-awaited appointment as governor-general of AOF. For details on de Coppet's service in Chad, see A. Gide (1927) and M. Allégret (1993). M. Perham (1983) visited the

de Coppets in 1932 and reports her impressions in her diary. I thank John Hargreaves for this information.

18. For details on de Coppet's policies towards Muslims, see Harrison, 1988, 183–93 and Bernard-Duquenet 1985, 88–89.

19. Person 1979, 91.

20. "Ordonnance no. 2563 AP," *Journal officiel du Sénégal*, no. 1889, 3 décembre 1936, pp. 948–52.

21. Lefranc 1965, 306; Delavignette 1981, 394.

22. Lefranc 1965, 301–7; Bernard-Duquenet 1985, 57–61; Jackson 1988, 154–58.

23. Bernard-Duquenet 1985, 77–79. It is important to note that the emphasis of these inquiries was on North Africa and Indochina, not on Sub-Saharan Africa.

24. "La commission est chargée de déterminer les besoins et les aspirations légitimes des populations demeurant dans les colonies, les protectorats et les mandats," *Bulletin officiel du Ministère des Colonies* 41, no. 2 (1937): 109.

25. *Bulletin officiel du Ministère des Colonies* 41, no. 5 (1937): 532–33.

26. Cohen 1972, 371. Lévy-Bruhl was the only member of the commission to actually write a final report, the subject of which was cannibalism in certain remote areas of Africa.

27. Suret-Canale 1961, 172–75. He explains in a footnote that Moran cited archival material which in theory was illegal, but laments that she often left out names of people and places (ibid.: 172, fn 1). Since Suret-Canale did not identify Moran, he probably knew nothing about her. Moreover, he omitted to include her name in his bibliography.

28. Moran 1934, 12.

29. ANS 17G/381/126, Rapport no. 2: "Les villages de colonisation de l'Office du Niger," p. 46.

30. "Lettre no. 467 du Gouveneur-Général de l'AEF au Gouveneur-Général de l'AOF, 26 mai 1937, Brazzaville," in V and M (see *supra* fn. 6). No details were found on this assignment.

31. Incidentally, Moran was eager to go back to French Equatorial Africa, but the governor-general of AEF had replied that there were no positions available for her there, which is why she served in AOF. For the bulk of official correspondence exchanged, refer to V and M (see *supra* fn. 6).

32. "Décision no. 2811 du 7 octobre 1937," *Centre d'archives d'outre-mer*, microfilm 17G381. It is very intriguing that decision no. 2811 was not reported in any of the relevant official journals. Indeed, neither the *Journal officiel du Sénégal*, the *Journal officiel du Soudan français*, nor the *Bulletin officiel du Ministère des Colonies* mention Denise Moran-Savineau's appointment, although information on who was hired as a typist-secretary to such-or-such department figures prominently. It is tempting to surmise that de Coppet's decision to appoint Moran was subject to criticism, and it was best not to publicize it.

33. ANS 17G/381/126, Rapport d'ensemble, no. 18.

34. ANS 17G/381/126, Rapport no. 16: "La Basse Guinée," p. 11.

35. It is important to mention that French West African colonies used French francs until 1946 when the F/CFA or *Colonies françaises d'Afrique* (now called the *Communauté financière africaine*), a currency pegged to the French franc, was introduced. Moreover, the French franc was dramatically devalued in 1936 during the Popular Front government. Subsequently, the prices of imported commodities such as rice escalated, (see Person 1979). Until the devaluation of 1960, the French currency was the franc, which was then converted to the "nouveau franc" at a rate of 100 to 1. These devaluations must be taken into account in order to appreciate the value of goods in 1930s terms.

36. *Pagne* is a unit of cloth approximately 4 by 2 meters.

37. ANS 17G/381/126, Rapport no. 16: "La Basse Guinée," pp. 23–24.

38. ANS 17G/381/126, Rapport d'ensemble, no. 18, p. 62; also Rapport no. 9: "Bobo, Marka, Lobi, Senoufo, etc."

39. These details are found in Rapport no. 9, pp. 28–30.

40. ANS 17G/381/126, Rapport d'ensemble, no. 18, p. 116.

41. ANS 17G/381/126, Rapport no. 13: "La Guinée orientale," pp. 20–21. Traders' husbands apparently complained that their women were often away on the road and did not share their earnings with them.

42. It is unclear exactly what amount is meant by a *mesure*.

43. ANS 17G/381/126, Rapport no. 6: "Le Dahomey," pp. 41–43.

44. ANS 17G/381/126, Rapport no. 12: "La Basse Côte d'Ivoire (ouest)," pp. 36–38.

45. Coquery-Vidrovitch 1976, 412.

46. ANS 17G/381/126, Rapport no. 12: "La Basse Côte d'Ivoire (ouest)," pp. 26–27.

47. Ibid., pp. 27–28.

48. In her final report, Moran further condemns French officials and businessmen for abuses and injustices committed; see ANS 17G/3281/126, Rapport d'ensemble, no. 18, p. 80.

49. Ibid.

50. ANS 17G/3281/126, Rapport no. 12: "La Basse Côte d'Ivoire (ouest)," p. 35.

51. For a study of this colonial venture, see Schreyger 1984.

52. Another critical assessment of the *Office du Niger* was produced by P. Herbart (1939). This is a pamphlet prefaced by André Gide, which I have not yet consulted. But I thank the board of editors of [*Cahiers d'Etudes africaines*] for bringing it to my attention.

53. ANS 17G/3281/126, Rapport no. 2: "Les villages de colonisation de l'Office du Niger," (49 pgs).

54. ANS 17G/3281/126, Rapport d'ensemble, no. 18.

55. Ibid., p. 95.

56. Ibid., p. 20.

57. ANS 17G/3281/126, Rapport no. 2: "Les villages de colonisation de l'Office du Niger," pp. 1–6.

58. *Colons* (settlers) were Africans brought in to work on the project. "'La visite officielle' n'a cependant pas manqué d'intérêt, ne fût-ce que pour avoir mis en lumière l'attitude des 'colonisateurs' à l'égard des colons . . . le ton est de maître à esclave. Nous le retrouverons partout employé, d'Européen à colon" (Rapport no. 2, pp. 8–9).

59. Ibid., p. 14.

60. Ibid., p. 16.

61. In her final report, Moran describes the *Office* as a "système d'économie dirigée par des Européens et *dont ils profitent*. Il est scandaleux qu'une entreprise européenne s'équilibre aux dépens des faibles. . . . C'est la pratique indirecte de l'esclavage" (ANS 17G/3281/126, Rapport d'ensemble, no. 18, p. 38).

62. ANS 17G/3281/126, Rapport no. 2: "Les villages de colonisation de l'Office du Niger," p. 6.

63. Ibid., p. 7.

64. Ibid., pp. 43–45.

65. Ibid., p. 36.

66. ANS 17G/381/126, Rapport no. 15: "Le Fouta Djallon," pp. 9–15.

67. Ibid., p. 11.

68. Ortoli 1939, 315–16.

69. Klein and Roberts 1994, 310.

70. Falola and Lovejoy 1994, 2.

71. ANS 17G/381/126, Rapport no. 8: "Ouagadougou," p. 25.

72. ANS 17G/381/126, Rapport no. 15: "Le Fouta Djallon," p. 26.

73. ANS 17G/381/126, Rapport no. 13: "La Guinée orientale," pp. 1–2.

74. ANS 17G/381/126, Rapport d'ensemble, no. 18, p. 102.

75. One exception is Deji Ogunremi (1975).

76. Roberts and Mann 1991, 5.

77. ANS 17G/381/126, Rapport d'ensemble, no. 18, p. 1.

78. To illustrate this point, one could cite the variations in length of sentences. For instance in the town of Allada, the sentence served by adulterous women was five months, whereas men served six months for the same crime (Rapport d'ensemble, no. 18, p. 31). In another case, among the Toma, judges replaced the death sentence for adultery with a compensation equal to the bridewealth. Moran reports that this "new legislation" was often abused by husbands who would falsely accuse their wives of adultery because it was lucrative.

79. In Moran's opinion, "il est impossible, actuellement de faire admettre le principe du consentement de la femme à son propre mariage. Les assesseurs rient au nez du président à cette suggestion" (ANS 17G/381/126, Rapport no. 8: "Ouagadougou," p. 26; see also Rapport d'ensemble, no. 18, p. 11).

80. ANS 17G/381/126, Rapport no. 12: "La Basse Côte d'Ivoire," p. 39. The same sentiments were expressed in Bamako where in 1936, 227 cases out of a total of 267 were

related to marriage and brought to court primarily by women. (Rapport no. 1: "La Femme et la famille à Bamako," p. 10.)

81. ANS 17G/381/126, Rapport no. 16: "La Basse Guinée," p. 28.

82. ANS 17G/381/126, Rapport d'ensemble, no. 18, p. 32.

83. Ibid., p. 33.

84. In Ouagadougou, Moran notes that only three women between 1936 and 1938 had been convicted, and explains their crimes (ANS 17G/381/126, Rapport no. 8: "Ouagadougou," p. 25); oftentimes she found that a woman could not go to court without the consent of her husband (Abidjan) (ANS 17G/381/126, Rapport no. 10: "La Basse Côte d'Ivoire (est)," p. 4; Rapport no. 11: "Abidjan et Bingerville—Grand Bassam," p. 20).

85. ANS 17G/381/126, Rapport d'ensemble, no. 18, p. 34.

86. In her final report Moran offers that "protégées par nous, les femmes commencent à se défendre elles-mêmes, voire à attaquer. Nous le verrons à l'occasion du divorce" (Rapport d'ensemble, no. 18, p. 18).

87. ANS 17G/381/126, Rapport no. 1: "Bamako," p. 10.

88. ANS 17G/381/126, Rapport d'ensemble, no. 18, p. 34.

89. Hay and Wright 1982. See Christelow 1991.

90. ANS 17G/381/126, Rapport no. 12: "La Basse Côte d'Ivoire (ouest)," p. 25.

91. Medical personnel often portrayed their clinics as sanctuaries and distributed free paraphernalia to attract new patients. See ANS 17G/381/126, Rapport no. 13: "La Guinée orientale."

92. For a lengthy chapter examining the obstacles the medical profession faced in the colonies, see ANS 17G/381/126, Rapport d'ensemble, no. 18.

93. Ibid., p. 172.

94. ANS 17G/381/126, Rapport no. 1: "Bamako," pp. 26–27.

95. ANS 17G/381/126, Rapport no. 13: "La Guinée orientale," p. 5. Moran explains that the men were not pleased with the situation because in the absence of their "hospitalized" wives, farming and cooking were left unattended.

96. *Journal officiel du Sénégal*, no. 1889, 3 décembre 1936, pp. 948–49.

97. Statistics of hospitalized births are probably difficult to find, even for the 1930s. Official records only contain general figures such as the total numbers of consultations per medical staff. See, for example, *Journal officiel du Soudan*, no. 1942, 11 novembre 1937, p. 800.

98. ANS 17G/381/126, Rapport d'ensemble, no. 18, pp. 168–85. Moran makes many interesting observations about African medical practices useful to researchers of medical history and anthropology.

99. *Journal officiel du Soudan,* no. 1942, 11 novembre 1937, pp. 788–89.

100. ANS 17G/381/126, Rapport d'ensemble, no. 18, pp. 145–46.

101. Moran criticized certain missionaries for collecting excessive donations, sometimes four times higher than taxes. She accused missionaries of substituting themselves for

the families of their followers and imposing Christian husbands upon young girls and pocketing the bridewealth if they were orphans (ANS 17G/381/126, Rapport d'ensemble, no. 18, p. 142; see also Rapport no. 12: "La Basse Côte d'Ivoire" for more detail). There are several examples of missionaries stepping over ethical boundaries, and some cases of suspected physical abuse.

102. ANS 17G/381/126, Rapport d'ensemble, no. 18, p. 164.

103. Bernard-Duquenet 1985, 87–88.

104. *Le Quotidien*, 7 octobre 1930, quoted in Knibiehler and Goutalier 1985, 226.

105. See note at end of essay.

106. Bernard-Duquenet 1985, 10.

A longer version of this paper was published in *Cahiers d'Etudes africaines*, 147, XXXVII-3, 1997, pp. 555–84. Earlier versions of this paper were presented at the African Studies Association meeting held in Toronto in November 1994, and at a workshop on Popular Front and Empire, University of Portsmouth, in February 1996. I am indebted to Mamadou Ndiaye for introducing me to the work of Denise Moran Savineau. Special thanks are due to Nancy Sweeney, David Robinson, Ellen Foley, Jim Jones, Liz MacGonagle, and Michel Brot for their comments and suggestions. I would like to thank the History Department and the African Studies Center at Michigan State University for their support and encouragement.

Note:

Yvonne Knibiehler and Régine Goutalier claim that sources written by European women exist, but they are not of an official nature since women were excluded from the French colonial administration. See Knibiehler and Goutalier 1987, 8. The dossier on which this essay is based—a report by Denise Moran Savineau compiled in the late 1930s—is rare indeed. Brought to my attention by Mamadou Ndiaye, the administrative assistant of the *Archives nationales du Sénégal*, "La famille en AOF: condition de la femme" was found lying on a dusty shelf, catalogued but unclassified. Moran Savineau's report has been cited by Echenberg and Filipovich (1986), Schreyger (1984), and Suret-Canale (1961). It is referenced as *Archives nationales du Sénégal* (hereafter ANS) 17G/381/126. A microfilm copy exists in the French colonial archives in Aix-en-Provence. (*Centre des archives d'Outre-mer*, 17G/381.)

Bibliography

Allégret, M. 1993. *Carnets du Congo: voyage avec André Gide*. Paris: Éditions du CNRS.

Bernard-Duquenet, N. 1985. *Le Sénégal et le Front populaire*. Paris: L'Harmattan.

Christelow, A. 1991. "Women and the law in early twentieth century Kano." In B. Mack and C. Coles, eds., *Hausa Women in the Twentieth Century*, 130–44. Madison: University of Wisconsin Press.

Cohen, W. B. 1972. "The colonial policy of the Popular Front." *French Historical Studies* 7 (3): 368–93.

Coquery-Vidrovitch, C. 1976. "L'Afrique coloniale française et la crise de 1930: crise structurelle et genèse du sous-développement." *Revue française d'Histoire d'Outre-Mer* 53: 232–33, 386–424.

Coquery-Vidrovitch, C. 1977 "Mutation de l'impérialisme colonial français dans les années 30." *African Economic History* 4: 103–52.

Deji Ogunremi. 1975. "Human porterage in Nigeria in the nineteenth century: A pillar in the indigenous economy." *Journal of the Historical Society of Nigeria* 8 (1): 37–59.

Delavignette, R. 1981. "La politique de Marius Moutet au Ministère des Colonies." In P. Renouvin and R. Rémond, eds., *Léon Blum, chef de gouvernement, 1936–1937*, 391–94. Paris: Presses de la Fondation nationale des sciences politiques (1st ed. 1967).

Echenberg, M., and J. Filipovich. 1986. "African military labour and the building of the Office du Niger installations, 1925–1950." *Journal of African History* 27 (3): 533–52.

Falola, T., and P. E. Lovejoy. 1994. "Pawnship in historical perspective." In T. Falola and P. E. Lovejoy, eds., *Pawnship in Africa: Debt Bondage in Historical Perspectives*. Boulder: Westview Press.

Gide, A. 1927. *Voyage au Congo: carnets de voyage; suivi de Le Retour du Tchad*. Paris: Gallimard.

Goyau, G. 1934. "L'action missionnaire pour la protection de la femme noire," *Annales coloniales*, août.

Harrison, C. 1988. *France and Islam in West Africa, 1860–1960*. Cambridge: Cambridge University Press.

Hay, M. J., and M. Wright, eds. 1982. *African Women and the Law: Historical Perspectives*. Boston: Boston University Press.

Herbart, P. 1939. *Le chancre du Niger*. Paris: Gallimard.

Iliffe, J. 1987. *African Poor*. Cambridge: Cambridge University Press.

Jackson, J. 1988. *The Popular Front in France Defending Democracy, 1934–38*. Cambridge: Cambridge University Press.

Julien, C.-A. 1981. "Léon Blum et les pays d'outre-mer." In P. Renouvin and R. Rémond, eds., *Léon Blum, chef de gouvernement, 1936–1937*, 377–90. Paris: Presses de la Fondation Nationals des Sciences Politiques (1st ed. 1967).

Klein, M., and R. Roberts. 1994. "The resurgence of pawning in French West Africa during the Depression of the 1930s." In T. Falola and P. E. Lovejoy, eds., *Pawnship in Africa: Debt Bondage in Historical Perspectives*, 303–20. Boulder: Westview Press.

Knibiehler, Y., and R. Goutalier. 1985. *La femme au temps des colonies*. Paris: Éditions Stock.

———. 1987. *Femmes et colonisation*. Aix-en-Provence: Institut d'histoire des pays d'outre-mer ('Études et documents').

Lefranc, G. 1965. *Histoire du Front populaire (1934–1938)*. Paris: Payot.

Manning, P. 1988. *Francophone Sub-Saharan Africa, 1880–1985*. Cambridge: Cambridge University Press.

Moran, D. 1934. *Tchad*. Paris: Gallimard.

Murphy, F. J. 1989. *Communists and Catholics in France, 1936–1939: The Politics of the Outstretched Hand*. Gainesville: University of Florida Press.

Ortoli, H. 1939. "Le gage de personnes au Soudan français." *Bulletin de l'Institut français de L'Afrique noire* 1 (1): 313–24.

Perham, M. 1983. *West African Passage: A Journey through Nigeria, Chad, and the Cameroons, 1931–1932*. London: P. Owen Publishers.

Person, Y. 1979. "Le Front populaire au Sénégal (mai 1936–octobre 1938)." *Le Mouvement social* 17 (2): 77–101.

Rabaut, J. 1978. *Histoire des féminismes français*. Paris: Éditions Stock.

Roberts, R., and K. Mann. 1991. "Law in colonial Africa." In K. Mann and R. Roberts, eds., *Law in Colonial Africa*, 3–58. Portsmouth: Heinemann.

Schreyger, E. 1984. *L'Office du Niger au Mali*. Paris: L'Harmattan.

Suret-Canale, J. 1961. *Afrique noire occidentale et centrale: l'ère coloniale (1900–1945)*. Paris: Éditions sociales.

Vérité, M. 1992. *Odette du Puigaudeau: une Bretonne au désert*. Paris: Éd. J. Picollec.

Labor Migration, Gender, and Social Transformation in Rural Mali

MARIA GROSZ-NGATÉ

L abor migration is a significant demographic and politico-economic phenomenon in Mali, as in neighboring Sahelian countries. Yet in contrast to
migration in Senegal and especially in Burkina Faso, labor migration in Mali
has attracted little attention on the part of researchers. As a result, available
data are largely restricted to aggregate statistics and fail to provide an appreciation of the long and complex history of migration in the country. Although
several "Women in Development" survey-based studies of women migrants in
the major urban centers of Mali[1] have recently started to improve our understanding of migration in Mali, these studies do not examine the rural context
or origins of the migrants. This chapter builds on recent theoretical developments which help us rethink connections between the rural and urban, the local
and global, and thus present an opportunity to take a fresh look at migration.

My own interest in labor migration stems from long-term research in an
area east of Segu locally known as Sana, which coincides with the administrative subdivision of the *Arrondissement de Sansanding*. The majority of Sana
inhabitants speak the Bamana language as their mother tongue, although most
of the citizens of Sinsanni and Shibla,[2] the two largest towns, identify as
Maraka rather than as Bamana. There are also Bozo speakers settled in villages
along the Niger River and a small population of semi-sedentary Fulbe dispersed throughout the province. Sana is densely populated so that villages are
within easy reach of each other. My research has concentrated on Bamana cultivators who engage in rain-fed production of millet and, to a lesser extent,
peanuts and fonio. In addition, most households cultivate 1–3 ha of irrigated
rice within the confines of the government rice development agency *Opération
Riz*. People identify themselves as "cultivators" (*cikèlaw*) if asked about their
occupation, but agriculture is not self-sustaining and the reproduction of social

life is predicated on a combination of agriculture and seasonal labor migration. Any analysis of rural social dynamics and cultural configurations must therefore take into account those who are away for periods of time, their projects, and their interactions with those who remain at home.

Exploring the local social context challenges us to rethink the analytical constructs which have been used to analyze rural society, even though the social analysis of African societies has undergone considerable changes over the past thirty-five years. For example, concepts like *lineage* and *tribe* have given way to *household* and *community* in recognition of integration into "wider stratified political and economic systems under a state form of government."[3] Similarly, the construction of typologies of local structures has been replaced by an emphasis on processes of change. These shifts, however, do not represent a uniform analytical framework: 'household' and 'community' originate in the study of European peasantries, and processes of change are conceptualized differently in neo-Marxist analyses than in studies drawing on dependency theory, for example. In recent years, researchers have stressed the connections between the 'local' and the 'global' (or the 'translocal' and the 'transnational') in recognition of the fluidity of boundaries of all kinds, but the challenge of conceptualizing these connections remains. We still seek ways to apprehend "continuity and change," as Jane Guyer noted more than fifteen years ago. Labor migration is only one of the phenomena that links local sociocultural formations with wider structures and processes. Studies of labor migration in Africa have concentrated above all on typologies of migration and on causes and consequences, the latter conceived mainly in terms of the impact on rural social structures and economy. This approach assumes that there is an active external force acting on a static local structure and overlooks the dynamic inherent in each that needs to be understood and whose interactions (and the meanings given to them) require analysis.

In this chapter, I concentrate on labor migration in Sana as a process linking local socio-cultural formations with wider structures and processes. Local social dynamics and cultural constructs shape labor migration, and, in turn, challenge these very same dynamics and constructs. This chapter explores issues that have arisen around migration—matters that have preoccupied villagers over the years—and suggests what they can tell us about social transformations in the Bamana villages of late-twentieth-century Mali. In short, this chapter seeks to elucidate social process and cultural meanings rather than characterize migratory flows or assess causes and economic impact. The focus is on the rural dimension of migration rather than the urban dimension or the regional and global historical forces that have helped produce migration. I have found it necessary to disaggregate labor migration into male and female migration. Men and women occupy different positions within the household and rural society, their objectives in migrating differ, and the tensions and ambiguities around their respective migration vary and meet with different responses. It will also become evident that 'male' and 'female' are not monolithic categories, but that the men and women involved are distinguished by generation and occupy specific social positions.

The Social Context of Migration in Sana

One of the fundamental social units in Sana is the household, an analytical construct that has gained currency in African studies only within the last twenty-five years. Its use in the African context has benefited from a feminist critique[6] that questioned an earlier conceptualization of the household as a solitary pooling and sharing unit. Research has shown that relationships within the household cannot be assumed and that internal differentiation (for example, age and gender hierarchies and the power relations these imply) needs to be elucidated. Moreover, households cannot be treated as isolated units but must be examined within a wider context. Taking into account these feminist concerns, the following sketch of the structure of Bamana households and their interrelations refers to the 1980s and 1990s.

Bamana households in Sana comprise people who cultivate and eat together. Ideally, they unite classificatory brothers,[7] their wives, sons- and daughters-in-law, and their children. However, many households consist of only a segment of these, often married brothers who are sons of the same mother as well as their offspring. Although labor migration enhances the possibilities for individual accumulation and may thus contribute to divisiveness, there is no evidence to support a direct relationship between accumulation and any increase in the establishment of nuclear units. Households have always experienced fission, and interviews with elders from different villages indicate that the anthropological model of a unified corporate kin group has rarely been the rule.

The eldest living man represents the household and makes decisions in consultation with the other adult men. He, or a younger man delegated by him, directs agricultural labor in the household fields and provides the grain and condiments for daily meals. A few large households also have subunits composed of different brothers or the sons of different wives who cultivate additional common fields, known as "evening fields" (*surò forow*). Where this is the case, each subunit derives one of its daily meals from the harvest of the evening field.[8] Married women and unmarried daughters work alongside men in the fields but can only cultivate their own plots if they receive permission from the household head. Women who are no longer required to participate in household agriculture, on the other hand, are entitled to their own field[9] if they wish to cultivate one and are able to pursue non-agricultural income-generating activities while other household members work in the fields. Following the harvest, the men and women who constitute the household's agricultural labor force also engage in various kinds of work—making mats or fans, spinning cotton, or cultivating onions, for example—that bring them a small income.

In addition to kin ties, a dense network of marriage alliances links households within the village and with others in neighboring villages and north into Kala. The preferred marriage is still one based on kin ties; that is, where an in-law relationship (*buranya*) has been transformed into kinship (*balimaya*) over generations.[10] Moreover, marriages are a highly desired form of inter-household ties as they turn neighbors into kin and in-laws with all of the social obligations this entails. To facilitate collaboration and enhance social life, members of village households participate in mutual aid groups and in various associations (*tònw*).[11] Although inter-village relations have for the most part been smooth over the past two decades, differential relations with the state have produced shifting solidarities on a few occasions.

"In the Interest of the Collectivity": Men in Migration

Male labor migration in Sana dates from the early part of the twentieth century when the French colonial government required that taxes be paid in cash rather than in kind. When attempts to impose cotton as a cash crop failed and the drought of 1912–13 devastated the region, households were increasingly compelled to look outside the province for the cash to pay taxes. Junior men were therefore delegated to leave in search of wage work and Senegal became a favorite destination. Given the distance, men would be gone for two or three years at a time. Migration, however, remained intermittent: not every junior man went on migration nor did those who left necessarily make more than one trip during their life time. In part, this was because departures had to be balanced with forced labor requirements that removed men from the household labor force periodically to participate in public works projects or act as messengers between the *cercle* government and the province. Other men, therefore, had to remain at home to ensure that work in the fields would be completed in a timely fashion.

The French colonial government abolished forced labor in 1946. By the 1950s, households began purchasing ploughs and oxen, thus increasing the requirement for cash. With forced labor no longer a drain, men became involved in migration to meet these needs. New opportunities within the Soudan (as Mali was called at the time) allowed men to make shorter trips to destinations closer to home and spend a few months away during the dry season, rather than leaving for two or three years at a time. The droughts of the early 1970s and 1983–84 further entrenched labor migration as a part of village life. The season of migration lengthened once again when technology shortened time-consuming labor processes: households adopted the plough for the cultivation of all crops, instead of confining it to peanuts, and began hiring tractors to thresh millet. At present, nearly all young men, beginning in late adolescence, leave every year for five to seven months. They continue to do this into their mid to late thirties unless the head of household dies prematurely or requires their assistance. Some go as far as Abidjan in Côte d'Ivoire to work as contractual laborers while others work in the 'informal' sector of Bamako and, more rarely, Segu. Despite the pervasiveness of labor migration, at least one adult man always remains at home during the dry season, except in the case of a few small households that have no sons earning cash. This is in stark contrast with practices elsewhere on the continent, particularly in southern Africa, where women are left in charge of rural households once labor migration becomes entrenched.

Men's involvement in migration is couched in the idiom of service to the collectivity. As members of a patrilineal household it is incumbent upon them to help maintain and, if possible, increase the patrimony. We leave "*ka so dila* (to put the house in order)," migrants first told me in 1981. Elders, too, stressed that migration was a necessity rather than a choice because the money for taxes, marriage expenses, and agricultural equipment could not be generated through agricultural production alone. At the same time, they noted that migration was no longer the same as during their own youth. One man who had made several trips during the late colonial period said: "We were dirty, we even looked like slaves; but see today's young men, they are clean and well-dressed." By pointing to the change in appearance, he commented not only on the difference between the work carried out then and now but also on the respectability—and therefore the desirability—of contemporary migration. Junior men themselves would sometimes say that they "missed Bamako" with its animation and excitement. Elder men acknowledged that it is impossible to prevent a young man from going, and thus admitted both the pleasurable side of migration and the fact that dependence on cash had diminished the authority they once enjoyed within the household. The major change between the early 1980s and the late 1990s is that a greater number of households, regardless of size, now accept that one of their members continue working in the city during the rainy season. They often accommodate a junior who wants to stay away even though this may put greater pressure on those at home.

The manner in which male family labor is reorganized in the context of contemporary needs and desires is evidence of a remarkable cohesiveness. It nonetheless makes power relations among the men of the household subject to continual renegotiation. This is best exemplified by the fact that, once in the city, migrants can delay returning home or change destination (for example, go to Abidjan from Bamako) against their elders' wishes. Elders then may feel compelled to send letters to Bamako exhorting their sons or younger brothers to return home as the cultivation season gets underway. And anxious mothers, worried that their sons' absences place too great a burden on household members, frequently query other returning migrants about their sons' plans.

Lewis[12] has argued that the *ci kè tòn* (the youth association composed of all the age sets until roughly the age of thirty-five) is instrumental in keeping young migrants at home for cultivation and thus indirectly maintaining the status quo of gerontocratic control. He contends that in the area near the Bani River where he conducted research in the mid-1970s villagers were loath to pay taxes with migrant earnings; the *tòn* helps make it possible to cover them with agricultural surplus. According to Lewis, villages with a strong *tòn* have less outmigration than villages with a weak *tòn*. He fails, however, to outline what makes a *tòn* strong or show just how the *tòn* checks the duration and permanence of migration, giving the impression that it is due to the moral force of the collectivity. Lewis does not say that the *tòn* works for a fee, therefore potentially favoring wealthier households, nor that it imposes fines—which may be very stiff—on members who neglect to participate. Although the system of fines is collectively decided and thus implies a political will, it still needs to be analyzed. In Sana, the *tòn* has at times turned down requests for work sessions when made by households from neighboring villages, judging it more important for members to labor in the fields of their respective households than to fill the *tòn* treasury. Unfortunately Lewis provides few ethnographic details to substantiate his argument so that it is difficult to assess differences in local conditions and social arrangements between Sana and the area along the Bani.

Apart from their ability to determine the timing of their return, migrants' control over their earnings contests household power relations. Ceding only a limited amount of cash to the household may introduce tensions between household head and migrant as well as between the juniors of a household. The ambiguity over the disposal of migration earnings is present in the very conception of work and its products: work on a collective project entitles each participant to a proportionate share of the product whereas the revenue of an individual project belongs entirely to the person who initiated and executed that project. This becomes problematic when applied to labor migration. Already in 1981 migrants did not agree on whether their work should be categorized as individual labor (*jòn foro* or *surò foro baara*) or as labor on behalf of the collectivity (*foroba baara*). Some held that it should be the latter, since wage labor is undertaken to provide for household needs. Others argued that it should be the former, since it is the individual who goes on migration and first satisfies his personal needs. Still others suggested that labor migration has an element of both categories.

It is recognized that the earning power of individuals varies and this is taken into consideration in evaluating a contribution, hence it is not differential contribution that is at issue but disproportionate withholding. No one objects to the migrant retaining earnings for small personal expenses and to purchase clothing, a radio, bicycle, or even a moped. The portion retained by the migrant, however, becomes a divisive issue and a "shameful matter" (*maloya ko*) for the household vis-à-vis other households if individual gain is visibly put above the common good or if it openly favors the "evening field."[13] One migrant, for example, was criticized for buying an oxen with his earnings. But he defended himself by saying that although it was his oxen, he was making it available to the household for pulling the plough. More frequently migrants use some of their earnings to buy small animals like goats or sheep. Interestingly, I have never heard any complaints that the migrant owes the household a certain level of contribution because those remaining behind have to work harder if he delays his return home. Outright requests for cash are generally made only when taxes or marriage payments are due, though migrants frequently told me that they preferred to go to Bamako rather than to Sinsanni or Segu because being within easy reach of home made it more difficult to save. A household head has little leverage against his junior unless the junior's wedding is still pending and the elder can warn that he will be unable to make an upcoming marriage payment without the potential bridegroom's remittance.

Handing over only a limited amount to the household head may be less an expression of individual self-interest than a manifestation of an already existing tension. The migrant may be signaling disagreement with the household head or differences among the men of the household which are threatening household unity. In the latter case, the migrant may cast his interests with a smaller unit within the household such as that of the evening field and deploy his earnings on its behalf, because household fission generally takes place along the lines of evening fields.

Endangering the Collectivity?: Women in Migration

Unmarried girls between the ages of approximately sixteen and twenty began migrating in the mid-1970s. Most go to Bamako to work as domestic servants in Malian households with the goal of earning cash to help their mothers prepare the "wedding goods" (*kònyò minanw*), a pattern established for other areas of Mali as well.[14] Wedding goods consist of things such as calabashes, kerosene lamps, flashlights, enamel bowls, blankets, and cloth that brides bring with them when they get married. Mothers are expected to accumulate these items on their daughters' behalf but have found it ever more difficult as goods considered necessary have increased in range and quantity. Initially, migration may have been precipitated by the penury created by the drought of the early 1970s when many women sold their cloth, gold, or animals to help prevent their families from starving. Girls going to the city reduced the number of mouths that had to be fed and provided a new opportunity for generating some income. Over time, with the continuation of migration even during periods of improved weather, migration has contributed to the inflation in wedding goods. Unlike their brothers, girls have no obligation to contribute to household needs and there is never any question over the allocation of their earnings.[15] Labor migration, however, effectively ends for girls at the time of marriage. A married woman does not migrate unless her husband asks her to accompany him, and this generally happens only if he stays in the city for more than one dry season.

When I first arrived in Sana in February 1981, girls were away working in Bamako but returned for the rainy season. Some left again when cultivation was completed in August; others stayed until after the harvest. Although the aims of female migration were not in question, there was a good deal of discussion by both women and men over some of its effects. Girls working in the city were said to be interacting with men in unseemly ways, becoming too intimate and risking pregnancy. In short, the city was thought to have a corrupting influence over which elders at home had no control. Mothers were concerned but felt that they had no choice except to let their daughters go, and fathers acquiesced.

In 1983, however, representatives from the various Sana Bamana villages (also referred to as the *Bamana tòn*) raised this matter at a meeting whose primary agenda was to discuss the growing burden of marriage expenses. The (male) elders in attendance debated and then concurred that no girls should henceforth go to Bamako. Any girl who contravened this prohibition would pay a fine of 25,000 Malian francs.[16] Each household was therefore obligated to help unmarried daughters find alternate ways of earning cash and prevent them from going to the capital city. Yet by the fall of 1986, girls from all but one village were again working in Bamako. A few were even staying there during the rainy season. When I inquired what had happened, I was told that the agreement had broken down; the fine was so high that once a household found itself in violation and was unable to pay, the prohibition lost its force and migration resumed.

That the perceived problem had not changed was driven home to me by a request made as I was getting ready for a trip from Bamako to Sana in December 1986. The brother of one of the girls (himself working in Bamako at the time) asked me to tell his eldest brother, who was also the head of household, to send someone to Bamako to get his sister because she was behaving very badly—"running after men," as he put it. I conveyed the message, but still did not find the girl at home during another visit several months later. When I asked about her, I was told that an elder brother had indeed gone to Bamako to fetch her but that she had left again after only a short stay, implying that they were unable to prevent her from leaving. In contrast, the one village that had collectively upheld the decision seemed to have no such problems. Their prohibition remains in force and has even been tightened: girls are not only prevented from going to Bamako' but also to Segu or Markala. They are only allowed to go to Sinsanni and Joro, where villagers regularly attend the weekly markets, and to Niono. Niono is a considerable distance to the north, but is seen as an agricultural town and girls going there generally work in the rice harvest and reside with a relative during their stay.

The debate over female migration, the way of dealing with perceived problems, and the failure to maintain the Sana-wide prohibition raises several questions: Why were objections to female migration couched in terms of a decline in morality rather than, for example, the nature, conditions, and rewards of domestic work? Why the focus on girls' promiscuity rather than on men's lack of restraint? Why did the prohibition against migration break down so quickly in all but one village? And why was one village able to prevail where the others failed?

To say, as some feminists might, that the preoccupation with girls' morality is an instance of a universal double standard that puts the burden on women to protect their virtue is not very useful. Pointing to a pattern does not help us understand the dynamics behind it or explain what happens in a particular place and at a particular point in time. De Jong has detailed how Jola villages in southern Senegal have used the *Kumpo* mask performance to control girls' labor migration to Dakar, but this performance did not involve a discourse on morality.[17] There is evidence that in colonial Zambia (then northern Rhodesia), however, women's departure for the urban areas generated a similar discourse on

morality.[18] According to Chauncey, women's migration deprived elders of agricultural labor and, more important, of the possibility to attract sons-in-law who
would provide bride service or its equivalent in cash and goods.[19] In short, the
concern with morality was closely tied to the threatened material interests of a
relatively privileged group within rural society. This is suggestive even though
the colonial Zambian case involves a difference in social structure (matrilineal
rather than patrilineal) and occurred under different historical circumstances.

Bamana girls participate in agriculture, but households are less dependent
on their labor because junior men and married women constitute the core of the
labor force. A girl's capacity for labor receives social recognition only upon
marriage when she joins her husband's household and is obligated to cultivate
alongside junior men. Household elders arrange marriages without obtaining
the consent of the potential bride or that of her mother. Migration raises the possibility that unmarried women will not return and is enhanced by the fact that
girls, unlike their male counterparts, have no share in the patrimony. Women's
control over property is limited to the wealth they themselves accumulate and
the opportunities for doing so are greater in the city than in the rural area, at
least during the agricultural off-season. In addition to such structural incentives,
staying in the city, despite the insecurities connected with life there, may be
preferable to an undesirable marriage. Malian law requires the consent of both
spouses to a conjugal union and would therefore support a recalcitrant girl.
Girls' refusal to return would not only undermine the marriage system, but also
increase the possibility that a greater number of men—whose search for wives
might become more precarious—would not return.

Male elders in the village that has upheld the prohibition contend that girls
change in the process of migration: while in Bamako, they often become
involved with a man and then decide that they do not want the one their elders
had chosen for them. It goes without saying that this jeopardizes the arrangement and, ultimately, social relations and the continuity of the patrilineal household. It also undermines the power of elders vis-à-vis women. When I asked if
migrating junior men might not also withdraw from an arranged match, elder
men asserted that this wouldn't happen, that men's interests lie with the interest
of the kin group. Evidence, however, contradicts this assertion of patrilineal ideology. I know of instances where marriage agreements were dissolved because
the bridegroom-designate decided that he did not want to marry the bride-to-be
despite the fact that, unlike their female counterparts, young men are asked for
their opinion before a marriage alliance is concluded.[20]

Male elders acknowledge that the prohibition makes the mothers' task of
preparing a trousseau for their daughters more difficult, yet contend that it

eliminates the earlier problems and therefore justifies the hardship. They *do* permit girls to migrate as soon as the wedding or a preliminary wedding ceremony (known as *singa*)[21] has been held, assuming the husband agrees. Frequently the couple migrates together from that point on. The advantage of migration to Bamako rather than to Niono or to rice fields near Kè-Macina to the east seems to lie more in the availability of work year-round. (Reports of what girls have brought back from their work in the rice harvest indicate that their earnings are not inferior to those in Bamako.) Girls say that work in Bamako is hard but that they like to go there more than anywhere else.

Mothers' main concern is that they might be shamed by a daughter who becomes pregnant in Bamako. Only recently did a woman friend tell me that 'you worry that your daughter might get pregnant in Bamako. But you counsel her and hope for the best.'[22] In spite of women's uppermost concern with their daughters' chastity, they—like their migrating daughters—say that girls' refusal of a designated marriage partner is the major reason for the prohibition in the village that has sustained it. Two young girls noted in the course of a conversation with me that another village had now instituted a similar prohibition and allowed that their own elders might yet do the same.[23]

I believe that the severe drought of 1983–84 hastened the demise of the prohibition on female migration in all but one village. Rainfall dropped to half the normal level during those years and dramatized the limited possibilities for generating cash locally. Desperate households might have permitted their daughters to depart in order to relieve pressure on the food supply, and their inability to pay the fine undermined the *tòn*. However, drought is only a context for change rather than its cause. That the agreement should have collapsed so quickly suggests that a Sana-wide *tòn* has less force than a village *tòn*; in short, individual households feel less bound by it. The reasons for this have to be sought in the history of Sana, in the tensions between household/kin group and non-kin collective interests, and in the effects of market relations on social solidarities. While wage labor is virtually absent in agriculture, commodities have become integral to social reproduction. The resumption of migration on the part of adolescent girls highlights that the items that currently constitute the wedding goods have become essential consumption goods for a young bride rather than dispensable luxuries. Women and men must concur in this or girls would not be leaving for Bamako, since most abide by their elders' wishes. Given the frequency with which weddings are postponed because a girl's trousseau is not ready, I asked some people if such postponements could not be avoided by having couples acquire any missing items jointly when they migrate after the wedding. A few men responded affirmatively, but others said that "people wouldn't agree to such a thing." And women did not like the proposition at all and found it unacceptable. Clearly, my suggestion would invite complications in the prevalent separation of spousal property, the control over and distribution of migration earnings, and the potential of *kònyò minanw* as a basis for women's greater autonomy.

Conclusion

In the effort to assist their mothers in preparing a trousseau, female migrants, like their male counterparts, have been drawn into wider sets of power relations that affect the construction of identity. While it is widely accepted that young men gain autonomy in the course of migration, the autonomy young women gain is perceived as a risk and a potential threat to the integrity of the collectivity. Girls' travel to and work in the city helps constitute them as independent agents and undermines kin-based power and the very conception of the household. The discourse on female morality and the efforts to keep girls from leaving for the city signal the ambivalence over this process.

The different significance attached to male and female migration is underlined by the nature of the response they have elicited. Men may return late or not at all for a given cultivating season, or they may make contributions perceived to be inadequate, but these problems are always dealt with by individual households. There has been no effort on the part of village elders to put collective pressure on young men to return home at particular times or make specific contributions to the household, nor has a *tòn* been put in place toward this end. Only when millet was still being threshed manually was a fine imposed on those who left after cultivation was finished and returned late or not at all for threshing. The risks men's actions might pose for the household (*du*) thus are not seen as something to be mitigated or regulated by communal intervention. This shows that once labor-saving technologies such as the plough or the threshing machine had become widely embraced, production and control of the labor force, like accumulation, were considered to be internal matters—issues to be resolved by the kin group segments encompassed by the household. It also highlights an inherent tension between a communal ethic and an emphasis on household (that is, kin group) control over production and its products, a tension Mali's first president, Modibo Keïta, ignored at his peril in some of his policies. Although there is a certain correlation between commoditization and greater stress on household control, this is not an entirely new phenomenon.

The responses to the concerns that have arisen in connection with the migration of men and women suggest that men are responsible to the household and women to the wider community. Women's actions potentially affect not single kin groups, but relations between kin groups that extend beyond the village. An initial response at the level of the province, which is the primary terrain for marriage alliances (or, more graphically, "marriage paths"—*furu siraw*), is therefore not surprising. Moreover, girls' refusal of a designated marriage partner challenges the control elder men still exercise over the constitution of those relations. The elders have accepted that young men have a say in the selection of their wives—men are asked if they agree to a match with a particular woman before negotiations go forward—but young women are not accorded the same privilege. I do not believe that this is simply a question of "patriarchal control" as an abstract universal phenomenon. Girls' actions threaten the existing process of household formation and raise the specter of social relations determined more by individual will than by principles inherited from the past, a form of chaos. This is not to argue that marriage alliances have continued unchanged.[24] Instead, I contend that girls' migration evokes such resistance and fears because it alters the balance of power between men and women as well as between the kin group and the individual. There may be some parallels between the focus on women's actions at the household level and the role often ascribed to women in nationalist movements since both involve the construction of an imagined community.

Notes

1. Diarra et Koné 1991; Institut des Sciences Humaines 1984; Vaa, Findley, and Diallo 1989; Van Westen and Klute 1986.

2. 'Sinsanni' became 'Sansanding' in French colonial records and 'Shibla' became 'Sibila.' Sansanding and Sibila remain the official names of these towns today.

3. Guyer 1981, 87.

4. Ibid., 1981.

5. For an overview of this vast multidisciplinary literature, see Stichter 1985.

6. See, for example, Dwyer and Bruce 1988; Guyer and Peters 1987; and Yanagisako 1984.

7. Classificatory brothers are men who are considered brothers in the local kinship system but who may not be brothers within the European kinship system.

8. Despite the name, "evening fields" are not cultivated in the afternoon or evening. They are simply secondary to the "common field" (*foroba*) and their cultivation is integrated with the cultivation of the *foroba*. Before labor migration became a widespread source of income, individual household members might also cultivate their own personal field known as *kò karila*, or "broken back."

9. These fields are also termed *kò karila* (broken back).

10. See Grosz-Ngaté 1988.

11. The most well-known of these in the literature on Mali is the "cultivation association" (*ci kè tòn*), sometimes referred to as the "youth association" (*kamalen tòn*).

12. See Lewis 1985.

13. "Evening field" refers not only to the field that constituent units within the household might cultivate, but also to those units themselves.

14. Institut des Sciences Humaines 1984; Diarra et Koné 1991.

15. Rosa de Jorio points out that this may be quite different in the cities where women are expected to contribute, if in varying amounts, to their paternal household. Personal communication, July 1998.

16. At a monthly wage of 7,500 Malian francs (MF), this was equivalent to more than three months of work in the city. Not being able to go to Bamako diminished earnings considerably since girls working in Sinsanni earned only 3,000 MF per month at the time. In the early 1980s, and until 1984 when Mali reintegrated the CFA zone, the currency was still the Malian franc. It equaled .50 CFA.

17. De Jong 1997.

18. Chauncey 1981; Hansen 1989.

19. Chauncey 1981.

20. In fact, I believe that such a rejection played a role in the case of the young woman, cited earlier, who has stayed in Bamako against her family's wishes.

21. A *singa* is a wedding where no transfer of wedding goods (*kònyò minanw*) takes place. It is held when the groom's family wants the wedding to take place but the bride's mother feels that the trousseau is incomplete. The *singa* represents a compromise because it integrates the bride into the household labor force during the cultivating season and allows the couple to live together. This arrangement may continue for two, or even three, rainy seasons before the wedding proper (*kònyò*) is held. I have no indication that *singa* weddings are more prevalent in marriages involving girls from that village.

22. I place this in single inverted commas because I did not retain her actual words in my notes. Although direct quotes make for livelier reading, I prefer not to take license with people's words.

23. They told me about a local girl who had recently left Bamako for Abidjan, where girls had not gone up to this point, because she wanted to avoid a marriage, arranged by her kinsmen, at all cost.

24. Grosz-Ngaté 1988.

Acknowledgments

My profound thanks to Rosa de Jorio, Shelley Feldman, and Karen Tranberg Hansen for their constructive readings of this essay.

Bibliography

Chauncey, George Jr. 1981. "The locus of reproduction: women's labour in the Zambian copperbelt, 1927–1953." *Journal of Southern African Studies* 7: 135–64.

De Jong, Ferdinand. 1997. "The power of a mask: a contextual analysis of the Senegalese *Kumpo* mask performance." *Focaal* 29: 37–56.

Diarra, Tiéman et Yaouga F. Koné. 1991. *Les migrations féminines au Mali. La main d'oeuvre domestique (Rapport final).* Bamako: Institut des Sciences Humaines.

Dwyer, Daisy, and Judith Bruce, eds. 1988. *A Home Divided: Women and Income in the Third World.* Stanford CA: Stanford University Press.

Grosz-Ngaté, Maria. 1988. "Monetization of bridewealth and the abandonment of 'kin roads' to marriage in Sana, Mali." *American Ethnologist* 15 (3): 501–14.

Guyer, Jane I. 1981. "Household and community in African studies." *The African Studies Review* 24 (2/3): 87–137.

Guyer, Jane I., and Pauline Peters, eds. 1987. "Conceptualizing the household: issues of theory and policy in Africa." *Development and Change* 18 (2). (Theme issue.)

Hansen, Karen Tranberg. 1989. *Distant Companions: Servants and Employers in Zambia, 1900–1985.* Ithaca and London: Cornell University Press.

Institut des Sciences Humaines. 1984. *L'exode des femmes au Mali. La main d'oeuvre domestique féminine à Bamako et à Ségou.* Bamako.

Lewis, John Van D. 1985. "Village-level restraints on the exodus from rural Mali." In *African Migration and National Development*, edited by Beverly Lindsay. University Park and London: The Pennsylvania State University.

Stichter, Sharon. 1985. *Migrant Laborers.* Cambridge UK: Cambridge University Press.

Vaa, Mariken, Sally E. Findley, and Assitan Diallo. 1989. "The gift economy: a study of women migrants' survival strategies in a low-income Bamako neighborhood." *Labour, Capital and Society* 22 (2): 234–60.

Van Westen, A. C. M., and M. C. Klute. 1986. "From Bamako, with love: a case study of migrants and their remittances." *Tijdschrift voor Economische en Sociale Geografie* 77: 42–49.

Yanagisako, Sylvia. 1984. "Explicating residence: a cultural analysis of changing households among Japanese-Americans." In *Households. Comparative and Historical Studies of the Domestic Group*, edited by Robert McNetting, Richard R. Wilk, and Eric J. Arnould. Berkeley: University of California Press.

Economic and Agricultural Policy Reform

Overview—MSU's Food Security Research and Outreach Program in Mali

JOHN M. STAATZ

Origin of the Program

In 1985, the Department of Agricultural Economics at MSU, in collaboration with Malian colleagues working in various ministries and research institutes, began a program of applied research and outreach focused on agricultural marketing reforms and on the potential roles for regional trade and cooperation in Mali's food security and economic growth strategies. The program also helped to strengthen Mali's public agricultural market information system and improve the strategic planning of agricultural research in the country.[1]

Analyzing the Market Reforms: The First Phase

The food security research program in Mali began as an effort to provide a stronger empirical base for implementing and evaluating the cereals market reform program, known by its French acronym, PRMC (*Programme de Restructuration du Marché Céréalier*).[2] This program, officially launched in 1981, aimed at transforming Malian agricultural production and marketing by abolishing the official state monopoly on grain trading and doing away with official prices, thereby creating incentives for the private sector (including farmers) to expand investment in grain production and marketing. Supporters of the reforms argued that the program would unleash strong market incentives and transform grain farming into a commercial activity. Critics replied that most Malian farmers had little capacity, because of poor technology and erratic weather, to respond to the reforms and that the benefits of market liberalization would likely be captured by a few large merchants.

Both sides were arguing on the basis of conventional wisdom(s) and ideology, but with very little empirical information to back up their arguments.

The MSU research program aimed to fill this empirical void, by creating a system that could observe farmer and trader behavior at several levels of the production and marketing system in order to determine which actors had the capacity and the willingness to respond to the reforms by expanding production and investment.

The first phase of the MSU work (1985–87) focused on the impact of the PRMC reforms in the southern "grain belt" of the country (the CMDT and OHV zones). The basic hypothesis was that the effects of the reforms would be most apparent in the grain-surplus producing zones of the country. Led by Josué Dioné and Niama Nango Dembélé, two Malians who were pursuing graduate degrees at Michigan State, the research program was carried out jointly with the *Commission Nationale d'Evaluation et de Suivi de la Stratégie Alimentaire* (CESA). Dioné's research focused on the food strategies of farmers in response to the reforms, while Dembélé's work focused on how traders, particularly cereals wholesalers, were responding to the changes brought about by the PRMC.[3]

Extending the Program

The initial research findings quickly influenced the debates within the PRMC during 1986 and 1987 and created the demand for further research in order to extend the results both geographically and over time, to see how traders and farmers modified their strategies as production conditions varied in different agro-climatic zones and as rainfall changed from year to year. The research and outreach program that emerged focused on four themes: (a) the ongoing impacts of the cereal market reforms in the southern regions of the country; (b) alternative public- and private-sector roles in assuring food security, particularly in the chronically grain-deficit region of northeastern Mali (Gao-Tombouctou); (c) access of farmers, traders, and consumers to market information; and (d) strengthening agricultural research by taking account of how interactions among policy reform, organization of the agricultural research system, and characteristics of the different technologies factors affect the payoffs to agronomic research.

Market reform and farmer strategies in southern Mali

The continuation of the research on market reform in southern Mali, led in the late-1980s by Niama Nango Dembélé, Philip Steffen, Victoire D'Agostino, Shelly Sundberg, and Mona Mehta, focused on how traders and farm households adapted their marketing and income strategies to cope with changing production conditions. These studies also examined the implications of these strategies for household food consumption and nutrition.[4] During this period, market integration also increased, the organization of the grain trade evolved rapidly in response to the ongoing reforms,[5] and the MSU-CESA studies continued to feed those results into the policy debate.[6] The researchers also evaluated the impact of PRMC measures aimed at strengthening the private sector's role in the market, particularly programs aimed at improving traders' and village associations' access to credit.[7]

Food security in the grain-deficit northeast

As the impacts of the market reforms in the southern, more densely populated areas of Mali became better understood, policy makers turned their attention to the potential effects of the reforms in the chronically grain-deficit regions of the northeast (Tombouctou and Gao regions).[8] These were areas where the state, through the national grain board (OPAM), had traditionally played a much greater role than in the south in assuring grain supplies because of the region's poor infrastructure and the political necessity of assuring grain supplies in an area where many had historically felt estranged from the central government in Bamako.[9]

The MSU-CESA research in the northeast, led by Philip Steffen, focused on the current and potential roles of the private and public sectors in helping assure grain supplies and food security in the northeast. The analysis involved both conceptual work on the changing role of a public grain board in a market economy characterized by weak infrastructure and periodic production and income shortfalls,[10] and empirical studies of the consumption and marketing strategies of farm households and traders in the northeast.

The research demonstrated that the private sector played a vital role in assuring the food security of the region, in contrast to the predominant view in Bamako that OPAM supplied most of the grain to the northeast. Rural households, particularly those in the more climatically vulnerable locations (the more northern areas and the areas away from the Niger River), followed a very diversified income strategy, focused on herding, trade, non-agricultural enterprises, emigration, and reliance on remittances from relatives. In contrast, households in the southern, on-river villages were much more dependent on their own agricultural production.[11] The less agricultural households depended heavily on purchases from private traders to assure their grain supplies. These households' diversified income strategies, combined with their purchases, allowed these households to have a more stable consumption of cereals throughout the year than the southern and on-river households that relied more on own production.[12]

The private traders of the Gao and Tombouctou area faced special challenges in meeting both the urban and the dispersed rural demand of the northeast because of the poor transport and communication infrastructure. In contrast to their southern counterparts, many grain merchants in the northeast were forced to hold inventories for up to several months (in contrast with only a few days for merchants in the south) due to their inability to transport grain (from suppliers) along the river in the dry season and ship grain to buyers in remote villages during the rainy season. Their large stocks of grain made these merchants particularly vulnerable to commercial losses when free distributions of food aid took place, reducing the commercial demand for their grain.[13] In addition, the traders in these regions generally believed they had poor market information, and thus were supportive of government efforts in the late 1980s to launch a public market information system (see below).

The importance of the private sector in helping assuring food supplies in the northeast implies that the rebellion of the early 1990s, which disrupted the traditional trading relationships and flows of products in the region, likely had a very severe impact on food security and real incomes in this area. It further suggests that re-establishing and strengthening those links will be vital to the recovery and development programs for the northeast.

Improved market information

As the market reforms continued, studies by MSU and others revealed that the lack of reliable market information seriously constrained farmers', traders', and consumers' ability to respond to the new opportunities opened by market liberalization. Farmers complained that the lack of reliable information on cereals prices in major markets prevented them from bargaining effectively with traders over prices for their crops. Consumers wanted to know where they could buy their staples most cheaply, particularly in large cities such as Bamako, which have many different neighborhood markets. Traders said that a lack of up-to-date information on grain prices and availability in various markets and on planned food aid distributions seriously hindered their developing effective business strategies.[14] Responding to this need, in 1988 USAID and the PRMC supported the creation of Mali's first public agricultural market information system, the *Système d'Information du Marché* (SIM). The SIM was created out of the merger of three existing data collection systems: the MSU-CESA panel of traders; a similar panel of semi-wholesalers in the center

of the country, interviewed regularly by a team financed by the Canadian
International Development Agency; and a retail grain price monitoring system
covering the regional capitals, run by OPAM.[15]

The SIM set up a network of enumerators (initially OPAM employees)
who reported weekly on price and supply conditions in more than fifty markets
throughout the country. This information was sent by radio-telephone to
Bamako, where it was compiled and analyzed by the SIM analytic staff based
at OPAM, and then diffused weekly by radio, television, and the written press.
In addition to regular weekly and monthly price reports, the SIM and affiliated
MSU researchers undertook studies of the evolving market structure,[16] developed improved data collection and analysis methods,[17] analyzed options for
restructuring the market information system as the market itself evolved,[18] and
attempted to measure the impact of the SIM's activities on market efficiency
and income distribution.[19]

In an effort to make the SIM more financially sustainable by linking it to
producers, in 1988 the SIM was transferred from OPAM to APCAM
(*Assemblée Permanente des Chambres d'Agriculture du Mali*). The system was
renamed the *Observatoire du Marché Agricole* (OMA) and modified as follows: coverage expanded to include horticultural, livestock, and fish products
in addition to cereals; decentralized supervision of data collection and diffusion;
the development of a broader range of information products, including short-
term market outlook bulletins and programs in marketing extension; and more
in-depth policy analysis based on SIM data.[20]

Improved planning of agricultural research

Much of the early debate surrounding the impact of cereals market reform centered on how farmers responded to new market incentives, using their existing
technologies. By the late 1980s, however, scientists at the *Institut d'Economie
Rurale* (IER), Mali's national agricultural research institute, were questioning
how the reforms would affect farmers' willingness to adopt the new crop varieties and other technologies that IER was developing. IER's previous research
had taken place in an environment of fixed prices and marketing quotas, and
consequently focused more on increasing yields per hectare than on market-
determined profitability of the new technologies. The market reforms forced
IER to re-examine its criteria for planning agricultural research. In response to
this challenge and to pressure from the World Bank to downsize and increase
its efficiency, IER began restructuring in the late 1980s and turned to MSU for
help in developing new research strategies.

MSU worked with IER to examine the implications of the market reforms for the organization of its research programs,[21] develop a new division of subsector economics that would focus on the evolution of agricultural markets and their implications for agricultural technology research, and carry out case studies to illustrate new approaches to incorporating market policy effects in the design and evaluation of new agricultural technologies.

The first of the case studies, carried out by Bruno Henry de Frahan in collaboration with IER's farming systems division, involved an ex-ante evaluation of the payoffs to extending farming systems research to the Mopti region. The analysis showed that the internal rate of return to investing in farming systems research in this region, in the then-current policy environment, was likely to be very low, around 2 percent.[22] Yet if key marketing, extension, credit and fiscal policy changes were implemented, the projected internal rate of return would increase to 26 percent. De Frahan's study thus clearly showed the synergies between policy reforms and agronomic research and the need to coordinate the two if the new technologies were to be attractive to farmers.

The second case study grew out of MSU's work with IER to develop a new division of commodity subsector economics studies, known in Mali as *économie des filières* (ECOFIL). A subsector (or *filière*) is defined as the vertical array of activities involved in the production and distribution of a given product, from input provision to on-farm production, all the way through distribution to the final consumer. The ECOFIL division was charged with examining how these various stages of production were organized and coordinated for key subsectors, and the implications of that organization for technical agricultural research. For example, how well do existing maize markets transmit information to farmers about millers' preferences for different varieties (based on the varieties' milling characteristics)? If these preferences are not transmitted, it is unlikely that farmers will pressure agricultural researchers to develop better milling varieties, and if the agricultural researchers do not regard merchants or millers as part of their clientele, it is unlikely that others will lobby for such varieties either. By looking at the whole range of activities linking farmer with consumer, the ECOFIL studies broadened the criteria for the breeding programs, which previously had focused mainly on increasing and stabilizing yields.

The maize study documented the importance of the CMDT's program of guaranteed prices for maize in the late 1970s and early 1980s in inducing farmers to intensify maize production. It also analyzed how the plunging maize prices that accompanied the market liberalization led farmers to abandon the intensification program. The study also went on to predict (correctly) that devaluation of the CFA franc and improved processing techniques for maize might lead higher maize prices and a re-adoption of more intensive production.[23] Many of the approaches developed in this pilot study have been adopted in subsequent studies by ECOFIL researchers.[24] MSU's collaboration with ECOFIL continued throughout the 1990s, both through research planning and carrying out specific studies.[25]

A Regional Perspective

Based on the successful food security studies in Mali and similar studies in Senegal, MSU developed a partnership with the *Institut du Sahel* (INSAH), a regional research institute based in Bamako, to carry out a program known as PRISAS that examined regional food security issues across the CILSS member states.[26] PRISAS aimed to strengthen (a) the capacity of national research institutions in the Sahel to carry out applied research on food security, and (b) the capacity of INSAH to help coordinate research on regionwide food security issues, through the following measures:

- Developing a Sahel-wide network of researchers and policy makers that exchanged research results and met to discuss ways of incorporating research results into improved food policies.
- Holding regional workshops to facilitate such exchanges between researchers and policy makers.
- Developing a series of background documents and reviews of the literature on food policy issues that served as reference documents for researchers throughout the subregion and as the basis for discussion during the regional workshops and seminars.
- Funding and backstopping collaborative research projects by members of the PRISAS network. The research projects were selected either because they developed research methods that were broadly applicable across the Sahel (e.g., the subsector approach to designing agricultural research, as pioneered by IER) or because they addressed issues of a regional nature (e.g., regional trade).
- Helping INSAH develop its long-range program for food-security research, as part of the CILSS program of strengthening regional food security policies.[27]

In January 1994, the former French colonies of West Africa devalued their common currency.[28] The CILSS member states voiced strong concerns about the effect of devaluation on the competitiveness of their predominantly rural economies and how the costs and benefits of this policy change would be shared among various groups in the population. In response, INSAH/PRISAS launched a major program of research on the impacts of the devaluation of the CFA franc on food security and real incomes in West Africa. By designing parallel studies in different countries, the research was able to identify the impact of differing national policies and institutions on the capacity of different groups to respond to the opportunities created by the devaluation. The research results were made available to policy makers through a series of national and regional workshops, policy bulletins, and in-depth research papers.[29] A key objective was to identify areas where strategic actions by governments, the private sector, and donors could augment the positive effects and limit the negative impacts of the devaluation on food security and income growth. Tefft's article in this volume is an example of the type of research carried out in this program, which allowed Malian researchers and policy makers to see more clearly the regional aspects of the challenges and opportunities facing them.

By 1998, the PRISAS devaluation studies were drawing to a close, and MSU's work with INSAH shifted to supporting its broader program in agrosocioeconomics (AGROSOC). That program provides research to undergird the CILSS Sahel 21 program, which is a strategic plan for agricultural transformation and broad-based economic growth in the Sahel, based on improved water management, expanded regional trade, decentralized natural resource management, and more productive agricultural research.

Summary

The MSU-Mali partnership in applied research and outreach on food security has been extraordinarily long-lived and productive. It has combined the best elements of the Land-Grant model of tying applied research on important practical problems to in-service and longer-term training and to policy extension. The articles in this section of the book provide a sampling of the results that have resulted from this partnership. The MSU team feels privileged to have worked with such skilled and dedicated Malian colleagues and looks forward to continuing this partnership into the future.

Notes

1. Many MSU faculty, graduate students, and Malian researchers have participated in these activities, which have also served as the basis for twenty master's theses and Ph.D. dissertations (twelve of them by Africans), both at MSU and in West Africa. The U.S. Agency for International Development (USAID) has provided financial and intellectual

support to the program through two Cooperative Agreements between USAID and MSU: the Food Security in Africa Cooperative Agreement (1985–94) and the Food Security II Cooperative Agreement (1994–2002).

2. See Dembélé and Staatz, and Dioné, in this volume, as well as Dioné (1989) for details on the PRMC.

3. The work was based on data gathered from a panel of nearly 200 farmers and 118 traders who were interviewed at least monthly over two years (1985–86) about their production, sales, and purchasing activities as well as their perceptions of the major opportunities and constraints they faced. See the chapters by Dioné and by Dembélé and Staatz for details.

4. See D'Agostino 1988a; Staatz, D'Agostino, and Sundberg 1990; and Maïga 1994.

5. Barry 1989; Mehta 1989; Dembélé 1994.

6. For example, D'Agostino 1988b; Dembélé 1988.

7. See Dembélé and Steffen 1987; D. Diarra 1993.

8. At the time of the studies (1988–89), the Gao region included what later became the region of Kidal.

9. See Diarrah, this volume. The MSU-CESA research in northeast Mali took place before the rebellion of the early 1990s.

10. See Steffen and Dembélé 1988; Steffen 1994.

11. Households in the northern villages covered by the surveys (Almoustrat and Temera) earned only 22 percent of their incomes from agriculture, livestock, and gathering of wild cereals. For the southern villages (Bara and Tessit), the figure was 55 percent. For the off-river villages (Almoustrat, Djebok, and Tessit), 25 percent of household income came from these sources, compared with 56 percent for the on-river villages (Temera and Bara). See Steffen 1995, 619–25.

12. Steffen 1995.

13. Free food-aid distributions in the northeast are typically untargeted, with all individuals within an area deemed "at risk" receiving an equal amount of aid, regardless of their ability to purchase food in the market. Although 85 percent of the thirty-one traders interviewed in the northeast believed that food aid disrupted the market, most declared that they believed it was necessary in times of crisis, and several large traders themselves made free distributions of food to the population in times of crisis. The traders' main complaint was that they were totally uninformed about the planned arrival and distribution of food aid and thus could not adjust their commercial strategies to accommodate it. See Steffen 1995, 448–52.

14. Dembélé and Steffen 1988.

15. Niama Nango Dembélé (and later James Tefft) served as technical advisors to the SIM while four SIM staff members studied in Michigan. For more information on the creation of the SIM, see Dembélé, Staatz, and Egg 1990.

16. See, for example, Traoré, Tefft, and Kéita 1992; Gabre-Madhin 1991; S. Diarra 1994, (Diarra et al. in this volume).

17. See SIM 1993.

18. See Aldridge 1992; Aldridge and Staatz 1993.

19. See, for example, Staatz and Dembélé 1992; Staatz, Dembélé, and Aldridge 1992.

20. Dembélé and Staatz 1998.

21. Staatz 1989.

22. The analysis of the case study is summarized in de Frahan 1990.

23. This pilot study of the maize subsector is summarized in Boughton 1994.

24. Boughton and Témé 1992.

25. Studies of the rice subsector, for example, are discussed in Mariko et al. 1998 and Dimithè in this volume.

26. PRISAS is *Programme Régional de Renforcement Institutionnel de Recherche sur la Sécurité Alimentaire au Sahel* (Regional Program for Strengthening Institutional Research Capacity on Food Security in the Sahel). INSAH is a research institute of CILSS (the Permanent Interstate Coordinating Committee to Combat Drought in the Sahel), whose member states are Mali, Senegal, the Gambia, Guinea Bissau, Mauritania, Cape Verde, Burkina Faso, Niger, and Chad.

27. For a list of the publications produced under the PRISAS program, see the PRISAS Fact Sheet on the Food Security II Project Web site: <http://www.aec.msu.edu/agecon/fs2/fact/idwp54i.htm>.

28. The common currency, the CFA Franc (CFAF), was devalued relative to the French franc (FF) for the first time since 1947. The devaluation, from 1 FF = 50 CFAF to 1 FF = 100 CFAF, was the largest change in macroeconomic policy in the region in several decades.

29. For summaries of the key results, see Kelly and Chohin-Kuper 1998; Reardon et al. 1998; Tefft et al. 1998; Yade, Kanté, and Staatz 1998; and Yade et al. 1999.

Bibliography

Aldridge, Kimberly M. 1992. "A framework for analyzing alternative institutional arrangements for the Cereals Market Information System in Mali." Master's thesis, Dept. of Agricultural Economics, Michigan State University.

Aldridge, Kimberly M., and John M. Staatz. 1993. "Lignes directrices pour l'analyse de la structure et de l'évolution du système d'information du Marché des Céréales au Mali." East Lansing: Michigan State University Agricultural Economics staff paper no. 93–55F.

Barry, Abdoul. 1994. "Comparative advantage, trade flows and prospects for regional agricultural market integration in West Africa: the case of Côte d'Ivoire and Mali." Ph.D. dissertation, Michigan State University.

Barry, Abdoul Wahab. 1989. "A study of cereal price inter-relationships across markets and commodities at the wholesale and retail levels in Mali." Master's thesis, Michigan State University.

Boughton, Duncan, and Bino Témé. 1992. "Farming systems and markets—combining analytical frameworks for development of commodity subsectors: the case of maize in southern Mali." Selected paper, Twelfth Annual Farming Systems Symposium, the Association for Farming Systems Research/Extension, East Lansing, September.

Boughton, Duncan. 1994. "A commodity subsector approach to the design of agricultural research: the case of maize in Mali." Ph.D. dissertation, Michigan State University.

D'Agostino, Victoire. 1988a. "Coarse grain production and transaction in Mali: farm household strategies and government policy." Master's thesis, Michigan State University.

————. 1988b. "La production et la commercialisation des céréales au Mali: résultats empiriques et implications en matière de politique." Document de travail 88–05. Bamako: Projet Sécurité Alimentaire MSU-CESA-USAID, November.

de Frahan, Bruno Henry. 1990. "The effects of interaction between technology, institutions and policy on the potential returns to farming systems research in semi-arid northeastern Mali." Ph.D. dissertation, Michigan State University.

Dembélé, Niama Nango and John M. Staatz. 1998. "Services d'information de marché pour le développement de l'agro-business et la croissance economique durable au Mali." *Policy Synthesis*, Food Security II Cooperative Agreement, Michigan State University, Dept. of Agricultural Economics, May.

Dembélé, Niama N., John M. Staatz, and Johny Egg. 1990. "L'expérience du Mali." Paper presented at CILSS/Club du Sahel Conference on Cereals Market Information Systems in the Sahel, Bamako, Mali, 23–25 April. Paris: OECD/Club du Sahel. (English version: "The Malian experience.")

Dembélé, Niama Nango, and Philip Steffen. 1987. "Evaluation conjointe des programmes de crédit PRMC aux associations villageoises et aux commerçants privés: campagne agricole 1986/87." Document de travail no. 87–04. Bamako: Projet Sécurité Alimentaire MSU-CESA-USAID, November.

————. 1988. "Approche méthodologique pour la mise en place d'un système d'information au Mali." Document de travail no. 88–01. Bamako: Projet Sécurité Alimentaire MSU-CESA-USAID, March.

Dembélé, Niama Nango. 1988. "Quelques eléments de performance de la commercialisation privée des céréales (mil-maïs-sorgho) au Mali." Document de travail no. 88–03. Bamako: Projet Sécurité Alimentaire MSU-CESA-USAID, October.

———. 1994. "Economic analysis of traders' response to cereals market reforms in Mali." Ph.D. dissertation, Michigan State University.

Diarra, Daouda. 1993. "Analyse economique de l'intégration spatiale des marchés céréaliers et de l'impact du crédit P.R.M.C. sur le revenu des producteurs agricoles au Mali." Thesis for Doctorat 3éme Cycle in Agricultural Economics, University of Abidjan.

———. 1994. "The role of small rice mills in the rice subsector of the Office du Niger, Mali." Plan B paper, Michigan State University.

Dimithè, Georges. 1997. "An economic analysis of the competitiveness of alternative rice production systems: the case of the bas-fonds rice production in Mali-sud." Ph.D. dissertation, Michigan State University.

Dioné, Josué. 1989. "Informing food security policy in Mali: interactions between technology, institutions, and market reforms." Ph.D. dissertation, Michigan State University.

———. "Sécurité alimentaire au Sahel: point sur les études et projet d'agenda de recherche." Research paper no. 90–02. PN-ABS-873. Bamako: PRISAS, Institut du Sahel, October.

Gabre-Madhin, Eleni. 1991. "Transfer costs of cereals marketing in Mali—implications for Mali's regional trade in West Africa." Master's thesis, Michigan State University.

Kelly, Valerie, and Anne Chohin-Kuper. 1998. *Food Security and Agricultural Subsectors in West Africa. Future Prospects and Key Issues Four Years after the Devaluation of the CFA Franc. Horticultural Subsector.* Policy Synthesis. Bamako: CILSS/INSAH.

Maïga, Younoussa. 1994. "Analyse de la demande des céréales en milieu urbain au Mali: le cas de la ville de Bamako." Thesis for Doctorat 3éme Cycle in Agricultural Economics, University of Abidjan.

Mariko, Dramane, Anne Chohin-Kuper, Valerie Kelly, and Diane Aissata Zouboye. 1998. "L'évolution de la filière riz à l'Office du Niger depuis la dévaluation du FCFA." Bamako: Institut d'Economie Rurale, Programme Economie des Filières and INSAH/PRISAS, August.

Mehta, Mona. 1989. "An analysis of the structure of the wholesale cereals market in Mali." Master's thesis, Michigan State University.

Reardon, Thomas, Bocar Diagana, Francis Akindes, Kimsyinga Savadogo, John Staatz, and Youssouf Camara. 1998. *Food Security and Agricultural*

Subsectors in West Africa. Future Prospects and Key Issues Four Years after the Devaluation of the CFA Franc. Consumption. Policy Synthesis. Bamako: CILSS/INSAH.

SIM *(System d'Information du Marché).* 1993. "Lancement d'une nouvelle méthodologie." Rapport Hebdomadaire, Bamako, week of 25–31 January.

Staatz, John M. 1989. "The role of market conditions in influencing the adoption of new agricultural technologies in Mali." East Lansing: Michigan State University Agricultural Economics staff paper no. 89–109, October. (French version: "Influence des conditions du marché sur l'adoption des nouvelles technologies agricoles au Mali.")

Staatz, John M., Victoire C. D'Agostino, and Shelly Sundberg. 1990. "Measuring food security in Africa: conceptual, empirical, and policy issues." *American Journal of Agricultural Economics* 72 (5): 1311–17.

Staatz, John M., and N. Nango Dembélé. 1992. "Has AID's investment in market-facilitating services had an impact?" East Lansing: Michigan State University, Agricultural Economics staff paper no. 92–93, December.

Staatz, John M., Nango Dembélé, and Kimberly Aldridge. 1992. "The role of market information systems in strengthening food security: lessons from Mali." East Lansing, Michigan State University Agricultural Economics staff paper no. 92–60.

Steffen, Philip, and Niama Nango Dembélé. 1988. "Une critique des rôles alternatifs pour l'OPAM sur le Marché Céréalier à travers un paradigme des biens publics." Document de travail no. 88–02. Bamako: Projet Sécurité Alimentaire MSU-CESA-USAID, August.

Steffen, Philip. 1994. "The structural transformation of OPAM, cereals marketing agency." *State-owned Enterprises in Africa,* edited by Barbara Grosh and Rwekeza S. Mukandala, pp. 221–44. Boulder: Lynne Reinner Publishers.

———. 1995. "The roles and limits of the cereals market in assuring food security in northeastern Mali." Ph.D. dissertation, Michigan State University.

Tefft, James, John Staatz, Josué Dioné, and Valerie Kelly. 1998. *Food Security and Agricultural Subsectors in West Africa. Future Prospects and Key Issues Four Years after the Devaluation of the CFA Franc. Cotton Subsector.* Policy Synthesis. Bamako: CILSS/INSAH.

Traoré, Abdramane, James F. Tefft, and Francis Kéita. 1992. "Pourquoi les prix des céréales sont-ils tellement élevés dans la région de Kayes?" Etude de Cas no. 1. Bamako: Ministère de l'Economie, des Finances et du Plan, Office des Produits Agricoles du Mali, Système d'Information du Marché, March.

Yade Mbaye, Bakary Kanté, and John Staatz. 1998. *Food Security and Agricultural Subsectors in West Africa. Future Prospects and Key Issues Four Years after the Devaluation of the CFA Franc. Beef Subsector.* Policy Synthesis. Bamako: CILSS/INSAH.

Yade, Mbaye, Anne Chohin-Kuper, Valerie Kelly, John Staatz, and James Tefft. 1999. "The role of regional trade in agricultural transformation: the case of West Africa following the devaluation of the CFA franc." Paper presented at the Tegemeo/ECAPAPA/MSU/USAID Workshop on Agricultural Transformation, Nairobi, 27–30 June 1999. East Lansing: Michigan State University Agricultural Economics staff paper no. 99–28, June.

Food Security Policy Reform in Mali and the Sahel

JOSUÉ DIONÉ

Introduction

The food crises of Mali and the other Sahelian countries during the 1970s and 1980s stemmed not only from the lingering effects of the severe droughts in the mid-1970s and early 1980s. Many observers of Sahelian development have concluded that poorly designed pricing and marketing policies distorted agricultural incentives and failed to address the major causes of the enduring food production gap throughout the subregion. In the late 1970s, many donors pressed for policy reforms to restore farmers' and private traders' investment incentives to increase food production and improve distribution. Under strong pressure from donors, the government of Mali agreed in March 1981 to carry out a series of policy reforms aimed at increasing official producer and consumer prices, liberalizing grain trade, and improving the efficiency of OPAM (*Office des Produits Agricoles du Mali*), the state grain board.

This chapter analyzes the impact of the process of market liberalization on food security in Mali during the decade of the 1980s. Based on the central thesis that output market liberalization is a necessary, but not sufficient, condition to improving food security in the Sahel, the chapter focuses on the interactive effects of technology, institutions, and policy reforms on food availability and access to food.[1]

The chapter is divided into five sections. The first section highlights the food security problems in the Sahel in general. The second section presents an overview of food and agricultural policies in Mali from 1928 to 1989. The third section discusses the objectives, implementation and achievements of the cereal market liberalization process in Mali, and outlines some of the major issues for the 1990s. The fourth section draws some policy implications for food security in the Sahel. And the final section discusses food security in Mali after the 1991 revolution that led to the democratization of the country.

Food Security Problems in the Sahel

The attention of the entire world was captivated by news of hundreds of thousands of people dying from hunger and suffering from starvation during the prolonged drought of the mid-1970s and early 1980s in the Sahel. The international donor community responded generously, yet the food production gap continued to widen. Even though per capita cereals production was declining, the bulk of the aid was not directed at improving domestic productivity in the major food crops.[2]

Following the disappointing performance of crop-production and integrated rural development projects during the 1960s and 1970s, donors turned their attention to policy reforms in the general framework of structural adjustment lending programs. In this framework, pricing and marketing policies, which traditionally subsidized consumers by depressing producer prices and accumulating budget deficits of the state grain boards, were perceived as major impediments to food security. Instead, output price and market liberalization were identified as the means to restore farmers' and traders' incentives to invest and to increase the production and improve the distribution of the basic food staples, especially cereals.

Food insecurity in Mali and throughout the Sahel, however, stems from a complex set of problems that cannot be solved by price and marketing reforms alone.[3] The picture is much more complex, and it is possible to identify at least five fundamental causes of food insecurity in the Sahel.

First, the overarching cause is poverty.[4] With per capita GNPs ranging between US$160 and US$260, five Sahelian countries were among the sixteen poorest nations in the world in 1987. All Sahelian countries were among the world's forty-three poorest countries.[5] Between 1965 and 1986, the average annual growth rate of per capita GNP was positive but less than 1.5 percent in four of the nine countries and negative in the other five countries. Although the bulk of the population still lives in the rural area and is engaged in agriculture, over one-fourth of the Sahelians experience what Professor Sen calls a "pull failure" in their food entitlements, that is, inadequate access to food because of the low level of their real incomes.[6] Failures in effective demand affect both the urban poor and food-deficit rural people (non-farmers as well as farmers), thus compounding constraints on the supply side of the Sahelian food-security equation.

Second, most Sahelian countries lack appropriate agricultural technology that farmers can readily adopt to expand and stabilize the production of rainfed millet, sorghum, and maize, which account for about 80 percent of total cereals consumption in the sub-region. As a result of heavy investments in export crops (especially groundnuts and cotton) since the colonial period, national research institutions have not focused on improving yields or stabilizing the output of rainfed cereals. As late as 1989, for example, there were no widespread high-yielding and drought- and disease-resistant varieties of millet, sorghum, and maize.[7] Growth in aggregate food supply from domestic production will most likely be limited as long as there are no viable technological options to increase and sustain productivity in the major rainfed cereals.

Third, the capacity of farmers in the Sahel to finance investments in agriculture is undermined by various agricultural surplus extraction strategies, including taxation of crop and livestock production and exports, overvaluation of exchange rates, and head taxes that are levied on some categories of the rural population. The composite effect of the tax burden is not offset by subsidized government credit programs. Hence, the supply response to higher grain prices is low.

Fourth, severe imperfections in labor markets, farm input supply markets, financial markets, and foodgrain markets are serious impediments to both improved availability of and access to food. Given the interactions among these different markets, their imperfections also have interactive effects on food availability (through production) and accessibility (through real income). Without a comprehensive view of market-related problems, the scope of actions undertaken to improve the efficiency in only one type of market (for example, the cereal market) will be constrained by prevailing imperfections in the other markets.

Fifth, rapid urbanization contributes to a shift in consumption patterns away from domestic production structures, hence to developing an unsustainable food-consumption profile. Both price and non-price factors—especially lagging processing and handling of local food products—stimulate an orientation of urban-consumption preferences toward relatively cheap imports of two "fast-food type" commodities: rice (mainly from Asia) and wheat. With an annual urban population growth rate of about 7 percent, per capita consumption of rice and wheat products in the Sahel rose by 29 percent between its average level in 1966–70 and that in 1976–80, while that of millet, sorghum, and maize fell by 12 percent.[8] Such a consumption profile is unsustainable because there is little hope in the medium term that domestic supply will respond adequately to the growing demand for rice and wheat. Moreover, the Sahelian countries' capacity to earn foreign exchange for grain imports is restricted by their declining competitiveness in the world oilseed-product markets.[9]

Evolution of Food and Agricultural Policy in Mali

The entire economy of Mali rests on the rural sector, which provides the bulk of employment, food (essentially cereals), and foreign exchange (cotton, livestock, and fish). Cereals provide approximately 70 percent of the total caloric consumption of Malians, and millet, sorghum, and maize account for 85 percent of this proportion. Mali is the Sahelian country best endowed with land suited for both rainfed and irrigated agriculture. But despite the relative abundance of land, Mali's agriculture has, just as in other Sahelian countries, progressively failed to produce enough foodgrain for a population growing at 2.5 percent per year.

The agricultural and food policy options followed by Mali after independence in 1960 were strongly determined by the 1928–59 colonial policy legacy in the French Soudan. Colonial policy was aimed at expanding the production of export crops needed by French industry.[10] Groundnut production spread successfully mainly because of the similarity of this crop to the local varieties of groundnuts grown for centuries. Success in developing cotton production was much slower. The first attempt to grow cotton under irrigation failed[11] and cotton production took off only after 1949, with the interventions of the *Compagnie Française pour le Développement des Fibres Textiles* (CFDT) in the country's high-potential rainfed areas. Throughout this period, agricultural research efforts were concentrated on developing improved seeds, fertilizers, pesticides, and farming techniques for these cash crops.

The production of these crops grew largely from the extension of cultivated land through the spread of animal traction and from the introduction of cash and cereal crop rotations. No significant research program was undertaken to improve food production. And instead of market incentives, head taxes and village-level quotas of cash crop delivery were established as means to increase market surplus. All important marketing activities were entrusted to French commercial companies holding monopoly rights and to Lebanese traders, thereby leaving only subsidiary assembly roles to domestic merchants.

Guided by an inherited anti-market and anti-merchant bias, misconception of the agricultural incentive system, and a high propensity for state interventionism and monopoly, Mali's leaders at independence opted for a radical socialist development path, which lasted from 1960 to 1968. Central planning was adopted, and implemented with French technical assistance, as the best way to achieve economic independence through a rapid development of agriculture, industrialization for agricultural input manufacturing and product processing, the systematic search for oil and mineral resources, and the implementation of mass-oriented social policies in education, health, administration, etc.[12] A total of thirty-three state enterprises were created between 1960 and 1968 to undertake or control virtually all the major economic activities, including agricultural input and credit distribution, product processing, domestic marketing, and exports.

Agricultural and food policy was dominated by the development of rice production under irrigation, implementation of crash-production projects in rainfed areas, collectivization of production, and compulsory marketing through OPAM—the state grain board created in 1964 in order to establish a legal monopoly in agricultural product marketing. Yet merchants continued to trade grain clandestinely on the private parallel market. The official consumer and producer prices for all major commodities embodied three conflicting objectives: (1) to increase rural incomes, (2) to provide cheap food (cereals) to urban consumers, and (3) to extract a surplus from agriculture to finance state investment in other economic sectors.[13] In reality, the last two objectives took priority and resulted in depressed official producer prices, the imposition on farmers of delivery quotas of cereals to OPAM, and the subsidization of consumers through urban consumer cooperatives at the expense of accumulating OPAM deficits.

Agricultural development and food policy remained essentially unchanged during the first two decades of Mali's independence. Even with the shift in the 1970s—with strong donor support—from commodity-based projects to integrated rural development programs, aggregate food production in Mali stagnated. In spite of the creation of twenty-six state-run integrated rural development projects (*Opérations de Développement Rural*), by 1981 basic investment in agricultural research and rural infrastructure remained insignificant, except for cotton.

The relative stagnation of food production led the country from its status as a net cereal exporter in the 1950s and early 1960s to becoming a net importer of increasing quantities of cereals after 1965. This deterioration in the country's food situation and the prolonged Sahelian drought led to Mali's food crisis.

The Cereal Market Liberalization

Official producer prices of cereals were raised after the end of the 1968–74 drought to stimulate domestic production. OPAM was mandated to sell cereals from both domestic production and commercial imports at official consumer prices set below the full cost of the cereals. The resulting consumer subsidies translated into an increased OPAM budget deficit that amounted to about

US$80 million by 1976–77.[14] Donor agencies in the late 1970s became concerned about OPAM's mismanagement and accumulating deficits, and many began to believe that OPAM's legal monopoly in grain marketing and the official price system was a major disincentive to domestic cereal production.[15] As a result, donors pushed for the establishment of the Cereal Market Restructuring Program (PRMC) in 1981. A group of ten major donors entered collectively into a policy dialogue with the government of Mali and they pledged multiyear shipments of food aid in exchange for a major overhaul of the government's cereals marketing policy.[16] The food aid was sold through commercial channels. The proceeds went into an account, jointly managed by the government of Mali and the PRMC donors, which financed mutually agreed-upon market reforms.

Objectives

Initially designed for the period between 1981 and 1987, the PRMC aimed explicitly at raising farmers' income through a gradual increase in official producer prices of cereals; liberalizing cereal trade through the elimination of OPAM's official monopoly and increased private trader participation; and improving OPAM's operating efficiency through the restructuring of this marketing parastatal.[17]

In the absence of adequate empirical information about the structure and conduct of domestic cereal production and marketing, the PRMC was based on the following assumptions:[18]

1. Farmers' production of coarse grains depended strongly on the prices farmers received for these crops, which were highly correlated with official producer prices;
2. Farmers constituted a homogenous group of net sellers of cereals, who would benefit from higher foodgrain prices;
3. No major constraints other than price disincentives hindered farmers' marginal propensity to invest in cereal production;
4. Private traders had the capacity and propensity to invest in response to new opportunities opened up by market liberalization;
5. The country would continue to experience cereal deficits, and thus needed food aid to support market liberalization;
6. OPAM should continue to exist to channel food aid and protect its politically influential clientele from higher grain prices.

Because the results of subsequent research showed most of these assumptions to be inaccurate, several adjustments were made in the cereal market liberalization program.

Implementation of the cereal market liberalization: 1981–89

Foodgrain production

Two of the major goals of the cereal market liberalization program were to raise farmers' incomes and to offer incentives to produce more cereals for the market. Yet foodgrain production in Mali has continued to be influenced more by rainfall than any other factor. An empirical study of farmers from 1985 to 1987 reveals that neither "getting prices right" nor producer floor prices are simple solutions to food insecurity problems in Mali.[19] First, severe liquidity problems restricted the ability of the government to sustain producer price supports through buffer-stock operations of the state grain board.

Second, research results raise serious concerns about the equity implications of increased cereal prices, even at the farm level.[20] Even following the two relatively abundant harvests of 1985 and 1986, up to 43 percent of the farm households of two of the best agricultural zones of Mali (CMDT and OHV) were net grain buyers (see table 1). These results are striking in that Mali is generally perceived as having a fairly egalitarian distribution of land. Only 53 percent of the farms were net grain sellers, and 90 percent of the total quantity of net sales came from only 28 percent of the farms. Most of the net cereal-buying households had poor access to extension services, input markets, and formal credit. As a result of their low investment capacity, these farmers used low-productivity technologies. The net sellers of cereals, in contrast, were essentially farm households located in the more humid southern part of the CMDT zone, with good access to improved farming techniques through relatively efficient systems of agricultural research, extension, input supply and credit, and were heavily engaged in cotton production.

This clearly illustrates the equity issue of what Timmer, Falcon, and Pearson have termed "the food-price dilemma."[21] In the short run, higher cereal prices would mainly benefit only a third of the farm households, while depressing the real income of at least 40 percent of them that are net foodgrain buyers. In fact, market demand for grain other than rice in Mali is essentially located in the rural areas (among non-farmers as well as a large number of food-deficit farmers). Millet, sorghum, and maize account for less than 45 percent of the total cereal consumption of the 20 percent of Mali's total population living in urban areas.[22]

Table 1. **Farmers' market transactions and net per capita availability of food-grains by rural development zone, rainfall subzone, and level of animal traction equipment, Mali (1985/86–1986/87).**

Zones/subzones and level of animal traction equipment	Percent of farm households with:		Average grain transactions per farm household (kg)			Net grain available per capita (kg)
	Net sales	Net Purchases	Sales	Purchases	Net sales	
South CMDT*	75.1	18.2	552	49	502	341
North CMDT	58.6	38.2	188	197	-9	286
South OHV*	35.9	58.9	49	151	-103	151
North OHV	15.2	82.7	119	629	-510	146
Total CMDT	66.7	28.3	368	124	244	310
Total OHV	24.9	71.6	86	406	-319	148
Total South**	62.4	31.4	389	82	306	273
Total North**	43.5	53.7	164	348	-184	241
Total Sample						
Equipped Farms	77.0	19.1	509	219	290	290
Semi-Equipped	45.2	51.7	173	185	-11	230
Non-Equipped	32.0	61.5	103	256	-153	201
Total	52.7	42.9	273	219	54	256

*CMDT is the largest cotton-producing zone; OHV is a zone with a similar agricultural potential but without significant cotton production.
**The south of each zone has higher rainfall and better agricultural land than the north.
Source: Dioné (1989), pp. 133, 147, 163, 193.

Given the generally low supply elasticity for food in the context of poor technology, infrastructure, and institutions in developing countries such as Mali, higher producer prices need a long gestation period and substantial complementary investment in research, extension, and other supporting services before they induce any significant effect on foodgrain availability and the real incomes of the rural poor.[23]

Third, adequate attention has not been paid to interactions between pricing and marketing policies and policies in other areas (especially fiscal policies), all of which may jeopardize farmers' food security in the short run and impede their capacity to invest and sustain capital formation in agriculture. For instance, in one of the survey zones (OHV), 37 percent of the farmers sold cereals without producing any real surplus beyond home-consumption requirements. In this zone, over half of the total grain sales were made at low prices during the first three months following harvest, and 71 percent of the grain sellers reported head tax payment as the most important motive for their sales.[24] About 72 percent of the farm households of the zone had to buy back cereals later in the year at higher prices than those at which they sold at harvest, often using very costly coping strategies—for example, cereal loans to be paid at next harvest, migration, and sale of family labor during the cropping season). Moreover, indirect farmer taxation through official cash-crop price schedules and head taxes compound farmers' weak self-financing capacity.[25] Restricted access to official credit further limits farmers' weak capacity to maintain their investment. Thus, about two-thirds of the OHV farmers who had historically invested in animal traction had also disinvested from it to generate cash to face both household food shortages and head tax payments in years of poor harvests.[26]

Fourth, the search for increased foodgrain production and accessibility in Mali has overlooked important synergies among cash crops and food crops. These synergies and differences in the performance of agricultural support institutions may lead to considerable gaps in productivity and growth between regions with similar agricultural potential. Our 1985–87 survey found that, relative to other zones, higher agricultural growth was achieved in the CMDT cotton zone through a strategy centered on a vertically coordinated set of activities (research, extension, input and credit distribution, processing and marketing, and investment in road infrastructure) for the long-term growth of cotton production and income. As a major cash crop with guaranteed outlets and prices, cotton gives farm households a privileged access to extension services, formal credit, input markets, and therefore to improved farming techniques for all major crops, particularly rainfed cereals that also benefit from residual cotton fertilizers through crop rotations. Thus, cotton income not only covers farmers' fixed cash liabilities (taxes and loans), but also gradually supports the development of food production and nonfarm activities. The CMDT cotton-farmers also produced on average 2.7 times as much per capita cereals as those in OHV, a zone with similar agricultural potential. After net outflows amounting to 10 percent of their own production, the farm households in the cotton zone still had enough foodgrain to meet their home-consumption needs (at 188 kg per capita per year) at least a full year beyond the two years of the survey. By contrast the farms in the non-cotton zone could barely meet their family foodgrain needs in spite of purchasing the equivalent to 16 percent of their own production.[27]

To summarize, there is more to improving food security at both the national and the farm-household levels in Mali than just improving grain pricing and marketing. In Professor Sen's terms, the "endowment bundles" and the "exchange entitlement mappings" are so interdependent in Mali that improving long-term access to food is almost synonymous with improving food and agricultural production. Mali still has to face the central issue of significantly raising the productivity of the agricultural sector. This requires that careful attention be paid to policies in other areas (agricultural research, extension, financing, taxation, employment generation, etc.) that have significant effects on farmers' opportunities and capacity to invest in agricultural production. It also requires a comprehensive strategy aimed at real income growth in agriculture through the development of improved policies and institutions, technology adoption, and capital formation.

Private foodgrain marketing

From 1981 to 1986, the government introduced several measures to improve the capacity of firms to market cereals. These included the abolition of OPAM's monopoly, the legalization of the private grain trade, and the removal of restrictions on interregional cereal trade. In reality, the abolition of OPAM's legal monopoly was largely symbolic, because the share of OPAM's grain marketing only exceeded 5 percent of total domestic production and one-third of the estimated total quantities traded in just three of the eleven years prior to the beginning of the reform in 1981.[28]

The legal action taken to promote private cereal trade nevertheless opened the door to new traders, who accounted for 39 percent of the 118 coarse grain wholesalers operating in four major cities in 1985. This led to some increase in specialization and scale of operations by longtime grain traders.[29] Hence, most consumers, including food-deficit farmers (who previously had little access to OPAM's subsidized supplies), have benefited from cost-savings resulting from free circulation of grain and larger-scale operations of grain merchants induced by the cereal market liberalization.[30]

The inability to support producer prices through the buffer-stock operations of OPAM led the PRMC in 1987 to launch a seasonal grain-trade credit program aimed at enabling private traders to buy more foodgrain in the post-harvest period and assume seasonal storage of cereals. This program encountered

several problems, including the complexity of loan procedures, the unwilling-
ness of traders to keep large grain stocks as a loan guarantee, poor access to
loans for those who lack political influence within the Chamber of Commerce,
and poor loan repayment records of the politically influential members of the
Chamber of Commerce.[31]

Even a significant improvement of this seasonal credit program would
leave several problems of the foodgrain distribution system unsolved.[32] First,
private traders still lack access to bank financing for long-term investment in
transportation and storage facilities. Second, very little basic investment has
been made to improve road infrastructure and facilitate grain transfer between
surplus and deficit areas. The government clearly faces a medium-term investment tradeoff between storage and transport facilities to improve the efficiency
of the private grain trade. Third, the government continues to show a high
propensity to control private traders' operations tightly and foodgrain exports
even following good harvests. These controls and regulations apply primarily
to trader registration, minimum stock levels, information about suppliers and
clients, and export authorization. Such restrictive conditions and high business
taxes impedes flexibility and overt competition in private grain trade.[33] Fourth,
a generalized liquidity crisis, which grew worse under a continuous government
fiscal crisis, results in the growing reluctance of private traders—who usually
play also the role of informal bankers—to extend additional credit in cereals to
increasingly insolvent civil servants, whose food security is more and more at
stake.

Finally, private grain traders are chronically subjected to unstable expectations caused by several types of risk. In the context of the thin and volatile
cereal markets in Mali, these include:

1. Uncertainty about supply from domestic production, which can be halved or
   doubled from one year to the next because of the vagaries of the weather;
2. Demand uncertainty resulting from the combination of unforeseen interventions of the public marketing system (OPAM) and food aid distributors, and
   the weakness and instability of consumers' real income;
3. Uncertainty about official cereal marketing and trade policies and regulations, which change constantly without prior consultation with, or notifica-
   tion to, private-sector participants; and
4. The absence of appropriate measures to induce the development of forward
   planning through enforceable contracting mechanisms.

These different kinds of risk and merchants' general lack of confidence in the
continuity of policies lead private traders to adopt short-run, small-scale, and

diversified trading strategies, which do not allow the whole food production and distribution system to benefit from all potential economies of larger-scale operations.

OPAM: The state grain board

The public sector received 92 percent of the total receipts from the sale of food aid provided through the PRMC food (about US$41 million) used over the first six years of the cereal market reform program. OPAM alone received, in addition to considerable donor technical assistance, 72.5 percent of this share of the public sector. This paradoxical outcome of the food aid program, which aimed primarily at increasing private-sector participation in foodgrain marketing, illustrates the political difficulty of this type of reform and the overriding concern of donors and the government of Mali to improve OPAM's financial situation. Access to these funds, along with drastic cuts in personnel (60 percent) and truck fleet (about two-thirds), improvement in stock management, and reduced consumer subsidies allowed OPAM to narrow its annual operating deficit by 68 percent between 1982 and 1986.[34] OPAM's financial improvement was also facilitated by poor harvests, which kept market prices above official producer prices from 1982 through the harvest of 1985, thereby reducing the domestic supply of cereals handled by the public sector. Because of the shortfall in production, receipts from sales of food aid (which increased from an annual average of 38,000 tons in the period 1978–81 to 125,000 tons in 1982–85) served as an effective means to finance the PRMC during the first five years of its existence.[35]

The sustainability of both supporting producer prices through direct public sector intervention in the market and financing the reform program only with food-aid sales was seriously challenged following two successive good harvests in 1985 and 1986. As a result of good rainfall, domestic production of millet, sorghum, and maize rose by 44 percent in 1985 relative to 1984. OPAM was then authorized to use PRMC funds and bank credit to support producer prices (which had fallen in November 1985 to 35 CFAF/kg for maize in major surplus zones) through buffer-stock purchases at the official producer price of 55 CFAF/kg.

Notwithstanding record public-sector purchases of nearly 83,000 tons of millet, sorghum, and maize between December 1985 and February 1986, actual producer prices of these cereals stayed around 50 CFAF/kg until March 1986, when OPAM ran out of money and withdrew from the market. Producer prices then fell to 42–45 CFAF/kg for millet and 31 CFAF/kg for maize. Unable to resell more than 43 percent of the total 103,000 tons of grain acquired through domestic purchases and food aid, OPAM was caught with most of its working capital tied up in cereal stocks in 1986, mainly because official sales prices were set too high above market prices.[36]

The situation grew even worse with a second good harvest in 1986, which exceeded the previous year's by 4 percent.[37] OPAM's intervention in 1986–87 was limited to purchasing 10,000 tons of domestic foodgrain to replenish the national security stock, since the parastatal was ineligible for new bank credit because of its incapacity to pay the loans contracted the previous year. Producer prices of rainfed cereals in major assembly markets fell an average of 25–31 percent compared with the previous year.[38]

These developments resulted in two major shifts in the policy-reform package. First, several donors gradually agreed to replace some of their food aid contribution with cash to be injected in the private grain marketing channels to support producer prices in years of abundant production. Second, by the end of 1987, the government of Mali abandoned the concept of official producer prices for millet, sorghum, and maize, and restricted OPAM's roles to (1) managing the national security stock; (2) managing and distributing food aid; (3) assuring, in complementarity with the private sector, adequate food supplies in chronically food-deficit areas; (4) developing and maintaining a market information system; and (5) providing other market facilitating services to private sector participants.[39]

The combination of a poor harvest in 1987 and a temporary ban on rice imports in early 1988 led foodgrain prices to rise enough to allow OPAM to sell off most of its commercial stocks and thus improve its financial situation. In addition, beginning in 1988, OPAM began specializing in producing and providing improved public-good type market services such as information and training for different market participants. The sustainability of these new developments, all initiated and supported mainly by donors' financial and technical assistance, represents a major challenge for the government of Mali in the 1990s.

Implications for the Sahel

Structural adjustment lending programs started in the 1980s and are now underway in thirty-two of the forty-five countries of sub-Saharan Africa. Mali was chosen by donors as a test case. Donors offered to provide multiyear food aid to help feed Mali's cities in exchange for foodgrain pricing and marketing policy reforms. The cereal market liberalization program in Mali was launched on the basis of implicit assumptions about both farmers' and traders' capacity and propensity to respond to cereal market incentives. Because most of the initial assumptions were unsubstantiated, numerous changes have been made in the program. As a result, some progress has been made since 1981: private grain trade has been legalized; cereals circulate more freely from suppliers to consumers; the roles of the public sector have been more appropriately redefined to some extent; and market facilitating services such as financing and information are improving.

Nevertheless, improving foodgrain pricing and marketing, however important, addresses only one of the five fundamental causes of food insecurity in Mali and the Sahel. The government of Mali and donors still must address several additional crucial issues. On the production side, the weakness of the national agricultural research system results in the lack of appropriate agricultural technology that farmers can adopt to increase and stabilize productivity in foodgrains. Farmers' capacity to respond to new market opportunities is severely undermined by heavy and rigid taxation and restricted access to more income-generating activities (such as cash-crop production), improved technologies, credit, input supplies, and efficient supporting institutions. These deficiencies critically hamper growth in food and agricultural production by impeding sustained capital formation through the adoption of more productive technologies in the rural area.

On the demand side, considerable instability in the cereal markets remains an unresolved issue for farmers and traders, as well as their clients. The rice production-consumption gap is also a major issue to address, since the demand for rice will continue to grow with urban population, while domestic production of rice under irrigation continues to be unable to compete with imported rice and no major prospect for expanding foreign-exchange earnings is in immediate sight. Above all, the entire foodgrain production-distribution system must cope with a persisting weakness of effective demand, which is characteristic of the general poverty and liquidity crisis of Malian consumers. The effects on food security of the cereal market liberalization will remain modest as long as adequate attention is not also paid to these other major issues.

Notwithstanding country-by-country differences in the Sahel, three major lessons emerge from Mali's experience with market liberalization. First, because structural adjustment programs involve tough political and institutional issues, and given the poor climatic, institutional, and technological context of the Sahel, food security policy reform in Sahelian countries must be perceived as a medium- to long-term battle. It is clearly not a short-term undertaking as the donors had perceived when the cereal market liberalization program was launched in 1981 in Mali. Second, the complexity of the food insecurity problems in the Sahel calls for a comprehensive approach to improving rural incomes across the board. Third, since severe resource limitations prevent Sahelian countries from simultaneously tackling all the major causes of their food insecurity, the prioritization and the sequencing of the reforms become crucial. Focusing on the root cause of food insecurity, poverty, should guide Sahelian governments' and donors' choice of actions. Since the bulk of the population of Mali and the Sahel are farmers, national food security policies must first deal with both sides of the food-security equation—increasing food availability and access to food—at the household level. Such national policies would require substantial and long-term commitment to invest primarily to increase the productivity of food staples, recapture domestic markets through improved competitiveness, and generate new employment and income streams for the rural as well as the urban poor. In this sense, food security in the Sahel also involves improving cash-crop production and nonfarm activities along with food-crop production.

Epilogue

by John Staatz

The preceding sections, written in 1989, chronicle Mali's experience with cereals market reform up to the end of the 1980s and its implications for food security. The 1991 popular revolt that led to the downfall of the Traoré regime and the subsequent democratization in Mali ushered in fundamental changes that broaden the options for addressing the food security challenges discussed above and increase the political urgency of doing so.

The key changes of 1990s that affect food security in Mali include democratization, decentralization, and the growth of civil society; the rebellion in the northeast and the subsequent peace agreement; payoffs to previous investments in technology and policy reforms, particularly in the rice subsector; and continued economic reforms, including both sectoral reforms and the 1994 devaluation of the CFA franc. Below, we briefly touch on some of the implications for these for the food security challenges facing Mali.

Democratization, decentralization, and the growth of civil society

Democratization has led to a flourishing of Malian civil society, including the emergence of independent farmer and consumer organizations. These potentially offer much greater scope for collective action, both in pressuring government

services to be more responsive to farmers' and consumers' needs, and in organizing additional services themselves. For example, the cotton farmers' union
(SYCOV) has been instrumental in bargaining with the state and the CMDT for
more favorable output prices for cotton farmers. Given the important role of cotton in strengthening farmers' capacity to produce cereals and in serving as an
engine of rural economic growth, such action can have major implications for
improved food security over the medium and long term. Similarly, the transfer
in 1998 of the agricultural market information system from OPAM to the
Assemblée Permanente des Chambres d'Agriculture du Mali (APCAM) offers
the possibility of improving the sustainability of this important service by lodg-
ing it with a politically influential group that has a strong incentive to lobby the
government to fund it. The creation of local communal governments in 1999 will
undoubtedly offer additional opportunities to mobilize local initiative to undertake actions (such as strengthening local road infrastructure) that will improve
food security.

Decentralization and democratization also pose new challenges for developing food security policies. Short-term pressures to address consumers' concerns about high grain prices in years of production shortfalls or heavy exports,
and farmers' concerns about low prices in years of abundant production, may
lead to policies to reverse market reforms (for example, blocking exports or
having OPAM engage in large-scale grain buying or selling operations). The
experience of the 1980s showed that such programs are very difficult to sustain
financially and administratively. With decentralization, such pressures are
likely to multiply on the local level, as local politicians try to respond to con-
stituents' immediate concerns. The challenge will be to develop policies and
programs that address these legitimate short-term concerns while at the same
time do not undermine the improvements in food system performance achieved
to date under the reforms. There is no simple formula for such policies, and
developing them will require careful analysis.

The rebellion and subsequent peace

The rebellion of the late 1980s and early 1990s illustrated the links between
food security and political stability. Building the peace in the northeast will
require that residents there have reliable access to food. Over the long term, the
only sustainable way of achieving such access is through private investments in
the food marketing system, combined with programs to increase incomes in the
region. Failure to achieve reliable food security could induce disaffected residents to pick up arms again.

Discussion of the food security challenges of the northeast are beyond the scope of this chapter,[40] but two points bear mentioning. First, the need to consolidate the peace in the northeast will mean that food security concerns will continue to be at the forefront of national and local policy makers' concerns in Mali. Second, the work of Steffen and others have shown the critical role that market relations and the private sector play in helping assure access to most residents of the north, particularly those who live away from the Niger River and engage primarily in non-cropping pursuits, such as nomadic herding. Helping the market reach these people more effectively, and at lower cost, will be a major challenge. A second will be to build safety nets to reach those without effective demand, but in a way that does not disrupt the market's ability to serve those who do have purchasing power.

Payoffs to previous investments, particularly in rice

The great success in the Malian food sector in the 1990s has been the rapid increase in rice production. Rice production more than doubled between 1987–88 and 1996–97, from 236,568 metric tons to 613,965 metric tons. The increase was fueled by a doubling of area in almost all regions of the country (not just the *Office du Niger*) and a 30 percent increase in yields nationally (resulting primarily from a doubling of yields in the *Office*).[41] Investments in rehabilitation of irrigation infrastructure in the *Office du Niger*, improved cultural practices (including the widespread adoption of transplanting in rehabilitated areas of the *Office*), better water management and improved rice varieties, and broader marketing opportunities for farmers following the liberalization of paddy marketing and milling in 1987 all contributed to the increase. Much more favorable farm prices following the CFA franc devaluation induced farmers to increase production further through continued area expansion, both within and outside the *Office*. The devaluation, by doubling the CFA franc price of imported rice, made Malian rice much more competitive with imports not only within Mali but throughout the CFA zone.

The growing rice production led Mali to near self-sufficiency in rice by the end of the 1990s, and policy discussions shifted from how to limit imports to how to promote exports.[42] The rice success story illustrates the importance of simultaneously addressing both technological and policy constraints to increased cereals production. Yet even with the phenomenal growth in production, rice still represented less than a quarter of total cereals production in Mali in the 1995–97 period.[43] The much more difficult challenges lie in creating the technological and policy conditions that will permit expansion and stabilization of rainfed cereals production (millet, sorghum, and maize). While maize pro-duction has increased by more than 40 percent between 1986 and 1997, progress on millet and sorghum, which together constitute more than 60 percent of Malian cereals production, has been much slower. There has been some tech-nological progress in developing shorter-cycle varieties that permit farmers to manage drought risk better (through helping stabilize yields), but major increases in yields and hence lower per-unit costs of production do not appear on the horizon.

Continued economic reform, including devaluation

The 1990s saw continued reforms in the cereals sector—for example, removal of licensing requirements for imports and exports, reduction of head taxes on farmers, and expansion of commercial courts to handle disputes among traders. These promoted greater internal and regional trade in Malian cereals. Better governmental financial management allowed civil servants to be paid on time, which increased overall liquidity in the market. The major macro-economic reform of the 1990s was the 1994 devaluation of the CFA franc, which in one day doubled the CFA franc border price of Malian imports and exports. This move greatly stimulated agricultural sectors oriented toward exports (cotton, livestock, and horticulture) and import-substitutes (such as rice).[44] In response, farmers increased production of these products; for example, cotton production doubled between 1994 and 1998. The higher prices and production raised real incomes of those farmers who had surplus to sell and helped re-ignite overall economic growth in Mali, which increased to over 5 percent per year over the period 1994–98.

But higher farm prices also translated into higher consumer prices, forcing urban (and probably some rural) consumers to reduce the quality and variety of their diet and cut back on non-food purchases.[45] It also raised concerns about growing social disparity, as those who were best able to take advantage of the new opportunities offered by the devaluation, at least immediately, were the larger, better-equipped farmers and herders. All this made more urgent the fun-damental need for poverty alleviation, which President Konaré identified as the main objective of his second term. For the cereals market, the main challenge remained: to make the market more predictable and stable and assure access to food for those lacking adequate income, while not undermining incentives of private sector actors (including farmers) to invest in the improvements neces-sary to drive down the real cost of food to consumers.

Remaining challenges

Despite the fundamental changes in Mali during the 1990s, many of the basic food security challenges facing the country remain the same as at the beginning of the decade.

On the supply side, structural problems imposed by slow technological progress in increasing millet and sorghum production, the small proportion of total production that is marketed, and poor physical infrastructure in remote zones result in volatile markets, where prices of these cereals may vary by a factor of 1:4 between years. Input delivery systems in areas without viable cash crops remain problematic, as do agricultural research and extension services. While the growth of civil society and the decentralization offer new options for addressing these problems, the basic question of how to make such supporting services financially sustainable has yet to be solved. On the demand side, poverty still limits effective demand, and there is a need to identify additional engines of growth for the economy beyond just cotton and livestock (both of which face environmental sustainability problems).

Improving access to food by the poor will, over the long term, only come about through reducing the real costs of food production and distribution, coupled with broad-based income growth. Given the predominantly rural nature of Mali, most of that growth must initially come from agriculture. The political reforms (particularly decentralization) offer the promise of harnessing local initiative to drive such growth. But those efforts will only be successful if the short-term problems of assuring access of food to the poor are addressed, but in ways that do not undermine the incentives for private actors to make the necessary investments in the food system that will lead to sustainable long-term food security.

Notes

1. Portions of this chapter are drawn from a paper originally presented at the IX World Congress for the International Economics Association in Athens, Greece, 28 August–1 September 1989, which drew on research conducted under the Food Security in Africa Cooperative Agreement DAN-1 190-A-00-4092-00 between the U.S. Agency for International Development (USAID) and Michigan State University (MSU) and under the CESA/MSU/USAID bilateral Food Security Project in Mali. The final content of the paper is, of course, the sole responsibility of the author and does not reflect official positions of either CESA or USAID.

   Empirical findings cited in this chapter about foodgrain producers and traders in Mali come from primary data collected between October 1985 and October 1987 by the CESA/MSU/USAID Food Security Research Project. Farm-level data were collected from a broad-based survey of 990 farm households and more in-depth, on-going surveys with a subsample of 190 farm households. The sample farm households came from six-teen villages, which were equally distributed between the south (about 1,000 mm of annual rainfall) and the north (approximately 700 mm of annual rainfall) of two savan-nah zones with similar agricultural resource endowments: the CMDT, which produces the bulk of cotton and has the best agricultural support institutions in Mali, and the OHV, which has a weaker institutional base. The 190 farm-household panel was roughly dis-tributed equally among three technological strata: farmers owning (1) a full set of ani-mal traction equipment, (2) an incomplete set of animal traction equipment, and (3) no such equipment.

Data on cereals sales and prices come from the farm surveys and from interviews with a panel of 118 coarse-grain wholesalers in four of the major cities (Koutiala and Sikasso in the surplus-producing zones, and Bamako and Mopti in major marketed-cereal consumption zones). Coarse-grain transaction (quantity and price) data were collected through repeated enumerator interviews, weekly in the major rural markets of the survey zones and monthly for farmers and wholesalers. These price data were complemented with PRMC data on retail cereal prices in the eight regional capitals of Mali. Less repet-itive questionnaires and informal interviews were used to collect basic information on farm household production and farmer and trader characteristics and perceptions.

2. For instance, de Lattre (1988) reports that of the total aid received by the Sahelian coun-tries, not much more than 25 percent was allocated to productive investment and only 4 percent was devoted to improving productivity in rainfed food crops. Delgado and Miller (1984) estimate that per capita production of foodgrain in the Sahel declined annually between 1961–65 and 1976–80 by 2 percent for millet, 1.3 percent for sorghum, 3 percent for maize, and 1.4 percent for rice.

3. Eicher 1982; Eicher 1988.

4. Sen 1981.

5. World Bank 1989.

6. Sen 1988.

7. In a few cases, some of the research on export crops has benefited food crops. For instance, since cotton, maize, and sorghum are often grown in rotation, the fertilizer residual from cotton is of benefit to sorghum and maize the following year.

8. Delgado and Miller 1984, 7.

9. There are no heat-tolerant wheat varieties and no improved rainfed rice varieties in the Sahel. Moreover, Berg (1989) shows that in spite of a 50 percent increase in world rice prices in 1988, the cost of rice produced under irrigation in the largest rice-consuming country of the Sahel (Senegal) amounted to 2.3–3.6 times the average landed price of broken rice imported from Thailand. While the Sahel's imports of rice and wheat prod-ucts continue to grow by nearly 8 percent per annum, FAO trade data indicate that Sahelian exports of groundnut products fell by 67 percent in quantity and 69 percent in value between 1976 and 1986 (FAO 1973–87).

10. Jones 1976, 20–23.

11. Amin 1965; de Wilde 1967; Jones 1976. The *Office du Niger* project was initiated in the late 1920s with the objective of irrigating 1.2 million hectares in the central delta of the

Niger River in order to create the "bread basket" of French colonial West Africa and to substitute for U.S. sources in supplying raw cotton to the French textile industry.

12. Amin 1965; Jones 1976; Bingen 1985.

13. Dioné and Staatz 1988, 144.

14. Humphreys 1986, 7.

15. de Meel 1978.

16. These donors were the World Food Program (which acted as secretariat of the program), Austria, Belgium, Canada, the European Community, France, Great Britain, the Netherlands, the United States, and West Germany.

17. Dioné and Dembélé 1978, 8–9.

18. Dioné and Staatz 1988, Staatz, Dioné, and Dembélé 1989, and Dioné 1989 give more details on the objectives and the implicit assumptions of the cereal market liberalization program in Mali.

19. Dioné 1989.

20. It is impossible to state unequivocally whether the PRMC actually raised producer prices because of the lack of data on the clandestine private system which, in most years, handled over 70 percent of the estimated total quantity of rainfed grain traded prior to cereal market liberalization.

21. Timmer, Falcon, and Pearson 1983.

22. Rogers and Lowdermilk 1988.

23. Estimates of the price elasticity of agricultural supply reported by various authors typically range from 0.2 to 0.7 in most developing countries and regions, including sub-Saharan Africa (Berg 1989, 13–18).

24. Dioné 1989.

25. Estimated rates of implicit farmer taxation through official price schedules in the 1970s are 24–61 percent for cotton and 48–65 percent for groundnuts (SATE 1982).

26. Dioné 1989.

27. Ibid., 357–58.

28. Dioné and Dembélé 1987, 21.

29. Mehta 1989.

30. D'Agostino 1988.

31. PRMC donors contributed funds to the seasonal credit program, which was administered through commercial banks and the Chamber of Commerce.

32. Dioné 1989, 324–33.

33. Since most traders are illiterate and do not keep formal accounts, business taxes are based on "guesstimates" of profits by agents of the ministry of finance. These estimated profits are taxed at 50 percent for companies and 30 percent for enterprises not set up as companies (Stryker et al. 1987).

34. Dioné and Staatz 1988, 150.

35. OSCE 1988.

36. République du Mali 1987.

37. OSCE 1988.

38. Dioné and Staatz 1988, 158.

39. Steffen, Dembélé, and Staatz 1988, 4–7.

40. See Steffen 1995.

41. MDRE 1998.

42. Barry, Diarra, and Diarra 1998.

43. MDRE 1998.

44. For details on the impact of the devaluation on agricultural production and food con-
    sumption, see Tefft et al. 1998; Yade et al. 1998; Kelly and Chohin-Kuper 1998; and
    Mariko et al. 1998.

45. Reardon et al. 1998.

Bibliography

Amin, S. 1965. *Trois Expériences Africaines de Développement: Le Mali, le
    Guinée et le Ghana.* Paris: Presses Universitaires de France.

Barry, Abdoul W., Salif B. Diarra, and Daouda Diarra. 1998. "Promouvoir les
    exportations de riz malien vers les pays de la sous-région." Rapport final.
    Equity and Growth through Economic Research (EAGER). Cambridge,
    MA: Associates for International Resources and Development.

Berg, E. 1989. "The competitiveness of Sahelian agriculture." In *Regional
    Cereals Markets in West Africa,* edited by Club du Sahel. Paris: OECD, pp.
    17–76.

Bingen, R. J. 1985. *Food Production and Rural Development: Lessons from
    Mali's Operation Riz-Segou.* Boulder: Westview Press.

D'Agostino, V. C. 1988. Coarse grain production and transactions in Mali: farm
    household strategies and government policy. Unpublished master's thesis,
    Michigan State University.

de Lattre, A. 1988. "What future for the Sahel?" *The OECD Observer,* 153:
    19–21.

Delgado, C., and C. Miller. 1984. "Changing food patterns in West Africa:
    implications for policy research." Compte-Rendu du Premier Atelier
    Interne du Projet Conjoint sur la Substitution des Céréales Importées pour
    les Céréales Traditionnelles en Afrique de l'Ouest. Washington, D.C.:
    IFPRI, pp. 1–20.

de Meel, H. 1978. *La Politique Céréaliére au Mali.* Rome: FAO.

de Wilde, J. C. 1967. *Experiences with Agricultural Development in Tropical Africa.* Baltimore: The Johns Hopkins University Press.

Dioné, J. 1989. "Informing food security policy in Mali: interactions between technology, institutions and market reforms." Unpublished Ph.D. dissertation, Michigan State University.

Dioné, J., and N. N. Dembélé. 1987. "Le Programme de Restructuration du Marché Céréalier au Mali (PRMC): Une analyse de ses objectifs, son fonctionnement et ses performances." Working paper no. 87–01. Bamako: MSU-CESA Food Security Project.

Dioné, J., and J. M. Staatz. 1988. "Market liberalization and food security in Mali." In *Southern Africa: Food Security Policy Options*, edited by M. Rukuni and Bernsten, R. H. Bernsten. Proceedings of the Third Annual Conference on Food Security Research in Southern Africa, 1–5 November 1987. Harare: UZ/MSU Food Security Research Project, pp. 143–70.

Eicher, C. K. 1982. "Facing up to Africa's food crisis." *Foreign Affairs* 61 (1): 154–74.

———. 1988. "Food security battles in sub-Saharan Africa." Plenary address (revised version) presented at the VII World Congress for Rural Sociology 26 June–12 July 1988, Bologna, Italy.

FAO (Food and Agriculture Organization). 1973–87. *FAO Trade Yearbook.* Vols. 27–41, Rome.

Humphreys, C. P. F. 1986. "Cereals policy reform in Mali." Draft report. Washington, D.C.: World Bank.

Jones, W. I. 1976. *Planning and Economic Policy: Socialist Mali and her Neighbors.* Washington, D.C.: Three Continents Press.

Kelly, Valerie, and Anne Chohin-Kuper. 1998. "Horticultural subsectors." *Food Security and Agricultural Subsectors in West Africa: Future prospects and key issues four years after the devaluation of the CFA franc.* Policy brief. Bamako: Institut du Sahel.

Mariko, Dramane, Anne Chohin-Kuper, Valerie Kelly, and Diane Aissata Zouboye. 1998. "L'évolution de la filière riz à l'Office du Niger depuis la dévaluation du CFAF." Bamako: Institut d'Economie Rurale, Programme Economie des Filières and INSAH/PRISAS.

Mehta, M. 1989. "An analysis of the structure of the wholesale cereals market in Mali." Unpublished master's thesis, Michigan State University.

MRDE (Ministère de Développement Rural et de l'Eau, République du Mali). 1998. *Receuil des Statistiques de Secteur Rural Malien.* Bamako.

OSCE (Office Statistique des Communautés Europénnes). 1988. *Statistiques de Base: Agriculture—Elevage.* Bamako: OSCE.

Reardon, Thomas, Bocar Diagana, Francis Akindes, Kimseyinga Savadogo, John Staatz, and Youssouf Camara. 1998. "Consumption." *Food Security and Agricultural Subsectors in West Africa: Future prospects and key issues four years after the devaluation of the CFA franc.* Policy brief. Bamako: Institut du Sahel.

République du Mali. 1987. "Evolution de la politique céréaliére." Paper prepared for the Séminaire National sur la Politique Céréali au Mali, 15–18 June 1987. Bamako: Ministère de Tutelle des Sociétés et Entreprises d'Etat.

Rogers, B. L., and M. L. Lowdermilk. 1988. "Food prices and food consumption in urban Mali." Final report of the Tufts/DNSI/USAID Food Price Project. Medford: Tufts University.

SATE. 1982. *Etude des Opérations de Développement Rural (ODR) et des Organismes Similaires: Premier Phase - Analyse et Bilan.* Paris: SATE.

Sen, A. 1981. *Poverty and Famines: An Essay On Entitlement and Deprivation.* Oxford: Clarendon Press.

———. 1988. "Food entitlements and economic chains." In *Science, Ethics, and Food*, edited by B. W. J. LeMay. Papers and Proceedings of a Colloquium organized by the Smithsonian Institution. Washington, D.C.: Smithsonian Institution Press, pp. 58–70.

Staatz, J. M., J. Dioné, and N. N. Dembélé. 1989. "Cereals market liberalization in Mali." *World Development* 17 (5): 703–18.

Steffen, P. N. 1995. "The roles and limits of the grain market in assuring household food security in northeastern Mali: implications for public policy." Unpublished Ph.D. dissertation, Michigan State University.

Steffen, P. N., N. N. Dembélé, and J. Staatz. 1988. "Une critique des rôles alternatifs pour l'OPAM sur le Marché Céréalier à travers des concepts de biens publics." Working paper no. 88–02. Bamako: CESA-MSU Food Security Project.

Stryker, J. D., J. J. Dethier, L. Peprah, and D. Breen. 1987. *Incentive Systems and Economic Policy Reform in Mali.* Washington, DC: AIRD.

Tefft, James, John Staatz, Josué Dioné, and Valerie Kelly. 1998. "Cotton subsector." *Food Security and Agricultural Subsectors in West Africa: Future prospects and key issues four years after the devaluation of the CFA franc.* Policy brief. Bamako: Institut du Sahel.

Timmer, C. Peter, Walter P. Falcon, and Scott R. Pearson. 1983. *Food Policy Analysis.* Baltimore: The Johns Hopkins University Press.

Weber, M. T., J. M. Staatz, J. H. Holtzman, E. W. Crawford, and R. Bernsten. 1988. "Informing food security decisions in Africa: empirical analysis and policy dialogue." *American Journal of Agricultural Economics* 70 (5): 1044–51.

World Bank. 1989. *World Development Report 1988.* New York: Oxford University Press.

Yade, Mbaye, Bakary Kanté, and John Staatz. 1998. "Beef sector." *Food Security and Agricultural Subsectors in West Africa: Future prospects and key issues four years after the devaluation of the CFA franc.* Policy brief. Bamako: Institut du Sahel.

The Response of Cereals Traders to Agricultural Market Reform in Mali

NIAMA NANGO DEMBÉLÉ AND JOHN M. STAATZ

Introduction

Since 1981, the government of Mali has undertaken a broad range of reforms aimed at fostering a much greater role for the private sector and market processes. These reforms have involved the sale of state enterprises, permitting private-sector (including independent farmer and trader organizations) competition and removal of domestic and international barriers to trade. These changes, combined with the liberty of association and expression that came with Mali's democratization starting in 1991, are having profound effects on the Malian economy and society.

Because of the importance of the cereals subsector in the Malian economy, the lead element of economic reform since 1981 program has been the liberalization of cereal marketing under the multidonor-financed cereals market restructuring program, known by its French acronym, PRMC (*Programme de Restructuration du Marché Céréalier*).

The effect of any policy reform depends on how economic actors react to it. For PRMC, success hinged upon whether private traders were willing to fill the vacuum created by the retreat of the public sector from direct involvement in cereals marketing. This willingness, in turn, depended on how the reforms affected the profitability and riskiness of investing in the cereals trade. This chapter discusses how Malian traders of coarse grains (millet, maize, and sorghum) have reacted to the cereals market reforms since 1981.[1]

145

A Brief History of the PRMC

Grain production in Mali

Approximately 70 percent of the total calories in the Malian diet come from cereals. Millet, maize, and sorghum (hereafter referred to as coarse grains) are the major rainfed staples, and, up until the mid-1980s, accounted for about 85 percent of the cereal calories, with rice providing most of the remaining 15 percent. Most rural residents produce at least some of their own cereals supplies, with the result that only about 15–20 percent of total grain production enters the market. In urban areas, consumers devote on average between 18 percent and 31 percent of their total expenditures to cereals (depending on the city); hence, cereal prices strongly influence urban real incomes.[2] Rice is much more important in the cities than in rural areas, accounting for more than half the cereals calories consumed in urban areas.

Grain production in Mali has historically been highly variable due to fluctuating rainfall. This variability, combined with a low percentage of total production entering the market, makes market prices and quantities highly volatile. For example, between 1986 and 1988, millet and sorghum prices varied by a factor of 1:4 from year to year.[3] Such instability makes cereal marketing risky, whether carried out by the public or private sector.

In recent years, millet and sorghum production has increased at roughly 2.7 percent per year, approximately the rate of population growth. Most of this growth has resulted from expansion of area cultivated, not an increase in yields. In contrast, technological progress in maize and rice production, combined with the impact of market reforms, have resulted in rapid expansion of the production of those two cereals (table 1). Thus, millet and sorghum, while still the most widely consumed cereals in Mali, represent a smaller share of total national production and consumption than when the market reforms began in 1981.

Genesis of the reforms

In 1964 the Malian government created an official grain marketing agency, the *Office Malien des Produits Agricoles* (OPAM), and granted OPAM a legal monopoly on the grain trade. Through OPAM, the government fixed official producer and consumer prices for cereals in order to (1) increase rural incomes, (2) provide cheap cereals to urban areas, and (3) extract a surplus from agriculture to finance state investment in other sectors.

Table 1. **Share of various cereals in Mali's total grain production**

Cereal	Annual Rate of Growth 1980-97 (%)	Share of Total Production in 1980 (%)	Share of Total Production in 1997 (%)
Millet & Sorghum	2.7	80	56
Maize	12.5	6	16
Rice	9.0	14	27
Total	4.7	100	100

Source: Egg 1999, p. 17.

Although the private trade was repressed, OPAM handled only between 20 and 40 percent of total grain marketed in the country.[4] Since only about 15 percent of total production was marketed, merely 3–6 percent of total production moved through OPAM at official prices.[5] The repression of the private trade, while not enough to eliminate it, undoubtedly increased transaction costs. In general, the government was more tolerant of the private trade during good production years, when supplies were abundant, than during years of shortage.

Until the mid-1960s, Mali was a net exporter of cereals. During the drought years of the late 1960s and early 1970s, however, Mali had to import large amounts of grain on both commercial and concessional terms. OPAM was obliged to sell the commercial imports at low official consumer prices, which led to an increasing budget deficit. In an effort to stimulate cereal production after the drought, the government raised official producer prices without a proportional increase in consumer prices. As a result, OPAM was forced to absorb the implicit consumer subsidies, and its cumulative budget deficit reached CFAF 20 billion (US$80 million) by 1976–77, equivalent to three times its annual grain sales.[6]

Donor pressure for cereal market reform mounted during the late 1970s as a result of OPAM's accumulating deficits (which the donors were increasingly reluctant to finance), concerns about OPAM mismanagement, and the perception that OPAM's official monopoly and the system of official prices acted as major disincentives to domestic grain production. In March 1981, the government of Mali agreed to a policy reform program that aimed at increasing producer and consumer prices, liberalizing grain trade, and improving OPAM's operating efficiency.

The reforms embodied in the PRMC were based on the idea of using food aid to finance market liberalization. In exchange for a series of proposed reforms, ten major international agencies and donors pledged multiyear shipments of program food aid. The food aid was sold, with the proceeds going into a common fund used to finance specific market restructuring actions agreed to by the donors and the Malian government.[7]

Long-term benefits were expected both at the trader and producer levels. For traders, potential benefits included a reduction in transaction costs, as private merchants no longer would be forced to operate clandestinely. This, in turn, was expected to lead to an increase in the scale and degree of specialization in trader's operations, thereby reducing marketing costs.[8] In principle, reducing the risk of trading cereals would stimulate entry into cereal marketing, thereby increasing farm level demand and hence farmers' incentives to produce cereals for the market. Moreover, eliminating restrictions on interregional grain shipments would allow equilibration of supply and demand over space, thereby helping eliminate localized gluts and shortages. This in turn would contribute to a more stable market, thereby encouraging greater private investment in grain production and marketing.[9]

Relation of the PRMC to Mali's structural adjustment program

The PRMC was related to, but not officially part of, a broader structural adjustment program (SAP) in Mali supported by the World Bank and the IMF. The SAP aimed first to re-establish macroeconomic balance by cutting government expenditures and improving revenue collection, as well as improving the efficiency of government services. These changes implied layoffs of government workers, changes in tax codes and collection policies, and closing of state enterprises, all of which affected the cereals trade.

Although the reform of cereals marketing played a key role in the broader process of economic reform undertaken as part of the structural adjustment process, the philosophy of the PRMC was not identical to that of the Bretton Woods institutions supporting the SAP.[10] The World Bank and the IMF focused mainly on getting the state out of direct buying and selling activities in the economy and refocusing on the production of facilitating services (effective law enforcement and other public goods), both to help reduce the government deficit and to open the economy to market forces. The PRMC, rather than just calling on the state to withdraw from the cereals market, attempted to "accompany" the state as it changed its role, through supporting government actions to reform the management of the grain board; to establish and manage a national emergency grain stock; to provide market information to consumers, farmers, and others in the private and public sectors; and to develop tools, such as the food crisis early warning system (*Système d'Alerte Précoce*), to prevent and mitigate disasters. Occasionally, this more supportive view of government action put the PRMC in disagreement with the Bank and the IMF regarding levels and types of government expenditures that should be accepted.

Phases of the reforms

Since 1981, the PRMC has gone through five phases (table 2). The objectives for each phase were mutually agreed to by the Malian government and the donor agencies supporting the reforms. These objectives fell into three main categories:[11]

- *Sectoral adjustment measures* These measures involved changing the roles of the state in cereals production and marketing, largely through the restructuring of OPAM and the *Office du Niger* (the largest government-supported rice production and marketing operation). The PRMC helped negotiate changes in their mandates (including elimination of their statutory monopolies in grain trade), provided assistance to improve their management, financed severance pay to the large number of employees who were laid off, and helped cover the organization's operating deficits as long as they met agreed-upon benchmarks for reform.
- *Market strengthening* This would be accomplished through assistance to the private sector as it took on greater responsibilities in the newly reformed markets. The PRMC financed supporting services to the private sector, such as the establishment of a public cereals market information system (SIM— *Système d'Information du Marché*), subsidized marketing credit to private traders and village associations, tested improved techniques for cereals cleaning and processing, and, for a brief time in the late 1980s, provided export subsidies.
- *Food crisis prevention and mitigation* The overall goal of the PRMC was, of course, to improve food security of the country by improving incentives to produce and market cereals efficiently. But in addition to this broad goal, the PRMC also supported activities aimed at dealing with short-term food crises. These activities included the financing of the national security stock, the food crisis early warning system, and the transport of food aid to areas requiring emergency food distribution.

Table 2. **Allocation of the PRMC budget by major category of activities (in millions of CFA francs)**

Objective	Phase I (1981–87)	Phase II (1988–90)	Phase III (1991–93)	Phase IV (1994–96)	Phase V (1997–99)
Sectoral Adjustment	11,051 (72%)	1,316 (11%)	2,311 (17%)	20 (0.4%)	525 (8%)
Strengthening the Market	1,102 (7%)	5,939 (51%)	5,958 (45%)	1,109 (25%)	658 (11%)
Food Crisis Prevention & Mitigation	1,526 (10%)	2,272 (19%)	4,426 (33%)	2,925 (65%)	4,928 (80%)
Other[a]	1,636 (11%)	2,185 (19%)	527 (4%)	448 (10%)	32 (0.5%)
Total	15,267 (100%)	11,721 (100%)	13,222 (100%)	4,502 (100%)	6,143 (100%)

Source: Egg (1999)

[a]Includes mainly operating costs of the PRMC.

Notably absent from the PRMC's activities were any actions aimed directly at improving farm-level food production. The PRMC defined its domain of action "from the farmer's field to the cooking pot," leaving issues of increasing farm-level productivity to others.

As shown in table 2, the share of the PRMC's financial resources devoted to these three objectives varied markedly in the different phases of the program. During the first seven years of the program (PRMC I), over 70 percent of the resources were devoted to sectoral adjustment activities, such as the improvement of OPAM's management. During this period, OPAM still tried to defend an official floor price for cereals, and the state required traders to have licenses to import or export coarse grains.[12]

Although the high proportion of PRMC resources going to sector adjustment activities led some observers to note the irony of a "market reform" program that devoted the bulk of its assistance to the state marketing board,[13] some of this assistance built the political support needed to allow the private sector to play a greater role in the system. (For example, some of the laid-off employees used their severance pay to finance their entry into private business and thus became supporters of a more liberalized market.)

The subsequent six years of the program (PRMC II and III, 1988–93) devoted roughly half of its budget to activities aimed at strengthening the role of the private sector through the provision of supporting services, such as credit and market information. Particularly important during this period was the establishment of the SIM, established in 1989, which for the first time provided consumers, farmers, and traders with an independent source of information on market prices and conditions. This information, broadcast weekly on the radio and television in French and local languages and published in newspapers, fundamentally changed the bargaining power between farmers and traders and contributed to greater market integration (see below).

As the liberalization consolidated its gains, attention shifted to helping those believed to have been bypassed by the reforms (poor consumers) or those at risk from the continuing instability in the market. During PRMC IV and V (1994–99), the majority of the budget has gone to food crisis and mitigation activities. Malian officials have become much more concerned about the vulnerability of the poor to such crises in recent years because of the large number of refugees returning to the Northeast following the peace settlement and because grain prices rose sharply following the 50 percent devaluation of the CFA franc in January 1994. Assuring secure and affordable food to returning refugees and former combatants in the Northeast is clearly important to consolidating the peace. The challenge was compounded by the effects of the devaluation. The now-cheaper CFA franc made Malian cereals much more competitive in neighboring countries, spurring exports, and increased the price of imported rice. As a result, nominal prices for rose sharply, threatening to price the poor out of the market. Indeed, one of the greatest challenges facing the Malian government in the future will be how to assure improved food access for the poor without reversing many of the gains achieved through the market reforms.

Traders' Response to the Reforms

Until 1981, OPAM enjoyed an official monopoly for all cereals transactions. OPAM agents and the local administration in rural areas, later expanded to include private merchants under contract, undertook direct purchases from farmers for OPAM. Indirect purchases were performed by cooperatives and *Opérations de Développement Rural* (ODRs). OPAM also pre-financed crop purchases from the production ODRs for resale to OPAM, paying for everything according to the annual *barème* or official price schedule. While private traders in the coarse grain trade were usually tolerated, they either worked openly as grain assemblers for OPAM (under contract) or clandestinely through networks of personal relationships with other traders and with agents of the state.

The PRMC reforms, by legalizing the private grain trade, attracted many more traders into the coarse grains market and increased competition. In addition, traders expanded their investments in the grain marketing business, particularly in storage and transport capacity. Many traders also changed their methods of operation, relying more on the open market than having to coordinate their economic activities solely through personal networks. As a result of these changes and of the improved market information and removal of restrictions on grain movements, Malian cereals markets became more integrated, both among themselves and with markets in neighboring countries.

In looking at the dynamics of trader response to the reforms, it is important to recognize that there were two distinct groups of traders involved in the coarse grains trade—"core" and "periphery" traders.[14]

The core comprises small-scale traders who lack sophisticated managerial skills. These traders also typically lack access to formal credit and to the court system to enforce contracts. The core deals largely with the domestic market and thereby plays a role in coordinating production and domestic consumption. Traditionally, these are the small-scale traders who had operated during the days of the OPAM monopoly to supply local towns with grain; they were not heavily involved in contracting with OPAM or with international trade.

The periphery comprises large-scale and skilled traders, many based in Bamako, who have access to formal credit market and to the court system to enforce contracts. They are often also involved in the import-export business and the rice trade. The periphery connects the domestic market to the international markets. It is responsible for most of the large-scale cereals exports and imports. Prior to the liberalization, many of these traders worked hand-in-glove with state enterprises.

Expanded entry into cereals marketing

As OPAM gradually withdrew from cereals marketing in the early and mid-1980s, wholesale coarse grain traders already in the market expanded operations and others entered the trade. The growth in the wholesale trade was faster for coarse grains than for rice.[15] The expansion in the number of traders also occurred more rapidly in Bamako (the main urban consumption market) than in secondary cities, such as Koutiala (in the main surplus producing zone) and Mopti.[16] For example, in 1985–86, 51 percent of Bamako coarse-grain wholesalers entered the market after liberalization, and many of these specialized in the grain trade. (Prior to the reforms, many grain traders diversified their operations to include other goods to reduce the risks involved in this illegal trade.) In contrast, only about a third of the wholesalers in Koutiala, Sikasso, and Mopti had entered the markets after the reforms.[17] Subsequent research in 1988–89 documented an expansion of market entry into the coarse grains trade in these other cities later in the decade and increased specialization among in the grain trade compared to the mid-1980s.[18]

Many of the initial entrants into the grain trade appeared to be smaller-scale traders in the core. These were the actors for which the former barriers to entry had been most daunting. Among the periphery, there was some restructuring of the trade, particularly as medium-sized urban firms formed joint ventures in an effort to improve their access to bank and PRMC credit.[19] A more recent phenomenon has been the entry of younger, recent graduates of secondary and post-secondary schools into the grain trade, particularly in the rice trade, but also coarse grains. These new entrants, operating on a smaller scale but with many of the stronger managerial skills of the periphery traders, may eventually serve as a bridge between the two groups.

As a result of the increased number of actors, the wider availability of market information, increased specialization, and removal of movement restrictions, the coarse grains trade became more competitive. Between 1986 and 1992, for example, marketing margins for millet and sorghum between Bamako and its two major supplying areas (Zangasso and Sirakorala) fell by 20 percent.[20] Most evidence suggests that the reduction in marketing margins was passed back to farmers in the form of higher prices.[21]

Expanded investment in the cereals trade

A major objective of the reforms was to increase the private sector's investment in the grain trade in order to improve efficiency and, it was hoped, increase market stability by inducing the private sector to hold greater stocks of grain. While it was anticipated that large traders would lead the way in making these investments, it was actually the smaller traders (the "core") who responded most dramatically. The lower margins in the grain trade, due to the greater competition, and the increased opportunities in other areas of the more liberalized economy, probably induced the larger traders in the periphery to invest elsewhere.[22]

Overall, coarse grains merchants increased their investments in transport and infrastructure dramatically in response to the reforms (figure 1). Dembélé

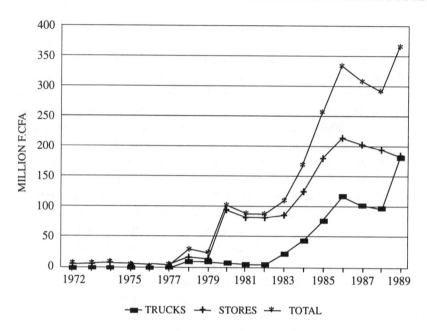

Figure 1. **Evolution of real net investment of a sample of 55 traders Mali (1972–89).**

found that for a sample of eighteen coarse-grain wholesalers from Bamako, Koutiala, and Mopti, net real investment in trucks and storage facilities grew at an annual rate of 19 percent between 1981 and 1989, with the increase in net investment split equally among the two (approximately 180 million CFA francs in each).[23] However, because there had been much less investment in trucks than in storage facilities by traders prior to the reforms, the annual rate of increase in trucking investment was much larger (53 percent) than for storage capacity (11 percent).

Average total storage capacity per trader (both rented and owned) rose from 61 tons to 761 tons between 1981 and 1989 for traders operating in Bamako, Koutiala, and Mopti, with the rate of growth of owned storage facilities outpacing the growth in use of rented facilities.[24] The increase in owned storage capacity may reflect a growing confidence of traders in the permanence of the market reforms and an improvement in incentives brought about by the overall liberalization of economic activities. Previous studies[25] found that urban traders tend to own more storage capacity than wholesale assemblers from producing zones and that urban cereals trade appears more concentrated than wholesale assembly. Thus, some of the increased profits that may have resulted from the concentration of the urban cereals trade appear to have been reinvested in marketing facilities.[26]

Two characteristics of the increased investment are particularly striking. First, in areas where feeder roads were good, wholesalers tended to substitute investment in trucking for investment in warehouse space. In other words, they found it more profitable and less risky to continue to have the bulk of the grain held in storage at the farm level and then draw it off the farm as needed through purchases, rather than to buy and hold the grain. Farmers probably preferred this approach as well, as they typically want to hold a substantial reserve in case the next year's rains are poor. In 1988, 74 percent of wholesalers and semi-wholesalers operating in major southern markets stored cereal for a week and a half or less. Only 16 percent of wholesalers and 13 percent of semi-wholesalers in 1988 stored cereal for more than three months.[27] The preference of traders for rapid turnover stock holding reflects not only the need to reduce the risk of storage activities that result from unexpected adverse price changes, but also the desire to reduce the cost of financing. A rapid turnover of cereals stocks constitutes an effective strategy to reduce the high interest rate costs of informal loans for traders with no access to formal credit markets. In contrast, in areas of poorer roads and limited physical access, particularly in the Northeast, traders have invested much more in storage capacity and hold grain for much longer periods, frequently up to three months.[28]

Second, the bulk of the new investment in storage and trucking facilities came from the smaller, more traditional traders (the "core"). Whereas traders in the periphery accounted for 93 percent of the net investment in storage before the reforms, that share had fallen to 55 percent by 1989. Similarly, traders who relied on relational contracting—informal or formal long-term agreements with trading partners, either within the country or outside— accounted for the bulk of net investment in storage and transport prior to the reforms, but their share fell dramatically after the reforms, as traders who relied on the spot market for sales increased their investments substantially.[29]

The picture that emerges is that prior to the reforms, the bulk of the investments were held by larger, more "modern" traders (the periphery) who were well linked into the official marketing system and the import-export business. Meanwhile, the more traditional wholesalers, who had a network of rural assembly agents to buy cereals from farmers and distribute them within the country, were forced to operate in a more clandestine manner that discouraged investments in visible assets such as warehouses and trucks. Trade was conducted in the shadows, with little reliance on the open spot market, at least for wholesale transactions. The reforms, by allowing these traders to operate more openly, stimulated their investments in storage and trucking, which likely allowed them to gain economies. The reforms also allowed greater use of the open spot market to coordinate economic activity. This, in turn, encouraged new entrants into the trade, as one now did not have to invest as much in developing a series of highly personalized relationships with other traders to succeed in the business. All of these changes lowered marketing costs, contributing to the reduced marketing margins discussed above.[30]

Impact on market integration

As a result of the freedom of traders to operate openly on the market, the improved market information, improved market infrastructure, and traders' investments in transport and storage, the integration of coarse grains markets with each other increased dramatically. Prices in one market were quickly transmitted to others, and traders moved cereals to areas where prices were most attractive. The average correlation of retail millet prices across major urban markets in Mali (a measure of market integration) increased from .70 in the mid-1980s to .97 during the 1990s.[31]

Statistical analysis also suggests that Malian markets, both for coarse grains and rice, became more integrated regionally and internationally, particularly following the CFA franc devaluation.[32] In addition, there is plenty of anecdotal evidence that the removal of import and export restrictions, both by Mali and its neighbors, has led to much greater trade flows and market integration. Regional trade flows of cereals (which are poorly captured in official statistics) appear to have increased sharply since the CFA franc devaluation of 1994, which made Malian grains much more competitive in the region compared with imports from throughout the CFA franc zone.[33] This increased regional market integration has had both positive and negative effects:

- It has resulted in more effective transmission of production incentives (in the form of prices) back to farmers and opened profitable new market opportunities for Malian traders and surplus coarse grain producers;
- It has led to greater physical availability of grain in food-deficit areas;
- It has put Malian consumers more clearly in competition with consumers in neighboring countries (particularly Côte d'Ivoire and Senegal) who have higher purchasing power, raising the risk that some Malian consumers may be priced out of the market;

- It has meant that market instability in neighboring countries such as Niger, where production is more unstable than in Mali, now spills over more into the Malian market.

Impact on market prices and availability

Nominal prices for coarse grains increased during the early years of the reform (1981–85), which were poor rainfall years (figure 2). They subsequently dropped in 1986 and fluctuated substantially from year-to-year between 1986 and 1993 but showed no distinct trend. Following the 1994 devaluation, nominal producer prices for coarse grains roughly doubled, as did consumer prices in Bamako. (If one takes a slightly longer-term perspective, nominal retail millet in Bamako increased only by approximately 25 percent between the years of 1990–93 and 1994–97; the increase immediately after the devaluation was more dramatic because prices had been exceptionally low in 1993.) In addition, prices became significantly more variable following the 1994 devaluation.[34] Indeed, one of the most striking features of coarse grain prices throughout the past eighteen years has been their high degree of instability. For example, between 1990 and 1996, average monthly retail millet prices in Bamako ranged between 70 CFAF/kg and 250 CFAF/kg.[35] Producer prices showed a similar pattern, and they were more volatile in percentage terms than were retail prices.

When prices are expressed in real terms (that is, when nominal prices are deflated by the GDP deflator), a different pattern emerges. Real retail prices of coarse grains in Bamako fell by approximately 20 percent during the period 1981–82 and 1997–98, although there were still substantial year-to-year fluctuations. Real producer prices showed a slight downward trend (but with substantial inter-annual variation) from 1981 until the CFA franc devaluation in January 1994; thereafter, real producer prices show an upward trend.[36] The rise in real producer prices since 1994 while consumer prices were still falling implies that marketing margins were falling, with the benefits being shared by both consumers and producers.

Even though real consumer prices of coarse grains were falling, they may not have seemed lower to many urban consumers, particularly in the post-devaluation period, because these consumers' incomes were falling even faster. The broader structural adjustment programs and the devaluation strongly turned the urban-rural terms of trade in favor of the countryside, reversing years of urban bias in Malian agricultural pricing policies. As the

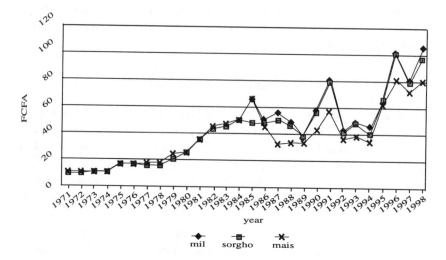

Figure 2. Nominal retail prices for millet, sorghum, and maize in Mali, 1971–98.

price of internationally traded goods, such as cereals, increased following the devaluation, the purchasing power of urban salaries eroded. Tefft et al. estimated that the real income of a typical Malian civil servant fell by 19 percent between 1994 and September 1997.[37] Thus, many urban residents associate the PRMC with higher, not lower, real prices.

The physical availability of cereals in most markets improved with the reforms, due to greater competition, improved flows between deficit and surplus areas, and improved consumer information about prices. This improved availability was especially important for rural grain-deficit households. During interviews carried out in 1987–88, members of such households in southern Mali (the OHV and CMDT zones) cited improved, less costly access to cereals in the markets as the major benefit to them of the reforms.[38]

Lessons Learned and Remaining Challenges

Several conclusions emerge from this review of the response of Malian coarse grain merchants to the market reforms undertaken by the PRMC.

Lessons

1. Effective market reform needs to be seen as an ongoing process, not a one-time event. The PRMC has gone on now for nearly two decades, and the

willingness of the Malians and donors to continue to work on the process of adjusting market policies and support programs has been an important key to the program's success. In contrast to reforms undertaken in some other countries, the PRMC did not focus on just the first-stage issues of sectoral adjustment ("getting the state out of the market"). It went on to tackle the much more challenging tasks of building an effective market system by redefining the rules of the game and providing supporting services to the private sector (such as improved market information). It also addressed the "second-generation" problems of the needs of those left behind by the reforms.

This willingness to see reform as an ongoing process has fostered greater collaboration between the donors and the Malian government, on the one hand, and between the government and the private sector on the other. The approach has also encouraged learning-by-doing, as the PRMC, other donors, and the Malian government have largely avoided doctrinaire approaches, preferring to invest in research to learn more about market processes, and to strengthen local analytic capacity to monitor and analyze agricultural markets, particularly through the SIM.

2. Market reforms were effective in increasing competition, lowering costs, and improving physical access to coarse grains by consumers. The removal of restrictions on who could legally trade grain led to an influx of new entrants and a greater reliance on the open market for coordinating economic activity. The increased competition, combined with better market information provided through PRMC-supported activities, led to lower marketing margins, which benefited both consumers and producers. In addition, food-deficit households in rural areas reported that it was now easier to find grain to buy when they needed it, as they no longer had to get authorizations to buy from OPAM and could buy in whatever quantities they needed.

3. Once convinced of the permanence of the reforms, coarse-grain traders invested substantially in market infrastructure. The greatest investments were in trucks and warehouses, with the type of investment depending critically on the state of the roads in the area where the trader operated. In areas of good roads, most coarse-grain storage continues to take place at the farm. In these areas, particularly in the production zones, traders focused more on truck ownership than investment in warehouses. In areas of poor infrastructure, such as the northeast, the lack of reliable transport requires traders to hold stocks for much longer periods, and hence they put more of their investments into expanded warehouse facilities.

The need of northern traders to hold stocks for longer periods puts them at greater risk of losses due to food-aid distributions. These findings imply that food-aid distribution in infrastructure-poor areas of the country should be well managed to avoid disrupting normal commercial storage activity.

4. Market reforms did not resolve all the problems of cereals marketing and food security in Mali. The market reforms were effective in reducing the costs of grain distribution, particularly in the south, where transport infrastructure was relatively good. They also substantially reduced the unsustainable government budget deficits incurred by the old official marketing system. Yet substantial problems remain in assuring reliable access of consumers to coarse grains in Mali. Most of these problems are due to *structural problems* in coarse grain production and transportation in Mali. These are problems that a program like the PRMC, which limits its actions just to marketing issues, is unlikely to resolve.

Challenges

1. Millet and sorghum production, which is highly dependent on rainfall, remains unstable. Production of these crops is highly variable, and growth in their production has resulted exclusively from area expansion, not yield increases. Until more improved, shorter-cycle varieties become available and technologies to conserve water and stabilize yields are more widely adopted, the erratic nature of sorghum and millet production is likely to continue. The contrast between the response of the rice subsector and the coarse grains subsector to the PRMC illustrates that policy reform by itself is unlikely to lead to a robust supply response.[39] Policy reform needs to be coupled with technological and institutional improvements in production and access to inputs.

2. Poor transport infrastructure in many areas of the country continues to limit access and contribute to local market instability. Although the PRMC reforms were very effective in strengthening the integration of coarse grain markets between major cities and within the rural areas of the south that benefited from a good network of feeder roads, the integration remained much weaker in more remote areas, particularly in the northeast.[40] Poor roads raise traders' costs and discourage trade, whether it is legal or not. A better use of food aid in these areas, as food for work devoted to the building of roads, could help ameliorate this situation.

3. Poverty continues to limit access to cereals in Mali. While the PRMC reforms were effective in lowering marketing costs (and thus helping hold

down cost of basic staples to consumers), there remain a large number of poor consumers in Mali who lack the purchasing power to assure their access to an adequate diet. The problem has become more acute as the Malian cereals markets have become better integrated with markets in Côte d'Ivoire and Senegal, countries with higher purchasing power whose consumers can outbid the Malian poor for available supplies. A market, no matter how efficient, only responds to those with *effective demand*, that is, needs backed up with purchasing power. Assuring poor people's access to adequate cereals will require a much broader effort to reduce poverty and develop targeted social safety nets in Mali. Promoting well-functioning markets for basic staples needs to be an important part of that strategy, but it cannot do the job by itself.

4. The threat of major drought remains. The PRMC has yet to be tested by a major drought. Although the early years of the reforms (1981–85) were very low-rainfall years, the reforms were in their nascent stages, OPAM was very active in the market, and the market was far from liberalized. Now, however, Malians rely almost entirely on the market for their grain supplies. It remains an open question whether, when faced with a major food crisis, the political support to maintain the market reforms would remain. This will depend in part on the rules that evolve to help the market deal with such a crisis. The temptation to restrict grain shipments, either to neighboring countries or across boundaries of the newly created rural communes, in order to maintain local supplies, could be very great. It is appropriate that the most recent phases of PRMC have focused much of their resources on crisis prevention and mitigation, for it is likely that a major drought will be the ultimate test of how committed Malians are to the reforms carried out since 1981 under the PRMC.

Notes

1. The focus in this chapter is on the coarse grains trade because these cereals historically have comprised the majority of the cereals consumed by Malians and because the response of the rice sector to the reforms is discussed by Diarra and Staatz and by Dimithè elsewhere in this book. Dioné (also in this volume) discusses coarse-grain farmers' responses to the reforms, so that topic is only discussed briefly in this chapter. The chapter draws heavily on a large body of research carried out by Malian, North American, and European researchers since 1985 and on a recent evaluation of the PRMC in which the authors participated (Dembélé, Traoré, and Staatz 1999; Shields, Staatz, and Dembélé 1999; Egg 1999).

2. Rogers and Lowdermilk 1988.

3. Staatz, Dioné, and Dembélé 1989.

4. Humphreys 1986, 5.

5. OPAM's share of rice marketing was much higher than its share of coarse grains as rice destined for the market was produced largely in government-run irrigation schemes, such as the *Office du Niger* (ON).

6. Humphreys 1986, 7.

7. The international agencies and donors included the World Food Programme (the project secretariat), Belgium, Canada, the European Community, France, Great Britain, the Netherlands, the United States, West Germany, and Austria. Over the period 1981–98, as Mali's food production has increased, many of the donors have replaced their food aid with cash contributions to the PRMC.

8. Berg 1978, 165–69; Wilcock, Roth, and Haykin 1987.

9. Staatz, Dioné, and Dembélé 1989.

10. Egg 1999.

11. Ibid.

12. The restrictions on the rice trade were removed even more slowly than those on the coarse grains, as the state tried to protect the value of its investments in the *Office du Niger* by continuing to protect the domestic rice industry. It was only in 1987 that farmers in the ON were allowed to sell their paddy to anyone other than the *Office*.

13. For example, Humphreys 1986 and Dioné (in this volume).

14. Dembélé 1994.

15. The rice market was dominated by four large import-export firms, which had the sole import licenses and also held contracts with the *Office du Niger* for most of the domestically produced rice destined for the commercial market.

16. In the secondary towns, particularly in the main production zones, wholesalers needed to develop networks of assemblers to buy from farmers, and government officials may have been slower in implementing the reforms.

17. Mehta 1989, 40.

18. Dembélé 1994.

19. Mehta 1989.

20. Staatz and Dembélé 1992.

21. Egg 1999.

22. Because of the dispersed nature of farmers' marketed surplus and of consumer demand in Mali, cereals marketing requires labor-intensive marketing techniques at the rural assembly and urban retailing level. Low-skilled and small-scale traders from the core are ready to supply the necessary labor at low returns because of lack of alternative employment. Thus, labor supply within the core is likely to be less responsive to changes in marketing margins. In contrast, traders from the periphery have alternative uses for their skills and their capital. Thus, the supply of skills and capital within the periphery may be very responsive to changes in marketing margins.

23. Dembélé 1994.

24. Ibid.

25. Mehta 1989 and Steffen 1995.

26. Dembélé 1994.

27. Ibid.

28. Steffen 1995.

29. Dembélé 1994.

30. Ibid.

31. Dembélé, Traoré, and Staatz 1999. The figures refer to the mean of pairwise correlations of retail market prices between Bamako, Mopti, Sikasso, and Ségou, and between those cities and the other regional capitals. Correlations for retail sorghum and maize prices showed very similar trends. The correlation coefficients for the 1980s may be biased downwards slightly due to the weaker quality of price data that existed before the creation of the cereals market information system (SIM).

32. Yade et al. 1999; Barry, Diarra, and Diarra 1998.

33. Observatoire des Marchés Agricoles 1999; Egg 1999.

34. Dembélé, Traoré, and Staatz 1999.

35. Ibid.

36. Egg 1999.

37. Tefft, Staatz, and Dioné 1997.

38. D'Agostino 1988.

39. See Diarra, Staatz and Dembélé in this volume.

40. Steffen 1995.

Bibliography

Barry, Abdoul W., Salif B. Diarra, and Daouda Diarra. 1998. "Promouvoir les exportations de riz malien vers les pays de la sous-région." Rapport final. Equity and Growth through Economic Research (EAGER) Project. Cambridge MA: Associates for International Development.

Berg, Elliot. 1979. "Reforming grain marketing systems in west Africa: a case study of Mali." In *Proceedings, International Workshop on Constraints to Development of Semi-Arid Tropical Agriculture*, 19–23 February, pp. 147–72. Hyderabad, India: ICRISAT.

D'Agostino, Victoire. 1988. "Coarse grain production and transaction in Mali: farm household strategies and government policy." Master's thesis, Michigan State University.

Dembélé, Niama Nango. 1994. "Economic analysis of trader's response to cereals market reforms in Mali." Ph.D. dissertation, Michigan State University.

Dembélé, Niama Nango, Abdramane Traoré, and John Staatz. 1999. "L'impact des réformes sur les indicateurs de performance du marché céréalier: Analyse des données de prix du SIM." Contribution to the PRMC study, *Etude sur l'impact de la libéralisaton sur le fonctionnement des filières céréalières au Mali*, Bamako.

Diarra, Salifou B., John M. Staatz, and Niama N. Dembélé. 2000. Chapter in this book. ("The reform of rice milling and marketing in the *Office du Niger:* Catalysts for an agricultural success story in Mali." In *Democracy and Development in Mali,* edited by R.J. Bingen, D. Robinson, and J.M. Staatz. East Lansing: Michigan State University Press.)

Dimithè, Georges. 2000. Chapter in this book. ("Small-scale inland valley swamp rice production: A viable enterprise in the grain-cotton farming system of southern Mali." In *Democracy and Development in Mali,* edited by R.J. Bingen, D. Robinson, and J.M. Staatz. East Lansing: Michigan State University Press.)

Dioné, Josué. 2000. Chapter in this book. ("Food security policy reform in Mali and the Sahel." In *Democracy and Development in Mali,* edited by R.J. Bingen, D. Robinson, and J.M. Staatz. East Lansing: Michigan State University Press.).

Egg, Johny. 1999. *Etude de l'Impact de la Libéralisation sur le Fonctionnement des Filières Céréalières au Mali: Rapport de Synthèse.* Bamako: Programme de Restructuration du Marché Céréalier/Commité d'Orientation et de Coordination du Système de Sécurité Alimentaire.

Humphreys, Charles P. 1986. "Cereal policy reform in Mali." Draft report. Washington, D.C.: World Bank.

Mehta, Mona. 1989. "An analysis of the structure of the wholesale cereals market in Mali." Master's thesis, Michigan State University.

Observatoire du Marché Agricole (Ministère du Développement et de l'Eau and Assemblée Permanente des Chambres d'Agriculture du Mali). 1999. *Bulletin de Conjoncture* 97–01(April).

Rogers, Beatrice L., and Melanee Lowdermilk. 1988. "Food prices and food consumption in urban Mali." Report presented at USAID seminar on cereals policy in the Sahel. Washington, D.C.: Tufts University School of Nutrition.

Shields, Will, John Staatz, and Niama Nango Dembélé. 1999. "Review of MSU studies on cereals market reforms in Mali." Contribution to Module 4 of the PRMC study, *Etude sur l'impact de la libéralisaton sur le fonctionnement des filières céréalières au Mali*, Bamako. Also available in

French under the title: "Synthèse des études faites par MSU sur les réformes des marchés de céréales au Mali."

Staatz, John M., Josué Dioné, and N. Niama Dembélé. 1989. "Cereals market liberalization in Mali." *World Development* 17 (5): 703–18.

Staatz, John M. and N. Nango Dembélé. 1992. "Has AID's investment in market-Facilitating services had an impact?" East Lansing: Michigan State University Agricultural Economics staff paper, no 92–93 (December).

Steffen, Philip. 1995. "The roles and limits of the cereals market in assuring food security in northeastern Mali." Ph.D. dissertation, Michigan State University.

Tefft, James, John Staatz, and Josué Dioné. 1997. "Impact of the CFA devaluation on sustainable growth for poverty alleviation: preliminary results." Bamako: INSAH/PRISAS.

Wilcock, David C., Alan D. Roth, and Stephen M. Haykin. 1987. "Cereals marketing liberalization in Mali: an economic policy reform assessment." Report to USAID, Bureau for Africa, Office of Development Planning. Washington DC: Robert R. Nathan Associates and Development Alternatives, Inc.

Yade, Mbaye, Anne Chohin-Kuper, Valerie Kelly, John Staatz, and James Tefft. 1999. "The role of regional trade in agriculture transformation: the case of West Africa." East Lansing: Michigan State University Department of Agricultural Economics staff paper no. 99–28.

The Reform of Rice Milling and Marketing in the *Office du Niger:* Catalysts for an Agricultural Success Story in Mali

SALIFOU BAKARY DIARRA, JOHN M. STAATZ,
AND NIAMA NANGO DEMBÉLÉ

Introduction

One of the great successes of Malian economic policy during the 1980s and 1990s has been the transformation of the rice subsector. Domestic production shot up dramatically, growing at an annual rate of 9 percent between 1980 and 1997, largely due to yield increases in the irrigated area of the *Office du Niger*. As a result, national rice production more than tripled between 1985 and 1998, from 214,000 m.t. (paddy) to 688,000 m.t.[1] At the same time, new macroeconomic and sectoral policies transformed the marketing system from a tight oligopoly that extracted rents from both consumers and producers to a competitive system that reduced marketing costs and effectively transmitted production incentives to farmers. The Malian experience in transforming its rice subsector in the *Office du Niger* (*Office*) illustrates the importance of combining changes in macroeconomic policy, improved technologies, and the institutional arrangements governing production in order to transform a food system. The liberalization of rice milling within the *Office*, particularly the introduction of small-scale rice mills, played a crucial role in this transformation, and is the main focus of this chapter.

Cereals marketing liberalization continues to be a centerpiece of development programs throughout sub-Saharan Africa. This chapter seeks to contribute to our understanding of this approach by examining the Malian experience with rice marketing reforms, and especially the role played by small, private rice mills in this process.

Following a brief historical overview of the *Office du Niger*, this chapter focuses on how changes in the rules regarding who could compete in rice milling in the *Office* combined with technological change in rice production and new macroeconomic policies (particularly the CFA franc devaluation) transformed rice production and marketing in the *Office*. The chapter pays particular attention to the synergies between technological changes in rice production, the introduction of new marketing and macroeconomic policies, and the evolution of institutions governing rice production in the *Office* on the transformation of agriculture in this region of Mali.

Importance of Rice in the Malian Economy

Rice is a major staple in Mali, particularly in urban areas, accounting for 16.7 percent of total per capita cereal consumption and 6.4 percent of the total expenses of Malian households in 1988–89. National rice consumption per capita averaged about 34 kg/year in that year, which in absolute terms is third among the cereals after millet and sorghum. Yet in urban areas, rice was the most widely consumed staple, with urban per capita consumption (58.0 kg) more than twice that of rural areas (24.3 kg). Thus, rice plays a strategic role in the Malian economy. Supply shortages or rising prices produce inflationary pressure on wages and have a potential of creating political instability.[2]

Because of the strategic importance of rice, the French colonial regime and later the Malian government were deeply involved in rice production and marketing until very recently. Rice is produced both in government-established irrigation projects, predominantly along the Niger and Bani rivers, and in lowland-inland swamps (*bas-fonds*), mainly in southern Mali (see Dimithè, this volume). The oldest and largest of the government-established rice production areas is the *Office du Niger*, which has historically produced nearly half of Mali's domestic rice production and the majority of the domestic rice entering the market. (Much of the *bas-fonds* production is for home consumption.) In order to understand the importance of the *Office* in Mali's food strategy, a brief historical overview is needed.

Historical overview of the Office du Niger

The *Office du Niger* is located along the central delta of the Niger River. The Markala dam (approximately 250 km downstream from Bamako) provides the primary water retention for the *Office*, while canals provide access to irrigation water from an area stretching northward to Niono and eastward to Macina (see figure 1). The history of the *Office* dates to the French colonial era of the early 1900s.

After achieving military control of what was called the Soudan in 1890, the colonial administration began using the newly constructed Dakar-Koulikoro

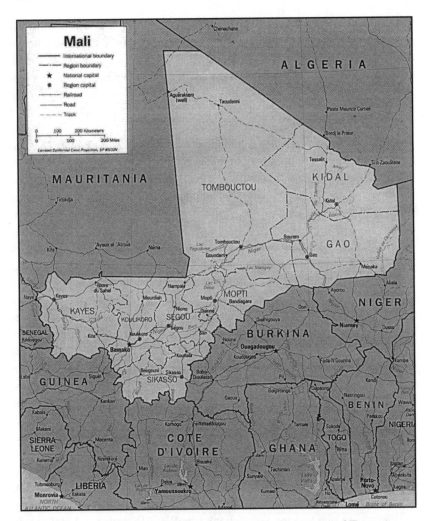

Figure 1. Location of the Office du Niger. Source: University of Texas map library web site.

railway to import cloth, salt, construction material, drinks, and equipment, and to export products of interest to French industry. These exports were limited to gum arabic, vine rubber, and ivory, as the Soudan showed no prospects for gold and high value crops such as coffee or cocoa.

In response, the French turned their attention to the agricultural potential believed to be available by irrigating the central delta of the Niger River. In the dreams of French colonial military engineers, the *Office du Niger* was supposed to bring over 1 million hectares of near-desert land into irrigated agricultural production. With strong support from the French cotton lobby, the colonial administration promoted what it hoped would become the metropole's main source of cotton, to be shipped to Europe by the ambitious, but never constructed, Trans-Saharan railway. Only after irrigated cotton in the area proved to be a failure did the colonial government consider turning the *Office du Niger* into the rice granary of French West Africa.

The *Office* was settled by smallholders, many of them migrants (*colons*) from what is now Burkina Faso. These smallholders leased land from the *Office* and were obliged to grow rice, for which the *Office* provided them—on credit— with water, seeds, fertilizer, and other inputs, as well as extension advice. The credit was recovered through the *Office*'s monopsony purchase rights to the output.

In his landmark assessment of the colonial investments in French West Africa, Samir Amin estimates that between 1928 and 1959 the French spent over $80 million, or almost 50 percent of the total investment in agriculture, solely on irrigation infrastructure and land reclamation in the *Office du Niger*. Despite these enormous investments, by the time of Mali's political independence, fewer than 20,000 hectares were being cultivated by fewer than 10,000 farmers.[3]

Consistent with its efforts to follow a socialist path to development, the Kéita regime invited both the Soviet Union and Chinese governments to continue investments in the *Office* through the 1960s and into the 1970s. Nevertheless, both the Soviets and Chinese also began to tire of facing of the huge problems associated with the *Office*. As they began to reduce their level of investment, the Traoré regime looked both to France and the World Bank as sources for continued investment.

In 1982, the government secured financing for a series of massive rehabilitation activities financed by the Netherlands (the ARPON project—11,500 ha), the French Development Fund (CFD—2,200 ha), the European Development Fund and the World Bank (the RETAIL project—2,800 ha). In 1983, more than $10 million was spent in these intensification and rehabilitation programs.[4] By the mid-1990s, these projects had rehabilitated almost 40 percent of the perimeters in the *Office*. In addition, each of these projects encouraged farmers to adopt improved production and harvesting practices.

Production levels

Until the great drought of 1972–74, Mali was basically self-sufficient in cereals, both for coarse grains (millet, sorghum, and maize) and for rice. From the

Table 1. **Rice production and imports in Mali.**

Year	Paddy	Milled Equivalent	Imports Supply	Total	% Dom. Production
1981/82	143500	78925	26000	104925	75%
1982/83	155000	85250	71131	156381	55%
1983/84	141500	77825	64754	142579	55%
1984/85	109354	60145	100200	160345	38%
1985/86	213841	117613	114000	231613	51%
1986/87	225138	123826	129100	252926	49%
1987/88	236568	130112	50000	180112	72%
1988/89	287797	158288	70281	228569	69%
1989/90	337749	185762	50500	236262	79%
1990/91	282366	155301	20000	175301	89%
1991/92	454349	249892	128400	378292	66%
1992/93	410018	225510	40000	265510	85%
1993/94	427609	235185	31500	266685	88%
1994/95	469127	258020	3600	261620	99%
1995/96	462702	254486	45700	300186	85%
1997/98	568375	312606	30000	342606	91%
1998/99	688125	378496	N.A.	N.A.	

Source: Direction Nationale de la Statistique for data. FAO database for trade data.

1970s to the mid-1980s, (with the exception of 1976 and 1977), Mali became a large importer of food and a perennial recipient of food aid. Despite the large amount of resources poured into the *Office* in the late 1970s and early 1980s, domestic rice production stagnated, and then dipped during the poor rainfall years of the early 1980s. Between 1981 and 1987, domestic rice production covered only 55 percent of the total Malian rice consumption, with the remainder being supplied by imports (table 1). While poor weather certainly contributed to the downturn in production in the early 1980s, the stagnation of production in the ON was fundamentally due to a lack of incentives for farmers to increase their production.[5] This lack of incentives resulted from the way in which rice production, processing, and marketing were organized in the *Office* prior to the 1986–87 marketing year.[6]

Organization of Rice Production and Marketing in the *Office du Niger*

Structure of production

Small-scale farming (4.7 to 8 hectares per household) predominates in the *Office*. Households lease land on an annual basis from the *Office* and agree to pay for water supply, the use of irrigation facilities, and other services. Until the mid-1990s, the *Office*, in return, delivered fertilizer and seed, offered credit to purchase farm equipment, maintained the irrigation, and guaranteed the purchase of paddy. In other words, the state controlled all input and output marketing, and paid an official price to farmers that did not fluctuate either seasonally or according to the quality of paddy produced. Until 1986–87, sales of paddy to anyone other than the *Office* were illegal.

Farmers in the *Office* are allocated land in one of the *Office*'s three production areas. The RETAIL project includes full water control and regular maintenance of the irrigation network, which allows double-cropping during the year. It is also the most intensive production system, with transplanting and the heavy use of chemical fertilizers. As a result, yields can exceed 5 tons per hectare. As of 1992, water charges were CFAF 42,000 per hectare and threshing services were billed at 8 percent of production.

In the ARPON project, the perimeters have not been systematically leveled; consequently, flooding is irregular. In the project's semi-intensive system, farmers use fewer inputs, and yields average 3.5 tons per hectare. Farmers paid less (CFAF 28,000 per hectare) for water, but still paid 8 percent of production for threshing services.

The non-restored areas still rely on gravity irrigation. The irrigation network in these areas is not maintained on a regular basis, farmers have access to fewer inputs, and as a result, yields are estimated at 2.5 tons per hectare. Nevertheless, farmers were charged CFAF 28,000 per hectare for water and 8 percent of their production for threshing services in the early 1990s.[7]

In principle, farmers who fail to respect the lease conditions are subject to eviction from their parcels. The number of evictions varies widely from year-to-year,[8] and in practice, those in default more often have the size of their parcels reduced. Most often, area cut from a resident's parcel is transferred to non-residents, or those who do not live within the *Office du Niger*. In the late

1980s, non-residents represented 28 percent of the total population in the *Office* and were assigned 20 percent of the total land. While some of these may have been employees of the *Office* who lived in nearby towns, there were also individuals who only had connections to *Office* executives, including those who lived elsewhere in the country. The nonresident farmers hire seasonal laborers for cultivation, and some evidence suggests that they not only are less productive than resident farmers, but tend to misuse the water and water systems. Moreover, the yields of non-residents tend to be significantly lower (45 percent) than those of established residents.[9]

Organization of rice marketing and processing

The organization of rice marketing and processing within the *Office* needs to be viewed in relation to the evolving organization of the entire rice subsector in Mali. Reforms in coarse grain marketing began in 1981 under the PRMC *(Programme de Restructuration du Marché Céréalier)*, but the rice subsector within the *Office* remained under strong government control until 1987.[10] The state, through the national grain board (OPAM), and the *Office*, continued to monopolize rice marketing and milling in the *Office*.

In part, the heavy state involvement in rice marketing in the ON was an attempt to protect the domestic rice industry from international competition, given the substantial investments the state had made in irrigation infrastructure in the *Office*, especially during the early 1980s. Protecting the domestic industry became both more necessary and more difficult starting in the mid-1980s because of the increasing overvaluation of the CFA franc. The overvaluation of the franc made imports, including rice from abroad, very cheap, undermining the competitiveness of Malian rice on the domestic market. The problem was compounded by the import policies of Mali's two non-CFA zone neighbors, Mauritania and Guinea. Both countries subsidized rice imports to keep prices low to urban consumers, and the large price differential between rice prices in these countries and in Mali encouraged large-scale smuggling into Mali, which further hurt the competitiveness of the *Office* rice.

The structure of the Malian wholesale market for rice further hindered competitive pricing. Rice imports were highly concentrated in the hands of the four largest rice traders in Bamako, who in 1988 were responsible for three-fourths of all rice imports.[11] This same small oligopoly of rice traders also held most of the contracts to buy domestic rice from OPAM (to whom the *Office* sold), and later, directly from the *Office*. They thus could tightly control retail rice prices, as semi-wholesalers and retailers had to go to these large wholesalers to get their

rice, both imported and domestic. As we will see below, one of the major benefits of the liberalization of rice milling in the*Office* was to break the power of
this oligopoly.

Organization of the Office rice subsector prior to 1987

Figure 2 illustrates the structure of the rice subsector in the *Office* between 1981
and 1987. Prior to the effective paddy market liberalization in 1987, the *Office*

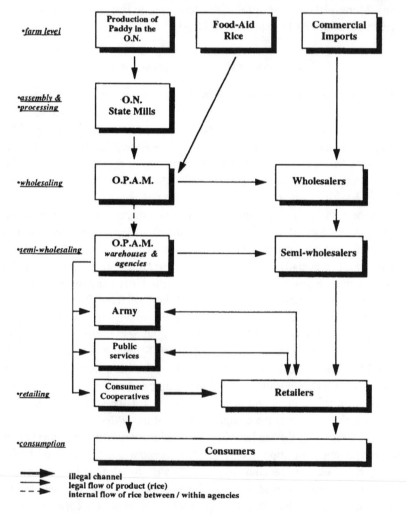

Figure 2. **Organization of the rice subsector in the *Office* between 1981 and
1987.**

handled all paddy assembly and processing within its boundaries This included assembly in the fields and transport to the milling plants in the *Office*. Once processed, the rice was marketed exclusively through OPAM, which in turn worked with the four major wholesalers to offer milled rice through consumer cooperatives, as well as to the army and other public organizations. OPAM also received all food aid rice imported into the country, while the same four wholesalers dominated the commercial imports as well. During this time, both producer and consumer prices were fixed by a national commission. These prices were set in relation to domestic production costs in the ON, not cheaper world prices, and as a result the four major rice importers were able to earn substantial profits on their imports.

Paddy in the *Office* destined for the market was processed in one of four state-owned large-scale mills, located at Molodo, N'Débougou, Kolongo, and Dogofri, which had a capacity of about 80,000 tons of paddy per year. Rice destined for home consumption was predominantly hand pounded. Private commercial milling of rice within the *Office* was illegal.

The 1987 reforms

Under strong pressure from the PRMC donors and the World Bank, the Malian government agreed in 1986 to a broad set of reforms in the operation of the *Office*. The key changes were embodied in a contract-plan between the state and the *Office*, which outlined changes in the *Office's* roles and set benchmarks for the ON to meet if it were to continue to receive agreed-upon support from the state. Two key elements of the contract-plan were more decentralized management of the irrigation perimeters and liberalization of paddy marketing (which became widely effective in 1987). The liberalization allowed farmers in the *Office* to sell their paddy to whomever they pleased and abolished the *Office*'s monopoly on rice milling within its boundaries. In addition, the *Office* was now required to market its rice directly to wholesalers rather than selling its grain to OPAM, which previously had handled the wholesaling operations for the *Office*. The marketing and milling reforms were strongly supported by the Dutch, whose foreign assistance programs began making small rice dehullers available to village associations and women's cooperatives in the *Office* in the late 1980s.

As a result of the marketing and milling reforms and the efforts of the Dutch and of various NGOs to promote small-scale rice mills in the *Office*, small dehullers began to appear in the *Office* in 1987. The mills were rapidly adopted by village associations (*associations villageoises,* or AVs), private entrepreneurs (typically farmers or local traders), and women's cooperatives.

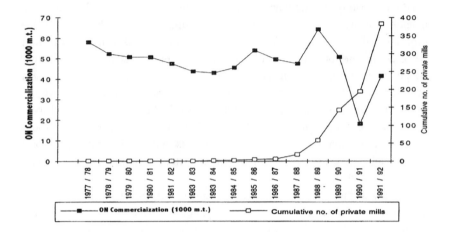

Figure 3. **Paddy commercialization through through the *Office* vs. growth in small rice mills**

Between 1987 and 1992, the number of small mills operating in the *Office* grew from one to 383, with a total milling capacity of approximately 210,000 m.t. (figure 3). As the small mills spread, the volume passing through the state mills fell because of the large mills' inability to offer prices as high as the small mills were paying for paddy. By 1992, 90 percent of the production in the RETAIL project zone was privately milled.

The small mills ranged in capacity from about 2 tons of paddy per day up to 30 tons/day. They had several advantages compared with the large state mills. Many of these small plate mills could be moved from village to village, which reduced the costs of hauling paddy long distances for processing. While the *Office* continued to pay a fixed price of 70 CFAF/kg of paddy, regardless of quality, the small mills were free to vary their prices according to market conditions. In practice, this meant that the small mills paid higher prices for paddy, particularly paddy of higher quality (for example, paddy that had been carefully dried and therefore converted to milled rice at a higher rate, because of fewer broken kernels). The small mills also offered higher prices to farmers located closest to major markets, where transport costs were lowest.

The small mills' operating costs were well below those of the large mills. A survey conducted in 1992 showed that it cost the small mills, on average, 4.3 CFAF to mill a kg of rice, compared with 17.6 CFAF/kg for the large state mills.[12] These cost differences were due to the lower capital and labor costs per kg of the small mills, their higher milling ratios (which reflected the poor state of repair of the state mills and the ability of the small mills, through their differential pricing, to attract better quality paddy), and their generally higher capacity utilization. As the small mills continued to attract more paddy from the state mills, the latter's unit costs continued to rise because of the large mills' falling capacity utilization.

In an attempt to protect some market share for the *Office*, which was falling because of increased competition from both the small mills and increased imports, the government began granting import licenses for rice only to those wholesalers who would agree to purchase from the *Office* a quantity of rice equal to the amount being imported. Because of resistance from importers and difficulties in enforcing the rule, this "twinning" arrangement lasted only a few months, and was replaced by a 32 percent ad valorem tax on all imports. The tax protected all domestic rice protection, whether from the *Office* or private mills, from foreign competition. It also allowed the state to capture the difference between the world price and the domestic price, which previously had been captured by the small oligopoly of rice importers.

The rapid spread of the small mills in the *Office* had profound effects on the organization of the rice subsector in the *Office* (figure 4). The large number of mills competed not only with the *Office* mills but also among themselves for paddy, which forced them to pass their cost savings back to farmers in the form of higher prices. In early 1992, for example, most of the small mills could afford to pay farmers an average price of between 72 and 82 CFAF/kg for their paddy and still earn a profit, compared to the 70 F CFAF/kg offered by the *Office* mills.[13]

Even more important, the spread of the small mills broke the market power of the four major rice importers, who had previously dominated the Malian rice market, both for domestic production and imports. Even after the PRMC reforms led to liberalization of imports, scale economies in importing were so large that the four main firms continued to dominate the import market. Thus, prior to the 1987 marketing reforms, all other rice wholesalers, semi-wholesalers, and retailers were obliged to go to these major players for their rice supplies. The emergence of the small mills gave smaller distributors an alternative source of supply, and many wholesalers and semi-wholesalers began buying directly in the *Office* from village associations and other owners of small mills. The competition for supplies helped bid up the prices paid to the small mills, and because of competition among the millers, these higher prices got passed back to farmers. On the retail side, competition among sellers, now freed from having to buy exclusively from the old oligopoly, led to lower marketing margins, thus holding down prices to consumers.

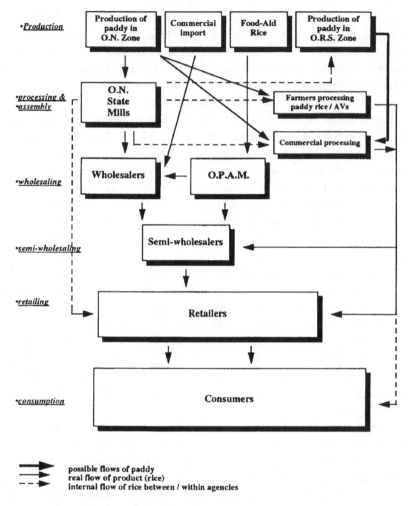

Figure 4. Organization of the rice subsector in the *Office* after 1987.

Because millers and retailers were now free to pay different prices for different qualities of paddy, millers began offering higher prices for varieties that consumers preferred and for paddy that had been carefully dried and hence would mill with fewer broken kernels. The ability of the market to pay premiums for higher quality rice led to a dramatic change in rice production technology. Farmers began to search for the varieties that consumers preferred (rather than focusing solely on agronomic yield), and adopted improved postharvest techniques to preserve paddy quality. The *Office* had tried in vain to extend such techniques prior to the liberalization, but now that farmers were being paid according to the quality of their paddy, *Office* extension agents found themselves deluged with farmers wanting to learn about these practices. This demand for new production technology complemented reforms launched in 1991 to involve farmers more in the management of the irrigation perimeters, making farmers more active participants in the basic decisions governing rice production in the *Office*.

As part of the marketing reforms, farmers were also given the freedom to pay their water and other input charges to the *Office* in cash, rather than in paddy (at the official price), as had previously been the case. Farmers argued strongly for this right so that they could take advantage of the higher cash prices offered by the small mills. Denied this secure source of paddy, the large mills' market share began to fall sharply.

As a result of all these changes, the small mills quickly became farmers' preferred outlets for their grain. The small mills offered custom milling services (milling farmers' rice for a fee), and many also began buying paddy directly, milling it, and reselling it themselves to wholesalers and retailers. In 1985–86, the year before the reforms, the *Office* marketed 65 percent of the total paddy produced in the *Office*, with most of the remainder going to home consumption. By 1989–90, the *Office's* share had fallen to 48 percent, and then plunged the following year to 13 percent (figure 3). The dramatic decline in *Office* processing in 1990–91 was due not only to the higher prices offered by the small mills, but also to breakdowns in several of the state mills, which prevented them from operating for several months. (Indeed, the *Office* was forced to subcontract with several of the small mills in 1991 to process over 40,000 tons of paddy on its behalf.)

With the repair of its mills, the *Office* was able increase its share back to 23 percent of total production in 1991–92, but the recovery was temporary. By 1994–95, the *Office* was no longer able to attract enough paddy to the large mills to operate them economically, and the mills closed in 1995. They remained closed until 1997, when they were sold to private entrepreneurs, including one of the former large rice importers. Yet even under private ownership and substantial refurbishing, the mills could not effectively compete with the small mills for paddy in 1998, and shut down again that year. This raises the question of the future role of large vs. small mills in the *Office*.

The economics of small vs. large rice mills

What is likely to be the future role of small vs. large rice mills in the *Office*? In a classic study, Timmer identifies four factors that determine the relative profitability of small vs. large rice mills: the technical efficiency of the mills, the relative price of milled rice vs. paddy, the relative price of capital vs. labor, and the discount rate. These factors will be important in determining the future structure of rice milling in the *Office*.[14]

- *Technical efficiency.* This term refers to the rate at which the mills can convert rough rice (paddy) into milled rice. While in most instances, one would expect modern industrial mills to have a higher milling ratio than the small mills, this was not the case in Mali in the early 1990s. The *Office* mills, which had not been adequately maintained, achieved a milling rate of about 65–67 percent in 1990–91, while the small mills varied between 65 and 70 percent.[15] The milling rate becomes particularly important when the price differential between paddy and milled rice is small (for example, when retail rice prices are held down by cheap imports or by price controls). In such a scenario, mills with higher technical efficiency gain significant advantages.[16] While the rehabilitation of the large mills by their private owners is likely to increase their technical efficiency, the likelihood of cheap imports or effective price controls for rice in Mali seems low in the near future, meaning that the small mills, on this account at least, are likely to remain competitive.
- *Relative paddy/milled rice prices.* If one type of mill can produce, for a given type of paddy, a higher quality rice that commands a premium on the market, then it will have an advantage relative to mills that produce lower quality output (more broken grains, for example). In the late 1980s and early 1990s, the large mills did poorly in this regard. Constrained to pay the same price for all paddy, regardless of quality, the large mills attracted the worst quality rough rice and hence often produced poor quality output. The *Office* also pooled all its milled rice together, regardless of quality, and thus did not exploit any of the profit opportunities available through developing niche markets for different qualities of grain. Some of the small millers were more successful in this regard, developing a reputation for producing high-quality products. It remains to be seen whether the new owners of the large mills will be more successful in producing high quality output that can command a premium price on the market. In theory, the large mills, if run well, should be capable of doing this.
- *Relative price of capital and labor.* The large mills substitute capital for labor and are more competitive when wage rates rise. Given that the devaluation has raised the price of imported capital, such as spare parts, relative to labor, one would expect the capital intensity of the large mills to work against their competitiveness in the near future.

The capital intensity of the large mills also makes capacity utilization very important for them. If the large mills cannot attract enough paddy to work close to capacity, their average fixed costs per kg of rice milled becomes very high. In the early 1990s, the large mills got into a vicious cycle: constrained by their inefficiencies, they were not able to offer farmers an attractive price for paddy. The large mills thus ran at low capacity (51 percent in 1991–92), driving up their unit costs and compounding their losses.

Thus, one of the future challenges for the large mills is to develop an assured supply of paddy. Some of the new owners have explored the possibility of undertaking large-scale rice production themselves to feed into their mills. Another alternative is to offer contracts to farmers that make it attractive for them to deliver paddy to the large mills rather than the small ones. This could involve factors other than just price—for example, assured market outlets and some guaranteed future price or guaranteed input provision.

- *Discount rate.* The discount rate is the rate at which future costs and benefits are discounted relative to the present. In commercial transactions, it is equivalent to the interest rate paid on borrowed or loaned capital. The large mills have relatively large initial investments and lower unit costs in the future, while the small mills, which have a larger labor cost per unit of output, incur a greater proportion of their costs in the future. Thus, the higher the discount rate (that is, the more future costs are discounted relative to the present), the greater the relative profitability of the small mills compared to the large mills. Thus, the large mills would be advantaged by programs that provided subsidized credit to investors. But barring such programs, it is likely that in a country as poor as Mali, the discount rate will remain high, working to the advantage of the small mills.

In summary, it is not apparent that simply privatizing the large mills will make them competitive with the small mills. Certainly, the experience of the first year of operation of the privatized large mills, when they had to shut down because they could not attract enough paddy to run their mills at a profitable level of capacity, is sobering. There are many characteristics of the small mills—such as flexibility of operation and greater use of low-cost labor (a relatively abundant resource in Mali)—that make them well suited to the Malian setting. It is, therefore, likely that the small mills will continue to be major players in the *Office*. The large mills may have a role, but it will take much more careful and innovative management than they have had in the past if these mills are to succeed.

Impact of the CFA franc devaluation

The January 1994 devaluation of the CFA franc by 50 percent ushered in a new era in the economics of rice production and milling in the *Office*. Overnight, the border price of rice, measured in CFA francs, doubled. This price increase had two effects. First, the price of rice on the Malian market quickly rose in response to the increase in import prices. The price of local rice in the Bamako (Niérala) market, for example, jumped 23 percent in the two weeks immediately following the devaluation.[17] Second, consumers quickly began to shift away from imported rice to Malian rice, which suddenly became cheaper than similar quality imported rice.

Immediately after the devaluation, policy makers and the general public expressed fears that the rapid increases in rice prices were the result of price gouging by wholesalers eager to take advantage of the higher import prices. Research by the agricultural market information system (SIM), however, quickly demonstrated that because of the competitive market structure that had resulted from the earlier reforms in the *Office*, almost all the increase in the consumer prices was passed back to farmers in the *Office*. Within two weeks of the devaluation, the share of the Bamako consumers price received by *Office* farmers jumped from 67 percent to 82 percent, while the wholesalers' share increased only from 2 percent to 3 percent.[18] This analysis quickly changed the policy debate. Instead of arguing about how to stop price gouging, debate focused on whether Malian rice could compete with imports not only in Mali but in neighboring countries as well.[19]

The higher producer prices resulting from the devaluation combined with the production and milling reforms initiated in the late 1980s to boost Malian rice production and yields even further (table 1). *Office* farmers increased rice yields substantially by switching from broadcast seeding to transplanting and by using more organic and inorganic fertilizer. There was also increased diversification into dry-season horticultural products such as onions and tomatoes. This diversification and input use increased the annual productivity of land and irrigation investments well beyond what could be produced with a single rice crop (or even a double rice crop, because dry-season rice yields are quite low). Both rice intensification and diversification into horticulture were stimulated by increased demand for the products. This demand came not only from Malian consumers but also from other countries in the region, primarily Côte d'Ivoire, but also Ghana.[20]

As Mali's rice production increased, it began to export small quantities of its higher quality rice to neighboring countries, particularly Côte d'Ivoire and

Burkina Faso, while continuing to import lower-cost Asian broken rice, which was consumed by low-income urbanites. This trade strengthens Mali's food security, as the country is able to use the export receipts from the high-quality rice to import a greater quantity of rice calories than it exports, due to the low cost of the Asian broken rice, which is considered a milling byproduct in most rice-consuming countries.[21]

The higher prices and increased productivity of Malian rice producers has allowed the government to eliminate the main import taxes on rice. Although the elimination of the import taxes removed a government source of revenue, it has also helped hold down consumer prices and is a sign that the Malian rice subsector can now compete without special tariff protection.

The problem of production credit

Although the reforms have boosted production, there remains a serious challenge: developing a sustainable system of production credit. Prior to the reforms, the *Office* automatically recovered production credit through its monopsony marketing of the paddy. After the liberalization, banks began extending credit through village associations, but this system collapsed in part because of the inexperience of the AVs in marketing and the lack of reliable contract enforcement between the AVs and traders. Several AVs sold paddy on credit to traders who failed to repay them, leaving the AVs with no funds to repay their production credit. Other AVs held paddy late into the season hoping to benefit from the higher prices, but in so doing, failed to repay their credit on time. The farmers complained that the banks had conspired with traders to require repayment of production credit within a few months of harvest (typically in March), which forced all the AVs to sell at that time, depressing prices.

Members of AVs that defaulted on their loans no longer had access to group credit and were forced to seek individual loans to purchase their inputs. This has caused serious problems of access to inputs, particularly for smaller farmers. Thus, a major challenge in the *Office*, as in much of sub-Saharan Africa, is to develop effective input delivery and credit systems to replace the automatic credit recovery that was a feature of the state monopoly marketing system.[22]

Conclusion

The marketing and milling reforms in the *Office du Niger* have helped bring about a remarkable transformation of rice production in Mali. The experience of market reform in the *Office* has also highlighted the following points concerning the nature of agricultural policy reform:

- Reforms that improve the transmission of consumer demand to farmers can play a critical role in inducing farmers to invest in their agricultural enterprises. The marketing reforms in the *Office* were essential in assuring that the higher prices that consumers were willing to pay for better-quality rice and the higher retail prices resulting from the devaluation were effectively transmitted to farmers. The strong demand by farmers for improved production and post-harvest technologies following the reforms, in contrast to farmers' indifference to extension programs that tried to spread these technologies prior to the reforms, testifies to the importance of market incentives in spurring farmers' interest and investment in new technologies.

- Market reforms and the devaluation were necessary but not sufficient conditions for the rapid increases in production. The data in table 1 show that production increases actually began in 1985–86, before the marketing reforms, in part in response to prior investments in rehabilitation of the irrigation infrastructure. But production accelerated after the marketing reforms of 1987, and particularly after the 1994 CFA franc devaluation.

- The contrast between the impact of policy reforms on rice production and its impact on coarse grain production[23] illustrates the synergies between changes in technologies (improved varieties, better planting techniques, and restored infrastructure), institutions governing production and marketing, and macroeconomic policy in transforming agricultural production systems. The PRMC led to important marketing reforms for both coarse grains and rice, and the devaluation boosted demand for both types of cereals. Yet production of coarse grains—which are grown under rainfed conditions, with fewer improved technologies, and often in places where the basic transportation infrastructure is much weaker than in the *Office*—has grown at less than 3 percent per year following the reforms, compared to a 9 percent annual growth rate for rice.[24] The marketing reforms in the *Office* were effective largely because farmers in the zone had the technical capacity to respond quickly by intensifying production. In areas where structural constraints are more binding (areas of variable rainfall, poor water control, and bad roads), policy reform by itself will be a much weaker instrument to increase agricultural production.

- The phasing of sectoral reforms and macroeconomic reforms was crucial in stimulating increased rice production. The marketing reforms introduced in 1987 broke the power of the small oligopoly that had previously dominated

Malian rice markets, thereby creating a much more competitive marketing system within the *Office*. Had these reforms not taken place *before* the CFA franc devaluation of 1994, it is likely that most of the higher prices resulting from the devaluation would have been captured by the oligopolists and not have been passed back to farmers. The competitive marketing system was thus essential in assuring that the increased production incentives reached farmers, and thereby helped stimulate the dramatic production increases that followed devaluation. This suggests that sectoral reforms often need to precede major macroeconomic reforms in order to give economies the flexibility they need to respond to the new macroeconomic incentives.

- Small, labor-intensive rice mills can effectively compete with large industrial mills in the Malian setting because they offer farmers low-cost milling services, flexibility (for example, some are mobile, and thus can be moved from village to village), and job creation. There may be a role for the newly privatized industrial mills, but their dominance of the market is not assured. It will be important for policy makers to avoid automatically favoring the large mills (viewing them as "modern"), but instead assure a level playing field between the two types of technologies.

- While the reforms have greatly improved output marketing, access to inputs and credit remain a problem. Lack of effective contract enforcement mechanisms (such as bonding of traders) and inexperience of AVs in marketing output pose serious challenges in assuring farmers in the *Office* reliable access to production inputs.

The role of the *Office du Niger* has evolved dramatically since the mid-1980s. Prior to 1987, it was an agency that was involved in all aspects of production, input and credit provision, and output processing and marketing. Now it is basically a provider of irrigation and extension services. The Malian government is currently considering the potential for private irrigation schemes in Mali. A major challenge for the future will be figuring out the appropriate and evolving role of the public and private sectors in rice production in Mali. The experience of policy reform in the 1980s and 1990s shows the importance of balancing these roles carefully in order to foster agricultural growth and food security.

Notes

1. Egg 1999.
2. Dimithè 1997.
3. Amin 1965; Jones 1976.

4. Dembélé 1990.

5. Kamuanga 1982.

6. In the *Office,* the main rice harvest begins in December and is marketed over the next several months; hence the 1986–87 marketing year refers to the period December 1986–November 1987. For brevity, we denote this marketing year as 1987 in this chapter. The Malian government officially allowed private traders to begin to buy paddy from the main harvest in the ON starting late in the 1985–86 marketing year. Because the market was opened to private traders so late in the season, they had very little involvement in marketing the crop in 1986. For this reason, we denote 1987 as the first year of the "effective" liberalization. See Sanogo 1988 for details.

7. Diarra 1994.

8. Samaké and Yung 1988.

9. Ibid.

10. See articles by Dioné and by Dembélé and Staatz in this volume for details on the PRMC.

11. Ceolo 1990. In contrast, in 1987–88, the four largest coarse grain traders handled only 42 percent of the coarse grains sold in Bamako (Mehta 1989).

12. Diarra 1994, 96.

13. Diarra 1994, 98.

14. Timmer 1998.

15. Diarra 1994.

16. Timmer 1998.

17. SIM, unpublished data.

18. The increase in the wholesalers' share was due primarily to higher costs, particularly transport, resulting from the devaluation (SIM 1994a).

19. SIM 1994b; Barry, Diarra, and Diarra 1998. The fact that the Malian government had the data-collection and analytic capacity to carry out these studies so soon after the devaluation is itself a tribute to the market reforms. The PRMC and USAID had funded the creation of the SIM in 1989 and strongly supported its development of local analytic capacity (see Dembélé and Staatz in this volume).

20. Yade et al. 1999; Mariko, Chohin-Kuper, and Kelly 1999.

21. Yade et al. 1999.

22. Kelly et al. 1999.

23. See Dembélé and Staatz in this volume.

24. Dembélé and Staatz in this volume. The production increases for coarse grains after the devaluation were also limited because farmers in the CMDT zone apparently shifted land out of these cereals and into cotton, whose price also shot up after devaluation. But even the increases in cotton production came about entirely through increases in area planted, in contrast to rice, where higher yields were the main source of production growth (Yade et al. 1999).

Bibliography

Amin, S. 1965. *Trois Expériences Africaines de Développement: Le Mali, le Guinée et le Ghana.* Paris: Presses Universitaires de France.

Barry, Abdoul W., Salif B. Diarra, and Daouda Diarra. 1998. "Promouvoir les exportations de riz malien vers les pays de la sous-région." Rapport final. Equity and Growth through Economic Research (EAGER). Cambridge, Mass.: Associates for International Resources and Development.

Ceolo, Serge. 1990. "Mission d'Evaluation de la Politique de Prix et de Commercialisatoin du Paddy et du Riz: Contrat-Plan Etat/Office du Niger." Version provisoire. Bamako: Office du Niger. September.

Dembélé, Niama Nango. 1990. "Rapport sur l'évaluation de la politique des prix and de commercialisation du paddy et du riz dans le cadre du contrat-plan Etat-Office du Niger." Ségou: République du Mali, Ministère de l'Agriculture, *Office du Niger.*

Dembélé, Niama Nango, and John M. Staatz. 2000. Chapter in this book. ("The response of cereals traders to agricultural market reform in Mali." In *Democracy and Development in Mali*, edited by R.J. Bingen, D. Robinson, and J.M. Staatz. East Lansing: Michigan State University Press.)

Diarra, Salifou. 1994. "The role of small rice mills in the rice subsector of the *Office du Niger*, Mali." Plan B paper, Michigan State University.

Dimithè, Georges. 1997. "An economic analysis of the competitiveness of alternative rice production systems: the case of the *bas-fonds* rice production in *Mali-sud*." Ph.D. dissertation, Michigan State University.

Dioné, Josué. 2000. Chapter in this book. ("Food security policy reform in Mali and the Sahel." In *Democracy and Development in Mali*, edited by R.J. Bingen, D. Robinson, and J.M. Staatz. East Lansing: Michigan State University Press.)

Egg, Johny. 1999. *Etude de l'Impact de la Libéralisation sur le Fonctionnement des Filières Céréalières au Mali: Rapport de Synthèse.* Bamako: Programme de Restructuration du Marché Céréalier/Comité d'Orientation et de Coordination du Système de Sécurité Alimentaire.

Jones, W. I. 1976. *Planning and Economic Policy: Socialist Mali and her Neighbors* Washington, D.C.: Three Continents Press.

Kamuanga, Mulumba. 1982. "Farm level study of the rice production system at the *Office du Niger* in Mali: an economic analysis." Unpublished Ph.D. dissertation, Michigan State University.

Kelly, Valerie A., Eric W. Crawford, Julie A. Howard, Thomas Jayne, John Staatz, and Michael T. Weber. 1999. "Towards a strategy for improving agricultural input markets in Africa." *Policy Synthesis*, Food Security II Cooperative Agreement. East Lansing: Department of Agricultural Economics, Michigan State University.

Mariko Dramane, Anne Chohin-Kuper, and Valerie Kelly. 1999. "La filière riz à l'Office du Niger au Mali. Une nouvelle dynamique depuis la dévaluation du Franc CFA." Bamako: IER/INSAH.

Mehta, Mona. 1989. "An analysis of the structure of the wholesale cereals market in Mali." Master's thesis, Michigan State University.

Samaké, A., and J. M. Yung. 1988. "Opinions et objectifs des riziculteurs de l'Office du Niger." Bamako: SEDES.

Sanogo, Ousmane. 1988. "Sythèse des études réalisées dans les zones de production rizicoles portant sur la libéralisation de la commercialisation du paddy." Bamako: Institut d'Economie Rurale, Division Planification et Evaluation. October.

SIM (Système d'Information du Marché). Unpublished data.

——. 1994a. "Aperçu sur le marché du riz à la suite de la dévaluation." *Rapport Spécial* no. 1 (February). Bamako.

——. 1994b. "Allez riz malien!" *Rapport Spécial* no. 2. (February). Bamako.

Timmer, C. Peter. 1998. "Choice of technique in rice milling in Java." In *International Agricultural Development* (3rd edition), edited by Carl K. Eicher and John M. Staatz. Baltimore: Johns Hopkins University Press.

Yade, Mbaye, Anne Chohin-Kuper, Valerie Kelly, John Staatz, and James Tefft. 1999. "The role of regional trade in agricultural transformation: the case of West Africa following the devaluation of the CFA franc." East Lansing: Michigan State University Agricultural Economics staff paper no. 99–29.

Small-Scale Inland Valley Swamp Rice Production: A Viable Enterprise in the Grain-Cotton Farming System of Southern Mali

GEORGES DIMITHÈ

Introduction

Until the early 1970s, Mali was self-sufficient in cereals. After the 1974 drought, food production failed to keep pace with the rapidly expanding demand for food, and between 1979 and 1991, per capita food production declined by an average of 0.7 percent per year.[1] As the gap between national food production and demand widened in the late 1980s, Mali became increasingly dependent on commercial imports and food aid. Rice imports alone accounted for approximately 26 percent of total rice consumption annually between 1984 and 1993. Agricultural productivity has improved since the early 1990s and Mali has significantly reduced cereal imports, especially rice. In order to improve food security, the government is seriously considering ways to intensify rice farming.

There are two basic interrelated ways for the government to stimulate increased domestic rice production. One involves policy reforms to transform the rice subsector and the entire food system and stimulate broad-based economic growth. Such policies could raise real incomes, and/or lower real rice prices while maintaining incentives to rice farmers, processors, wholesalers, and retailers. The challenge is to identify such policies and to implement them successfully. Historically, government initiatives designed to achieve these goals focused on policies that artificially raised food prices for producers and lowered them for consumers through subsidies. However, because such policies have become fiscally unsustainable, food market reforms have been launched in Mali and throughout Africa.

A second approach involves increasing farm-level productivity through investments in agricultural research and extension that account for local resources and farm-level conditions. The success of this approach, however, depends upon more than investments in research and extension. Complementary improvements in the tax code, better supply markets, and investments that strengthen marketing infrastructure—that is, roads linking production and consumption areas, market facilities, and market information systems—are also needed.

This chapter examines this second approach. The discussion is organized in four parts. The first part highlights the importance of rice in Mali. The second part presents an overview of *bas-fond* (inland valley swamp) rice production, including the land tenure and the institutional environment under which farmers operate. The third part examines the potential for *bas-fond* rice production. And the fourth part focuses on the potential of the *bas-fonds* to increase rural household incomes and thereby increase household access to food.[2]

Rice is an Important Staple in Mali

Mali's agricultural sector is characterized by a low level of diversity and a high degree of production variability that often leads to food deficits. The principal crops are cotton, cereals (sorghum, millet, rice, and maize), and groundnuts. Cotton, the main cash crop, is grown mostly in the southern part of the country by smallholders under a marketing guarantee with the *Compagnie Malienne pour le Développement des Fibres Textiles* (CMDT). As such, cotton provides greater financial security to farmers than do food crops, as inputs (seed, fertilizer, pesticides, in-kind loans for animal traction) are guaranteed by the CMDT. Millet, sorghum, and maize are the major rainfed staple crops and they account for more than 80 percent of total area planted and more than 75 percent of total grain production. Rice, the only cereal grown under irrigation in this drought-prone country, offers the greatest potential for significant yield increases. It accounts for about 11 percent of total area planted, and 16 percent of total grain production.

Cereals are the staple of the Malian diet and provide approximately 79 percent (1,770 kcal/year/individual) of the total human energy supply.[3] Millet, sorghum, and maize account for about 85 percent of these cereal calories while rice provides the remaining 15 percent[4] and accounts for about 6.4 percent of the total expenses of Malian households.[5]

According to Mali's most recent (1988–89) nationwide consumption expenditure survey,[6] national rice consumption per capita averages about 34 kg per annum, and is higher in urban areas (58.0 kg/year) than in rural areas (24.3

kg/year). While rice is currently only third among cereals in terms of per capita consumption, Mali's strategic development plan[7] projects that per capita rice consumption will increase at an annual rate of 2.1 percent in urban areas and 0.4 percent in rural areas. Because the demand for rice is growing rapidly among urban consumers, who represent more than 25 percent of the population and tend to be politically active, the government places a high priority on increasing rice production to satisfy this growing demand.

Irrigation Potential and Rice Production Systems

Mali's agricultural potential is limited by irregular and low rainfall, ranging from 200 mm in the north to 1,400 mm in the south. The country has the largest irrigable land potential (that is, land that could be developed for irrigated crop production) of any Sahelian country, estimated from 500,000 to 2,000,000 hectares.[8] To develop its vast irrigable land potential and thereby lessen the unfavorable effects of the irregular rainfall pattern, Mali has established several government-managed irrigation schemes along the Niger and Senegal Rivers and other small rivers in the south of the country. The government also encourages communities to develop farmer-managed schemes in *bas-fonds* and flooded plains. As a result of these investments, Mali currently has approximately 263,880 hectares in rice production.[9]

Based on water source and the level of water flow control, the country's rice production systems can be classified into three subsystems: (1) the fully controlled irrigation subsystems in large (*Office du Niger*, Baguinéda, Manantali, and Selingué) or small perimeters along the Niger (1,700 km) and Senegal Rivers; (2) the partially controlled irrigation subsystems which are found in smaller irrigated perimeters (*Opération Riz Ségou, Opération Riz Mopti, Opération Riz Sikasso*) and smaller rivers in the south; and (3) the largely undeveloped traditional flooded plains and *bas-fond* subsystems, which are found mostly in southern Mali. Currently, the largest share (48 percent) of the rice area (126,078 ha) is found in the flooded plains, followed by the fully irrigated subsystem (25 percent; 65,953 ha), the traditional *bas-fond* (14 percent; 37,263 ha), and the partially irrigated (13 percent; 34,588 ha) subsystems.[10]

Past government efforts to increase rice production have focused on both expanding and rehabilitating the intensive irrigated areas (fully and partially controlled irrigation subsystems) and increasing yields in these schemes. Rehabilitating and expanding those irrigation systems, however, is costly. For example, the World Bank estimated that in 1989 the cost of a typical irrigation perimeter with full water control (canals and diversion dam) was 2.6 million

CFAF/ha (US$8,161).[11] As a result, in recent years the government has sought to exploit the untapped potential of the *bas-fond* and flooded plains rice production systems.

Mali-Sud *Bas-fond* Rice Production

Southern Mali's (Mali-Sud) *bas-fonds* are narrow inland valley swamps that used to be permanent rivers, but have dried up with declining rainfall. During the rainy season, the water table in these swamps rises due to overflow from small rivers, seepage, and slope surface runoff from adjacent upland, generally supplying water throughout the growing season. The standing water level in these *bas-fonds* ranges from a shallow/medium depth (25–50 cm for 2–5 months) to deep water (50–100 cm). They may extend over 25 km in length and vary from approximately 10 m wide in the upper levels to about 100 m in their lower stretches. These *bas-fonds* are largely undeveloped (that is, little or no water control infrastructure) and are primarily cultivated by women (88 percent), principally to assure household self-sufficiency in rice.

Mali-Sud possesses the largest potential for *bas-fonds* in Mali, equal to about 3–5 percent of the total Mali-Sud land area. A partial inventory conducted by CMDT in 1992 revealed a potential of 48,657 ha of *bas-fond*, with only 5 percent of hectares under some type of water control.[12] Despite their small size (average 0.3 ha), Mali-Sud's well-watered *bas-fonds* offer farmers an opportunity to produce rice during the rainy season and to cultivate various upland crops in the valleys during the dry season. While this potential is important, it has not been fully utilized. Understanding this underutilization requires an examination of *bas-fond* land tenure, the gender composition of *bas-fond* farmers, and the institutional environment under which they operate.

Land tenure

Throughout Mali-Sud, land tenure is based on customary law which is heavily patriarchal. Land is communally owned and community members hold usufruct rights (i.e., they have a use right without the possibility to sell). Generally, the valley belongs to the first settlers in the village, who often constitute the dominant lineage. While these first settlers have superior rights over land, individual plots are assigned to each household at its request, for as long as the plot is continually cultivated. There is no land market in the village, nor do farmers rent land for cash or in-kind payments. Generally, the usufruct rights in both the *bas-fond* and the upland applies only during the rainy season.

During the dry season, random grazing is practiced, except in the plots with vegetables.

While this strong gender-based tenure system makes it extremely difficult for women to own upland plots, they have access to *bas-fond* land through their husband or their household heads. Previously, *bas-fond* land distribution took place at two levels: village and household. At the village level, the "chief of the lands" (*dougou kolo tigui*), who in some cases is also the village chief (*dougou tigui*), allocated land parcels to the head of the household. In return, each household head paid a symbolic price of 10 cola nuts. After *bas-fond* land has been allocated to a household, the household head partitions the household's share among the wives who wish to have a plot. Each time a new wife joins the family, the household reapportions its land to accommodate the newcomer. Over time, as more and more women became interested in rice farming, a third level of *bas-fond* land allocation developed and newly married women began to acquire rice plots from their aging mothers-in-law. This practice of reapportioning household land has resulted into multiple small, but extremely valuable, parcels.

The changing gender composition

Bas-fond rice production used to be a male-dominated activity but, according to conventional wisdom, as rice production became less profitable due to declining rainfall and soil fertility, men tended to abandon this activity to women. *Bas-fond* area is limited, and cotton and maize production represent more profitable activities.

Initially, only older women, who were unable to work on upland crops, cultivated *bas-fond* rice. Over time, more and more young women have become involved in *bas-fond* rice production. This appears to have occurred as the spread of animal traction has reduced the demand for labor in the upland fields, and as rice has become more important in the lives of women. Men decide on the use of upland crop production and these cereals, considered essential for the household's food security, are stored in the household granary under the husband's control. In contrast, women have discretionary power over the use of their rice harvest. This harvest is often used to complement the upland harvest, but it symbolizes a gender-based social freedom for women by increasing their ability to satisfy their needs and social obligations (for example, welcoming visitors). As a result, the rice harvest tends to be stored in each wife's personal granary.

The institutional environment

The behavior and performance of *bas-fond* rice farmers depend on a wide range
of factors, including the institutional environment that defines the set of opportunities available to them. This environment consists of the national research
institute, the government agency responsible for promoting cotton production
(CMDT), the market information system (SIM), as well as government policies.

Bas-fond rice research in Mali was launched in the mid-1980s by the
national agricultural research institute—*Institut d'Economie Rurale* (IER)—
through its Farming Systems Research Program (ESPGRN) and the *Bas-Fond*
Rice Projects (PRBF), both based in Sikasso, as well as the Subsector
Economics Program (ECOFIL) based in Bamako.[13] Research activities in the
bas-fond are not only limited in scope, but also they are site specific.
Consequently, the current knowledge concerning the *bas-fond* agroecosystem
still has substantial gaps.

The CMDT provides extension services for *bas-fond* rice production
through its *Bureau d'Etude* and *Projet Petits Bas-Fonds* and the Production
Systems Monitoring and Evaluation Office. The primary activity of *Bureau
d'Etude* and *Projet Petits Bas-Fonds* is to improve the traditional *bas-fonds* by
(1) evaluating the technical and economic feasibility of water control investments in interested villages, and (2) constructing and maintaining water control
infrastructure in *bas-fonds* that justify investment.

Careful management (not just the control) of the water flow is essential to
fully exploit crop production. Water management involves providing water at
various stages of the plant growth, or removing excess water. Water control
lessens weed competition and encourages better and more stable plant growth.
Improved water management also:

1. Allows farmers to cultivate a larger *bas-fond* area;
2. Maintains water and reduces drought-induced risks, which can increase
   the rate of adoption of new technologies and the returns to research and
   extension;
3. Controls non-aquatic weed pressure and thereby releases labor for other
   activities, especially when land preparation is done properly;
4. Offers farmers the opportunity to increase their land use intensity by allowing them to first plant crops such as maize, followed by transplanted rice;
5. Helps manage labor allocation between upland and *bas-fond* fields;
6. Reduces soil erosion when infrastructure such as contour ridges are used;
7. Encourages men who had abandoned rice production because of declining
   rainfall to return to *bas-fond* rice production.

For many fields, however, effective plot-level water control does not exist because fields do not have internal dikes.

Potential Contribution of *Bas-fond* Rice Production to Increase the Food Supply

The potential contribution of *bas-fond* rice production can be assessed in terms of the per capita quantity of paddy rice produced in each village, and what this production level represents in the total domestic rice supply in comparison with commercial imports and food aid. Table 1 presents the yields from selected *bas-fond* villages and per capita milled rice production. In six of the ten villages, per

Table 1. **Contribution of *bas-fond* rice production, Mali, cropping season 1995–96.**

Location	Bas-Fond Area Cultivated (ha)	Village Population	Yield (kg paddy/ ha)	Total Paddy Production (t)	Per Capita Milled Rice Production[a](kg)
Kado	108	3,542	1,099	119	22
Diassola	3	221	2,989	9	26
Kafuziéla	69	1,625	886	61	26
Solo	32	1,400	1,940	62	29
Niéna	128	3,457	1,433	183	34
Banko	35	806	1,465	51	41
Faradié	34	398	1,046	36	58
Sola	300	1,900	591	177	61
Péniasso	125	840	1,011	126	98
Longorola	330	540	1,826	603	725
Mali-Sud	48,657[b]	-	1,216[c]	59,167[d]	-

(a) Computed using a 65 percent milling recovery rate.
(b) Total potentially cultivatable *bas-fond* area in Mali-Sud, based on a *bas-fond* inventory conducted by the CMDT in 1992.
(c) Assuming rice yields in the *bas-fond* area are equal to the average yield in the 12 surveyed villages.
(d) Estimated by multiplying the total potentially cultivatable *bas-fond* area by the assumed yield.
Source: Dimithè (1997).

Table 2. **Potential** *bas-fond* **and flooded plains rice production, as a percentage**[a] **of the rice supply from** *Office du Niger*, **commercial imports, and food aid.**

Rice Supply Source	*Bas-Fond* [b]	*Bas-Fond* & Plains[c]
Office du Niger [d]	31	143
Commercial Imports [e]	26	119
Food aid [f]	160	128
Commercial Imports & Food aid [g]	22	102

(a) *Bas-fond* (flooded plains) production potential divided by the respective rice supply sources.

(b) Estimated *bas-fond* production potential, 210,368 mt.

(c) Estimated flooded plains production potential, 189,091 mt.

(d) Average amount of rice supplied by the *Office du Niger* over the period 1991–95, 226,000 mt.

(e) Commercial imports (rice) in 1991, 226,000 mt.

(f) Food aid (rice) in 1991, 37,000 mt.

(g) Total commercial imports plus food aid, 263,000 mt.

capita milled rice production is higher than or equal to national average rice consumption (34 kg/person/year). In other words, *bas-fond* villages with surplus production of paddy could have rice to sell to deficit areas.

The importance of this contribution nationally is reflected when the "potential" level of *bas-fond* rice production is compared with the rice supply from the *Office du Niger*, as well as with commercial imports and food aid to Mali (table 2). Currently, only part of Mali-Sud's *bas-fond* area is planted to rice. However, if all of Mali-Sud *bas-fonds* (48,657 ha) were brought into production, and assuming the average yield observed in this study (1,216 kg/ha), 59,167 mt of paddy could be produced. This represents about 31 percent of the total paddy produced by the *Office du Niger* annually over the last five years, 26 percent of commercial rice imports, and 160 percent of food aid (rice) to Mali in 1991.

Only part of Mali-Sud's flooded plains are currently planted to rice. However, if all of Mali-Sud's flooded plains (173,000 ha) were brought into production, and assuming the average yield observed in the *bas-fonds*, 189,091 mt of paddy could be produced. This represents about 111 percent of the total paddy produced by the *Office du Niger* annually over the last five years, 93 percent of commercial rice imports, and 569 percent of food aid (rice).

Clearly, developing the untapped potential of Mali-Sud's *bas-fond* and flooded plains would significantly contribute to the government's effort to boost domestic rice production and thereby ensure an adequate food supply for all. This contribution could be even more significant if greater attention were given to addressing constraints that limit intensification of these systems. However, before investing in the development and intensification of traditional rice production, it is necessary to establish its profitability to farmers and to the country as a whole.

Potential Contribution of *Bas-fond* Rice Production to Increase Rural Household Income

The first part of this chapter documented the current level of rice production in the *bas-fonds*, and estimated its potential contribution to the national rice food supply. This section focuses on assessing whether *bas-fond* farmers would be willing to produce more rice by analyzing the profitability of the *bas-fond* rice enterprises, relative to upland crops which compete with rice for farmers' labor. To analyze the profitability of *bas-fond* rice production, rice farmers are grouped into four production systems (table 3) that are defined by their unique combination of inputs—water control, variety, fertilizer, and herbicide application.[14]

Since the *bas-fonds* are cultivated by small-scale farmers who also cultivate upland crops, the profitability of *bas-fond* rice production should account for the opportunity cost of not producing upland crops. By definition, the opportunity cost of family labor is the net return to labor from the best farmers' alternative, which is forgone by producing rice. Typically, farmers have a variety of revenue opportunities, including crop production and processing, livestock, handicrafts, hunting, and urban remittances. A study conducted in Mali-Sud by Giraudy and Niang[15] revealed that sources of revenues most cited by farmers are cotton (62 percent of the production units [Pus] surveyed) and

Table 3. **Predominant systems of *bas-fond* rice production, Mali-Sud.**

Production Systems	Water control	Varieties	Fertilizer	Herbicide
Purely Traditional	none	traditional	none	none
Macro-Semi-Intensive	yes	traditional	none	none
Micro-Semi-Intensive	none	traditional	none	some
Intensive	yes	improved	some	some

cereals (48 percent). Among the cereals, sorghum ranks first (22 percent), followed by millet (14 percent), maize (11 percent), rice (2 percent), and finger millet (1 percent). Given the difficulties in accurately estimating the opportunity cost of family labor, however, *bas-fond* financial profitability can be assessed in three ways.

First, an analysis can compare the returns to a day of family labor from alternative *bas-fond* rice production systems. While this identifies the systems' net returns to family labor relative to each other, it does not necessarily imply that they are profitable. Second, these returns can be compared with the opportunity cost of labor, based on the assumption that the next best alternative for family labor is to seek a wage employment. Nevertheless, it's recognized that rural wage labor may not represent a viable alternative to rice farming because such opportunities in these villages are seasonal and limited.[16]

Third, we can analyze the profitability of *bas-fond* rice production by comparing its net returns to family labor with its corresponding values from cotton, maize, and sorghum/millet, the main upland crops competing with rice for farmers' labor.

Relative profitability of alternative bas-fond *rice production systems*

Table 4 shows that, for all systems, the returns per day of family labor in rice (ranging from 1,374 to 2,971 CFAF/day) are higher than the opportunity cost of labor, estimated at 500 CFAF/day. Similarly, the cost of producing a kilogram of paddy (ranging from 43 to 78 CFAF/kg) is lower than the output farm-gate producer price (115 CFAF). These results indicate that these systems could be financially profitable. Among the four systems studied, the most profitable is the *micro-semi-intensive* system, which also has the lowest production costs, largely because of the use of herbicides to substitute for hired labor in weed control.

It is important to note that the results reported in table 4 are based on a single year of data. In addition, they do not account for the production risks associated with the prevailing erratic rainfall and poor water control in these *bas-fonds*. However, sensitivity analysis shows that, under the *traditional* production system, a 32 percent yield decrease would be necessary for farmers' net returns to fall to zero (break-even), *ceteris paribus*. The same estimate is 38 percent for the *macro-semi-intensive* system, 63 percent for the *micro-semi-intensive* system, and 35 percent for the *intensive* system.[17] Furthermore, the distribution of the net returns to labor among farmers in each of these systems shows that the profitability of the enterprise varies even within a given system.

Table 4. **Comparative financial budgets for the** *bas-fond* **rice enterprises, Mali, rainy season 1995–96.**

Production Systems	(CFAF/ha)				(CFAF/kg)	(CFAF/day)
	Gross Revenues[a]	Total Variable Costs[b]	Total Fixed Costs[b]	Total Production Costs[b]	Paddy Production Costs[C]	Net Return/ Day of Family Labor
Purely Traditional	117415	58815	0.00	58815	78	1374
Macro-Semi-Intensive	141680	69492	0	69492	72	1934
Micro-Semi-Intensive	163645	40338	0	40338	43	2971
Intensive	272090	147407	0	147407	74	2194

(a)   Paddy is valued at 115 CFAF/kg. The currency exchange rate in 1996 was US $1 = 560 CFAF.
(b)   Excluding family labor.
(c)   Excluding family labor valued at 500 CFAF/day of farm work.
Source: Dimithè (1997).

From a production risk standpoint, the micro-semi-intensive system continues to be the most attractive of all four systems.

Profitability of bas-fond *rice production relative to upland crops production*

Bas-fonds are complex production environments in which water availability, soil texture, and related physical and chemical properties vary along the toposequence.[18] Furthermore, because small-scale farmers cultivate upland and *bas-fond* fields, the interrelationships that link upland and *bas-fond* activities are a particularly important dimension of the *bas-fond* agroecosystems. In this context, the successful promotion of *bas-fond* rice production will depend in part on its profitability relative to the main competing upland crops—cotton, maize, and sorghum/millet. The financial enterprise budgets for the cotton, maize, and sorghum/millet enterprises are summarized in table 5.

Among upland crops, maize and then sorghum/millet are the most profitable, followed by cotton which yields the lowest return to a day of family labor. The returns for a day of family labor from the rice, maize, and sorghum/millet enterprises are higher than the opportunity cost of wage labor (500 CFAF/day), regardless of the level of mechanization. The return per day of family labor from cotton is higher than a daily wage only when the farmer

Table 5. **Comparative financial budgets for maize, sorghum, and cotton enterprises in the *bas-fond* villages, by level of mechanization, Mali, rainy season 1995–96.[19]**

	Gross Revenues[a]	Total Variable Costs[b]	Total Fixed Costs[b]	Total Production Costs[b]	Net Return to Family Labor	Net Return/ Day of Family Labor
Manual						
Maize	87,150	1,272	0	1,272	85,878	1,128
Sorghum/millet	62,550	1,272	0	1,272	61,278	823
Cotton	160,580	62,222	0	62,222	98,358	485
One implement						
Maize	106,275	34,717	1,123	35,840	70,435	1,157
Sorghum/millet	73,350	3,136	6,359	9,495	63,855	1,072
Cotton	184,140	64,086	24,093	88,179	95,961	591
More than one implement						
Maize	119,100	34,848	3,962	38,810	80,290	1,318
Sorghum/millet	86,310	4,663	24,343	29,006	57,304	962
Cotton	234,670	65,613	113,705	179,318	55,352	341

(a)   Maize is valued at 75 CFAF/kg, sorghum/millet at 90 CFAF/kg, and cotton at 115 CFAF/kg.

Source: Adapted from Giraudy and Niang (1994) in Dimithè (1997).

uses one implement. But in comparison, all four *bas-fond* rice production systems (table 4) yield higher returns for a day of family labor than any of the three upland crop enterprises.

These calculations assume that the fixed costs in *bas-fond* rice production (especially the cost of water control infrastructure) are zero because they are borne by CMDT. As these costs are transferred to farmers, the profitability of *bas-fond* rice production relative to upland crops would diminish. As this happens, a key question will be whether greater intensification of *bas-fond* rice production would induce a significant number of farmers to abandon or reduce cotton cultivation, and thereby decrease its production.

Currently cotton appears unprofitable because almost all fixed costs of upland crops are attributed to cotton production. Cotton production drives the household farm enterprises and the other crops free-ride on cotton for fixed investments. As a result, they tend to appear profitable compared to cotton. But because cotton ensures farmers' access to inputs (which go to food crops) via the cotton development agency's (CMDT) credit system and guarantees an income from sales, farmers have greater flexibility in deciding when to market their food crops. Furthermore, for the country as a whole, cotton production offers important growth linkages with the livestock and processing sub-sectors, as well as demand and fiscal linkages. Cotton seed is sold as livestock feed, while ginning will create important processing opportunities.

Compared to the upland crops, *bas-fond* rice production is a meaningful complementary source of income for farmers, especially for women. While several constraints would have to be relaxed to extend and intensify *bas-fond* rice production, the associated relative financial profitability and utility value suggest that if given greater attention, the *bas-fonds* could make a major contribution to raising rural household incomes and thereby increase household access to food and reduce food insecurity.

Competitiveness

Competitiveness can be defined as the ability of a given system to produce rice of a specific quality, at a given point in time, in a specific market, at a lower unit cost than another rice production system. This definition recognizes that competitiveness is a relative term. For example, a given rice production system can be more competitive than another rice production system in the regional market at a specific time in the year, for a given rice quality. At the same time, it might be less competitive than the same production system in a local market, given consumer preferences and transportation costs. The immediate implication of this definition is that evaluating the competitiveness of different rice production systems requires that these systems be compared at different market levels, for the same rice quality, and during the same time period. In the following analysis, Sikasso, Bougouni, and Bamako are used as output markets. *Bas-fond* rice quality is categorized as 45 percent broken rice, which is comparable in quality to Thai A1 super.

To assess the competitiveness of alternative production systems, comparing production costs is often inconclusive because these costs are frequently distorted by government policies or market failures. As a result, a crop can be profitable for farmers (for example, because of price subsidies), even though its production may not represent an efficient use of resources from the point of view of the country. Conversely, a crop can be unprofitable for farmers, even though its production represents an efficient use of the country's resources.

The domestic resource cost (DRC) framework offers what Michael Morris describes as a way to "see-through market distortions" in order to measure competitiveness empirically by generating quantitative indicators of the efficiency of using domestic resources to produce a given crop. In this framework, the measure of efficiency is social profit, defined as each production system's net contribution per hectare of cultivated land to the national income.[20]

First, DRC ratios are estimated for subsistence and commercial *bas-fond* farms.[21] To determine these DRC ratios, fertilizer and paddy market prices were adjusted to reflect their social value, and the cost items are grouped into their tradable and nontradable components. In this process, the costs of CMDT investments to control water, which were excluded in the financial analysis because they are borne by CMDT, are included. In addition, secondary data are used to estimate similar budgets and DRC ratios for two commercial rice production systems managed by the *Office du Niger*—a rehabilitated perimeter in Niono and a non-rehabilitated perimeter in Macina. All these DRC ratios are estimated by varying the distance between each of the central markets under consideration and the village where the rice was produced.[22] Figures 1 to 4 illustrate results for the *bas-fond* systems; table 6 shows the results for the *Office du Niger* systems.

Figure 1 shows how the DRC ratios for subsistence *bas-fond* systems vary over space, as the distance between the production/consumption point and Bamako increases. Figure 1 also shows that the four systems have DRCs that are less than 0.7, regardless of the distance between the production/consumption point and Bamako. In other words, producing rice for home consumption in any of the Mali-Sud *bas-fond* systems is a better use of domestic resources than shipping rice from outside the region into Mali-Sud to feed these farm households. It is important to note, however, that this result does not account for the production risks associated with erratic rainfall and poor water control in the *bas-fonds*.

Figures 2, 3, and 4 illustrate how DRC ratios for commercial *bas-fond* rice production systems vary over space, depending on the market in which the farmers sell their rice. These figures show that the further the production site is from the sale point, the less competitive these systems become. However, the production site would have to be very far from the market for any of the *bas-fond* systems to lose their competitiveness in those three output markets.

More specifically, figure 2 shows that, if commercial *bas-fond* farmers sell their rice in Bamako, the *macro-semi-intensive* system is not competitive (DRC>1), regardless of the distance between Bamako and the production site.

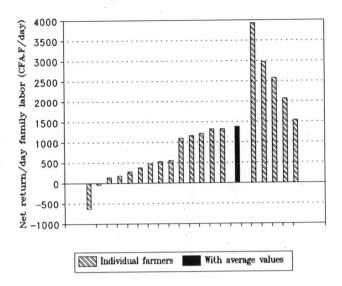

Figure 1. Distribution of net returns per day of family labor among sampled farmers (N=19) following the *bas-fond traditional* rice production system, Mali, 1996.

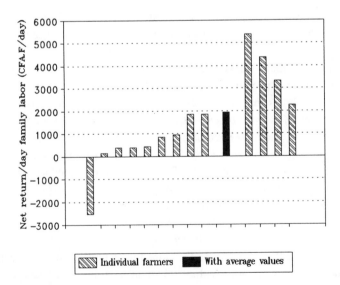

Figure 2. Distribution of net returns per day of family labor among sampled farmers (N=13) following the *bas-fond macro-semi-intensive* rice production system, Mali, 1996.

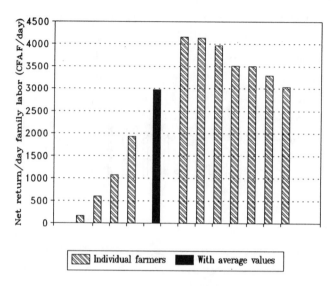

Figure 3. **Distribution of net returns per day of family labor among sampled farmers (N=11) following the *bas-fond micro-semi-intensive* rice production system, Mali, 1996.**

In contrast, the *intensive* system is competitive (DRC<1) in Bamako if the production site is less than 740 km away from Bamako. Rice produced in both the *traditional* and the *micro-semi-intensive bas-fond* production systems is competitive in the Bamako market for farms located less than 1,000 km away from Bamako, which include all Mali-Sud's *bas-fond* rice production sites.

    Figure 3 shows that, while not competitive when Bamako is the output market (figure 2), the *macro-semi-intensive* production system is competitive if *bas-fond* farmers within 288 km of Bougouni sell their rice in this town's market, which is closer to the rice production area than Bamako. Similarly, the *intensive* system is competitive in the Bougouni market if produced within 945 km of Bougouni. Rice from both the *traditional* and the *micro-semi-intensive bas-fond* rice productions are competitive in the Bougouni market for farms located less than 1,000 km from Bougouni.

    Finally, figure 4 shows that, the *macro-semi-intensive* production system is competitive in the Sikasso market, the closest main city to the production sites, if production occurs on farms within 408 km of Sikasso and farmers sell in this market. Similarly, the other three systems are competitive in Sikasso as long as the production site is within 1,000 km of the city.

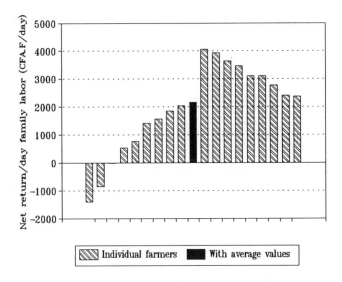

Figure 4. **Distribution of net returns per day of family labor among sampled farmers (N=18) following the *bas-fond intensive* rice production system, Mali, 1996.**

Table 6 summarizes the DRC ratios associated with commercial *Office du Niger* production systems. When family labor is valued at 500 CFAF/day, rice harvested from these two systems is not competitive in any of the three markets. However, if the opportunity cost of family labor is assumed to be zero, rice produced in both of these two systems is only competitive in Sikasso.

Comparing the *bas-fond* (figures 2–4) to the *Office du Niger* (table 6) systems indicates that, within 1,000 km of the *bas-fond* production area, rice from the *bas-fond* systems would be more competitive than rice of the same quality harvested from any of the *Office du Niger* systems, if sold either in Bougouni (figure 3) or Sikasso (figure 4). The same conclusion holds if farmers sell their rice harvest in Bamako, except that in this case the competitive superiority of the *bas-fond's macro-semi-intensive* systems is limited to 700 km. Clearly, this result leads to the conclusion that, from the national perspective, it is less costly to produce 45 percent broken rice quality in the *bas-fonds* than in perimeters managed by the *Office du Niger*, assuming farmers' harvests are sold either in Bamako, Bougouni, or Sikasso.

Table 6. DRC ratios[a] for commercial *Office du Niger* rice production, by sale point, Mali, 1996

Production Systems	Family labor wage rate = 500 CFAF/day			Family labor wage rate = 0 CFAF/day		
	Bamako	Bougouni	Sikasso	Bamako	Bougouni	Sikasso
Rehab. perimeter	1.295	1.264	1.179	1.066	1.042	0.974
Non-rehab. perimeter	1.275	1.243	1.147	1.080	1.053	0.971

(a) Computed as the ratio of domestic factor cost to value added measured in social prices, where value added is the value of total production less the cost of tradable inputs.
Source: Dimithè (1997).

Conclusion

For three fundamental reasons, *bas-fond* rice production could be a major contribution to improving household food security in Mali. First, if all Mali-Sud *bas-fonds* were brought into production, it would represent about 31 percent of the total amount of paddy produced in the *Office du Niger* annually over the last five years, and 22 percent of commercial imports and food aid to Mali. If all Mali-Sud *bas-fonds* and flooded plains were brought into production, this could supply about 43 percent more paddy than the average annual quantity of paddy produced in the *Office du Niger* over the last five years, and roughly the same amount of annual imports through commercial imports and food aid.

Second, it makes sense for *bas-fond* farmers to produce rice because this enterprise is not only financially profitable, but it also yields higher returns to a day of family labor than the three upland crop enterprises. Hence, by increasing rural incomes, *bas-fond* production raises rural households' access to food. Finally, the *bas-fond* rice production enterprise also makes sense from the national perspective. The DRC ratios show that the contribution of *bas-fond* rice production to Mali's economy is sufficiently large to justify the resources required to develop these systems. In addition, *bas-fond* rice production uses domestic resources more efficiently than the two *Office du Niger* systems studied (that is, the non-rehabilitated perimeter of Macina and the rehabilitated perimeter of Niono).

Given the positive financial and economic performance of *bas-fond* rice production, there are two complementary (farm-level) ways to bring about increases in production. One is through an extensification strategy that expands the current technology over a wider production area. The preceding analysis of the profitability of *bas-fond* rice production is an analysis of this option. Currently, only parts of the *bas-fonds* are utilized because of poor water control conditions. In order to fully utilize the total potential area of Mali-Sud *bas-fonds*, it would be necessary to improve the water control system and address other constraints faced by *bas-fond* rice farmers, especially labor constraints of hand weeding. The existing quality and effectiveness of water control infrastructure—that is, dams across streams with no internal control of the water level—can be improved with complementary investments in plot-level water control (for example, internal bonding) and a system of canals.

The high profitability of the *micro-semi-intensive system* compared with other systems indicates that given the current degree of water control in the *bas-fonds*, insufficient labor for weeding is the most serious production constraint. The share of labor costs in the total production cost (relative to other cost items) in each of the four most common *bas-fond* systems suggests that, if scientists succeed in identifying relatively low-cost labor-saving technologies, the financial profitability of these systems could be significantly higher. Efforts to reduce labor costs should assess the potential of reducing labor input through the substitution of adapted and economically justifiable labor-saving technologies such as herbicide, mechanical threshing, sickle harvesting, and better water control systems to reduce weeds.

A complementary way to increase *bas-fond* rice production is through an intensification strategy involving the use of yield-increasing modern inputs such as improved varieties, herbicide and fertilizer applications, and accounting for local resources and farmers' specific conditions. While the analysis of the profitability of rice in this chapter focuses on current technology, intensifying *bas-fond* rice production requires addressing a number of constraints.[23]

First, because the varieties farmers currently plant were developed for a much drier area, their yields tend to be lower compared to those observed in the *Office du Niger*. The intensification of *bas-fond* rice farming will depend heavily upon the development of high-yielding varieties. However, transferring on-station results to the complex *bas-fond* environment represents an enormous challenge for Malian researchers because they must develop higher-yielding varieties that are appropriate for the more unstable *bas-fond* environment with poor water control.[24] Short-term rapid yield increases can be achieved through traditional plant breeding strategies that rely on selecting appropriate genetic material from the world collection, producing crosses, and screening the most promising selections under farmers' agro-environments. For this effort to succeed, however, scientists will need to adopt a participatory approach in order to combine the experimental knowledge of farmers and more formal scientific understanding. The *bas-fond* plant breeding program should give priority to: (1) yield potential and stability, (2) the growth duration of the rice plant in relation to the length of the flooding period and the water level, (3) the potential for double cropping, and (4) plant characteristics, including resistance to diseases and water stress, height and architecture in relation to the water level.

Second, the yield potential of improved varieties will not be realized in farmers' fields unless scientists also develop appropriate complementary technologies to relax fertility, pest, and disease constraints, and to improve water control. Indeed, it is important to recognize that currently the most pressing constraint on higher rice yields is not the physiological potential of the varieties farmers plant. Rather, inadequate water control, soil infertility, pests, and diseases are the key factors that prevent farmers from fully exploiting the full potential of the varieties they currently plant.

Third, *bas-fond* rice research activities in Mali have been limited in scope due to limited funding and human capital. Unless sufficient financial support is available, it will be impossible to carry out the research required to generate appropriate technologies suitable for intensifying *bas-fond* rice farming. Thus, for these efforts to succeed, the Malian agricultural research system must mobilize a political constituency in support of agricultural research. However, as is the case throughout West Africa, Malian researchers have not been strong advocates for public investment in research. As funding from the government and the donor community continues to dwindle, there is an increasing need for researchers to become proactive advocates of the value of agricultural research, especially given the limited political power of the farmers.

Finally, efforts to modernize rice farming in Mali have largely centered on promoting the adoption of modern varieties and increased use of fertilizer and herbicide, all of which require capital. Yet, although *bas-fond* rice farmers are predominantly women (88 percent), existing institutional arrangements do not provide women direct access to new rice technologies and other resources such as credit. Currently, the main source of improved technology is the CMDT, a government agency that only provides credit to cotton farmers. Because all cotton farmers are men, many of whom are not willing to borrow for their wives, very few women farmers have access to modern inputs. This condition is worsened by the patriarchal nature of the rural social structure which tends not to expect women to generate household income. As a result, women have limited access to household resources for investing in rice.

Notes

1. World Bank 1993.

2. The discussion in this chapter is based on secondary data and survey-generated data collected from a random sample of 334 farmers selected from a purposive sample of twelve *bas-fond* villages in Mali-Sud, during the cropping season 1995–96.

3. Samega 1991.

4. Staatz et al. 1989.

5. DNSI 1994a, 1994b.

6. Ibid.

7. Ministère de l'Agriculture, de l'Elevage, et de l'Environnement 1992a, 1992b, 1992c.

8. World Bank 1992.

9. Haïdara et al. 1998.

10. Ibid.

11. World Bank 1992.

12. CMDT 1992.

13. Ahmadi et al. 1995.

14. Inputs are valued at the market prices farmers paid for, non-purchased resources are valued at their opportunity costs, and outputs are valued at the average farm-gate price received by farmers at harvest.

15. Giraudy and Niang 1994.

16. Dimithè 1997.

17. Ibid.

18. Carsky and Masajo 1992.

19. The data used to develop these budgets are adapted from a study conducted within the cotton development agency (CMDT) by Giraudy and Niang (1994) and labor data collected by IER's Farming Systems Research Program in 1988 and 1989.

20. Morris 1990. The DRC framework generates two measures of the relative efficiency of alternative production systems: net social profit (NSP) and the domestic resource cost (DRC) ratio. However, both indicators lead to the same conclusions. The NSP indicates the contribution of each rice production system to national income, measured in terms of social net returns to family labor and management. In contrast, the DRC ratio, which is a restatement of the NSP expressed as a unitless ratio, indicates the efficiency of each alternative system in using domestic resources to earn or save one unit of foreign exchange. It is computed as the ratio of domestic factor cost to value added measured in social prices, where value added is the value of total production less the cost of tradable inputs. This chapter uses the DRC ratio.

21. *Bas-fond* farms that consume all of the rice they produce are defined as subsistence farms; *bas-fond* farms that sell all of their production are considered to be commercial farms.

22. A detailed discussion of these estimations is reported in Dimithè 1997.

23. Dimithè 1997.

24. Ibid.

Acknowledgement

This essay is a revised version of the author's article, "Potential Contribution of *Bas-Fond* Rice Production for Improving Food Security in Mali," published in *Food Policy*. Both the article and this essay are extracted from "An Economic Analysis of the Competitiveness of Alternative Rice Production Systems: the Case of *Bas-Fond* Rice Production in Mali-Sud," by Georges Dimithè (Unpublished Ph.D. dissertation, 1997. Department of Agricultural Economics, Michigan State University). Requirements for the degree of doctor of philosophy under the title "An Economic Analysis of the Competitiveness of Alternative Rice Production Systems: The Case of *Bas-Fond* Rice Production in Mali-Sud." Funding for this research was provided by the Food Security II Cooperative Agreement (AEP-5459-A-00-2041-00) between Michigan State University (MSU) and the United States Agency for International Development (USAID) through the Africa Bureau, Office of Sustainable Development, Productive Sectors, Growth and Environment Division, Technology Development and Transfer Unit (AFR/SD/PSGE/TDT), the Mali Research Institute (IER)/Inland Valley Consortium in Mali, and the West African Rice Development Association (WARDA). The field survey was conducted by the MSU Food Security II project, in collaboration with the Malian national research institute's subsector economic research program (ECOFIL), and its Farming Systems and *Bas-Fond* Rice Research programs. I am greatly indebted to Dr. J. M. Staatz, Dr. R. Bernsten, and Dr. R. J. Bingen, professors at MSU, for their invaluable contributions when reviewing the early drafts. I am also grateful to IER/ECOFIL researchers for their assistance during field work. The opinions reported in this chapter are the author's and do not necessarily reflect those of WARDA, IER, or MSU.

Bibliography

Ahmadi, N., B. Traoré, F. Blanchet, O. Lefay, J. Montillet, et M. Simpara. 1995. "Riziculture de Bas-Fond et Aménagents peu Coûteux au Mali-Sud: De la Parcelle au Terroir, Optimisation d'Innovations Techniques par une démarche Intégrée et Participative." Colloque International CNRS/CIRAD sur l'Avenir de la Riziculture en Afrique de l'Ouest, Bordeaux, 4–7 avril 1995.

Carsky, R. J., and T. M. Masajo. 1992. "Effect of toposequence position on the performance of rice varieties in inland valley of West Africa." IITA/ Resource and Crop Management Research Monograph No. 9.

Compagnie Malienne pour le Développement des Textiles (CMDT). 1992. Inventaire des Plaines et Bas-fonds. Direction Régionale/Sikasso.

Dimithè, Georges. 1997. "An economic analysis of the competitiveness of alternative rice production systems: The case of *bas-fond* rice production in

Mali-Sud." Unpublished Ph.D. dissertation. Department of Agricultural Economics, Michigan State University.

Direction Nationale de la Statistique et de l'Informatique (DNSI). 1994a. Enquête Budget Consommation 1988–1989. Volume 0: Résultats Bruts. Bamako.

————. 1994b. Enquête Agricole de Conjoncture Campagne 1993/1994: Résultats Définitifs. Bamako.

Giraudy, F. et M. Niang. 1994. "Revenus Paysans en Zone Mali-Sud: Première Partie: Revenus et Dépenses des Individus et des Exploitations." Compagnie Maliénne de Développement des Textiles (CMDT)/Suivi Evaluation.

Haïdara et al. 1998. "Memorandum de Politiques sur la Filière Rizicole Nationale. Version Définitive." Ministère du Développement Rural/Cellule de Planification et de Statistiques/Micro Projet de Formation à la MAP.

Mikklesen, Duane S., and Suraijit K. De Datta. 1991. "Rice culture." In *Rice* (2nd edition), edited by Bor S. Luh. New York: Van Nostrand Reinhold.

Ministère de l'Agriculture, de l'Elevage et de l'Environnement. 1992a. Schéma Directeur du Secteur Développement Rural: volume 2—Stratégies de Développement.

————. 1992b. Schéma Directeur du Secteur Développement Rural: volume 3—Plan d'Action.

————. 1992c. Schéma Directeur du Secteur Développement Rural: volume 1—Stratégie Générale.

Morris, M. L. 1990. *Determining Comparative Advantage through DRC Analysis: Guidelines Emerging from CIMMYT's Experience.* CIMMYT Economics Paper No. 1. Mexico.

Samega, D. 1991. "Situation Alimentaire et Nutritionelle à partir des Résultats de l'EBC 1988-1989." Direction Nationale de la Statistique et de l'Informatique, Mali.

Staatz, M. J., J. Dioné, and N. N. Dembélé. 1989. "Cereals market liberalization in Mali." *World Development* 17 (5): 703–18.

World Bank. 1989. World Development Report 1989. Washington, D.C.

————. 1992. Mali Irrigation Policy Report. APD/SD/AR. Washington, D.C.

————. 1993. World Development Report 1993. Washington, D.C.

Cotton in Mali: The "White Revolution" and Development

JAMES TEFFT

I t is no oversimplification to state that as cotton goes, so go the prospects for development in Mali. Cotton has always figured predominantly in the country's economic and social life, and a good year for cotton production and marketing is also usually a good year for food production and overall economic progress. But the contribution of cotton to Malian development continues to be risky and uncertain.

From the mid-1970s through the late 1980s, cotton production grew rapidly, despite large fluctuations in world prices and some unprofitable years. In the early 1990s, low world prices, an overvalued CFA[1] franc and low productivity growth created a crisis situation that, in retrospect, was averted only by the January 1994 50 percent devaluation of the CFA franc and the subsequent doubling of world market prices for cotton. Helped by good rains, the area under cultivation and the production of seed (unginned) cotton production rose dramatically. Exports increased and despite farmers' increased production costs, net income rose for most of them. In the same manner, although the cost of producing cotton lint (ginned cotton) has more than doubled since devaluation, higher world prices have permitted the parastatal production and marketing agency, the CMDT (*Compagnie Malienne pour le Développement des Fibres Textiles*), to earn windfall profits.

Although cotton has performed relatively well since the 1994 devaluation, the continued reliance on cotton to drive the country's development raises three key challenges. First, the large expansion in the area under cultivation, the decreased use of fallow periods between cropping cycles, and the absence of sufficient organic and inorganic fertilization suggest that environmental degradation and soil fertility problems may constrain both cotton and cereals production over the long term. Second, the volatility of world cotton prices and the competitive nature of international markets mean that continuing efforts must be made to improve productivity at both farm and industrial levels. Since the solution to these first two challenges will undoubtedly require substantial financial resources, deciding how to use subsector profits for reinvestment in the cotton subsector, for financing the government's budget, or for strategic investment in other sectors of the economy presents a third major challenge for the Malian government.

The manner in which the government addresses these issues will depend greatly on the future evolution of the structure and organization of cotton production and marketing as well as the complementary public development activities in the cotton zones. More specifically, continued improvements in the productivity of cotton will be directly affected by the government's decision either to maintain its current integrated system of production and marketing, or to follow demands from the IMF-World Bank for the liberalization of the cotton subsector and the privatization of the CMDT.[2]

In the discussion on restructuring the subsector, the fundamental question comes down to this: What is the best way of organizing individual and collective action to improve productivity at different levels of the subsector, and to improve coordination among those levels, while taking into account economies of scale and avoiding rent-seeking behavior? In short, restructuring the cotton subsector involves determining the appropriate roles for various actors (CMDT, farmers, private business, and government agencies) and empowering them with the legal, financial, organizational, and technical resources needed to successfully carry out those roles.[3]

The ability of the government to effectively analyze these different issues and future options facing the cotton subsector depends, in turn, on the development of an independent policy analysis capacity capable of examining the complex and dynamic interactions between government policies, technological change, institutional reform, human capital, and their relationship to external factors in the international and national economy.

The information presented in this chapter on the response of farmers and the CMDT in the post-devaluation period (1994–98) discusses factors affecting current and future subsector performance and offers some insights on guidelines for future investment. Following a brief historical overview of the cotton subsector, the second part of the chapter discusses the 1994 devaluation of the CFA and the responses to this devaluation by farmers and the CMDT. The chapter concludes with a look at the kinds of constraints, opportunities, and challenges raised by the production of cotton for development in Mali.

Foundations of the "White Revolution"

The historical success of cotton in Mali can be attributed to a 50-year period of experience in developing an integrated and carefully coordinated set of activities critical to producing and marketing a quality product.[4] The approach begins with a varietal breeding research program that integrates Mali's national agricultural research program at the *Institut d'Economie Rurale* (IER) into a network of other West and Central African breeding programs managed by CIRAD, the French *Centre de coopération internationale en recherche agronomique pour le développement.* A credit system managed by the CMDT[5] facilitates the purchase of equipment and supplies, and an extensive network of CMDT field agents closely monitor all phases of production. Continued association with the CFDT *(Compagnie Française pour le Développement des Fibres Textiles)* allows the CMDT to receive technical expertise for its ginning operations. Moreover, the CMDT relies almost exclusively on COPACO, the marketing arm of the CFDT, to market the largest share of its cotton along with that from several other West African countries. This relationship has allowed the CMDT to develop a market identity for Malian cotton and to benefit from economies of scale that would not otherwise be possible. [6]

Largely as a result of this highly integrated management and commercial system, the area under cotton cultivation expanded rapidly between 1960 and 1964. More impressively, from the mid-1960s through the mid-1970s, cotton yields increased by 12 percent per year—from 322 kg/ha to 1,156 kg/ha—finally reaching 1,300 kg/ha in the early 1990s. Similarly, the varietal breeding program has developed varieties with ginning ratios that are among the highest in the world.[7] Equally important, cotton producers have tended to be among the most successful food crop producers. Thus, while the levels of cereal production for the country as a whole have varied widely since the 1960s, per capita coarse grain production relative to regional averages is much higher in CMDT zones because farmers have access to CMDT-supplied fertilizer, equipment, and higher yielding maize varieties.

The mid-1980s malaise

In the mid-1980s, the world price of cotton dropped precipitously. The average market year price according to Cotlook Index A[8] fell 21 percent from US$0.88/lb in 1983/84 to US$0.69/lb in 1984/85. It then dropped another 29 percent to US$0.49/lb in 1985/86.[9] Prices bounced back 27 percent in 1986/87, but were canceled out by the 23 percent depreciation of the dollar relative to the French franc.

In 1985/86, the CMDT's total per kilo unit cost to produce cotton fiber averaged 505 CFAF, 130 CFAF/kg higher than the average sales price (375 CFAF/kg). As a condition of financial assistance to overcome its almost 9 billion CFAF deficit during 1985/86, several foreign aid agencies required the CMDT to undertake a series of cost-saving measures as one means to move toward financial equilibrium. These measures included a reduction in input subsidies, sub-contracting for lower cost transportation, freezing producer prices at 85 CFAF/kg, enforcing more rigorous management practices, and assuming direct control over cotton exports.[10] These measures helped reduce the total unit cost 14 percent to approximately 435 CFAF/kg and thereby allowed the CMDT to break even in the following two growing seasons.[11]

Devaluation and Cotton

The January 1994 devaluation of the CFA franc was aimed at reducing the heavy dependence of the West Africa franc zone on imports, stimulating export production and import substitution, and shifting consumer demand towards more locally produced goods and services. The ultimate goal was to stimulate self-sustaining, broad-based economic growth, which would reduce Mali's widespread poverty and food insecurity.[12]

The means by which devaluation of a currency is supposed to change economic incentives are well known. By modifying the exchange rate, a devaluation raises the price of imports relative to domestically produced goods, discourages imports, and stimulates demand for local goods. In doing so, a devaluation increases the incentives to produce internationally traded goods, such as cotton. But with a commodity like cotton in Mali, where the price paid to the farmer is fixed institutionally by the CMDT, farmer incentives to increase cotton production (and thereby exports) are improved only as the increase in the international market sales price of cotton is reflected in higher prices paid to farmers. In addition, this higher price must be superior to the farmers' increased cost for the imported inputs used to produce cotton.[13]

In response to the higher world cotton lint sales price, the CMDT raised the nominal producer price of cotton 65 percent from 85 to 140 CFA francs per kilo between 1994 and 1998. Moreover, when a 35 percent rebate share from the CMDT's profits, or 30 CFAF/kg for each of the last three seasons, is added to this price, this doubles the farmers' total price per kilo of cotton. In real terms, the average producer price increased 39 percent over the five-year period.

Despite these increases, however, the farmers' share of total export value changed little after the 1994 devaluation. The smaller, incremental increases in the base producer price and rebate lagged behind the immediate large jump in total export value in 1994. The combined effect of the rising world market price and the appreciation of the U.S. dollar relative to the French franc was superior to the increase in nominal producer prices in 1994 and 1995, thereby decreasing the farmers' share to 39 percent. But subsequent increases in the price paid to farmers, together with the annual drop in world prices beginning in 1995/96, slowly brought the farmers' share back close to pre-devaluation levels (54 percent). Some observers argue that liberalizing the cotton subsector would increase producers' price share to levels in other countries (>70 percent), leading in turn to higher incomes and greater growth.

Improved farm-level prices spurred large increases in cotton production and in the quantity of cotton ginned. Annual growth rates averaged 21 percent between 1994/95 and 1997/98, almost double the 11 percent annual rate over the period 1961 to 1993. [14] For the most part, a significant expansion in the area cultivated in cotton explains this growth. In contrast, cotton yields dropped 18 percent from the 1990/91–1993/94 average level of 1,285 kg/ha to the 1994/95–1997/98 average of 1,110 kg/ha. [15]

Gross cotton fiber sales revenues increased from 43 billion CFAF in 1992/93 to approximately 200 billion CFAF in 1997/98, a gain of 365 percent. While the CMDT lost 65 CFAF for every kilogram of cotton lint sold in the years immediately preceding devaluation, gross profits per kilogram of cotton fiber after devaluation ranged from 262 CFA to 347 CFA between 1994 and 1997.

When viewed from the perspective of the Malian economy, the value of all cotton product exports—lint (98 percent), fabric, cotton seed oil, and cake— increased at an annual rate of over 19 percent between 1993 and 1999, a cumulative jump of 188 percent. Cotton's share of the value of all exports increased from 27 percent in 1993 to 50 percent in 1999, a gain of 84 percent. This large increase in export earnings helped the Malian government meet its growing debt service requirements in the first years after devaluation.

Cotton After Devaluation

Farm-level production trends and practices

The annual growth rates over the last four years—1995 to 1999—for area cultivated, cotton yields, and production listed by CMDT production zone (see table 1) underscore a general trend toward extensification and decline in land

Table 1. Average annual growth rates of area cultivated, yields and production in CMDT zones, 1994/1995–1997/1998.

CMDT Zone	Area cultivated, growth rate			Yield, growth rate			Production, growth rate		
	Cotton	Cereals	Total	Cotton	Maize	Millet-Sorghum	Cotton	Maize	Millet-Sorghum
Fana	24	11	15	-2.5	0.9	-0.8	20	16	9.0
Bougouni	24	13	16	-1.1	3.4	0.3	23	17	9.6
Sikasso	22	9	14	-1.3	2.1	-3.4	21	15	1.6
Koutiala	25	11	15	-6.8	-1.3	-3.9	16	14	6.2
San	20	26	22	1.6	0.2	-1.3	22	16	26.0
Total	25	14	17	-3.1	1.3	-2.6	21	16	10.5

Source: CMDT 1999

Table 2. Post-devaluation changes in area planted to cotton and cereals, CMDT zones.

CMDT Zone	Cotton				Cereals				Total	
	Hectares		% Cotton in Total Hectares		Hectares		% Cereals in Total Hectares		Hectares	
	93/94	97/98	93/94	97/98	93/94	97/98	93/94	97/98	93/94	97/98
Fana	1.75	3.6	25	33	4.1	5.6	59	51	7	10.9
Bougouni	.99	1.9	21	28	2.9	3.8	61	55	4.7	7
Sikasso	1.64	3.0	26	34	3.9	4.5	61	51	6.4	8.8
Koutiala	1.7	3.7	23	32	4.6	6.4	63	55	7.3	11.7
San	0.4	0.6	16	15	1.4	2.7	65	73	2.2	3.7
Kita		1.4		27		2.7		53		5.1
Average Change	85%		30		29%		-10%		45%	

Source: CMDT 1999

productivity. Area planted to both cotton and cereals grew rapidly after devaluation.[16] While earlier studies indicated some substitution of cotton for food crops in 1994 and 1995, as table 1 indicates, the area planted in cereals also increased after devaluation, albeit at a slower rate than cotton (table 2).[17] Most farmers have increased the area cultivated by reducing fallow periods and clearing new lands, the latter behavior predominant in the relatively newer production zones (for example, Bougouni, Kita).

Giraudy notes that farmers replaced the traditional five- to seven-year fallow period on 50 percent of their holdings with almost continuous cropping, although they still manage to keep the other one-half of their fields in a ten- to thirteen-year fallow system.[18] Kébé and Brons point out that in zones where there is human and animal demographic pressure on the land, many farmers have begun putting fallow land into production out of fear of losing their customary rights to a given parcel.[19]

On a per farm basis, the higher growth in area cultivated to cotton relative to cereals increased the percentage of the area in cotton on a farm from 23 to 30 percent, while reducing the area planted to cereals from 61 to 55 percent[20] and the slower rate of growth in the total area in cereals relative to cotton may raise some concerns, the total area planted to cereals rose 29 percent in four years from 3.4 to 4.4 hectares per farm. With the exception of the San zone, area cultivated to other crops also increased 0.4 hectares on average, representing a 50 percent increase. Overall, total farm size increased on average by 45 percent after devaluation.

Farmers were able to increase total area planted at such a fast rate after devaluation because of the growing availability and use of animal traction equipment. Since devaluation, the number of manual or nonequipped farms (type D) declined on average by 24 percent.[21] The number of farms in groups B and C increased in almost all zones, averaging respectively 6 and 11 percent. Changes in the best-equipped group (A) varied by zone; the number of type A farmers in Fana and Koutiala (with the most equipped farms) increased 6 and 17 percent respectively while the numbers fell between 4 and 8 percent in other zones. The growing numbers of semi-equipped farms are due primarily to the breakup of large, well-equipped (type A) extended family farms into more independent production units. This has resulted in a larger number of partially equipped farms and contributed to the cultivation of a larger percentage of marginal land.[22]

CMDT farming system surveys show that higher maize yields led to a 13.5 percent increase in average farm maize production (1,357 to 1,906 kg). This improvement offset the 12 percent drop in production for other coarse grains

Table 3. **Average annual gross cereal production, per capita (kg/person) by region and CMDT production zone (1989/1990–1997/1998).**

Region	CMDT zone	Regional average, kg/person	CMDT zone average, kg/person
Kayes		133	
	Kita		223
Koulikoro		225	
	Fana		407
Sikasso		311	
	Bougouni		241
	Koutiala		454
Segou		306	
	San		132
National		184	
CMDT			314

Source: DNSI 1999; CMDT 1999

(4,183 to 3,692 kg) resulting in a 1.0 percent increase in total cereal production (5,540 to 5,598 kg) among CMDT households.[23]

This growth represents a positive development in light of the 1.75 percent annual decrease in per capita coarse grain production in Mali over the last twelve years and highlights once again the beneficial effect of cotton production on cereals. The results in table 3 that compare mean annual per capita cereal production of CMDT farmers with the government's regional averages, reconfirm findings from previous studies that coarse grain production is higher among cotton farmers than non-cotton producers. Additional research has shown that better equipped cotton farms are more productive with higher yields for both cotton and coarse grains.[24]

With respect to cotton yields, outside of the Kita zone where CMDT is less than five years old, agronomic yields have been declining since 1992/93. Between 1994/95 and 1997/98, average cotton yields decreased 12 percent, from 1,196 to 1,058 kg/ha, while maize jumped 5 percent, from 1,925 kg/ha to 2,024 kg/ha. It is interesting to note that yields for all crops in the Koutiala zone, the heart of cotton country, have been decreasing faster than other zones.[25]

Input use, labor, and farm profitability

Inputs

Farmers' incentive to use fertilizer is dictated largely by the price of inputs that is, agricultural equipment and supplies) relative to the sales price of seed cotton. Since devaluation, the input-output price ratio has improved by 33 percent, indicating a relatively greater incentive to use inputs on cotton. The CMDT reports that the percentage of farmland in their zone receiving inputs increased from 32 to 43 percent between 1994/95 to 1997/98.[26] Determining the actual change in input use after devaluation with a reasonable degree of precision is complicated by the different results from the CMDT's and IER's farming system surveys. The CMDT reports a 12 percent rise in use of NPK (nitrogen-phosphorus-potassium fertilizer) between 1994/95 and 1997/98. IER findings for the period 1993/94 to 1996/97, on the other hand, show a change of -1 percent, -3 percent, 18 percent, and -15 percent respectively for farm types A, B, C, and D. Despite these variable results, both surveys report fertilizer levels that are on average 75 percent of recommended levels for NPKsb (NPK plus sulfur and boron) and 105–121 percent for urea). [27]

IER and CMDT report that some farmers, particularly those with less-equipped farms, use a part of their cotton fertilizer (NPKsb) on maize because of food security objectives, because they know that the high-yielding maize varieties are responsive to inputs, and because of their inability to procure quality fertilizer on credit at prices comparable to those offered by the CMDT.

Both surveys report increased use of organic matter for the semi- and fully equipped farms, but only minimal amounts applied by nonequipped farms. This augmentation can be partially explained by the price increase of inorganic fertilizers relative to organic matter and the tendency of some farmers to substitute manure for mineral fertilizer. This improvement has been facilitated by an increase in the total number of carts owned by cotton farmers (an 11 percent rate of growth between 1993/94 and 1997/98) as well as the increase in animals.

For coarse grains, better-equipped farmers increased the quantity of fertilizer (NPK) used on maize by over 100 percent after devaluation.[28] The quantity of urea also increased among the equipped farms. Doucouré and Healy report that the percentage of maize fields receiving fertilizer increased from 50 to 67 percent between 1994/95 and 1997/98.[29] As with cotton, these levels for maize fertilizer, while encouraging, are still below recommended levels. Since maize is traditionally used as an early-harvested, hungry-season crop and is not the principal cereal consumed by households in the CMDT zone, the increase in both area planted to maize and quantity of fertilizer used leads one to question whether farmers have begun to grow it as a cash crop.[30] If so, this would not be entirely surprising, given the higher prices of all cereals—maize in particular—after devaluation, and the increased demand from the Côte d'Ivoire and Senegal.

The pattern of extensification and less intensive production (that is, insufficient fertilizer) is consistent with the many observers' perceptions that while not as profitable on a per hectare basis as intensive production, extensive production may be a less risky, less costly strategy for low-income farmers to use in an environment characterized by insufficient and unequally spaced rainfall, variable cereal prices, and uncertain markets.[31] Farmers' priorities in the short run appear to be largely determined by their primary interest in meeting their food needs and maintaining a certain standard of living in the least risky way possible. Malian cotton farmers, like many people in Mali who are confronted with the basic problem of survival, focus on the potential short-term benefit of using the recommended technologies not necessarily only with cotton, but for the total contribution to their overall objectives.[32]

Labor

One of the strengths of the CMDT cotton sector in terms of its profitability and competitive position has been the use of unpaid family labor. There is unfortunately a lack of accurate data on the changes in the type and quantity of labor used after devaluation. Given the large increase in area cultivated to all crops and the relatively smaller increase in farm household size, labor requirements undoubtedly increased. With a higher number of fully equipped farms able to meet many labor requirements more effectively, harvesting cotton remains the primary task where the availability of labor may present a problem for many households. For the semi-equipped and nonequipped households, there is an additional demand for labor for weeding.

Research by IER's farming system team over the last ten years has estimated the number of person-days per hectare required to produce cotton and different cereals at the following rates: millet/sorghum—60; maize—90; cotton—170.[33] With cereal and cotton area increasing respectively by 1.06 and 1.12 hectares, this represents an increase of 286 additional person-days of labor.

Costs of production

The cost of inputs rose on average 37 percent between 1993/94 and 1997/98 ranging from 42,000 to 60,000 CFAF per hectare depending on estimates of the quantities of inputs used and degree of mechanization. Unlike the 65 percent increase in the price of fertilizer, the rise in total input costs was moderated by the change in type and reductions in the quantity of insecticide needed.

Despite the drop in cotton yields between 1993/94 and 1997/98, gross income per hectare of seed cotton grew on average 60 percent. For maize, the gross nominal income per hectare grew between 113 and 170 percent for the better-equipped farms with smaller increases for the less mechanized ones.[34] In real terms, average gross income per hectare of cotton and maize increased respectively 14 and 30 percent over the four-year period.[35]

A comparison of gross returns to labor for cotton and maize is strongly dependent on estimates of labor demands for different cropping activities and the manner in which equipment depreciation is shared between crops. Estimating labor requirements and valuing family labor is a highly politicized undertaking because the method used affects estimates of production costs, net profits and subsequently the negotiations between farmers and the CMDT on a "fair return" or "fair price" for seed cotton.

Using IER's estimate of ninety person-days of labor for maize and fifty-eight person-days for cotton,[36] the returns to labor are more profitable for cotton than for maize only for the most mechanized farmers (type A). However, for the semi- and nonequipped farms, returns for maize are equal to or superior to those for cotton. In valuing family labor at the post-devaluation salaried labor rate of 750 CFAF/person/day for the fifty-eight-day season (up 50 percent from 1993) in order to estimate the returns to management, capital, and risk, Kébé et al. note that most farms lost money on cotton.[37]

These average figures hide the variation between differently equipped farms. The results are strongly dependent on changes in the estimated yields in the different samples (CMDT and IER). The lack of accurate data on equipment depreciation and changes in family, salaried, and social group labor requirements prevents more precise analysis of net farm profits.

Impact and response of the CMDT

After devaluation, the total average delivered unit cost of production of cotton, that is, all the costs to produce, gin, and transport one kilogram of cotton to a European port (CIF—cost, insurance, freight—Rotterdam), jumped from 384 CFAF/kg in 1992/93 to 670 CFAF/kg in 1996/97, an increase of 75 percent. This represents a 17 percent increase in real terms. For the 1998/99 season, costs were projected to rise 11 percent to approximately 743 CFAF/kg.[38]

Table 4 shows the real increase of the different costs comprising the total delivered cost of cotton. Notable among the expenses included, in the line item

Table 4. **Real change in CMDT's total delivered unit cost of cotton to Europe: percent (%) change from 1992/1993 to 1996/1997.**

Unit of cost	% change
Producer price for cotton	-1%
Production and collection costs *(collection, marketing, extension, roads, overhead)*	57%
DELIVERED UNIT COST TO GIN	11%
Ginning, financing, handling and storage	35%
UNIT COST OF COTTON AT GIN	15%
FOB costs *(transport: Bamako-Dakar/Abidjan)*	-1%
CIF costs *(Dakar/Abidjan-Europe)*	39%
DELIVERED UNIT COST TO EUROPEAN PORT	17%

Source: CMDT Annual Reports; Waddell 1997

entitled "non seed cotton costs to gin," is a 30 and 94 percent increase respectively in overhead and cotton development activity costs.[39] A more recent audit of the CMDT revealed, however, a much larger increase of 112 percent in overhead costs between 1994/95 and 1996/97.[40] Over this same three-year period, inflation increased only 5.7 percent,[41] yet the total unit cost rose 17 percent. While the difference between the two studies' estimates of overhead costs can be attributed to different accounting methods, the higher cost inflation for this line item relative to others is an indication to many observers of the need to restructure the CMDT. Among the many expenditures that contribute to higher overhead costs, SEC-Diarra/BAC+ point out that the average CMDT employee salary increased more than 82 percent in real terms between 1993/94 and 1997/98.[42] This augmentation is huge compared to the 3 percent fall in the real wages of government civil servants.[43]

The non-seed cotton costs to gin also include many other expenditures—charges for extension services, research, and rural road maintenance, for example. In fact, rural road maintenance costs financed by the CMDT grew from 161 million CFAF in 1993/94 to 1.1 billion CFAF in 1997/98. Donors' investments in new roads and major repairs, however, totaled 9.4 billion over three years for 1,205 kilometers. With many of these expenditures, the issue is not so much a question of whether it should be done, but who can provide the service most effectively and cheaply. The recent audit by SEC-Diarra/BAC+ provides several examples:

- Transport costs have been higher than necessary because of continued use of the more expensive CMDT truck pool rather than private truckers. Average cost per ton kilometer for CMDT trucks averages 128 versus 65 CFAF for private truckers. While the CMDT has emphasized use of loaded round trips (transport inputs and animal feed to the village where they pick up cotton to transport to the gin), organizational problems have required the CMDT to make many one-way trips, thereby adding to total transport costs.[44]
- Ginning-related costs and associated financing charges for constructing new gins rose respectively 38 and 28 percent. Part of the higher ginning costs are due to expensive energy charges from using more costly, CMDT-operated generators for only five-six months per year during the ginning season. Several recently constructed gins powered by CMDT generators cost double the amount to run than those supplied by *Energie du Mali* (EDM—the Malian electrical company) or HUICOMA *(Huilerie Cotonnière du Mali)*, the seed cotton processor subsidiary generators. Energy costs could be reduced by connecting CMDT generators to the EDM grid.[45]
- The relatively small change in export costs (that is, FOB) provides a good example of the positive effect of increased competition. After a small increase in 1994, FOB costs for exported cotton decreased 5 percent between 1994 and 1998. This positive development can be attributed to the greater use of containerization and competition among forwarding agents.[46]

Prices and profits

The average annual market season sales price of cotton rose dramatically after devaluation from 319 CFAF/kg in 1992/93 to 877 in 1996/97. In their analysis of sales transactions over the last three years, SEC-Diarra/BAC+ show that private traders who export a small percentage of CMDT cotton (2–8 percent) sold cotton at prices 15–23 percent higher than prices received by COPACO.[47] They also report that in recent years, Malian cotton has been selling at lower prices compared to that from Benin, Côte d'Ivoire, and Togo. This comes on top of historically lower prices for West African cotton. Over the last fifteen years, the Cotlook West African franc zone cotton price index had prices of US$0.01/lb (15 CFAF/kg) less than similar grades included in the Cotlook A index.[48] This less-than-optimum performance calls attention to the need to reconsider the channels through which the CMDT sells most of its cotton as well as renewed efforts to improve quality.

In addition to earnings on cotton exports, CMDT sales of cotton seed[49] to HUICOMA, its processing subsidiary, increased from 4 to 11 CFAF/kg since devaluation. This is less than a third of the price received by cotton companies in Côte d'Ivoire and Benin (SEC-Diarra/BAC+ 1998).[50] In 1997/98, the CMDT earned 2 billion CFAF on the sale of 186,000 tons of cotton seed.

Profitability

As noted earlier, gross sales revenues increased substantially since devaluation, increasing 365 percent from 43 billion CFAF in 1992/93 to 201 billion in 1997/98. These revenues do not include, however, the proceeds from the sale of cotton seed to HUICOMA; these earnings are not part of the profits shared with the Malian government and farmers. Gross sales revenues also exclude economies earned by the CMDT in cotton ginning at an average cost less than the target operating costs established in the contract plan. In 1997/98, this bonus amounted to 10 billion CFAF for the CMDT.[51]

Gross profit is calculated by subtracting the average total delivered unit cost for cotton from gross sales revenues. Under the 1994–98 contract plan, the CMDT, farmers, and the government agreed that a 65 percent surcharge on the share of the cotton price exceeding 900 CFAF/kg would be paid from gross sales revenues. These revenues would also finance a contribution to the price stabilization fund that would be used to support the base producer price during periods when the world market prices were low. According to the contract plan, the annual contribution to the price stabilization fund is based on the amount required to maintain the total fund value to 25 percent of the current year's total seed cotton production valued at the current producer price.

Having deducted the surcharge and price stabilization fund contribution, the resulting net profit is shared among the beneficiaries as follows: farmers— 35 percent; CMDT—30 percent; government—35 percent. Since the government and the CFDT own respectively 60 and 40 percent of CMDT shares, the effective profit sharing is the following: producers—35 percent; government— 53 percent; CFDT—12 percent. For the 1996/97 season, the CMDT earned 170 billion CFAF in gross sales with total charges coming to 123 billion CFAF. With the average cotton sales price below 900 CFAF/kg, no surcharge was paid. The CMDT contributed 2.9 billion CFAF to increase the stabilization fund to 14.75 billion. Net profits were shared in the following percentages: farmer rebate— 15.5 billion CFAF; Malian government—10.07 billion CFAF; CMDT—19 billion CFAF.[52]

Use and Investment of Devaluation Gains

The potential for devaluation to have a positive impact on long-run productivity growth depends on how various actors who benefit from devaluation reinvest their new income. A key question for the cotton subsector is how the increased earnings stemming from devaluation will be channeled back into public and private investments that contribute to improve productivity of their respective operations. Whether this will occur will depend largely on how profits are shared, on individual producers' investment and consumption decisions, and on public decisions regarding taxation and public expenditures.

Farmers

Kébé et al. report that for those farms that earned additional income after devaluation there was a general pattern of greater expenditure in consumer goods (such as radios, televisions, cement and roofing for houses, bicycles, motorcycles, sewing machines, generators) than in directly productive agricultural investments. Surveys conducted in 1996/97 show that most purchases were made in cash.[53] These results do not necessarily contradict CMDT data showing greater acquisition of plows, oxen, and carts beginning in 1996/97.[54]

While no exact data exist, there is increasing evidence that farmers are being solicited to use their "new" income, together with additional loans, for "unproductive" purchases that do not contribute to gains in productivity. These consumer loans have led to over-indebtedness of many village-level farmer associations who have had to assume the unpaid debt of their members.[55] In order to counteract this tendency, several banks have already agreed to give priority to loans for productive purposes over the purchase of consumer goods.[56]

In addition to the purchase of consumer goods and equipment, cattle have traditionally been used as a storehouse for wealth in rural Mali. Between 1993 and 1998, the CMDT reports that average farm holdings in the CMDT increased 9 percent. Average annual growth in cattle herds slowed substantially from 25 to 1 percent over this five-year period. A considerable portion of cattle herds in Fana and San have actually been sold off since devaluation, spurred by profitable trade with coastal countries. Average annual growth in the number of draft oxen per farm also slowed from a 7.5 pre-devaluation rate to 2 percent since 1994. The growing size of cattle herds and use of oxen in the CMDT zone have helped break the traditional distinction between farmers and livestock breeders.

Increased village association revenues earned from marketing and cotton assembly fees have continued to be invested in social infrastructure, most notably new schools and community health centers. These cotton funds have enabled villages in the cotton zone to successfully participate in the government's push to increase schooling rates and improve access to medical care.

CMDT

Following devaluation, the CMDT used profits to reimburse debt and tax arrears totaling 40 billion CFAF. During the cotton crisis of the early 1990s, when the CMDT was losing money on every kilogram of cotton sold, the government bailed out the CMDT with 10.3 billion CFAF. As part of its assistance to Mali after devaluation, the French government canceled 8.4 billion in debt owed, but required the CMDT to reimburse the Malian government. The accelerated payment, tax arrears, and fees totaled 21 billion CFAF.

The majority of the CMDT's share of devaluation gains has been focused on modernizing and expanding ginning capacity. In mid-1994, the CMDT initiated an investment program to modernize existing gins and its truck pool used for seed cotton transport, and purchase four new gins. In addition to the improvement in the quality and yield of the ginned cotton, modernization added 15,500 tons of capacity. The addition of four new gins in 1995/96 and 1996/97 plus four more phased over three years (1998/99–2000/01) will expand ginning capacity to 559,067 tons in 1998/99 and 711,557 tons in 2000/01.[57] The French Development Agency (AFD), the CMDT, the West African Development Bank, and other banks are financing respectively 30, 26, 34, and 10 percent of the cost of new gins.[58]

Challenges for the Future

The preceding discussion has shown that the CMDT's and farmers' production and investment strategies after devaluation have focused on output expansion through extensification with relatively minimal attention to improving productivity. This approach remains profitable as long as world prices remain stable and high. Any prolonged drop in world market prices or a continual increase in production costs could very easily push the subsector back into the red, potentially leading to a reduction in farmer prices. This section examines three long-term strategic issues that could help avoid this situation as well as solidify future growth of the cotton sector and its role as a catalyst of economic development in Mali: subsector reorganization; sustainability of cotton production; and strategic reinvestment for broader economic growth.

Reorganization of the subsector

The World Bank/French debate

Throughout the historical development of the cotton subsector, the CMDT and CFDT have responded to problems and crises by taking minimal steps to improve finances (that is, get out of the red), making changes to dysfunctional areas while maintaining the same basic, integrated structure and waiting for prices to rise.[59] Following a series of discussions among the World Bank, the French government, and cotton companies in the franc zone (including the CMDT) on the most appropriate model for the future development of the subsector, the situation is a little different. To simplify a very complex debate: The French government and the CMDT advocate maintaining the status quo and keeping a successful integrated subsector. The World Bank, on the other hand, while recognizing the important achievements recorded by the CMDT and CFDT over the last twenty-five years, argues for privatization of cotton companies and liberalization of the subsector. Their assumption is that greater competition will lead to (1) higher producer prices and farmer incomes, (2) greater cost efficiencies that will foster more rapid growth, (3) increased rural and urban employment, and (4) greater tax and foreign exchange earnings. In essence, the debate centers around a tradeoff between coordination and disciplining the system to be more cost-conscious.[60]

In the short term, it appears that the CMDT, CFDT, and the Malian government will continue to maintain the same basic integrated structure while undertaking incremental changes to improve efficiency and performance. This decision should not preclude the Malian government, however, from continuing to reflect on ways to improve the productivity and sustainability of the cotton subsector in the future, especially with respect to changes in institutional structure, and to develop the capacity of other actors to undertake public service development activities formerly implemented by the CMDT.

As noted earlier, the historical partnership with the CFDT and CIRAD (research) and French development agencies (*Ministère de Coopération*, AFD) has benefited the cotton subsector in many areas, most notably in the areas of research, ginning, and marketing expertise; funding for development related activities; and financing for investment (gins and roads) and deficits in crisis years. Any major changes to the organization and structure of the subsector and the relationship between the CFDT and CMDT will need to be preceded by careful examination of their implications for the future relationship with these French institutions and the services provided by them.

Varietal research is one area where the French institutions have been particularly important. While there is a lack of exact accounting of donors' contributions to the research budget, French financing of cotton research has been quite substantial. Future productivity improvements may depend, however, on access to a variety of performance-enhancing genetics (for example those containing the Bt gene)[61] recently developed by multinational agro-chemical pharmaceutical firms. Developing the most appropriate organizational structure and institutional relationships—international partnerships or contractual mechanisms—may prove to be an important prerequisite to gain access to this technology. While an integrated subsector may possess advantages in developing close relations with these companies and obtaining access to the results of ongoing varietal and biological research, the interest of the giant multinationals in investing in Mali will depend in part on the protection of their intellectual property rights over these seed varieties. Establishing mechanisms to assure enforceable contracts thus becomes very important.[62]

Streamlining the CMDT

Today, more than ever, the risks of volatility in the world market and the dependence on cotton revenues require a redoubling of efforts to reduce the total delivered unit cost of cotton in order to maintain the subsector's competitiveness and the profits to which it has grown accustomed. This effort to create a leaner, more profitable and competitive subsector requires a reexamination of alternative, more efficient and less costly methods to carry out the different functions of the subsector. As mentioned earlier, a recent audit has outlined a series of potential measures to reduce costs, many of which involve the transfer of certain functions to other actors (for example, greater use of private transport).[63]

The manner in which certain functions, particularly public service ones, are delegated to other actors becomes especially important as the CMDT sheds general development activities to focus on its industrial and marketing operations. While not directly related to producing cotton, the CMDT, as part of its former rural development mandate, implemented a wide range of activities (for example, veterinary services for animal traction, blacksmith, functional literacy/numeracy, health centers) that contributed to the development of rural areas and thus indirectly to cotton production. As the CMDT continues to jettison these important, but non-essential activities, the Malian government needs to empower the relevant actors (village associations, farmer organizations, community health centers, decentralized government structures) with the legal, financial, organizational, and technical resources needed to carry out those roles.[64]

While the separation of cotton-specific from public service activities will help to reduce the CMDT's costs, reducing the large overhead presents another difficult challenge (and fodder for proponents of privatization). In a call for more stringent audits and financial accountability, a recent audit recommends improvements to the computerized accounting system and a more effective management planning system with more realistic annual budgeting, especially for costs associated with inputs.[65] The recent dismissal of top CMDT officials for alleged mismanagement is an indication of the current efforts to improve operating efficiency.[66]

Recent studies have suggested that the price stabilization fund be dismantled with most of the assets used to finance farmers' participation in the CMDT's capital. Since farmers already share in corporate profits, the actual effect of this action on farmer decision making and subsector performance would depend on the details of farmer participation. Although farmers would be a minority shareholder (20 percent),[67] their greater involvement in future management and policy decisions could conceivably help future restructuring efforts. Some observers question whether this new institutional arrangement in which farmers and the CMDT become closer corporate partners may affect the ability of Mali's cotton subsector to evolve in the future (that is, toward privatization and liberalization) as both sides seek to maintain the status quo.

If the price stabilization fund is used to finance farmers' participation, an effective mechanism to manage world market price risks to replace the fund will need to be developed.[68] This question is part of the larger issue of minimizing price and exchange risk. Prior large fluctuations in world market prices and the subsequent loss of profitability underline the importance of developing a price system that achieves a balance between the stability needed to assure a constant level of production required by actors to have profitable investments, and flexibility to adjust producer prices when the world market falls. In the same vein, the transmission of international market risks are affected by exchange rates. Since the ability of the subsector to maintain its future competitiveness may also depend on exchange rate policy, Mali, along with other cotton-producing countries in the CFA franc zone, could benefit from analysis of the experiences of other cotton-producing countries that are organized differently, have flexible exchange rate policies and use an alternative price system.

As Mali works to create a leaner, more profitable and competitive subsector by instituting more efficient and less costly methods to carry out the different functions in the system, past experiences of restructuring subsectors in other countries or for other commodities reminds us of the importance of implementing changes gradually. Whether or not restructuring disrupts the coordination between various levels of a subsector depends on the capacity of new actors to carry out new functions, the efficiency of economic governance systems, and the mechanisms for the enforcement of contracts.[69]

Cotton production sustainability

The current pattern of extensification—in which farmers are using insufficient quantities of mineral and organic fertilizers, reducing fallow periods, and not following recommended cropping practices and conservation measures—has negatively affected soil fertility. In their efforts to assure food and income security in the least risky way possible, farmers tend to focus on the potential short-term benefit of using the recommended technologies while discounting the long-term financial returns to soil recapitalization stemming from current investments in fertilizer. The second major challenge consists of modifying cropping practices for cotton and other crops in a manner that responds to the immediate needs of farmers while providing the nutrients needed to sustain soil fertility.

How to promote greater use of intensification practices and conservation measures and sustainable productivity growth is a difficult task for which the multiple factors affecting its outcome may differ by farm type and region. Foremost among the factors affecting environmentally sustainable production are the following: lower input prices, effective pesticide management, a concerted soil conservation plan, and a land tenure management program.[70]

Inputs

Reducing the cost of fertilizer to farmers is very important to encouraging use at recommended levels. The recommendation in a recent audit to develop a more transparent, competitive bid tender system for input imports, to closely monitor costs and to separate the input budget from the CMDT's general budget are constructive suggestions to reduce costs.[71] If the establishment of a competitive system can contribute to a lower unit cost of fertilizer, its efficient functioning will first require that new actors receive professional training, have access to market information, and have a viable credit system. Pooling purchases at the regional level for a single formula of fertilizer and greater use of bulk blends are two additional cost-cutting actions that merit greater study. Investments of a public nature are also indispensable for the development of a legal system, mechanisms for contract enforcement, and efficient input markets for all crops.[72]

Increased use of organic matter depends on intensive livestock production as well as the means to transport manure to fields. The need to equip farm households currently lacking animal traction equipment and to replace old and worn-out farming equipment on many other farms calls, in turn, for a review of policies and other factors that may constrain imports and local manufacture of agricultural equipment.

Effective pest management is another factor critical to sustainable cotton production. Although the CMDT's conscientious approach to pest management through the uniform use of lower cost pesticide "cocktails" throughout the zone has slowed the onset of pest resistance, there is a growing concern that resistance is developing in certain areas and that the pesticides are becoming ineffective. If pesticide resistance persists and Mali continues on the pesticide "treadmill," it may be necessary to use more powerful and expensive pesticides whose cost can only be supported by a commensurate increase in productivity.[73] Future restructuring of input distribution in Mali will need to pay particular attention to plant protection policy and input quality and may call for the establishment of an industry oversight committee to coordinate and monitor future actions.

Conservation measures

IER surveys in the mid-1990s showed that farmers undertake little conservation work—spreading organic matter and anti-erosion work—preferring commerce, horticulture, and seasonal work in Côte d'Ivoire to diversify income sources.[74] Despite many successful projects implemented over the last ten years to address environmental problems, the CMDT estimates that only 28 percent of farms use anti-erosion techniques.[75] The increased cultivation of marginal lands and low farmer application rate of conservation measures would appear to justify a more concerted, focused program to deal with soil fertility and erosion problems; and an examination of land tenure issues would need to figure predominantly in any conservation program. The nature of communal land use rights seems to have a detrimental effect on farmers' interest in undertaking long-term soil conservation measures (on fields whose future use is not guaranteed). Notwithstanding these efforts, a community-based approach and participation of farmer organizations would appear to offer possible solutions to environmental problems.

The transfer of functions to farmer organizations would, however, need to be preceded by successful resolution of several internal problems including generational conflicts and those between new associations created for remunerative activities and traditional ones, increased economic differentiation in villages leading to smaller associations grouped around smaller family units, loss of confidence with CMDT agents, and credit problems due to unreimbursed individual credit secured by communal collateral.[76] To be more effective, farmer organizations also need to increase the numbers of functionally literate and numerate members and improve financial management. Improved performance of these structures will depend in large part on the creation of an appropriate institutional and legal environment that assures the establishment and respect of transparent working rules acceptable to all the actors.[77]

Tapping the gains for broader growth

No matter what form the future reorganization of the subsector may take, improving the productivity, sustainability, and competitiveness of cotton production and marketing will require significant private and public investments. To date, cotton profits have been used by the CMDT primarily to expand ginning capacity needed to absorb the large production increases resulting from the acreage expansion. There has been relatively little noticeable increase in investment in productivity-enhancing measures required to improve yields at the farm level and reduce costs throughout the subsector.

A large share of cotton profits continues to be transferred to the government. Aside from the apparent reduction in the government's debt service ratio and budget deficit, it is difficult to ascertain precisely how the Malian government has employed post-devaluation cotton profits. Regardless of who implements the many public development activities formerly performed by the CMDT in the future (decentralized government units, farmer organizations, private business), outside of finding alternative sources of revenue (for example, local taxes) the government will at least for the short term need to continue its financial support. In the same vein, continued improvement in schooling rates and access to health care will require sustained government investment for many years.

To date, the Malian government has relied heavily on foreign aid to finance its budget and development programs. Since the mid-1980s, foreign aid has represented 27 percent of Mali's budgetary revenues. And since 1993, donors have financed 80 percent of Mali's annual special investment budget. Although donors can make a positive contribution to future development in Mali, it would appear a risky strategy to link Mali's future to this aid. In this context and given the important share of profits received by the Malian government and the CMDT, it is critically important to rethink the distribution and use of cotton profits.

Continuing to transfer a large share of cotton profits to non-cotton uses at the expense of productive reinvestment in actions to improve the long-term sustainability, productivity, and competitiveness of the cotton subsector would be equivalent to killing the goose that lays the golden eggs. In the same vein, the Malian government cannot overlook the importance of using these funds to finance the annual operating and political expedient payment of civil servant salaries.

At the same time, Mali cannot disregard the strategic investments required to foster greater economic growth. While investment in sustainable and productive agriculture advocated earlier addresses one aspect of Mali's food security problem (increasing per capita food production), improving incomes through job creation represents a major challenge and enormous need of investment demand. After a decade of consistent efforts to improve schooling rates, thousands of young people hit the job market each year with close to 3,000 graduates (and even greater numbers of unskilled young) not being able to find work. With minimal civil servant hiring and a drop in government expenditure on civil servant salaries (from 29 to 27 percent of the government budget between 1996 and 1998), there is little public capacity to absorb these new entrants.[78]

Freeing up a part of the government's limited resources to reinvest in growth sectors capable of generating jobs poses a difficult task to the resource-constrained Malian government. Determining first which sectors have the most potential to create jobs and increase value added, and second how to most effectively invest available funds in these sectors to achieve these results remain critical questions. Since agriculture is still the foundation of the Malian economy, generating 40 percent of value added, and since many products have become more competitive on regional markets after devaluation, upstream and downstream investments that support initiatives to increase value added in these areas (for example, textiles, livestock, and food processing) would appear to offer many possibilities.

There is no question that public monies can only satisfy a small portion of the investment required to stimulate growth in these sectors and generate jobs and income. But with a dearth of private investment in Mali and reticence of investors to commit funds to risky investments in undeveloped sectors, additional public investment in infrastructure (for example, roads, electricity), commercial courts, market development, and training for private sector actors may be critical to encouraging private investments and assuring their future success.

Developing appropriate responses to these challenges depend largely on the capability of the Malian government, in partnership with all economic actors, to continuously monitor and modify the complex and dynamic interactions between policies, institutional reform, technological change, and human capital as Mali seeks to improve human welfare and develop in a very competitive global economy.

Notes

1. *Communauté Financière d'Afrique*, the African Financial Community unit of currency.
2. CFDT 1998.
3. Tefft et al. 1998.

4. The population living in what is now called Mali has grown cotton for centuries. During the colonial era, the French colonial regime began to grow cotton for export only in the 1920s. In 1949, a French parastatal, the CFDT *(Compagnie Française pour le Développement des Fibres Textiles)*, began its cotton production and marketing program. Based on an approach involving intensive agricultural extension with small-scale farmers, the CFDT increased area planted from 1,000 hectares (ha) in 1949 to 32,000 ha in 1960. The CFDT continued its monopoly control over cotton production, processing and marketing until 1974 when the government and the CFDT agreed to create the CMDT with 60 percent Malian government and 40 percent CFDT capital. With financing from the World Bank, *Fonds d'Aide et de Coopération* (FAC), *Caisse Centrale de Coopération Economique* (CCCE), the International Fund for Agricultural Development (IFAD), and other bilateral donor agencies, several rural development programs have been financed since the mid-1970s in the region covered by the CMDT (Dioné 1990; Bingen 1998).

5. With more recent involvement of the *Banque Nationale de Développement Agricole* (BNDA).

6. ICAC 1996; Bingen 1998.

7. The ginning ratio is the percentage of lint ginned per kilogram of seed cotton.

8. Cotlook Index A is an "average of the cheapest five quotations from a selection of the principal upland cottons traded internationally" (Cotlook 1999).

9. ICAC 1996.

10. This involved replacing the state import-export agency, SOMIEX, which had been created shortly after political independence in order to handle the importation and exportation of all food and agricultural products.

11. In 1988/89, additional reforms designed to increase CMDT's efficiency and productivity included (1) changing the CMDT from a parastatal agency to a semi-public, limited liability, industrial corporation *(société anonyme à caractère industriel)*; (2) developing a contract plan between the CMDT and the government; and (3) involving farmers on the board of directors (Coopération Française 1991).

12. Tefft, Staatz, Dioné 1997.

13. Ibid.; Dibley et al. 1996; Yade et al. 1999.

14. Cotton production in the OHVN zone grew even faster than the CMDT zones (30 percent annually; 155 percent cumulatively over four years, albeit from a smaller base). The OHVN *(Opération Haute Vallée du Niger)* is the rural development area to the west of the CMDT zone in the Niger River basin.

15. CMDT 1999.

16. The opportunity for farmers to plant more acreage to cotton and increase seed cotton production is due to the increase in ginning capacity and corresponding elimination of production quotas after devaluation.

17. Giraudy and Niang 1996; Diakité et al. 1996; CMDT 1999.

18. Giraudy 1999.

19. Kébé and Brons 1994.

20. In the more arid northern San zone, however, farmers increased the area cultivated in cereals at double the rate of other zones, and even faster than cotton.

21. Mali has made considerable progress since the 1970s to increase the number of farms with animal traction equipment. In addition to its direct effect on increasing cultivated area through a reduction of labor inputs, the availability of animal traction equipment has a positive impact on yields through improved and timely land preparation, early planting, and weeding. Better-equipped farms also appear to have a greater tendency to use other technological improvements (Dioné 1990). The CMDT classifies farms in four categories by degree of mechanization: type A—farm with at least two complete traction units (that is, two oxen and two plows or one plow and one multiculteur and at least six head of cattle); type B—farm with one complete set of traction equipment without cattle herd; type C—farm with one partial set of traction equipment and animal traction experience; type D—farm with no traction equipment and no animal traction experience (Kébé et al. 1998).

22. Kébé et al. 1998.

23. Doucouré and Healy 1999.

24. Dioné 1990; Raymond and Fok 1994; Kébé et al. 1998.

25. In addition, with the opening of the new Kita zone (located in the western Kayes region) to cotton production in 1995/96, more than 13,000 farms now grow cotton on 21,000 ha and had a total cotton production of 27,000 tons in 1997/98.

26. Doucouré and Healy 1999.

27. Kébé et al. 1998; Doucouré and Healy 1999.

28. Kébé et al. 1998.

29. Doucouré and Healy 1999.

30. Ibid.

31. Giraudy 1999.

32. Tefft et al. 1998.

33. Kébé et al. 1998.

34. Ibid.

35. Ibid.; Doucouré and Healy 1999.

36. This represents only those days during peak work periods for which there may be an alternative remunerative activity. But this estimate does not include labor required for productivity-enhancing measures in the off-season (for example, manure spreading). The incentive for family and salaried laborers to perform this work would be partly determined by relative remuneration received in alternative activities (for example, work in Bamako and Côte d'Ivoire).

37. Kébé et al. 1998.

38. SEC-Diarra/BAC+ 1998; Waddell 1997.

39. Waddell 1997.

40. SEC-Diarra/BAC+ 1998.

41. This period began in 1995, after the 32 percent increase in inflation in 1994.

42. SEC-Diarra/BAC+ 1998.

43. Tefft, Yade, Chohin 1997.

44. SEC-Diarra/BAC+ 1998.

45. Ibid.

46. Ibid.

47. Ibid.

48. Ibid.; J. M. Consultants 1995.

49. That is, what is separated from the cotton during the ginning process.

50. SEC-Diarra/BAC+ 1998.

51. Waddell 1997; Waddell 1998; SEC-Diarra/BAC+ 1998.

52. Waddell 1998.

53. Kébé et al. 1998.

54. CMDT 1999.

55. Kébé and Kébé-Sidibé 1997.

56. SEC-Diarra/BAC+ 1998.

57. Based on operations of 150 days per year with a ginning yield of 42 percent (Waddell 1997).

58. The CMDT also invested 1 billion CFAF in the following companies in which it is a shareholder (percent of shares): COPACO—the marketing arm of CMDT (6 percent), SOSEA—*Société de services pour l'Europe et pour l'Afrique* (2.5 percent), HUICOMA—*Huilerie Cotonnière du Mali* (54 percent), SMPC—*Société Malienne des Produits Chimiques* (25 percent), SEPT-SA—*Société d'exploitation du phosphate de Tilemsi* (36 percent), SMECMA-SA—*Société Malienne des Equipement de Construction et des Matérials Agricoles* (34 percent). Many are recent acquisitions.

59. Bingen 1998; Deveze 1994.

60. CFDT 1998.

61. Bt cotton refers to genetically engineered cotton seed that is modified to contain a gene that allows the plant to produce a protein from the bacterium called *Bacillus thuringiensis* (bt) which kills the heliothis caterpillar when it feeds on the plant.

62. Tefft et al. 1998.

63. SEC-Diarra/BAC+ 1998.

64. Tefft et al. 1998.

65. SEC-Diarra/BAC+ 1998.

66. Agence France Presse 1999.

67. Following this capital offering, the CMDT would retain 47.27 percent and the CFDT 31.52 percent (SEC-Diarra/BAC+ 1998).

68. Many observers questioned whether the stabilization fund could ever be effectively used since the contract plan allowed the CMDT to borrow from it to finance input and cotton purchases without direct reimbursements, raising questions as to its liquidity.

69. Tefft et al. 1998.

70. Declining yields are not due to non-performing seed varieties. Yields obtained in on-farm trials and by the most productive farmers are 20–50 percent higher than average yields (Dembélé 1996; CMDT/Sikasso 1998).

71. SEC-Diarra/BAC+ 1998.
72. Tefft et al. 1998.
73. Van der Valk 1999.
74. Kébé and Brons 1994.
75. CMDT 1998.
76. Kébé et al. 1998.
77. The recent local elections and creation of new, decentralized governmental units will clearly influence these developments and call for additional training of other actors.
78. DNP/DNSI 1999.

Bibliography

Agence France Presse. 1999. "Limogeage d'une dizaine de personnes à la société malienne des textiles." 20 June. Paris: AFP.

Bingen, R. James. 1998. "Cotton, democracy and development in West Africa." *Journal of Modern African Studies* 36 (2): 265–85.

CFDT (Compagnie Française pour le Développement des Fibres Textiles). 1998. "Contresens et contre-vérités sur les filières cotonnières africaines éléments de réponse à un document provisoire abondamment diffusé." *Coton et Développement* No 26 (Avril-Mai-Juin): 2.

CMDT (Compagnie Malienne pour le Développement des Fibres Textiles). 1998. "Annuaire Statistique 97/98, Résultats de l'Enquête Agricole Permanente." Novembre. Bamako: CMDT/ DPCG.

———. 1999. "Rapport Annuel de la CMDT, Campagne 1997–98," Annexes. Bamako: CMDT.

CMDT/Sikasso, Direction Régionale de Sikasso. 1998. "Elements d'analyse de l'évolution des rendements du coton de la campagne 1994/96 à la campagne 1997/98." Sikasso: CMDT.

Coopération Française. 1991. *Le Coton en Afrique de l'Ouest et du Centre, Situation et Perspectives*. Paris: Ministère de la Coopération et du Développement.

Cotlook Limited Services. 1999. Database. London.

Dembélé, Siaka. 1996. "Recherche cotonnière au Mali; présentation sommaire de quelques résultats saillants." Bamako: Institut d'Economie Rurale.

Devèze, Jean-Claude. 1994. "Les zones cotonnières entre développement, ajustement et dévaluation: Réflexions sur le rôle du coton en Afrique Francophone de l'Ouest et du Centre." Paris: Département des Politiques et Etudes, Caisse Française de Développement.

Diakité, Lamissa, Demba Kébé, and Hamady Djouara. 1996. "Incidence de la dévaluation du franc CFA sur le comportement des producteurs de coton dans les régions CMDT de Sikasso et de Koutiala." Bamako: IER/ECOFIL-PRISAS.

Dibley, David, Thomas Reardon, and John Staatz. 1996. "How does a devaluation affect an economy? Lessons from Africa, Asia and Latin America." July. East Lansing: Michigan State University Agricultural Economics Staff Paper No. 96–105.

Dioné, Josue. 1990. "Informing food security policy in Mali: Interactions between technology, institutions and market reforms." Ph.D. dissertation. Michigan State University, Department of Agricultural Economics.

Doucouré, Cheik Oumar, and Seàn Healy. 1999. "Evolution des systèmes de production de 94/95 à 97/98: Impact sur les revenus paysans." Bamako: CMDT/DPCG.

DNSI (Direction Nationale de la Statistique et de l'Informatique). 1999. Database.

DNP/DNSI. 1999. "Situation économique et sociale du Mali en 1998 et perspectives pour 1999." Bamako: Ministère de l'Economie du Plan et de l'Intégration.

Giraudy, François, and Mamadou Niang. 1996. "Impact de la dévaluation sur les systèmes de production et les revenus paysans en zone Mali-Sud." Bamako: CMDT.

Giraudy, François. 1999. "Culture attelée, culture cotonnière, crédit et intensification de l'agriculture." Coton et Développement 29 (Janvier-Février-Mars): 20–24.

ICAC (International Cotton Advisory Committee). 1996. "Marketing cotton in Francophone Africa." Cotton: Review of the World Situation. March-April: 9–14.

J. M. Consultants. 1995. "La compétitivité du coton dans le monde, Pays hors zone franc." Paris: Ministère de la Coopération.

Kébé, Demba, and Johan Brons. 1994. "Quand le rythme du tam-tam change." Document No 94/25. Bamako: Institut d'Economie Rurale/ESPGRN.

Kébé, Demba, and Marie-Cécile Kébé-Sidibé. 1997. "Etude diagnostique de la crise des associations villageoises en zone CMDT." Bamako: Institut d'Economie Rurale/ESPGRN.

Kébé, Demba, Lamissa Diakité, and Hamady Diawara. 1998. "Impact de la dévaluation du FCFA sur la productivité, la rentabilité et les performances de la filière coton (Cas du Mali)." Bamako: PRISAS/INSAH-ECOFIL/IER.

Raymond, Georges, and Michel Fok. 1994. "Relations entre coton et vivrier en Afrique de l'Ouest et du Centre, le coton affame les populations? Une fausse affirmation." Montpellier: CIRAD.

SEC-Diarra/BAC+. 1998. "Evaluation technique de la filière coton, dans le cadre de l'exécution du contrat-plan etat - CMDT - exploitations agricoles (1994–1998), 2nd phase de l'étude, Bilan diagnostic du secteur cotonnier, perspectives d'évolution à moyen terme, recommendations." Rapport provisoire. Bamako: Cellule d'Appui à la Mise en Oeuvre du Plan d'Action (CAMOPA), Ministère du Développement Rural et de l'Eau (MDRE).

Tefft, James, John Staatz, and Josué Dioné. 1997. "Impact of the CFA devaluation on sustainable growth for poverty alleviation: preliminary results." Paper presented at the World Bank Conference on Poverty Alleviation, Stockholm, Sweden, October 1997.

Tefft, James, Mbaye Yade, and Anne Chohin. 1997. "Evolution des prix relatifs et effets sur les revenus et la sécurité alimentaire suite à la dévaluation du franc CFA – Synthèse." In Sahelian Studies and Research—La dévaluation du franc cfa en Afrique de l'Ouest, Quel bilan trois ans après?, edited by Abdoul Aziz Ly. Number 0, July-December 1997. Bamako: Institut du Sahel.

Tefft, James, John Staatz, Josué Dioné, and Valerie Kelly. 1998. "Food security and agricultural subsectors in West Africa, future prospects and key issues four years after devaluation of the CFA franc, cotton subsector." Bamako: INSAH/CILSS.

Van der Valk, Harold. 1999. FAO/Institut du Sahel/CILSS, personal communication.

Waddell, Alain. 1997. "Rapport financier: application des mécanismes de rémunération et de stabilisation de la filière coton." Etude Realisée à la Demande du Comité de Suivi et de Gestion du Contrat-Plan Etat/CMDT/Producteurs. Bamako: CMDT.

Waddell, Alain. 1998. "Etude concernant la contribution de la CMDT aux recettes fiscales de l'état." Rapport principal, vol.1. Bamako: Ministère des Finances.

Yade, Mbaye, Anne Chohin-Kuper, Valerie Kelly, John Staatz, and James Tefft. 1999. "The role of regional trade in agricultural transformation: the case of West Africa following devaluation of the CFA franc." Paper presented at the Workshop on Agricultural Transformation, Nairobi, Kenya, 27–30 June.

Political
Innovation

Overview–The Malian Path to Democracy and Development

R. JAMES BINGEN

Mali's modern political history deserves close inspection for its contribution to the knowledge and practice of democracy and development. Since the creation of the First Republic in 1960, Mali's largely under-recognized political journey offers important evidence that can enhance our understanding and appreciation of the various ways in which democracies continue to be constructed little by little across Africa. Over the last thirty years we have witnessed the enduring nature of historic forms of popular control and the continuing demand for democratic accountability in which the Malian people have found the means to assure that their leaders answer for their actions. The Malian journey has not been smooth, nor free of breakdowns and roadblocks along the way. But the journey continues. A Malian graduate of MSU captured the essential and driving spirit for this journey: "Our democracy is young. But its future is bright if all of us, both men and women, will work together in good faith to assure that our beloved country continues to serve as one example for the rest of Africa" (personal communication, anonymous).

When Modibo Kéita and the *Union Soudanaise-Rassemblement Démocratique Africain* (US-RDA) helped achieve Mali's political independence in 1960, the new political leaders never questioned the need for ambitious state investments to mobilize the capital required for rapid economic growth. The central political issue was not whether the government should direct the economy, but which specific measures to use to achieve economic decolonization and economic independence from the French commercial monopolies (see Clark).

In the countryside the Malian model of "rural socialism" encouraged smallholder production and idealized the village as a model of socialist organization. While the subject of some debate among the government's planners, the model protected peasant production units while relying heavily on political mobilization and control. The Kéita regime believed that new village-level party committees could both revitalize traditional productive forces and create new political leadership in the countryside. At the same time, Kéita reorganized the territorial administration of government in order to bring government closer to the people. The ironic result of these measures, however, was that Kéita wiped out the very local structures that offered the most potential for promoting local responsibility (see Rawson).

Most observers acknowledge that Kéita's policies did achieve a measure of economic decolonization. But it is also widely acknowledged that the regime failed to construct rural socialism. On the contrary, in the face of peasant resistance, the party's increasingly repressive and authoritarian pressure in the countryside contributed to the government's demise. The effort by party militants to confiscate food grains signaled the political bankruptcy of Malian socialism, and there was little popular discontent when the regime fell to Traoré's coup d'état in November 1968.

The Traoré regime justified its takeover on the grounds that Kéita's policies no longer represented the views of most Malians. The new National Liberation Committee (CMLN) was intended to rebuild majority rule and guide the country with a more open door policy to foreign assistance. The new regime successfully forestalled calls from many aid agencies to "liberalize" the economy until 1981 when it finally agreed to several IMF and World Bank fiscal and economic policies in return for significant budget support. Private commercial trading of food grains became the key feature of the government's Third Economic Plan (1981–85). After almost twenty years of strained relations between the state and private traders, this new, more liberal grain trade policy represented a significant step toward removing a long-standing source of political opposition.

In the countryside, the Traoré regime sought a new form of cooperation by creating official *Tons villageois* modeled on traditional forms of village mutual aid groups. Reminiscent of Kéita's appeal to the "new man in the countryside," these new *Tons* were intended to be the base of collective action for rebuilding rural Mali.

If the regime had been able to move beyond its rhetoric of collaboration with the country's producers and traders, it might have been able to chart a new future for Mali. In the short term, such rhetoric at least assured some degree of continued international political confidence and a flow of foreign aid. In retrospect, however, it is clear that the regime was neither willing to transfer a full measure of responsibility to the countryside nor accept the economic uncertainties of unfettered private investment interests in the economy.

The regime's new official party, the *Union Démocratique du Peuple Malien* (UDPM) was intended to achieve political legitimacy, both domestically and in the international arena by promising a new era of political freedom and openness in Malian politics. Outwardly moving toward constitutional government, the regime became increasingly repressive in response to a series of student demonstrations that started in the late 1970s. Moreover, government programs and policies in response to the international calls for "economic liberalization" became the means to consolidate economic opportunities and investments by small numbers of individuals within, or favored by the Traoré government.

As the winds of revolt and democracy began blowing across Africa, Traoré reluctantly responded to both international and domestic demands for political liberalization by allowing a free press to emerge in Mali for the first time since independence (see Clark in this volume). On the other hand, Traoré refused the increasingly vocal demands for multiple political parties. Instead, Traoré mistakenly assumed that he could control the emerging political interests through a series of nationwide "democratic conferences" organized by the official UDPM. Ironically reminiscent of the failure of the Kéita regime's increased militancy in the face of popular resistance in the late 1960s, Traoré's murderous armed efforts to suppress a series of public demonstrations in early 1991 are now just a painful memory along the Malian road to democracy.

Mali's National Conference, held in late 1991 and described in Clark's review of contemporary Malian political history, represents one of the few national conferences that led to a successful transition from an authoritarian to a government founded on democratic principles. Alpha Oumar Konaré, as first president of the Third Republic, is acutely aware of the continuing challenges that will face the young republic for many years. "Democratic struggle is conducted on a daily basis. And once the democratic option has been chosen, there is no turning back. It is not easy and it cannot be done alone. It requires team work. While everyone has an interest and position to defend, everyone needs to make sure that what prevails is best for all."[1]

Education, health, decentralization, and regional integration are among the key issues before the current government. According to President Konaré:

> The low level of education jeopardizes democratic and economic development. Out of 1.5 million children throughout the country, one million do not attend school. And out of the few who have the opportunity to attend school, the dropout rate is very high. Only one in five of those who start first grade reach the sixth grade of elementary school. Moreover, there are significant regional disparities in educational opportunities that must be rectified.

> Democratization in the absence of a literate population may be possible, but
> shallow. Learning how to read and write is a fundamental act of liberation. The
> lack of access to education for a significant segment of the population impedes
> their participation in the country's social debate and makes this group depen-
> dent upon those with even the most minimal literacy skills.

Davis explores another dimension of this issue in his discussion of civil society
and political socialization. His findings, however, strengthen President
Konaré's concerns about the need for more educational opportunity. Based on
the findings from numerous studies of group membership and political values,
Davis expected to find that different types of groups in Mali might socialize
members to hold political values such as compromise, trust, tolerance, and efficacy. Instead, he found that the low levels of involvement in group decision
making and leadership selection do not foster these types of values. Moreover,
group membership did not foster a sense of political efficacy or tolerance.
Clearly, in addition to the challenge of broadening educational opportunities,
the country must find ways to strengthen civic education and associational
capacity-building that increases meaningful participation for large numbers of
women, youth, and smallholders.

At the same time, the country faces a health situation of crisis proportions:

> One Malian child out of four does not live more than five years. Thirteen out
> of every one hundred children die before reaching one year of age, and most
> of these die because they do not have access to immunizations. In addition, 50
> percent of Malians do not have access to drinking water, 13 percent suffer
> from malnutrition, and 70 percent of Malian women live at a considerable dis-
> tance from a health center.

Mezey's chapter on how a more democratic Mali might be able to address rural
women's use of and access to health care on women's health issues provides
additional and disquieting confirmation of President Konaré's concerns. Based
on extensive interviews in Sansanding, Mezey found that it is important to
identify women's low social and economic status and particular illnesses that
result from gender discrimination in order to address female health problems.
In particular, Mezey suggests that the most effective way to address women's
health issues is to link care with reproductive health concerns. While women
have high levels of anxiety related to reproductive illnesses, they have little
confidence in government medical facilities and instead seek help from
marabouts and traditional healers. In particular, women are unwilling to discuss

their illnesses, whether reproductive or not, with male health care workers. In response, Mezey suggests that health care programs should collaborate with educational and economic institutions to ensure that Malian women become equal citizens with men. She also argues for innovative financing schemes that help local groups of women and men to meet health care expenses. "Decentralization and regional integration will also be important steps toward democratization. Decentralization allows more grassroots involvement as well as the opportunity to listen to the concerns of the people, to identify their pre-occupations and to improve popular participation in the management of public affairs and good governance."

As Rawson asks in his chapter, however, will real authority and adequate resources devolve to new local authorities? The answer is not clear since Malian history offers abundant evidence of authoritarianism and centralizing tendencies as well as village governance and customary checks and balances. The critical issue posed by Rawson is how current leadership, with due regard to historic values, can move beyond the structures it inherited from thirty years of post-independence Jacobin politics. At a minimum, it will be critical, Rawson argues, to reform the culture of governance at the center so that the national adminis-tration sees itself as a complement to, not a supervisor of, local government. "Decentralization remains at root a question of political will."

Finally, President Konaré believes that:

> [R]egional integration is another way of deepening democracy. In fact, it may be among the best weapons to struggle against many forms of fundamental-ism, as well as to stop regionalism and ethnic conflicts. This broader context allows us to move beyond a framework of dependency. For example, it is important to think about ways to combine decentralization with regional inte-gration in order to renew partnership and cooperation in order to empower local communities within the context of a larger market.

Bingen's discussion of Malian agrarian politics suggests that networks of pro-ducers' associations might offer at least one way for combining decentralization and regional integration. A decentralized structure of government would clearly open multiple new opportunities for political expression by many of the coun-try's emerging agricultural groups. In principle, greater decentralization of gov-ernmental structures should create more avenues for political access by local groups. At the same time, the capacity for cross-national communication pro-vides new political opportunities and expanded resources that can turn previ-ously local groups into significant national and sometimes regional actors.

Grassroots regional networking among producer groups might offer a historically significant means to realize the challenge of democratization, decentralization, and regional integration. The key lies in creating the conditions that
allow the Malian people to move beyond the art of the possible to the art of creating new possibilities.

Note

1. This quotation and all those in the remainder of this section are taken from remarks
   made by President Konaré in the session on education, democracy, and development at
   the MSU Symposium on Democracy and Development in Mali held on 8 May 1998.

From Military Dictatorship to Democracy: The Democratization Process in Mali

ANDREW F. CLARK

Democratization in Africa

This essay analyzes the successful, and largely peaceful, transition from military dictatorship to civilian democracy in Mali. Unlike most other nations, Mali held a national conference, wrote a constitution, and held elections after deposing a repressive military regime. Because of its openness and success, the democratization process in Mali—and in particular the use of a national conference—can serve as an indicator of what might happen in other areas of Africa experimenting with democracy. The rapidity of the transformation, however, does leave some questions unanswered.[1]

The recent, still unfolding democratization process in much of Africa contrasts dramatically with the first decades of African independence in the 1960s and 1970s when the United States and the Soviet Union, joined by former colonial powers Britain, France, and Belgium, played active and often decisive roles in preserving the post-colonial status quo. Each side had its protégés in power and every effort was taken to insure their survival, even in the face of internal and external opposition. In many African countries during the early years of independence, the existing order meant unsavory, usually military, dictators or one-party states closely linked to the Western or Eastern blocs economically, militarily, and ideologically. West Africa suffered particularly from military dictatorships supported by the British and the French who sought to preserve their economic and military interests in the region.

Although civilian government in Africa does not necessarily equate with political freedom, three countries in West Africa—Senegal, The Gambia, and Côte d'Ivoire (until recently)—have managed to retain civilian rule since independence. The remaining thirteen nations in the region have been led by

military governments.[2] The Gambia, ruled by Daouda Jawara after independence from Britain in 1965, and Côte d'Ivoire, headed by Félix Houphouet-
Boigny after independence from France in 1960, functioned as one-party states.
Senegal, in theory, had a multiparty system since independence from France in
1960. But the government party, the *Parti Socialiste*, headed initially by
Léopold Sédar Senghor and then by his hand-picked successor, Abdou Diouf,
retains a commanding hold on the electoral and political processes. In recent
elections, opposition parties have gained votes, yet the ruling party has been
accused of irregular election practices and indirect suppression of its opponents.

The end of the Cold War has had serious and perhaps unexpected global
implications. Western governments and media focused on the remarkable
events in Eastern Europe and Germany, ignoring the broader ramifications for
the non-western world. The media largely ignored less dramatic but equally
important transformations throughout Africa, following the general pattern of
neglect or focusing selectively, erratically, and briefly on Africa.[3] The transition
to democracy in Africa continues to be long and complicated, demanding serious, sustained coverage and analysis. The process, when generally peaceful,
does not produce sound bites or graphic, compelling images of starvation and
massacre for television. The western media prefers instant product to unfolding
process. Consequently, there has been little attention paid to democratization
movements throughout Africa, and virtually no coverage of the rapid pace of
change in several West African countries, the region of Africa that consistently
receives the least amount of coverage in the United States. The British and
French media pay closer attention to events in West Africa, although they too
tend to focus on troubled spots.

Because the industrialized world no longer considers most African countries strategically or politically important on a global or even continental scale,
Africans have been able to pursue much-needed and long-delayed experiments in more open and responsible political systems without outside objections or interference. Opposition groups no longer face the combined forces of
the existing ruling elites and their Cold War or post-colonial sponsors.
Attempts at constitutional democratic reform have achieved varying degrees
of success in West Africa. In some situations, violent uprisings sparked
changes, whereas in others, violence erupted after the democratization process
had already begun. Whatever the chronology or outcome, the volatile political
situation in many West African countries has not changed with the end of the
Cold War, and there is little expectation, either in Africa or abroad, that general, lasting stability is imminent. Nevertheless, signs do exist that renewed
"winds of change" sweeping across the African continent in the 1990s can be

labeled the decade of "second independence" for many West African states that achieved formal independence in 1960.

The National Conference in Africa

Perhaps the most interesting case of the transition to democracy in West Africa centers on the use of a national conference in the early stages of the process. Between 1990 and mid-1992, opposition groups in ten countries (Benin, Burkina Faso, Cameroon, Côte d'Ivoire, Madagascar, Mali, Niger, the People's Republic of Congo, Togo, and Zaire) demanded some form of national conference to determine the political future of their countries. The results of the conferences have ranged from successful to disastrous. In Benin, Congo, and Mali, for example, the conferences led to elections in which the incumbent government lost and conceded power, whereas in Togo, the government won the election. In Zaire, on the other hand, President Mobutu Sésé Séko threatened the participants in the national conference, refused to abide by its pronouncements, and never permitted elections.[4]

The national conference, essentially a francophone phenomenon, is a uniquely African contribution to the democratization process in the post-Cold War era.[5] The conference, which usually lasts several weeks, consists of representatives of all major groups in the country, including political parties, military officials, union leaders, educators, territorial or regional figures, and others involved in national politics. Observers from the diplomatic corps and international aid agencies often attend. Current government ministers may take the lead in the early days of the conference, gradually turning over decisions to a coalition. The conference generally elects a prime minister as new head of government, reducing the incumbent president to a mere figurehead. Discussions center on, among other local topics, the transition to democracy, presidential powers, the role of the military, organization and funding of political parties, and the drafting of a new constitution and electoral code.

The conference also sets the dates for elections—usually within the year—for local, legislative, and national offices. Because of its diverse composition, the national conferences generally carry a good deal of legitimacy among the elite, with their recommendations usually accepted by all parties involved, although the conference in Zaire collapsed because of opposition from Mobutu Sésé Séko. Popular participation in elections establishes the legitimacy of the national conference at the local level. The final result of the process is usually the installation of a democratically elected, civilian head of state with broad support from both the elite and the masses.[6]

National conferences, depending on their relationship to the incumbent government, can be divided into two types: those with limited autonomy and those with full autonomy.[7] A conference with limited autonomy functions within parameters demarcated by the government, considering and endorsing an agenda established, or at least outlined, by the rulers in power. This type of conference aims at dialogue, reconciliation, and opening up the political process. The outcome is generally an already-declared goal, usually elections for a new government. Benin and Mali had this form of limited autonomy national conference, and both were successful. The other type, a conference with full autonomy, operates completely outside the government and is considerably more revolutionary than a limited-autonomy conference. Its aims include the overthrow of the existing rulers and the establishment of an entirely new political order. In Togo, Congo, and Zaire, the conferences functioned with full autonomy, and all failed to achieve their goals. The lesson may be that a national conference with limited autonomy has more chances of a successful conclusion than one with complete autonomy from the current government.

The national conferences in Benin and Mali, both of which fall into the limited-autonomy category, have paved the way for new governments. Both nations successfully made the transformation from military dicatorship to freely elected civilian rule in two years.[8] While the Malian experience may appear unique, it is remarkable for its achievements and can serve as an inspiration to other popular movements in the region and in other parts of Africa and the Third World. Mali also deserves recognition and support from the American and other Western governments for its steady transition to democracy.

The Case of Mali: Background and Context

The landlocked West African nation of Mali is unquestionably one of the world's poorest countries. Most of the country's numerous ethnic groups, including the numerically dominant Bamana (often called the Bambara), the Mande (or Mandinka), the Fulbe (or Fulani), the Tuareg, and the Songhay, are Muslim. Tensions have traditionally existed between the largely nomadic Berber Tuaregs and other groups, primarily farmers. Subsistence agriculture and pastoralism, both severely affected by drought and increasing desertification in recent years, comprise the nation's struggling and stagnant economy. Much of Mali (*Mali inutile*) lies within the Sahara Desert while the more densely populated and considerably smaller southern area (*Mali utile*) occupies the Sahelian zone. Life expectancy and adult literacy are low, and infant mortality is high. Per capita income hovers around $250 annually. Despite some aid relief, particularly by the French, Mali has no prospect of ever paying its enormous international debts. Much foreign aid went to the military and to efforts to suppress numerous Tuareg revolts in the north. Even by West African standards, Mali is desperately and perhaps perpetually poor.[9]

During French colonial rule, which lasted from approximately the 1890s until 1960, the area of present-day Mali formed the colony of *Soudan Français,* or French Sudan, an artificial, administrative creation of colonialism. The French quickly realized that the region held few prospects for profit since the costs of administering the colony were greater than the benefits it produced. The end of the trans-Saharan trade and the growth of regions along the West African coast sealed the economic and political fate of the interior French Sudan. Having occupied the largely uninhabitable and resource-devoid territory, the French continued to administer it without enthusiasm or any attempt to develop the area.[10]

With the approach of independence in the 1950s, the few political leaders in the French Sudan, encouraged by the departing French, sought political and economic union with their more prosperous and coastal neighbor, Senegal. Consequently, during the transition to independence, the present countries of Mali and Senegal, led respectively by Modibo Kéita and Léopold Senghor, formed the Mali Federation. The origins of today's political parties can be traced to the period of decolonization following World War II. Independence for the federation became effective on 20 June 1960.[11]

Relations between the two former colonies, and their ambitious leaders, soured immediately. The more radical and better disciplined Malians posed a threat to the accommodationist Senegalese on a number of issues: Africanization of the administration, relations with France, command of the army, and Malian withdrawal of support for Senghor's candidacy as president of the federation. In August 1960, the Senegalese and Malian sides mobilized their military forces and war threatened to erupt. Fortunately, the situation was resolved peacefully, and Mali and Senegal each declared their unilateral independence. Mali, however, blocked all communications with Senegal for three years and closed the Bamako-Dakar railroad that linked the two countries and gave Mali access to the port at Dakar. Both nations, but particularly Mali, experienced severe economic dislocation. The western region of Mali, centered on Kayes, was devastated by the closure of the railroad and the border with Senegal. Tensions between Senegal and Mali continued for several years. In the dispute, the French generally sided with their close ally and admirer, Léopold Senghor, further angering the Malian leadership.[12]

Modibo Kéita, Mali's first president, reacted to the break-up of the Mali Federation and French support for Senegal by seeking closer ties to the Soviet bloc. In 1961 he received loans and aid from the Soviet Union, China, and Czechoslovakia. He proclaimed a policy of state socialism, established a centralized economy, and instituted a one-party state.[13] Inefficient state-run marketing and distribution systems had negative impacts. Because of low official produce prices, farmers sold their crops on the black market or smuggled their products to neighboring countries, especially the more prosperous Senegal and Côte d'Ivoire. Kéita's attempt to function outside the French-sponsored African Financial Community (CFA franc zone) also proved disastrous. The Malian franc was worthless outside the country. Economic conditions worsened, all political opposition was suppressed, and Kéita became increasingly dogmatic and dictatorial.[14]

In 1968, Kéita was overthrown by a military coup d'état, led by General Moussa Traoré.[15] Because of the hardships caused by Kéita's socialist policies, and the contrasting prosperity of its neighbors, most Malians welcomed the change of government, even if it meant military rule. The French and other Western nations were relieved that the socialist Kéita was out of power, and hoped that Traoré would seek better relations with the West. General Traoré established a Military Committee for National Liberation, citing the failure of Kéita's fiscal policies at solving the nation's economic troubles. He modified some of the centralized economic structures, improved relations with neighbors, including Senegal, and eventually joined the CFA franc zone by adopting the CFA franc. He headed the nation's one legal political party, the Malian People's Democratic Union (UDPM).[16]

The Malian economy remained in dire straits and, despite the military government's efforts, there was no improvement in living standards for the Malian people. The appalling poverty of most people contrasted dramatically with the increasing wealth and opulence of Traoré, his relatives and associates. Corruption was rampant from the national to local levels. Traoré brutally suppressed all political opposition, particularly among the country's intellectuals, many of whom went into exile in France or Senegal. Student demonstrations and labor strikes occurred periodically but were quickly crushed, resulting in school closings, massive arrests, and many deaths. People even began to long for the days of Modibo Kéita whose government they remembered as inefficient but not as obscenely corrupt and repressive as that of General Moussa Traoré.[17]

Traoré held onto power through his control of the military, as head of the one official party, and through the repression of all dissent. He also had the tacit support of the French who saw no alternative to his military rule. Traoré continued to rule Mali as a virtual police state while its economy worsened. The severe Sahelian drought of the 1970s and again in the early 1980s profoundly affected the country. Numerous international agencies worked in the region, although under strict government control. Other moneys were funneled into the military and used to attack Tuareg rebel camps in the north of the country.[18]

Conditions deteriorated markedly in the late 1980s. Both civil servants, who formed most of the country's salaried work force, and the rank and file soldiers in Mali's relatively large military frequently went unpaid for weeks at a time. At one point, the armed forces threatened to mutiny and received their pay promptly. In 1990 and 1991, civil servants undertook a series of strikes, primarily centered on the capital of Bamako, although initially they were poorly organized and ineffective. Nevertheless, the strikes did demonstrate the mounting frustrations of different civilian groups of Malians with the Traoré regime. The armed forces broke up all public demonstrations, and the National Assembly, consisting only of members belonging to Traoré's party, issued hasty proclamations in support of the head of state. As long as Traoré had military support, he held onto power.

The Democratization Process in Mali (1990–92)

In mid-1990, under the pressure of international events and growing tensions in Mali—especially within the armed forces, President Traoré proposed some minor liberalization of politics within his single party, the Malian People's Democratic Union. He adamantly refused to consider any new political parties. This delaying tactic infuriated the civilian opposition who sought Traoré's resignation and the complete opening up of the political process. Opponents formed several political organizations, including the National Committee for Democratic Revival (CNID), the Students Association of Mali (AEEM), and the Democratic Alliance of Mali (ADEMA), one of whose key figures was Dr. Alpha Oumar Konaré.

In 1983, Dr. Konaré, a respected scholar, founded *Jamana*, a highly successful cultural cooperative which sponsored forums, festivals, publications, and literacy programs. The cooperative also established museum-documentation centers, craft workshops, an independent printing and publishing company, and Mali's first private radio station. Under Traoré's dictatorship, groups such as *Jamana* provided Malians with subtle yet meaningful avenues of political criticism and debate. Because theoretically *Jamana* was not a political party, it could operate legally and openly. In 1990, the association merged into a broad-based coalition, still officially a non-political organization. It participated actively with student groups and unions.[19]

The critical phase in the opposition to Traoré and the reform movement began in March 1991. Demonstrations and riots occurred in several cities, the most violent erupting in Bamako on 22 and 23 March. People rioted in the downtown market and shopping areas, burning several buildings and looting stores. The riots quickly became insurrections as demonstrators marched on government buildings, demanding the resignation of the president. The armed forces, hastily sent out onto the streets with orders to shoot to kill if necessary to restore order, put down the insurrection without respect for human life. In one incident, government forces reportedly trapped demonstrators and onlookers in a downtown shopping center, blocked the exits, and then set fire to the place. At least sixty-five people died in that one fire alone.

The overall numbers of civilians killed and wounded in Bamako in the days of violence remain unclear. Government figures range from fifty to 100, while opposition groups claim that at least 200 people were killed, with many more wounded, in the first days of the insurrection alone. Violent demonstrations in other cities resulted in more deaths and injuries. There is no way to determine if people died at the hands of the armed forces or in the general chaos of the riots and demonstrations. Traoré declared a state of emergency and imposed a dusk-to-dawn curfew throughout the country. Borders and airports were also closed.[20]

Opposition leaders met in Bamako on 24 March 1991, to form a Committee for the Coordination of Opposition. Led by Konaré, ADEMA, which had already established a strong, broad-based support network in both rural and urban areas, proclaimed itself a political party and participated actively in the meeting. The committee called for Traoré's immediate resignation, an end to the state of emergency and national curfew, the dissolution of the one-party National Assembly, and the drafting of a new constitution. The committee also endorsed the largely successful nationwide strike initiated by the National Workers Union of Mali, which began on 25 March 1991, to protest the government's actions and to force Traoré to give up power.

That same day, numerous international organizations protested the violence in Mali. The second-in-command of the government party, Djibril Diallo, resigned, and, in a token gesture, the government freed about thirty political prisoners in Bamako. It is unknown how many political detainees were being held; the more senior political prisoners were not held in Bamako but in the Saharan region of the country. New rioting occurred in the capital outside the central prison, which the armed forces crushed. No other opposition demands were met. The situation remained tense and unresolved throughout the country.

On the morning of March 26, the head of the Malian lawyers' association unexpectedly announced that President Traoré had been arrested during the night. The army and security forces that had overthrown him formed a National Reconciliation Council led by Lt.-Colonel Amadou Toumani Touré. The new leadership issued a proclamation, citing the number of people killed in demonstrations, the Traoré regime's corruption, and the country's desperate economic situation as justification for their overthrow of the Traoré government. The new leaders announced that Traoré was still alive and that he and his ministers would be placed on trial. The council claimed it sought eventually to return the country to civilian rule through open, competitive elections. It promised to implement the demands forwarded by civilian opposition leaders.[21]

Despite the promising steps of Touré's National Reconciliation Council, the opposition committee opposed all military participation in the new government and refused to accept the military National Reconciliation Council as the appropriate or legitimate organization to head a transitional government. ADEMA led the opposition to the military government. In a compromise, Lt.-Col. Touré established a coalition of civilians and the military named the Transition Committee for the Well-Being of the People (CTSP), with Konaré and ADEMA playing a prominent role. The CTSP immediately nominated Soumana Sacko, a civilian, as prime minister. More significantly, the group announced steps toward a democratic transition and civilian rule, including a national conference of all groups to decide the exact process and timing for elections and a new constitution. The opposition, with Dr. Alpha Konaré playing a leading role, agreed to work with the transition committee and participate in a national conference.

The CTSP effectively determined the nature and process of the transition toward democratic rule in Mali. The main goal of the initial conference called by the transition committee was to restore peace and reconcile the different factions within the country. The final result of the conference, a change to civilian rule, was already decided. The CTSP coalition created the necessary institutions based on two official documents. The first document, which outlined the political principles to form the basis of the new society, replaced the old constitution until a new one could be drawn up and adopted. This proclamation determined the powers of the CTSP, president, government, and judiciary, and also outlined the final steps of the transition. The second text to be presented to the conference concerned the formation of political parties and their funding. The CTSP also officially convened the national conference whose main agenda included writing three main documents: the political parties charters, the electoral code, and the new constitution.

The national conference, lasting several weeks, took place in Bamako in late 1991. Participants included representatives from the transitional government, all opposition and political groups, and the major trade unions. Members of the diplomatic corps and representatives from some of the major international aid and finance agencies also attended. The goal of the conveners was to include all segments of Malian society, although in reality the political, military, economic, and intellectual elite of the country predominated.

The conference opened with a speech by Lt.-Col. Touré endorsing the gathering, and directing the participants to address the major political problems facing the country. The delegates dissolved the National Assembly and abolished the existing constitution. The conference then considered the documents prepared and presented by the transitional military government. Because the responsible ministers had technical experience and were familiar with the wishes of the opposition, all three documents—the electoral code, the charters for the political parties, and the new institutions to run the government—received approval from the conference without amendments.

The conference adopted a rather complex electoral process. Forty-seven different political parties received approval to participate in the elections. Many of these parties consisted of only a few members and had no national base for support. A series of five elections—one for municipal positions, two for the national assembly, and two for the presidency—were agreed upon.[22] By allowing two elections for the national assembly and the presidency, the conference apparently sought to permit all parties some participation in the initial stage, and then to winnow out those groups not having wide-based support.

Voting, starting with municipal, then national assembly, and finally presidential elections, began shortly after the end of the meetings.[23] A referendum held on 12 January 1992, approved the new constitution. The first round of legislative elections occurred on 23 February and the second round, among the remaining eleven parties, took place on 8 March. ADEMA, led by Alpha Oumar Konaré, won seventy-three of the 115 seats. The presidential elections were held on 22 March and 5 April. Ten candidates contested the first round. On the second ballot, Alpha Konaré was elected with 69 percent of the votes, finishing first in every region of the country and among Malians living abroad.[24]

Several factors contributed to the success of ADEMA in general and Alpha Konaré in particular. ADEMA already had a communications base and widespread support in both rural and urban areas before it officially became a political party in 1991. The party ran candidates in every region. In addition, the reputation of Alpha Konaré, leader of ADEMA, assisted party candidates in municipal and assembly elections. Teachers and medical personnel formed the core of the party's rural support, where most voters lived. Konaré himself visited every part of the country during the elections. Other presidential candidates, focusing on the towns, delegated authority to colleagues, especially in the countryside, whereas Konaré undertook the campaign personally in both rural and urban areas. It is likely that the Malian people, particularly in the countryside, responded to seeing and hearing personally such a prominent Malian.

Dr. Alpha Oumar Konaré was inaugurated on 8 June 1992, and his prime minister formed the first government of the third Malian Republic on the following day. President Konaré instituted a series of reforms while implementing the decisions of the national conference. The political situation in Mali progressed with no further violence. Lt.-Col. Amadou Touré remained as head of the military. Former President Traoré was tried, convicted, and sentenced to death, but in late 1997, Konaré commuted the death sentences of Moussa Traoré and twenty of his followers to life imprisonment.

The new civilian government began the daunting task of dealing with Mali's enormous economic problems, with mixed success. Slow economic development, hampered by the devaluation of the CFA franc in 1994, sparked periodic violent student protests and the rise of some virulent opposition groups centered in Bamako. The government did reach a fragile-but-holding peace settlement with Tuareg rebels in the far north of the country in 1995.

The political scene has been increasingly turbulent since the 13 April 1997 parliamentary elections were canceled by the Constitutional Court because of "poor organization." In the subsequent presidential election on 11 May 1997, Konaré was re-elected to his second and last (under the constitution) five-year term. The legislative elections were repeated in July 1997 and were won by ADEMA. Local elections, postponed twice, were scheduled for late April 1998, with probable success for ADEMA.

Some small opposition groups have refused to recognize the president and other institutions in the country. The opposition alliance is demanding the resignation of the government, dissolution of the national electoral commission, and the release of all those arrested during anti-government rallies and demonstrations before and after the elections. Conciliation efforts are underway to resolve the crisis. The majority of the Malian population, however, apparently accepts the legitimacy of the current government and the results of the elections.

Conclusion

Despite the outbreak of violence in March 1991, the transition from military rule to democracy in Mali can be judged a remarkable success. Ideally, the process should have occurred without bloodshed, although this was highly unlikely given that the entrenched military regime of Moussa Traoré responded to demonstrations with excessive force. By mid-March 1991, the government had little control over its armed forces in the streets of the nation's cities. The same armed forces overthrew Traoré a few days later. The escalating public demonstrations and violence forced the government to grant some concessions, including liberalization of the press, the right to strike, and the recognition of opposition political parties. The violence also facilitated the removal of the existing military government and permitted Lt.-Col. Amadou Touré to institute political reforms that eventually, and rather rapidly, led to democratically elected civilian rule in a country that had no experience with an open electoral process.

The Malian democratization process involved the overthrow of the existing military government and its replacement with a transitional body that oversaw the national conference, leading to open, competitive elections. In other countries, where no interim committees have been installed, the incumbent regimes can easily determine the outcome in advance or halt the process altogether, as happened in Zaire. One of the key elements in predicting the success of the transition involves the status of the existing leaders, most notably the head of state when the transition is initiated. In order to work, the national conference must have autonomy from the government but function within parameters set by the government in power. The process also must be supervised by someone other than a head of state who has ruled for many years, otherwise the focus of the movement becomes the removal of the individual leader, or a coup d'état, rather than the complex process of replacing a military regime with a freely elected civilian government. Conferences with full autonomy have so far been unsuccessful.

The success of the Malian process can be traced to several factors, but most notably to the seizure of the democratic initiative by political forces acting outside of the state through a national conference. Other factors included the removal of the existing Traoré military government before convening the national conference, the enlightened rule and compromises of Lt.-Col. Amadou Touré, the inclusiveness and partial autonomy of the national conference, and the presence of a national figure such as Dr. Alpha Oumar Konaré who emerged a clear victor in the national elections. With any of these factors missing, the process could easily have been derailed or abandoned at any stage. In addition, the conference possessed a considerable degree of legitimacy in the view of the military, political opposition groups, and—finally and most important—the Malian people.

Legitimacy poses one of the major problems faced by all new governments and is of particular concern in other African countries engaged in the democratization process.[25] In the Malian case, Lt.-Col. Touré had both military and popular support because of his overthrow of the despised Traoré regime, as well as his promise and quick moves to initiate a process of democratization. The national conference, composed of appointed individuals and groups rather than elected officials, achieved legitimacy because of its broad representation and the nature of its public debates. The ultimate outcome—democratic elections for local, national, presidential, and judicial positions—was already determined before the conference and provided an opportunity for the Malian people to validate and legitimize the conference's work.

The electoral difficulties in 1997 apparently have been resolved in favor of the legitimacy of the Konaré government, and municipal elections were finally held in June 1999. Mali's transition to democracy continues. The stumbling blocks encountered along the way do not detract from the immense achievement of the Malian people.

Notes

1. R. Vengroff, "Governance and the transition to democracy: Political parties and the party system in Mali," *Journal of Modern African Studies* 31, no. 4 (1993): 541–62; and J. Nzouankeu, "The role of the national conference in the transition to democracy in Africa: The case of Benin and Mali," *Issue* 21, nos. 1–2 (1993): 44–50.

2. The region commonly known as West Africa includes Benin, Burkina Faso, Cape Verde, Côte d'Ivoire, The Gambia, Ghana, Guinea, Guinea-Bissau, Liberia, Mali, Mauritania, Niger, Nigeria, Senegal, Sierra Leone, and Togo.

3. F. Ogundimu, "Images of Africa on U.S. television," *Issue* 22, no. 1 (1994): 7–11; and J. Domatob, "Coverage of Africa in American popular magazines," *Issue* 22, no. 1 (1994): 24–29.

4. "Focus—Toward a new African political order: African perspectives on democratization and regional conflict managment," *Issue* 21, nos. 1–2 (1993): also see J. Nyang'oro, "Reform politics and the democratization process in Africa," *African Studies Review* 37, no. 1 (1994): 141.

5. F. Eboussi Boulaga, *Les conférences nationales en Afrique noire: Une affaire à suivre* (Paris: Karthala, 1993); J. Nyang'oro, "Reform politics," and P. Robinson, "The national conference phenomenon in francophone Africa," *Comparative Studies in Society and History*, forthcoming. For a comparison between Benin and Mali, see Nzouankeu, "The role of the national conference."

6. G. Martin, "Preface: Democratic transition in Africa," *Issue* 21, nos. 1–2 (1993): 6.

7. Nzouankeu, "The role of the national conference," 47.

8. For the military's role in the democratization process, see R. Luckham, "The military, militarization and democratization in Africa: A survey of literature and issues," *African Studies Review* 37, no. 2 (1994): 13–75.

9. A thorough but dated country study of Mali is the *U.S. Area Handbook for Mali* (Washington D.C.: Government Printing Office, 1976). See also R. Imperato, *Historical Dictionary of Mali* (Metuchen, N.J.: Scarecrow Press, 1986).

10. For a history of the colonial period, see J. Suret-Canale, *French Colonialism in Tropical Africa, 1900–1945* (London: Frank Cass, 1972). Also see chapter in this book by David Robinson, "French Africans. . . ," in R.J. Bingen, D. Robinson, and J.M. Staatz, eds., *Democracy and Development in Mali* (East Lansing: Michigan State University Press).

11. P. Imperato, *Mali: A Search for Direction* (Boulder, Colo.: Westview Press, 1989); W. Foltz, *From French West Africa to the Mali Federation* (New Haven and London: Yale University Press, 1965); and D. Kurtz, "Political integration in Africa: The Mali federation," *Journal of Modern African Studies* 8, no. 3 (1970): 405–23. For a biography of Senghor, see J. Vaillant, *Black, French and African: A Life of Leopold Sedar Senghor* (Cambridge, Mass.: Harvard University Press, 1990).

12. For a comprehensive history of Senegal, see A. Clark and L. Phillips, *Historical Dictionary of Senegal* (Metuchen, N.J.: Scarecrow Press, 1994).

13. K. Grundy, "Mali: The propects of planned socialism," in M. Friedland and P. Rosenberg eds., *African Socialism* (Stanford: Stanford University Press, 1965), 28–45.

14. G. Martin, "Socialism, economic development and planning in Mali, 1960–1968," *Canadian Journal of African Studies* 10, no.1 (1976): 23–47.

15. A contemporary account is "Mali: Kéita overthrown," *Africa Confidential* 9, no. 23 (1968): 2–3.

16. Imperato, *Mali: A Search for Direction.*

17. M. Schatzberg, *The Coup and After: Continuity or Change in Malian Politics?* (Madison: University of Wisconsin Press, 1972); and M. Wolpin, "Dependency and conservative militarism in Mali," *Journal of Modern African Studies* 13, no. 4 (1975): 281–95.

18. See the chronology in Imperato, *Historical Dictionary of Mali,* 12–24. For an analysis of the military regime to the mid-1970s, see V. Bennet, "Military government in Mali," *Journal of Modern African Studies* 13, no. 2 (1975): 249–66.

19. F. Ramsay, *Africa: Global Studies* (Guilford, N.C.: Dushkin Publishing, 1993), 46.

20. Daily events were covered in the Senegalese national newspaper, *Le Soleil,* and summarized periodically in the weekly magazines *West Africa* and *Jeune Afrique.* See also Nzouankeu, "The role of the national conference," 46.

21. Information based on reporting in *Le Soleil.* See also Nzouankeu, 46.

22. Vengroff, "Governance and the transition to democracy: political parties and the party system in Mali," *Journal of Modern African Studies* 31, no. 4 (1993): 544.

23. Election data are contained in the official publication, *Direction national de l'administration territoriale* (Bamako: Malian Government Printing Office, 1992). See also Vengroff, "Governance and the transition to democracy," 544.

24. Election results were printed in *Le Soleil.* See also Nzouankeu, "The role of the national conference," 46–47; and Vengroff, "Governance and the transition to democracy," 544.

25. On legitimacy, see, e.g., G. Hyden, "Governance and the study of politics," in G. Hyden and M. Bratton eds., *Governance and Politics in Africa* (Boulder, Colo.: Westview Press, 1992).

Dimensions of Decentralization in Mali

DAVID RAWSON

The Drive to Decentralize

In 1991, Mali's revolutionary elite met at the National Conference to set out the boundaries of the new national order. The conference report concluded in part that the previous administration was inefficient, incompetent, and oblivious to the needs of the nation, that state intervention in rural areas had only reinforced central power, and that existing notions of decentralization followed the logic of neocolonial administration. As a cure to these ills, the National Conference recommended:

- A redefinition of the mission and structures of territorial administration,
- Transfer of competencies to decentralized structures in order to promote real development,
- The redefinition of local collectivities, territorial collectivities, and territorial public establishments *in harmony with the new political context* on the one hand and *the activity and interests of concerned populations* on the other hand. (Italics added.)

The National Conference wanted radical change in the way state business was conducted across the territory. It called for "the abandonment of that type of administration" that did not respond to the requirements of a new "democratic and multiparty" Mali. Building this new Mali required "the purging of the command structure of territorial administration before electoral consultation," and the "reorganization of territorial administration."[1] This essay argues that "the new political context" constituted the driving force behind the formulation of a framework for decentralization over the past five years and that the evolving nature of this political context constitutes the greatest challenge to implementation of the decentralization effort.

But as Mali continues to rebuild its domestic foundations, several questions remain. Will the revolutionary coalition that called for decentralization six years ago hold to its vision? Will real authority and adequate resources devolve to new local authorities? Will Bamako dictate what local authorities may decide, as traditionally done, or will a new spirit of collaboration and constitutional participation evolve between the center and localities? The answers to these questions will have to await the pounding out of political grist within the mortar of Malian history.

Historical Perspectives on Decentralization

Malian scholars have recently emphasized the decentralized nature of Malian patterns of governance. The major political constructions in Malian history "are, of their essence, decentralized," claims Tingé Coulibaly.[2] Within Mande politics, says Mody Sissoko, decentralized institutions resisted all unifying movements "by the nature of things."[3] Policymakers also evoke the vibrancy of village life, the deference which precolonial and colonial empires paid to village or canton chiefs, and the counterweight which custom and religion offered against central authority. Many argue that the empowerment of localities will restore an equilibrium long recognized in Malian administrative patterns.[4]

Malian history is replete with authoritarianism and centralizing tendencies as well as village governance and customary checks and balances. Understanding these historic institutions contributes to our comprehension of the current decentralizing dynamic, especially as Malian leaders seek legitimization in history for a decentralized future.

Malian history is rich with well-known precedents for decentralization. Al Umari noted that Ghanaian kings gave autonomy to gold-producing areas because when they tried to extend authority over those areas, "the gold there begins to decrease."[5] In a similar vein, the division of labor within the occupational caste system of Mande society and Mali empire guaranteed rights and autonomy to persons within customary trade specialties. Throughout Sahelian history, traders, building on relations of confidence rather than force, established commercial networks that transcended political domain and control.[6]

Custom and council in Sudanic courts also limited autocratic tendencies. Al-Idrisi describes a practice among Ghanaian kings of "keeping close to the people and upholding justice among them," in which king awaits the assembly of his counselors before riding at their head through the streets where "anyone who has suffered injustice or misfortune confronts him and stays there until the wrong is remedied."[7] Al Bakri tells us of blind old Basi who exercised his "love of justice" through the advice whispered by his ministers.[8] Even Ibn Battuta's descriptions of elaborate ritual at Mansa Sulayman's council underscores the importance of his deputy Qanja, Dugha the interpreter, and the *farari* elders (each with his followers) in assuring access to the sultan and in upholding a system characterized by a "lack of oppression."[9]

Religious communities also provided an alternative to the rapacious centralizing tendencies of the ruler's court. The epic of Askia Mohammed—full as it is of fury, rivalry, and conquest—underscores the special status and peaceful existence of the wise Islamic counselor, Modi Baja:

> None of Modi Baja's people suffered;
> From that day to the present,
> Our Lord did not make their lives hard.[10]

In both the Mali and Songhay empires, the preacher (*khatib*) or Islamic judge (*qadi*) offered a countervailing pole of authority, ensuring the rule of law under the Maliki tradition and providing refuge within their mosques and cities against arbitrary actions of the emperor's court. Ibn Battuta reports, "It is their custom there that they seek sanctuary in the mosque, or if that is not possible, then in the house of the *khatib*."[11] Islam not only provided a counterweight to centralizing power but a model for decentralized governance. In Timbuktu, as in Djenne or other Islamic centers, the local religious community, *jamaa*, provided parish governance within a rule of law in the several districts of the city.

Biton Coulibaly: the father of decentralization?

Malian enthusiasts for decentralization often cite Biton Coulibaly as avatar and model for establishing state power within a decentralized structure. Many argue that the dominance of Bamana as the language of exchange and the preeminence of Bamana/Mande personalities in Mali's contemporary political history grounds Mali's core political culture in a Bamana ethos. In this context, what do Biton's political achievements offer for contemporary Malians? For example, was his use of the associational age group (*ton*) an affirming tradition or a revolutionary use of a traditional institution? Roberts emphasizes that the change of the *ton* from a social/occupational association to a militarizing institution gave rise to slave raiding and an oppressive authoritarian regime.[12] Person sees Biton's use of the *ton* as a "rupture with the lineage system of the Bamana" and the creation of a new mode for social mobilization and "a more or less egalitarian ideology of the society."[13]

Different interpretations of how Biton financed his new order also illustrate these divergent political tendencies. The original gifts given by *ton* leaders to Biton's mother were customary appreciations of the help and protection she had given them and voluntary recognition of Biton's leadership. As described in the Ségou Bamana epic, the gifts underline the social contract that bound the *ton* to Biton and the voluntary, communal basis of contributions to his cause:

> They said; "Hey look at this.
> When Biton came to power,
> We all said his mother did nothing to command us
> He himself did not shoot to capture us
> There was no force,
> The Council set the manner of choosing him. . . ."
> The Bamana said, "Things have become very good for us.
> Let us put our hands together
> We will give what we can to Biton's mother at Sekoro."
> They said, "Things have become good for us."
> This became a permanent custom.[14]

When Big Bina of Fabugu, a free *ton* member (*tonden*), realized that the levy was being made permanent, he refused to pay. "This yearly tribute will never end. It will become a custom, but I will not pay it this year." The association sent men to destroy his house and take his family into slavery, thus creating the first elements of the *ton* slave caste (*tonjonw*).[15] The gift became a tribute. The *ton*, originally a voluntary association "joined by choice to accomplish a common purpose,"[16] became a means to consolidate power. Over time, and especially under Ngolo Diarra, the free *tondenw* lost rights and become assimilated into the warrior slave caste *tonjonw*. The *ton* leader (*tontigi*) became the wielder of power (*fangama*). Equality gave way to authoritarian ascendancy.[17]

The Biton model encompasses the paradoxes that beset local governance while offering a basis for contemporary aspirations toward tolerance and secularism. The greater Ségou community included Somono, Marka, and Peul ethnic groups that pursued their respective occupations and, as long as they paid tribute, were allowed to pursue their own interests under the protection of Bamana rulers.[18] During much of the Bamana empire this same tolerance was accorded smaller polities and states on the periphery who were left to rule themselves.[19]

Decentralized dimensions of French rule

If the authoritarian slaving state of Ségou had dimensions of decentralized rule and tolerance, so too did the hierarchical French colonial power reinforce decentralizing tendencies within the Malian polity. The centralizing ethos of French colonial administration coupled Cartesian logic with republican rigor, Roman law, and French civilizing mission. Moreover, the French notion of effective administration and social service delivery paralleled its top-down notions of political control and influence.

In a country as diverse and large as Mali, however, French administration experienced the same limitations of distance and locality that the great empires had confronted centuries earlier. Efforts to impose uniform codes gave way to local practices. Islamic or customary courts were used as the courts of first instance. Major local languages—Bambara, Songhay, or Arabic—served as languages of social interaction. *Cercle* administrators, in the name of local security and administrative effectiveness, championed local views against the edicts of the center.[20]

The colonial government also gave limited jurisdiction to communal councils first in Bamako, then in regional centers like Kayes, Ségou, and Mopti. In 1958, a number of other cities were added to the list of full-practice communes.[21] Consequently, many local authorities today see decentralization as a process of recapturing the authority and responsibility their predecessors exercised forty years ago. In addition, representative government through the Constitutive Assembly, from 1945 to the US-RDA (*Union Soudanaise du Rassemblement Démocratique Africain*) proclamation of independence in 1960, touched all localities. Intense party competition between PSP (*Parti Progressiste Soudanais*) and US-RDA to capture the provinces and win the national vote (1947, 1952, 1957) engaged ordinary Malians in determining their own future. Associational activity—whether in veterans groups, unions, or party organization—proved valuable in group decision making and collective action.

What does this historical perspective suggest for future decentralized institutions in Mali? Associational activity has existed in varying degrees of autonomy from political authority for centuries; civil society is not a new idea in Mali. Associations have been based on trades, age affiliation, religious and ceremonial vocations, or producer groups, always with inter-penetration and cross-fertilization within society. The colonial government overrode some of the traditional forces of local control and associational activity while cultivating new ones, particularly in the introduction of political pluralism and electoral choice. There are strong reasons to believe that pluralism and decentralized governance are historically "the Malian way." The critical question is how current leadership, with due regard to historic values, can move beyond the structures it inherited from thirty years of post-independence Jacobin politics.

The Jacobin State

Those revolutionary Parisians who covenanted to common political vision in 1789 at the Dominican monastery of Saint Jacques might have a hard time recognizing the political structures that emerged in the Malian postcolonial state as Jacobin. Yet this designation, commonly applied to the Traoré regime, even more aptly fits the institutional dynamics of the Modibo Kéita era. These regimes were Jacobin in their focus on the nation state, in their insistence on a lay and republican government, and in their demand for conformity to a new normative order. The two regimes may especially be considered Jacobin in their assertion of Party discipline over constituted political institutions, in the techniques of mass mobilization, and in their belief that moral and deliberative authority came from the center. In Mali, from 1960 onward, polity and economy were directed from the top.[22]

The Socialist Era

It is ironic that the drive to organizational conformity wiped out many institutions whose structures offered the best potential for growth in local control and responsibility. One of the first acts of the US-RDA leadership was to sack all the *cercle* commandants who had over the years developed local savvy and promoted regional loyalties, and replace them with administrators politically linked to the Party. The new leaders also abolished the institution of canton chief, thus doing away with the possibility of delegated authority at the local level.[23] All opposition political voices were required to join the US-RDA, eliminating political pluralism as an arena for expression of local interests.

The regime developed its own approach to decentralization. As enshrined in the new republic's constitution, decentralization allowed territorial collectivities to administer "themselves freely by elected councils and under conditions foreseen in the law." However, "the delegate of the Government has charge of the interests of the Republic, administrative control and respect of laws."[24] The ideological commitment to local government and the deconcentration of social services was balanced against the larger and more centralized "interests of the Republic."

Reflecting the US-RDA's paternalistic view of the masses, Dr. Seydou Badian Kouyaté, minister for Plan and Rural Development, said, "To develop this country is to permit the rural majority to put itself in the rhythm of productivity required by state needs and objectives. . . . Renovation has as its first step the modernization of agriculture, the source which feeds the national revenue."[25] This renovation was to take place through a complex system of agricultural extension, model collective farms, and cooperatives for the sale of agricultural products and consumer goods for the rural population.[26]

This scheme was based upon two important assumptions: the use of state services to force modernization in the rural sector, and the need for the state to capture the rural economy. First, "it was a matter of arranging that the new leadership would exercise its authority according to the principles of the Party which had established as an objective the improvement of conditions of existence for the laboring masses."[27] State agents were to be the force of change within decentralized cooperative action. Second, the party and government recognized the rural areas as the source of Mali's productive wealth and wanted to tap that potential for the development of a modern, urban industrial society. Thus, the cooperative network was part of a larger plan to sell agricultural supplies and consumer goods to farmers while exercising monopoly control on marketing of farm production.

Inevitably such control of influence and wealth at the center generated divisions between the administration and within the Party. The rural development schemes gave extraordinary powers to the Minister for Plan and Rural Development, leading to resentment among others in the administration. The US-RDA also split between the conservative elements, whose base among Mali's commercial class was being eroded, and the progressives, who wanted to press forward with further socialization of Malian society and economy. Progressive party leadership affirmed the primacy of "policy over technicity," and in 1966 created the National Committee for Defense of the Revolution and six commissars to oversee conformity with party objectives.[28]

Thus, in the first seven years after independence, as realities diverged from socialist ideology, the response was not to change doctrine but to multiply instruments of supervision and control from the center. The dual problem of stagnation of production and disintegration of a marketing network were directly related to forced collectivization of farm fields and nationalization of commerce.[29] The party misjudged the power of village elders and the attachment of Malians to personal property. Nor could it produce economic growth with its dominant agricultural sector in disarray. The Kéita regime tried to cover the costs of its ambitious program by borrowing and printing money.

France offered to subsidize a return to the Franc zone but only with the conditions that applied to other members of the monetary zone: better control of public finance, reduction of public employment, state enterprises to be put on a business footing, control of credit, and devaluation of the Malian franc by 50 percent.

The agreements should have brought quick relief to Mali's economy with an injection of budget support and French treasury backing of Mali's currency.[30] The policy discipline required by these agreements would dramatically change the regime's social development strategy. President Kéita initially played down the accords' import, but the party commissions called for new measures of state investment that would undercut the agreements. Then in November 1968, President Kéita publicly called the Franco-Malian Agreements a mistake and said, "We must be prepared to break them."[31] Within a few days, he was overthrown in a military coup.

Military rule

On 19 November 1968, military officers constituting themselves as the Military Committee for National Liberation (CMLN) took power, promising a return to civilian rule in six months. They stayed nearly twenty-three years. The "liberation" in the committee's title meant the liberation of Malian villagers from the effort of the socialist state to control and reorder their lives. Liberation did not mean, however, freedom from economic control. For at least a decade, the CMLN held a public commitment to its own brand of "Malian socialism." The CMLN disbanded the labor unions and reorganized a quiescent union directorate committed to "responsible participation"; state enterprises were seen as the "people's inheritance," requiring protection and expansion. These enterprises also provided the quickest means of enriching military officers who managed them.[32]

Instead of assuring local governance through a cooperative structure, the CMLN freed villagers from cooperative oversight and ensured security by directly appointing officials at all levels of local authority. In addition, the committee established "Rural Development Operations" to "assure the harmonious establishment of rural development programs." The Operations sought to provide extension services—technical control and appropriate inputs from central government to specific productive sectors, a bureaucratization of rural production that brought some economic growth to respective zones but enormously benefited the administrative elite and enhanced central government control over rural areas. So, while local governance reverted to village elders, territorial administration and economic control was kept firmly in the hands of the military regime. The suppression of a parallel cooperative structure with attendant services left functional ministries sole occupants of the terrain with an enhanced emphasis on control of extension and social services from the center.[33]

In response to the drought of 1972–73, along with challenges to the CMLN from within and without, the military leaders decided to broaden the regime. The result was a new constitution, ratified by popular referendum in 1974 but not to take effect until five years later. This constitution transmuted the previous regime's dreams for the primacy of a single party into law with a provision making the party the highest organ of the state and its secretary-general the Chief of State. President Traoré, like his predecessor, saw the party as the means for mobilizing people to create an independent national economy. But as a commentator noted, "The UDPM (*Union Démocratique du Peuple Malien*) never received the support it needed to root itself in national environment while assuring the mobilization of the people and favoring their participation [in national life]."[34]

Meanwhile, the regime put forward a far-reaching reform of territorial administration. Like all measures of this era, the new provisions proceeded not out of parliamentary deliberation but as an ordinance decreed by the military committee. *Ordonnance 77–44* set up a new system of territorial administration by region, *cercle, arrondissement*, commune, village, nomadic faction, and the district of Bamako. Development committees and indirectly elected councils were to be established at the region, *cercle*, and arrondissement. At the lowest (village or nomadic faction) level, the new ordinance annulled regulations on communal governance drafted in the Kéita regime. Village chiefs were elected under terms of pre-independence regulations, but were sanctioned by the territorial administration and councils. The *chef* was now "the representative of the *chef d'arrondissement*" and hence of the territorial administration. The village council, combining the advisory and consultative roles of higher development committees and councils, looked into "all economic, social, technical and cultural matters."[35]

In 1988, the *Fonds de Développement Régional et Local* was established to assist in self-financing of local development initiatives. Arguments over which layer of administration would receive what proportion of the fund kept it from being fully operational. Moreover, a considerable part of the fund was diverted in those last years of Traoré's one-party state into building up party offices in localities rather than in productive development projects.[36]

The Traoré regime accentuated the consolidation at the center by abolishing the communal authorities and making all territorial offices from governor on down appointive, usually from military ranks. Maintaining the supremacy of the military oligarchy became the controlling motive. The Traoré regime was as committed as Kéita's socialist ideologues to the consolidation of economic control at the center and the protection of that control through political indoctrination. Individual rights and freedoms were overridden in the first order by the exigencies of socialist doctrine and in the second by the *raison d'étre* of a military regime. Decentralization of authority could only take on an instrumental purpose in making these regimes more sure and effective.

In the late 1970s, President Traoré's military regime had broadened its base by creating a one party state. In the early 1980s, it had adjusted its statist economic doctrines to accommodate donor-imposed economic reform. It initiated a form of consultative process in local administration and, in the late 1980s, developed a decentralized strategy for social services. But despite this reform, the regime could not withstand the triple threat of economic sclerosis, civil war, and agitation for political pluralism. The liberalization of the economy had not been accompanied by any improvement in the government's management of finances. Employees were not paid. The CFA remained overvalued, undercutting the industrial and export sectors. Even the military saw their materiel disintegrate and their wages decrease, while commanders at the top siphoned off the nation's wealth.[37]

In the far north, years of exploitative governmental presence coupled with the mid-1980s drought and the growing demand for autonomy or independence brought the outbreak of a rebellion. Just when the regime could least afford it, it had to concentrate resources and men in fighting a desert insurgency. Meanwhile, back in the capital city, the impetus for freedom of expression and political pluralism grew with each passing month. In March 1991, students and workers were joined in the streets by disaffected women leaders, bureaucrats, and intellectuals. When the military tried to control massive street demonstrations by firing on the crowd, a popular insurrection ensued. A small group of officers led by the Commander of the Presidential Guard, Lt. Col. A. T. Touré, brought the "revolution" to its denouement by finally arresting President Traoré and top members of his regime, hesitantly setting up the Transitional Committee for the Salvation of the People, and calling for a National Conference.[38]

Decentralization as a Democratic Option

The National Conference of August 1991 called for "a true policy of decentralization and administration for development" to remedy Mali's post-independence experience of centralized administration; that is, a truncated socialist experiment using instruments of state "to improve the conditions of existence for the laboring masses" and a quarter-century of military/single party rule. Those who took the reigns of power during the "Revolution of '91" countered this history by a clear commitment to fundamental freedoms, by negotiating and drafting fundamental texts and laws for a decentralized state, by establishing deconcentrated state services, and, eventually, by devolving political authority.

Transition doctrines

The constitution that emanated from the August 1991 National Conference reverted back to the 1960 Constitution's formula in its definition of territorial organization—collectivities would administer themselves freely through elected councils. But the mood of the conference challenged the "Jacobin assumptions" of both the Kéita and Traoré eras. For one thing, the new constitution starts out with an affirmation of individual rights within a rule of law, whereas the 1960 US-RDA Constitution enshrines the "Republic . . . indivisible, democratic, lay and social," and the 1974 Traoré Constitution begins by establishing the party as the first institution of state. While the Kéita regime determinedly pursued a socialist agenda and the Traoré regime gave up its control of economic institutions out of necessity, the 1991 Constitution sanctions the right to property and freedom of enterprise.[39] Moreover, in reviewing documents of the 1991 transition period, one sees the arrogance of the previous regimes (ideological rectitude of the US-RDA or might-makes-right of the Traoré regime) giving way to a genuine consultative process as National Conference leaders grappled with setting Mali off on a new course.

Finally, there is throughout the documents of the transition period a concern with the plight of rural areas. The National Conference calls for "the transfer of authority to decentralized structures so as to promote a real development of local populations."[40] The constitution establishes a High Council for Collectivities to press regional and local development at the national level. Interim President A. T. Touré's "State of the Nation" report notes that "the economic and social crisis which Mali has known for the last thirty years has been felt most heavily by the rural populations," recognizes the heavy weight of the administration on rural populations, and recommends an effective "policy of decentralization" as the cure for this malaise.[41]

It is as though the founders of the Third Republic wanted to distinguish themselves in every regard from policies and positions of predecessor states.

While the Traoré regime was the strawman against which these re-orientations were assessed, both previous Republics are the effective foils of this flight from economic centralism, state control, and social engineering. As the head of Mali's decentralization mission noted some years later, "to choose centralism, even democratic centralism, as the royal road to decentralization is to engage in pious wishes."[42] Regarding the local institutions presumably set up by the Traoré regime under *Ordonnance 77–44*, Sy argues, "[T]hey never functioned. Instead, the administrative commanders were rewarded for executing at the base the orders given from the top." In Dr. Sy's view, the previous regimes saw grass roots development in "a desire to do good to men in spite of themselves, or sometimes against themselves."[43] Thus, rejecting previous approaches to local governance and local development, the National Conference issued a clarion call for "the transfer of authority to decentralized structures so as to promote a real development of local populations."

Documents of decentralization

The process of that transfer was more complex than any of the conference delegates might have imagined. It required a five-year progression of public commitments, legislative drafting, field surveys, educational programs, and local elections. The first step in that process came out of necessity—settlement of the Northern rebellion occasioned by memories of the government repression from 1961–63, by three decades of often exploitative administration, and by disastrous effects of droughts on the North's fragile economy. After three years of fitful battle which only demonstrated the Malian army's incompetence against the nomadic warriors and its frustrated brutality against civilian populations, the interim government decided to press for a political settlement.

The ensuing agreement, the *Pacte National*, began to define the parameters of decentralized governance in Mali. The Northerners wanted what they believed they had been promised in *Ordonnance 77–44*, an immediate voice in how their lands were to be developed and direct control over development implementation. Negotiators won an agreement that gave them authority to organize community life, assure local control of public order, manage patrimony of land, define development programs, and bring linkage with development partners under their control.[44] The *Pacte's* guarantees were imprecise and its timelines unrealistically tight. The agreement fell off track as fighting broke out again. Eventually, by working through local community leaders, Malian authorities were able to reestablish a cease-fire, conduct a donor's roundtable on the North, and signal the end of the war in the *Flame de la Paix* ceremonies in March 1996.

Progress thereafter on integration of faction elements into Malian armed services and economic reintegration of ex-combatants was rather swift. Devolution of authority has been much slower, although the North now exercises a limited sort of self-government through the *Colleges Transitoires d'Arrondissements*. In effect, the devolution of authority to the North was held hostage to the slow process of setting up local authorities in the South. While decentralization and derogation of autonomy to ungovernable regions of the North seemed easy enough to concede, giving those same rights to the South where the administration, government, and legislators had so many vested interests was another matter. So the process of setting up decentralized territorial administration had to await long preparation, vigorous debate, and extensive education campaigns across the country.

Legislating decentralization

Between 1992 and 1997, in addition to approving constitutional provisions on territorial administration, the National Assembly voted through eleven bills setting up the framework of decentralized government. The first of these, voted on 29 January 1993, gave substance to the constitutional provisions on free administration: "...the Region, the District of Bamako, the *Cercle* and the urban and rural commune are endowed with a corporate personality and financial autonomy." While the legislation provides that boundaries of territorial collectivities and the principles of devolution of public goods are to be set by national law, the bill gives collectivities the responsibilities (again to be defined by subsequent law) for conception, programming, and implementation of economic social and cultural development within their respective territories. Most importantly, the state is to transfer to the collectivity resources necessary for the normal exercise of those responsibilities.[45]

Another eight statutes began to fill out this framework. If territorial entities were autonomous, what was the status of civil servants within those entities? That was answered by a law on the status of civil servants, a law on the nomination and attribution of state representatives to the collectivities, and two statutes treating the District of Bamako and its functionaries. If the territorial entities were autonomous, what became of state services and state property within their boundaries? A law on devolution of state services and one on transfer of state domain filled in that gap. Once endowed with civil servants and public property, how was the now autonomous entity to support them? The most recent two laws covered financial resources of the communes and of the District of Bamako.

A perusal of this extensive legislation underscores the Third Republic's seriousness of purpose in pushing forward the agenda of decentralization. Many of the provisions were heatedly debated in drafting committees and in the National Assembly, and it took more than three years to put together the necessary corpus of law. The process also illustrates how far removed the previous regimes had been from anything resembling real decentralization. There was nothing on the books before 1992 even closely resembling the subsequent practical delineation of measures that would create really autonomous territorial collectivities.

Decentralization through découpage

Decentralization of territorial authority is fundamentally a question of land. Since colonial days, all land in Mali belonged to the state unless private title had been specifically granted. With decentralization, the question was how to pass on control over public domain, agricultural land, forests, pastures, and fishing and mineral rights. *Law No. 96—050* covered the establishment and management of domain in territorial collectivities. Its formula was to give to the collectivity responsibility for management, improvement, and conservation of public land but in "collaboration with professional organizations and technical services in conformity with laws and regulations."[46] A larger question was what would be the territorial limits of the "collectivity"? Under the centralized appointive structure of *Ordonnance 77–44*, the state was represented by an administrator and by social services at the arrondissement level. Now the arrondissement was being wiped out, with the commune forming the smallest administrative unit. Within most urban areas, commune lines were already drawn, but how were rural areas to be delimited?

To deal with the problem, the Decentralization Mission organized regional and local groups for education and mobilization (GREM/GLEM) to structure debate among local populations about decentralization. A typical group might include leaders of civil society, political party representatives, religious leaders, members of professional organizations, and businessmen.[47] Members of these informal groupings were then put together with representatives of Territorial Administration in *Commissions de Découpages* to divide the arrondissement into communes. Armed with a manual giving population figures of villages within the zone, the commission was to consult with villagers as to how to organize into communes based on criteria of social solidarity, economic viability, and logic of geography and space.[48]

These commissions worked the ground for several months, in some cases taking proposals back several times to local populations. In some instances villages that had been merged into one commune refused to deal with each other; in other instances populations solicited consolidation. The proposed "Découpage" law encompassing the conclusions of the commissions was vociferously contested in the National Assembly. The draft law proposed 643 communes; legislators poured over maps, reviewed population and other characteristics of villages, took in complaints, and ended up by eliminating four rural communes, adding forty-three new ones and transferring some villages from one side to another. In all, 701 communes were given legal birth.[49]

What complicated the issue was that these newly delimited communes had been "collectivities" before—as village, chief seat of the arrondissement, or emerging town gathered around a market on a new highway. Will elected communal counselors reflect old loyalties or new ambitions; will they build a sense of participation and community or propagate new divisions within the body politic? The intensity of the debate engendered in setting up the communal structure demonstrates that Malians, always politically interested, are most directly engaged when it comes to local issues. That is why the holding of these elections is so important to Mali's future and why President Konaré on the thirty-seventh anniversary of Malian independence said, "Since our country is mostly of a rural nature, I would say without hesitation that the last important reform at the end of this century is decentralization, which remains the strongest political justification for democracy."[50]

Implementing Decentralization

The territorial reorganization this study surveys is a work in progress. For all the effort already deployed, for all the eloquent statements positing decentralization as a great national ambition, the process will not find real form until communal councils have been elected and the infrastructure for local governance established. Holding elections for councils—which will range according to population density from eleven to forty-five members, with both party and independent candidates in the running, and with the results to be determined on the proportion of the vote gained—will be a daunting task.

The political challenge

People of good will were looking hopefully to the communal elections as the arena in which multiparty politics would get its second wind. But efforts to bring boycotting parties to the contest have failed; the political impasse, originating in the administratively flawed legislatives of April 1997, remains. The dominance of the majority party and recalcitrance of historic opposition parties can only weaken the openness of the atmosphere in which local polling takes place. Moreover, the same opposition forces that joined the cry for decentralization in 1991 and approved decentralization measures in the National Assembly over the last five years now raises concerns about the process. In a February 1997 meeting with President Konaré, boycotting leaders asserted that fundamental policy differences on decentralization, the electoral process, and equal access to media stood between the government and the opposition.[51] Decentralization has become official doctrine, yet the opposition challenges it as ill-advised and unworkable.

There are signs, however, that the very process of holding local elections is breaking down the conceits of "democratic centralism" by which political elites in Bamako practiced armchair leadership of parties around the country. Political leaders in regional capitals are anxious to join the fray, believing they can win. In several instances, such leadership joined with other parties in revising the electoral lists against party headquarters' wishes. Some party leaders have split away so they can stand for local elections. Others may authorize their members to run as independent candidates. Setting up decentralized structures may cure the close-mindedness of Malian elite politics.

One can only hope that the communal elections take place so that the real process of having local groups determine their collective future can begin. Should the communal elections be moderately successful, a number of outstanding issues will remain. What Mali will have at the end of this exercise is a restructuring of territorial administration in which the local populations have been consulted to an unusual degree in determining what the "collectivity" will be. That collectivity, however, will enjoy only delegated powers. These are not jurisdictions where the decisions of councils have the power of law. Rather all decisions taken by regional, *cercle*, or communal councils must conform to laws established by national institutions. Rights to communal property may be ceded or withdrawn by an act of government; communal budgets have to be approved by the state delegate. What kind of local taxes may be established and at what levels has already been decided at the national level.

The center knows best

Behind these structural realities lurks the mandarin conceit that intellectuals in the capital city know best what is needed in the provinces, that the best administrator is not a locally elected official but an experienced bureaucrat appointed

by central authority. Should the electoral process falter or a post-election council be found wanting, there are those within the central administration quite
willing to use the law or arguments of contingency to reassert control over the
local administration. Already, the failure to hold communal elections before
the end of the mandate of municipal councils in autonomous communes has
resulted in their being disbanded and *délégations spéciales* being appointed in
their place. The enthusiasm with which veterans of territorial administration
again took over the reigns of local government and put to rights the presumed
failings of their elected predecessors illustrates the limited support which the
decentralization process may have among the officials who must help make it
a success. Moreover, the mandate of these delegations has twice been renewed
without argument from any political front; Malian politicians appear more at
ease with appointed officialdom than with elected office holders.

The process of decentralization, for all the well-intentioned consultation
of the population on territorial boundaries, has engaged learned bureaucrats at
the center in establishing modalities for subdividing national territorial administration and delegating to localities some responsibilities for that administration. Perhaps it was necessarily a top-down exercise. But in reading the
legislation as it details just how the process will work, one senses the pater-
nalist heart of yore. Can the people really be trusted to run their own affairs, to
choose the modalities of their own governance? What if they want more than
what they have been given in the decentralization process? When asked how
decentralization will function, respondents in the region all too often remark,
"The Decentralization Mission has made us understand that. . . ." At this point
in the exercise, we are a long way from the ideal of participatory democracy
which "ought to render to each person the power to influence the condition
under which decisions are made."[52]

The Decentralization Mission insists that the communal institutions must
be put in place and then each commune will grapple with issues of empowerment, responsibility, and financial accountability. The government is currently
elaborating measures to facilitate and order that process: training programs,
common administrative forms, personnel and organization data banks, new
procedures for tax collection, and allocation of start-up funds.[53] But it will also
be necessary, as some strategists now realize, to reform the culture of governance at the center so that the national administration sees itself as a complement to, not a supervisor of, local government. The local stake in the nature of
the process has not been fully appreciated either by administrators at the center or potential leaders in the hinterland.

Making cooperatives work

There is a counter current at work across the land. The "spirit of Ségou" has brought about a flowering of associational activity in towns and cities across Mali. Producer groups, parent/child associations, health center committees, independent rural radio stations, women's organizations, human rights organizations, and nongovernmental organizations of all sorts have flourished.[54] Without waiting for communal councils to be set up or *cercle* councils to oversee deconcentrated services, these associations are carving out their own control over school construction, health care, or civic education in the local arena.

This flowering has yet to be fully recognized by central authority. A case in point is the status of cooperatives now burgeoning across the country: agricultural production groups, transport collectives, economic initiative groups (GIE), or savings and loan networks. The last law on cooperatives dates back to the Traoré era and keeps direct control of cooperatives, in the tradition of Kéita regime, under the minister of Rural Development.[55] Proposed revisions would adapt the law to the new atmosphere in civil society across the country, make recognition procedures simple, and create a national supervisory board, rather than have cooperative affairs directed by a functional ministry. But the Ministry of Rural Development has refused to sign off on the project and thus to give up putative control over horses that have long since escaped the barn.

It may well be that not having a functioning law on cooperatives does no harm as long as associations are able to form and function. The situation of rural radio stations illustrates this sort of laissez faire principle. The government has been unable to keep up with the demand for authorizations to use air space and instead lets stations flourish without trying to police them. This growth in rural radio stations has been a boon to development and an embellishment on Mali's international image as a promoter of free expression and human rights. In the case of cooperatives, however, the questions of who belongs, who controls, and who gains are bound to invite government intervention. What would happen, for example, if an elected council at the *cercle* level decided to assert control over a producer's cooperative that had not been able to establish its legal status?

Cooperative action has given a whole new dimension to community life at the local level that the current laws for decentralization do not take into account. Some legal recognition of this cooperative renaissance is certainly necessary if it is to take root and endure. Helping good governance get implanted at the local level while nurturing the precious plants of free associational activity remains the coming challenge for Malian authorities and donors alike. Decentralization

of territorial administration with delegation of some responsibility and authority to local levels can set a political framework for this activity, but the future
of development in Mali is villagers pursuing their own interests and determining for themselves what the political agenda will be.

Evolving political context

Six years ago, the National Conference set a new vision for a Mali that was
"democratic and multiparty," and ordained a reordering of the territorial administration. In those six years, authorities in Bamako have slowly established the
framework for decentralization and prepared for communal elections. During
this period they have also reestablished "the ensemble constituted by institutions, procedures, analyses and reflections, calculations and tactics" that we call
the central state.[56] To use a common measure of African state practice, over the
past five years, rule in Mali has become less personalized with democratic institutions beginning to assert their appropriate role, while freedoms of expression,
enterprise, and assembly have been exercised. There was a certain delegation of
authority with the reinstitution of autonomous communes in 1992 and a very
considerable effort to involve local populations in delivery of social services.
Free press and radio have helped maintain a fairly high interest among ordinary
Malians in political discourse, although the electoral difficulties beginning in
April have caused a significant part of the electorate once again to disdain political participation—witness the low turnout at legislative elections.[57]

The fundamental question is whether this record constitutes a successful
transition to the democratic and pluralist Mali that the National Conference
envisaged, or a "partial liberalization of an authoritarian state" as some in the
opposition claim. In its vision of human rights, support for individual initiative, the rule of law, and democratic consultation, the Third Republic stands in
vivid contrast to its two predecessors. But has the articulate vision drawn
behind it the structural change that will perpetuate this change? After the re-
establishment of national institutions in recent elections, does Mali remain a
model for democracy in Africa or does it join the mainstream of failed or partially achieved democratic experiments?[58] Until the final plank of the National
Conference, the "decentralization of administrative structures," is in place,
Mali's 1991 revolution remains partial.

The administrative tendency toward control from the center remains. Has
the political will to override centralist tendencies survived the changing political context? The failure over five years to achieve decentralization gives us
caution. President Konaré, the embodiment of that political will, affirms that

he will step down at the end of his current term. His party, ADEMA, now over-whelmingly dominates state institutions. Will other ADEMA leaders see local governance, as did the Kéita and Traoré regimes before it, as a means of reg-ulating individuals and organizing space, goods, and riches, or as a way of let-ting people take over their own government? The political context has mutated; the prospect of a contest for succession in four years may well dim ADEMA's enthusiasm for dispersal of power.

On the other hand, the current refusal of a significant part of the opposi-tion to participate in national elections suggests a "decay in institutional capac-ity to generate new forms of consensus about the basic rules in politics."[59] That opposition claims it has no other recourse since rules of the game have been dictated by the majority. But absent at least an effort to contest within the polit-ical process, that opposition, in its academic conceits and urban focus, may be becoming irrelevant to the process of politics in Mali.

Over the past five years, constitutional changes and legislative reforms have significantly altered the rules of political competition. It is not yet clear whether these changes were imposed by the dominant classes for their own end or established to open the arena to effective political discourse among masses.[60] Both the ruling majority and the recalcitrant opposition are almost exclusively urban. During those five years, these elite coalitions collaborated in the management of state politics, including the elaboration of decentraliza-tion law. Now the elite debate has coalesced around the issue of whether to pursue the democratic process or abort it to return to a transition under a "gov-ernment of national union." On all other issues, fragmentation and personal-ization of the political demarche remain the rule of the day. Power remains based "on loose alliances of elite factions."[61]

In 1991, the National Conference posited decentralization as the antidote to the administrative centralism of previous Republics. That political context has now shifted: there is a competition for perpetuity at the center that may obstruct the political elite's stated intention of empowering localities. Decentralization remains at root a question of political will. We can still hope that the leaders of Mali on all sides of current issues will claim the future and permit a genuine devolution of political authority in the implementation of decentralized government.

Notes

1. *République du Mali, Actes de la Conférence Nationale du Mali*, Bamako, 20 August 1991: 133.

2. Tingé Coulibaly, "La décentralization aujourd'hui," *Le Républicain* 138 (3 May 1995).

3. Sékéné Mody Sissoko, "Décentralisation," *L'Indépendant* 14 (1995).

4. Sébastien Diallo, "Pour que le Mali profond retrouve son âme!" *Le Démocrate Malien* (July 1995): 61.

5. N. Levtzion and J. F. P. Hopkins, *Corpus of Early Arabic Sources for West African History* (London: Cambridge University Press, 1981), 26.

6. For a description of the pervasiveness of these "Wangara" traders, see Nehemia Levtzion, *Ancient Ghana and Mali* (London: Methuen and Co., 1973), 165–70.

7. Levtzion and Hopkins, 110.

8. Ibid., 79.

9. Ibid., 240–91, 296.

10. Thomas A. Hale and Nouhou Malio, *The Epic of Askia Mohammed* (Bloomington: Indiana University Press, 1996), 27.

11. Levtzion and Hopkins, 295; Levtzion, 201. Also see, Mahmoud Kat ben El-Hadj El-Motaouakkel Kati, *Tarikh El-Fettach*, O. Houdas and M. Delafosse, eds. (Paris: Librarie d'Amerique et d'Orient, 1964), 224, in which Tarikh el Fettach records that "in the kingdom of Mansa Musa no one is allowed to shake his hand but his *qadi*," and that the *qadi* El Aqib enjoyed a fame "as great as that of Askia Daoud and his son Askia El Hadj."

12. Richard Roberts, *Warriors, Merchants and Slaves* (Stanford: Stanford University Press, 1989), 19; cited in Sundiata A. Djata, *The Bamana Empire by the Niger* (Princeton: Markus Wiener Publications, 1997), 13.

13. Yves Person, "Ngolo Tara ou la Force de Ségou," in *Les Africains*, André Julien, ed. (Paris: Edition T. A., 1978), 282; cited in Djata, 14. Also see, Jean Bazin, "Recherches sur les formations socio-politiques anciennes en pays Bambara," *Etudes Maliennes* 1 (1970): 3; cited in Djata, 15. Bazin argues that the political model of Biton's rule was ancient and that Biton was more of "a renewal than an origin."

14. David C. Conrad, ed. *A State of Intrigue: The Epic of Bamana Segou according to Tayiru Banbera* (Oxford: Oxford University Press, 1990), 96.

15. Ibid., 98–99.

16. Ibid., 3n.

17. See Adame Ba Konaré, *L'épopée de Ségou* (Lausanne: Pierre Marcel Favre, 1957), 94, for an argument that power was exercised in Ségou as violent force.

18. Djata, 22.

19. Ibid., 186. The Coulibaly and the Diarra clans did not seek to impose their clan-based religion either.

20. An element in the preservation of Bamara identity, for example, was the articulation to foreigners (French administrators and colonial ethnographers) of what the Bamana thought they were. Djata, 183.

21. "Loi No. 551489 du 18 novembre 1955." *Journal Officiel de la République Francaise* (19 November 1995): 11274–78. Also see, Jennifer Seely, "Democratization in Mali," unpublished paper, American Embassy Bamako, Mali, 1996, 3.

22. It is particularly true that the ideologue of the Kéita era was, like the Jacobin, "not revolutionary in that he believed in heaven, or even in that he believed in a special kind of heaven, but in that he attempted to realize his heaven here on earth." Clarence Crane Brinton, *The Jacobins* (New York: The Macmillan Company, 1930), 239 and 137–83.

23. Jeanne A. Toungara, "Kinship, politics and democratization among the Malinke of northwest Côte d'Ivoire," in *The Younger Brother in Mande*, 52–53, Jan Jansen and Clemens Zober, eds. (Leiden: Research School CNWS, 1994); also see Seely, 3.

24. République du Mali, *Constitution*, Loi No. 60–1, 22 September 1960.

25. Cheick Oumar Diarrah, *Le Mali de Modibo Kéita* (Paris: Editions l'Harmattan, 1986), 72.

26. Ibid., 75–77.

27. Ibid., 38.

28. Ibid., 41, 149, 156. Party leaders later divided the national territory into twenty-three zones and gave to the *chef de zone* full powers of oversight in political, economic, and social/cultural domains.

29. Ibid., 107–15.

30. Ibid., 116–28.

31. Ibid., 177.

32. Cheick Oumar Diarrah, *Vers la Troisième République du Mali* (Paris: Editions l'Harmattan, 1991), 69. If an officer were powerful enough, a state enterprise might be diverted directly to one's profit, as when Minister of Defense Dounkara disbanded the trucking parastatal and channeled its assets into his own company.

33. *Ordonnance No. 22 CMLN*, "Portant institution des Opérations de Développement Rural," 24 mars 1972; and Cheick Oumar Diarrah, *Mali bilan d'une gestion désastreuse* (Paris: Editions l'Harmattan, 1990), 109–12. Gerard notes how the Ministry of Education tried in vain to monopolize basic education in the 1970s, attempting by regulation to close Islamic schools. In the same time frame, authorities put Catholic religious in prison for violating the state monopoly on the sale or distribution of medicine. See Etienne Gerard, *La tentation du savoir en Afrique* (Paris: Editions Karthala, 1997), ch. 5.

34. CERDES, *Le processus démocratique Malien de 1960 à nos jours* (Bamako: Editions Donneya, 1997), 30. Also see David P. Rawson, "Mali: soldiers as politicians," in Isaac James Mowoe, ed., *The Performance of Soldier as Governors* (Washington: University Press of America, 1980), 290–304, for a discussion of Traoré's efforts to return to "normal constitutional life."

35. Comité Militaire de Libération Nationale, *Ordonnance No. 77–44*, "Portant réorganisation territoriale et administrative de la République du Mali," 2 June 1974.

36. Patrick Meagher and Georges Korsun, *Decentralized Public Finance and Effective Governance in West Africa* (College Park: Institutional Reforms and Informal Sector, 1997), B-2.

37. CERDES, 31–32.

38. Ibid., 32–36.

39. Présidence du Comité de Transition pour le Salut du Peuple, *Décret No. 92-073/P-CTSP*, "Portant promulgation de la Constitution," in Primature-Mission de Décentralisation, *Lois et Décrets de la Décentralisation*, February 1997.

40. *Actes de la Conférence Nationale du Mali*, 133.

41. Diarrah, 1991, 208.

42. M. Ousmane Sy, "La décentralisation en chantier," *Le Démocrate Malien*, July 1995: 11.

43. Sy, 11.

44. Secrétariat Général du Gouvernement, "Pacte National conclu entre le gouvernement de la République du Mali et les mouvements et fronts unifiés de l'Azawad consacrant le statut particulier du Nord du Mali," 11 April 1992, Title III, A-G.

45. *Loi 93–008* "Déterminant les conditions de la libre administration des collectivites territoriales," 11 February 1993, in *Lois et Décrets*, 12.

46. *Loi 96–050* "Portant principes de constitution et gestion du domaine des collectivites territoriales," 16 October 1996, in *Lois et Décrets*, 72.

47. "Les groupes régionaux d'étude et de mobilization," in *Le Démocrate Malien*, 21–22.

48. "Les commissions de découpage," in *Le Démocrate Malien*, 27–29.

49. Primature-Mission de Décentralisation, *Loi 96–059* "Portant création de communes," 10 November 1996, 5–9.

50. Alpha Oumar Konaré, "Address to the Nation," *Essor*, 22 September 1997.

51. "Alpha invite le COPPO a produire un argumentaire écrit," *Le Matin* (February 1998): 1.

52. See Robert Cummings Neville, *The Cosmology of Freedom* (Albany: State University of New York Press, 1995), 344.

53. Mission de Décentralisation, Présidence de la République, "Groupe de travail pour le démarrage des communes," April 1998: 2–4.

54. For a review of projects reflecting the "spirit of Ségou," see *On ne ramasse pas une pierre avec un seul doigt* (Bamako: Foundation Charles Leopold Mayer, 1994).

55. Présidence de la République, *Loi 86–62 ANRM*, "Régissant le mouvement coopératif en République du Mali," 10 June 1988.

56. See Achille Mbembe, "Pouvoir, violence et accumulation," in J. F. Bayart, A. Mbembe, C. Toulabor, *Le politique par le bas en Afrique noire* (Paris: Editions Karthala, 1992), 250–52.

57. Goran Hyden, "Governance and the study of politics," in *Governance and Politics in Africa*, Goran Hyden and Michael Bratton, eds. (Boulder: Lynne Rienner, 1992), 23. Hyden offers the following negative characteristics of politics in Africa: personalized nature of rule; frequent violations of human rights; lack of delegation by central authorities; and tendency for individuals to withdraw from politics.

58. Michael Bratton and Nicolas van de Walle, "Toward governance in Africa: popular demands and state responses," in Hyden and Bratton, 51.

59. Ibid., 49–50.

60. J. F. Bayart, "La revanche des sociétés africaines," in *La politique par le bas*, 100.

61. Michael Bratton and Donald Rothchild, "The institutional bases of governance in Africa," in Hyden and Bratton, 272.

The opinions in this essay are those of the author and do not necessarily represent the views of the United States government.

Classrooms of Democracy? The Educational Prospects of Malian Civil Society

JOHN UNIACK DAVIS

Chaque heure qui passe apporte un supplément d'ignition au creuset où fusionne le monde. Nous n'avons pas eu le même passé, vous et nous, mais nous aurons le même avenir, rigoureusement. L'ère des destinées singulières est révolue.[1]

Introduction

Primary among the dramatic changes that have swept a shrinking world in the past decade is the advent of democracy in many contexts previously deemed inhospitable due to a lack of certain prerequisites. For example, democratic transitions of varying degrees have been undertaken in over half of Africa's countries. While the routinization of competitive electoral processes gives reason to be hopeful regarding prospects for stable democratic governance, the long-term consolidation of democratic rule is an even more challenging undertaking. In this vein, many in the international donor community have chosen to promote and support local associations as the building blocks of democracy. For instance, the United States Agency for International Development (USAID) is promoting democratic governance in twenty-four sub-Saharan African countries, and most of these programs include civil society capacity-building as an essential element of their programming. In fact, in the Republic of Mali, the promotion of capacity-building among community organizations and local non-governmental organizations (NGOs) is the sole focus of USAID's "Democratic Governance Strategic Objective" (DGSO). In Mali alone, USAID is spending nearly $4 million a year on such programs.[2] With such resources being committed, it is worth examining the assumptions behind the supposed democratic effects of civil society.

Having an associational sphere distinct from the state can serve an interest aggregation, or pluralist, function and it can also serve to socialize members to hold political values such as compromise, trust, tolerance, and efficacy which are believed desirable for long-term democratic stability. In this chapter, I evaluate this supposed socialization function of civil society using both organizational-level data and individual political attitudes data gathered in the Republic of Mali.

The chapter is organized in the following manner. This introduction is followed by a brief discussion of the key issues involved in positing a socialization function of civil society. Next, the general case of the Malian democratic transition is introduced, along with background information concerning the socioeconomic context of the study. I then describe local organizational characteristics along four dimensions based on extensive interviews in six Malian villages. This ethnographic material is supplemented with an analysis of a twenty-one-village survey on organizational participation and political attitudes. The chapter concludes with a summary and tentative conclusions regarding the nature of associational life in rural southern Mali.

Democratization, Civil Society, Political Socialization

During the "third wave" of democratization—that is, since the 1970s—there has been a renewed interest in factors which facilitate democratic transitions as well as those that contribute to a subsequent consolidation of democracy.[3] Indeed, in recent years, elites in most of the world's nation-states have come to profess that the best form of government is a democracy,[4] and the end of the Cold War has engendered an unprecedented level of American interest in spreading the gospel of democracy throughout the world.[5] For example, the United States Agency for International Development (USAID) has placed a great deal of faith in the possibility of civil society organizations serving a vital role in promoting democratic governance in Africa, both in their direct contribution to democratic development, as well as by inculcating democratic habits and values in individual citizens.[6]

Those who count on the democratic socialization effects of the associations that constitute civil society make *two assumptions*. First, they assume that there is something inherently democratic about associations. Second, they assume that exposure to these positive characteristics will induce individual members to have more democratic values. To test empirically the potential of local organizations to contribute to democratic consolidation in this manner, one must evaluate both of these assumptions.

In order to examine the assumption that there is something democratic about the associations that make up civil society, we must be clear about what is meant by the term. Most analysts agree that it is an arena beyond the household in which organizations interact with the state, influence the state, but are distinct from the state and do not vie for state power, as "political society" does. Many object to including organizations that do not directly interact with the state in the category of civil society.[7] Others employ a broader definition, seeing the essential democratic characteristic of civil society in its being an alternative center of social organization, regardless of the thematic content of its organizations' activities.[8] For the purposes of the present study, this broad, inclusive definition is employed.

Civil society, at its best, has been described as having both pluralist and educational functions in the stability and performance of a democratic polity.[9] In serving as the locus of organized collective action, civil society performs its pluralist function and "forms a bulwark against despotic tendencies in political life."[10] In this aspect, the external relations of organizations are of concern, particularly their autonomy, strength, and openness of membership. By most definitions of civil society, its organizations must necessarily be *autonomous* from the state or its local representatives and membership must be *voluntary* in nature. Civil society also can serve an educational function, socializing support of democracy through participation in democratic structures. In this function, the inclusiveness and transparency of internal procedures of *leadership selection and decision making* are most important.[11]

Some do not see civil society as in and of itself a panacea for anti-democratic tendencies. Fatton suggests that civil society is a necessary but not sufficient condition for the existence of "civic community,"[12] which is characterized by "an active, public-spirited citizenry, by egalitarian political relations, and by a social fabric of trust and cooperation."[13]

Another important issue to consider when assessing the democratic potential of civil society concerns the cultural and political context in which it evolves. While "modern" civil society has preceded democratization in many cases, "the development of civil society and democracy are occurring in much of Africa as parallel and related processes."[14] Indeed, regions of the world that have historically been populated by authoritarian regimes pose interesting issues for students of participation. In Africa, informal organizational activity flourished even where authoritarian control was most evident.[15] State-society relations have been suggested to be mutually beneficial and not a zero-sum game. As such, civil society could be an important factor in democratic political development.[16]

African societies differ from the networks which constitute civil society in the West in the way that they have held together according to kinship ties and age groups rather than by bonds of impersonal interest. While many precolonial cultures in Africa included a plethora of informal associations, their ascriptive nature set them apart from their counterparts in Europe and the United States. Célestin Monga argues that African civil society cannot be easily assessed in European terms, not least because "in the African case the leadership, membership, and functioning of such structures are often shrouded in mystery."[17] Consequently, one cannot assume that organizational participation means the same thing there that it does in Europe and the United States. As the late Ernest Gellner put it, "a modern conception of freedom includes the requirement that identities be chosen rather than ascribed."[18]

While the first assumption made by those advocating the desirable effects of civil society is organizational in nature, the second takes as its unit of analysis the individual—what effect can one expect organizational participation to have on its members? The study of political socialization has long been a preoccupation of Western political science. Some have suggested that the exposure of citizens to democratic institutions from a young age performs the function of inculcating values presumed to be favorable to democracy, such as efficacy, compromise, trust, and tolerance.[19] While most of this body of work has focused on childhood political socialization, certain scholars have acknowledged that beliefs and attitudes are not established immutably in childhood.[20] Research on 'political learning' has attempted to identify the sources of changes in political beliefs among adults.[21]

Most attention to socialization has examined the role of electoral institutions,[22] though adult experiences in non-political associations have also been suggested to be a source of the learning of political culture.[23] Robert Putnam has argued that membership in horizontally-ordered groups such as cooperatives, sports clubs, and mutual aid societies should be positively correlated with good government and that institutional changes are reflected in corresponding, but gradual, changes in values.[24] For example, organizational activism can foster solidarity which contributes to individual feelings of competence or efficacy with regard to the larger political system. Similarly, exposure to the give and take of diverse groups within an organization can contribute to broader feelings of tolerance for different ethnicities or ideological points of view. On the eve of the current dramatic transitions, Muller, Seligson, and Turan echoed this point of view, suggesting that in nations with authoritarian pasts or where electoral institutions have harbored clientelistic networks, "norms of democratic governance may be learned through participation in local organizations."[25]

Of course, as discussed above, civil society cannot be assumed to embody the values of anywhere but the milieu in which it evolves. Larry Diamond makes this point, saying that democratic values will be acquired in civil society only if the organizations which make it up "function democratically in their internal processes of *decision making* and *leadership selection.*"[26] Michael Bratton makes a similar point, arguing that one cannot expect organizations with liberal characteristics to emerge from a "neopatrimonial" political culture.[27]

This is a venerable discussion. Tocqueville spoke of civic organizations as "classrooms of democracy" in the American context a century and a half ago. More recently, in their classic tome, *The Civic Culture*, Almond and Verba spoke of an emerging world-political culture in which "the participation explosion" would be key—democracy was held to entail more than just formal institutions.[28] While political culture arguments had all but disappeared from the theoretical radar screen by the 1980s, the emergence of nascent democracies in cultural contexts very different from those studied by Almond and Verba and their contemporaries has led to a renewal of interest in this and related topics.

Much of the empirical literature on civil society concerns the pluralist function.[29] Compared to the plethora of theoretical articles on civil society, as well as articles describing the interest aggregation function, there is a dearth of empirical testing of the socialization function. The current study describes the types of associations most familiar to rural citizens in one African country. To evaluate the external characteristics of organizations, assess their fit with the Western notion of civil society, and gauge internal levels of democratic procedure, local-level rural organizations in Mali are evaluated according to observations on four dimensions:

1. Is membership *ascriptive* or *voluntary*?
2. Is the organization *autonomous* from control by the state and traditional authorities? In other words, do external authorities have any significant control over organizational activities?
3. Is *leadership selection* conducted in an inclusive fashion? Is there any evidence of any kind of systematic participation by the rank and file in this process?
4. Are *decisions* made inclusively? Again, do procedures exist which ensure systematic participation by the general membership?

Only through this examination of procedures and characteristics can one evaluate whether the much-vaunted socialization potential of civil society organizations is plausible. Following a section describing the context of the present study, these organizations will be described. Their characteristics will then be linked to the values of organizational members, particularly with respect to political efficacy and tolerance, to test socialization effects.

The Malian Context

Democratic advances in Mali over the past seven years have been widely lauded as emblematic of the rosy prospects for democratic consolidation on the continent.[30] In spite of more cautious recent assessments,[31] the political openness of Mali, coupled with its rich tradition of associational life, make it a propitious venue in which to examine citizen participation in the process of democratic consolidation.

Before the pro-democracy mass demonstrations in March 1991 toppled the Traoré regime, Mali had been ruled since independence by two authoritarian governments. Modibo Kéita's single-party *Union Soudanaise–Rassemblement Démocratique Africain* (US-RDA) regime (1960–68) pursued a relatively coherent developmental vision, but its socialist ideology became excessively rigid and over-centralized. Rural people complained of statist interference in agricultural production, including their subsistence millet crop. Traoré's military oligarchy (1968–91) spawned frequent charges of corruption but remained in power until the brutal massacre of at least 200 pro-democracy demonstrators outraged the public and led to his ouster by sympathetic military officers. Colonel Amadou Toumany Touré served as interim head of state from March 1991 until he shepherded in the country's first democratically elected president, Alpha Oumar Konaré, in June 1992. Konaré was elected to a second five-year term in May 1997, but the election was tarnished by an opposition boycott, two rounds of flawed legislative elections, and dissatisfied opposition parties. It is still uncertain (late 1998) when the long-planned and frequently postponed municipal elections, which will bring into existence the new decentralized communes, will take place. [NOTE: Municipal elections were held in June 1999.] Despite continuing challenges to the viability of the Konaré government, the country is still viewed as hosting a fairly propitious climate for the survival and consolidation of democracy. Indeed, President Konaré recently stated that, without an effort to strengthen opposition political parties, Mali's "level of democratic culture will not evolve."[32] It remains to be seen how the government and the opposition will bridge their differences and move forward with the process of both institution-building and broader democratic consolidation.

The research on which this chapter is based took place in Mali's southern, cotton-producing zone. This zone provides an interesting context in which to study nascent rural civil society because of its vibrant associational life and the great variety of organizational combinations at the village level.

Mali's cotton-producing parastatal, the *Compagnie Malienne pour le Développement des Fibres Textiles* (CMDT) oversees production and economic development in a zone more than 700 kilometers long and 400 kilometers wide.[33] The CMDT zone extends throughout the southeast corner of the country, along Mali's borders with Burkina Faso, Côte d'Ivoire, and Guinea.[34]

The present study employed both ethnographic and quantitative methodological techniques. A discussion of the sampling and data collection methodologies employed is included in appendix 1. Briefly, the study combines semi-structured interviews with survey data on political attitudes among rural leaders.[35] The diverse methods are employed in order to discern both broad contours as well as the rich detail of associational life in southern Mali. The challenges of employing survey research in very different socio-linguistic contexts are well known. Primary among these challenges are issues such as conceptual equivalence which require the careful translation and back-translation of survey instruments. This research was conducted while conscientiously heeding such concerns. Consequently, the rich qualitative data and the broad survey results contribute a useful complementarity to the analysis.

The villages used for semi-structured interviews on organizational dynamics were chosen in order to ensure variation in terms of distance and remoteness from Bamako, organizational type, and—to some degree—ethnicity. After making a purposive selection of five of the twenty-one villages surveyed, a Bambara cotton-producing village from the OHVN (*Opération Haute Vallée du Niger*) zone was added.

Organizational Characteristics and Political Socialization in Rural Southern Mali

Local rural organizations

Informal associations rooted in indigenous cultural institutions have existed in West African villages since long before French colonial penetration.[36] Traditional age class associations among both males and females and cultural associations organized around traditional religion and indigenous medicine as groups have long had important economic and social roles.[37] Since independence, Mali's leaders have promoted village and village organizations in keeping with the country's economic development policy.[38] Nevertheless, farmers have remained the least represented at national debates on agricultural development planning and have been excluded from policy decisions that affect them.[39] This section reviews diverse types of organizations and summarizes the internal dynamics found most commonly at the local level in southern Malian villages: formal *associations villageoises* (AVs), women's groups, youth groups, and hunters' associations. The AVs have come into existence only since independence, while the other groups are contemporary versions of informal groups that have existed since precolonial times.

1. *Associations villageoises* (AV)

During French colonial rule, as well as after independence, a number of pseudo-cooperative farmer organizations were established as part of the country's rural development policy.[40] While all of these organizations sought to promote the capacity of farmers to defend their collective interests, these organizations did not emerge as a result of farmer initiative, and membership was compulsory.[41] These organizations were all subject to repeated official interference, even to the point of the government's choosing their leaders and dictating the manner in which they operated. They routinely served such purposes as tax collection, compulsory cultivation of collective fields by villagers, and forced marketing of food grains at official prices.

More autonomous groups emerged in the CMDT zone in the mid-1970s.[42] Farmers, frustrated that some tasks critical to the marketing of cotton, such as weighing and valuing output, were performed by CMDT agents rather than locals, demanded that these tasks be assigned to literate villagers (mostly school drop-outs). This proposal was well-received by CMDT officials because they saw in it a mechanism for collecting delinquent loans (incurred during the drought period of the early 1970s), and thereby cutting administrative costs by substituting unpaid officials for paid officials.[43] It also gave the government a basis for co-opting villagers.[44]

Organizational autonomy. In the cotton zone, AVs have been created in a top-down manner. If a village wants to create an AV, it must conform to the CMDT requirements. For example, at least two villagers must be literate in Bambara and agree to train other villagers in order to ensure that a minimum threshold of administrative competence exists in the association.

AVs serve as versatile vehicles of agricultural development policy but are primarily devoted to the needs of cotton producers rather than non-cash-crop producers. Activities include the collective purchase of agricultural inputs on credit, village-wide collection of cotton at harvest, stocking food grains for sale during periods of food insecurity, securing credit for investments in livestock or farm equipment, equipment rental to other villages, collective labor for private individuals and in other villages (*jekabaara*), and farming the association's collective field (*foroba*).

AVs have formal bank accounts, the contents of which they use for a variety of purposes. AV expenditures include the purchase and maintenance of agricultural equipment, advance money for the purchase of agricultural inputs for the AV, loans to members in financial crisis (for which, depending on the village, they may or may not be required to pay interest), and contributions to local development projects, including road and school construction.

Membership. Drawing upon the model of traditional age group associations, AVs are created as largely ascriptive associations in which all adult residents of a village are considered to be members. However, as some AVs evolve into more commercial voluntary associations, they tend to focus on issues of interest to cotton producers, then some villagers choose not to participate. Because they are accustomed to ascriptive groups, many villagers do not understand fully the concept of a voluntary association. For example, the leaders of two AVs both believe that all villagers were automatically members of SYCOV, the national cotton producers' union, even though they were aware that "membership" required the purchase of a union card. Similarly, although the CMDT states that all villagers are members of their village's AV, in practice most AV officers observe that only cotton producers are members. In yet another case, all villagers are required to do collective AV work whether or not they grow cotton, the rationale being that there are some benefits from the functioning of an AV—such as school and road projects and access to credit—that all residents of a village enjoy. This village discourages "free riding" by levying fines on those who do not show up on designated community work days.

Leadership selection. Largely because of strict guidelines promulgated by the CMDT, AVs have boards with ten or more officers and, at least on paper, a clear division of labor. The large number of officers allows villages to balance loyalty, trust, and competence in whom they choose. Consequently, many villages have two officers for every post, often an older man who is respected in the village and a younger man who is literate and numerate.

Elders exercise considerable control over officer selection and prominent families are disproportionately represented on AV boards, though some villages have innovative representational procedures. In one village, for example, each extended family (*gwa*) must have at least one member among the ten principal officers. In another, the association gets considerable input from the CMDT in choosing officers. One village studied enjoys complete autonomy from CMDT agents because the current chief's predecessor and a previous

CMDT agent both died under mysterious circumstances after a quarrel over land tenure issues. Villagers fervently believe that the chief killed them using supernatural powers. The chief's scary reputation threatens AV autonomy because no villager dares to controvert his will.

Officers are generally, though not exclusively, middle-aged men. In just two of the five AV villages studies, women or young men serve on the board. This means that the majority of village adults are under-represented in debates pertaining to a developmental vision for the village. Further, there is little turnover in officers. In most villages, officers remain in their positions until they choose to step down or are asked to step down for malfeasance. AVs often wrestle with problems concerning honesty of their officers, however. A big problem is asymmetry in numeracy, which leads numerate officers to attempt to exploit their positions. Three of the five AV villages in this study reported this problem.

Decision making. Many AV decisions are consensus-based among officers, with non-officers having little direct say. While chiefs have considerable input into most AV affairs, the increased prominence of AVs at the village level could be perceived as a challenge to the authority of the chiefship (*chefferie*).[45] AVs handle larger amounts of money than chiefs and it is in the chief's interest to have some control over those funds. AVs also have an interest in amicable relations with village elders. In one village, the AV secretary frankly acknowledges that he and other founders of the AV had proposed a self-effacing son of the chief as their president in order to pursue their developmental objectives with minimal interference from the chief and elders. Of course, this action is also perfectly consistent with a culture that values consensus and social cohesion over conflict.

2. Women's groups

In the cotton zone, ascriptive women's groups, formal or informal, have become standard features of the rural landscape. It is often unclear whether these groups have been initiated by local representatives of the government's territorial administration or by village women themselves. Some groups are formally recognized by Malian authorities, while others are entirely informal. The groups that participated in this study had generally existed for ten to thirty or more years. Often, women have long worked together informally in their mutual economic interest. For example, before the formation of its present multivalent group in one village, women had long cooperated to process and commercialize shea nut butter (*situlu*).

Women's groups serve a variety of purposes. They are the locus of women's collective activity in a village and as such mobilize women to serve village needs. They generate income and allow members to meet the costs of meal condiments and clothing for themselves and their children. Women's groups perform a vital role in serving as a means for women to help each other fulfill these responsibilities.

In order to generate income, groups often cultivate a common field (*foroba*) or vegetable garden, do collective work for others, sell millet and rice to provide village food security during the lean pre-harvest months, sell shea nut butter, provide interest-accruing loans to members (and, occasionally, village men), and charge fines to members who are late for collective work endeavors. Some women's groups also engage in a wide array of small commercial activities including dyeing fabric, making soap, and raising chickens. Because women's education still lags in Mali, young men often perform supporting roles in these groups, primarily helping with bookkeeping and associated recordkeeping.[46] Expenses incurred by women's groups include the costs for food and transport for women going to classes to become literacy trainers, upkeep of local maternity clinics (*jiginiso*) and funds for infant nutrition, contributions to the chief for expenses incurred hosting guests, and maintenance of common grain mills or water pumps.

Organizational autonomy. The structure of women's groups varies by village. In some large villages one umbrella group unites all village women and smaller groups exist in each *quartier*. The village-wide group only meets during the less demanding months of the dry season, while the smaller groups cooperate on work projects throughout the year. In another arrangement subgroups for young women and older women, all married, exist within a single village-wide group. Sometimes sub-groups raise their own funds while in other cases women's communal funds are centralized at the level of a village-wide group.

Membership. Only married women take part in the activities of the women's associations in the six villages studied in detail. Unmarried women are normally members of a village's youth group until they marry, at which time they cease to be members of the youth group and become members of the women's group. In some villages, elderly women do not participate in the main village women's group but have their own informal group led by the first married among them.

Leadership selection. Leadership selection in women's groups is often heavily influenced by village chiefs and elders. The selection of a president is based more on a subjective perception of trustworthiness (*danaya*) and loyalty than on capability, though other posts are often filled based on competence. Often, either the president or the vice president of a women's group is the chief's wife. The presidents of women's groups are usually in their forties, if not older, but notable exceptions exist.

Women's group leaders are generally not chosen for a specific term of office but rather remain in office until they become too old, move away, or lose the community's confidence. When a president dies or steps down, a village chief and elders normally have a direct or indirect hand in the selection of a successor. In one village, the chief and elders appoint all nine members of the board of the village women's group. In another, women have little say in village affairs in general but are left to their own devices in leadership selection; the men technically have a final say over women's leaders, but in practice always tacitly approve the women's choices. In yet another village, the chief appoints the women's president, but women then assist her in selecting the other five officers. In practice, most women concede that they choose officers who they know will not elicit objections from the chief.

Decision making. Among the women's groups examined, presidents held enormous sway over the decisions. In all cases, either the president alone or the president in concert with other officers made decisions and then relayed them to the general membership, normally with no formal discussion by the group at large. In one case, the women's president acknowledged the value of discussion by the board—"A single person cannot solve all problems; several people's ideas can result in a better idea"—and board members are allowed to challenge the president's proposals, but the membership at large always accepts a decision by the board. In another village, the four most important officers (president, vice president, and two treasurers) present their views on an issue to the membership at large and the members are allowed to make alternative proposals if they are not happy with a proposal from the officers. In practice, the membership usually acquiesces with little discussion.

The degree to which women influence village-wide decisions varies somewhat but is generally quite low. In an extreme example, the *matronne* of the village maternity clinic stated that women participate less in village affairs in [this village] than in all five other villages in which she had worked: "Here, women do what their husbands tell them to do, end of story." As a case in point, the men manage the most important women's project in the village—the maternity clinic management committee consists of the midwife and eight men. No members from the women's group are on that committee. An elder in one village neatly summed up women's involvement by saying, "Of course women participate in village decisions—we make a decision and then inform them."

3. Youth groups

One type of association with very deep origins in the culture of southern Mali is the youth group. These ascriptive associations have roots in solidarity age groupings and communal work groups such as the *ciketon* that have existed since long before colonial rule, and have evolved in recent years through a phase as formal youth groups organized by the Kéita and Traoré regimes. Any effort to understand the role of local-level associations in Africa must be informed by an awareness of the fluid nature of organizational distinctions. For example, asking villagers where one informal group leaves off and another begins is often confusing and imprecise. It appears, however, that most villages have merged their *ciketon* with a more formal grouping (often with official recognition) that has emerged since independence. These groups provide a locus for social activity among younger villagers and a structure through which village leaders can mobilize a robust labor pool for arduous collective endeavors. In some villages, however, the increase in importance of AVs has resulted in a corresponding decrease in the importance of traditionally rooted youth groups.[47]

In five of the six villages studied, all unmarried women and all men aged fifteen to thirty-five or forty, depending on the village, are members of a youth group. The women, however, serve primarily as sources of encouragement for the men, bringing water and food to work parties, and singing as the men work. None of the six youth associations studied had female officers, but only one had no female members.

Youth groups are structures that make young men available to perform tasks of benefit to the community. They repair village buildings, fix roads, clear fields, load trucks, and stock agricultural input warehouses. They perform both unpaid collective work for their village as well as paid collective work for their own budget. They levy fines against members who are disrespectful of others in the group or show up late for collective work endeavors. With revenues from collective work, youth groups often invest in technology such as generators, microphones, and speaker systems to facilitate more lively *fêtes* (*nyenaje*). Other expenses include helping sick villagers, assisting in funeral costs, helping with members' marriages or baptisms, and providing no-interest loans to members in financial difficulty. The biggest expenses are those related to throwing parties for village youth, a practice that has existed for generations.

Leadership selection. In four of the six villages, the president of the youth group was the oldest member of the group and had succeeded someone who had stepped down because he had passed the age limit. Youth group presidents generally had traveled less and were less literate than young men with key AV positions. Other officers are often chosen based on competence. Often the president chooses his fellow officers with substantial oversight from elders; the members remain passive in the process. There are some cases where the organization actively nominates officers. In these cases, the organization at large nominates officer candidates but the president has the final decision. In any case, the boards of officers of these youth groups are generally smaller and less formal than the boards of AVs.

Decision making. Decision-making procedures vary widely by youth group. In one village, the youth group is firmly controlled by the powerful chief. No important decision is finalized without his approval. In other villages, the youth group president, sometimes aided by other board members, makes firm decisions with little or no input from members. In others, major decisions are made by the association's board with input from the membership at large in a general assembly, with the chief only intervening in cases of serious conflict.

Organizational autonomy. Village elders have a strong hand in the affairs of youth groups. Because everyone in a village knows everyone else and will have to live with them side-by-side for their entire lives, and because youth group officers are the offspring of village elders, youth groups virtually never challenge the wishes of their elders.

4. Hunters' groups

Hunter's associations (*donsotonw*) have roots deep in the pre-Islamic religious traditions of Malian ethnic groups.[48] In former times, hunters often were given the task of defending their village if it was threatened by outsiders or neighboring villages. To this day, Mali's hunters elicit a warm emotional response even from urban dwellers. This deep cultural and religious significance makes hunters wary of discussing their organizations with strangers for fear of inadvertently divulging secret rites. In cases where hunters were interviewed, however, they provided a rich window into associational patterns that have existed in Mali since long before colonial rule.

Hunters' groups tend to be most active during the dry season, when game is easier to spot and agricultural work is minimal, freeing them up to pursue their avocation. In some villages, all hunters are given a quota of game to kill during the dry season. Those hunters who fail to meet the quota are required to provide millet beer (*chiapalo*) and chickens for the hunters' end-of-season ceremonies. In another village, violations of association rules are penalized by a fine, in the form of cola nuts, beer or a goat, depending on the severity of the offense. If activities are undertaken during the rainy season, they may consist of hunters working the fields of their president or performing collective work or working a collective field in order to raise money for association expenses.

The hunters' associations studied usually had an informal fund (as opposed to a formal bank account) entrusted to their president. The principal expenses of hunters' associations include giving or loaning money to members in financial difficulty, paying for expenses of members who have to travel to meetings, hosting hunters from other villages, and throwing big ceremonial *fêtes*.

Membership. Hunters' associations clearly constitute the most voluntary of the associations in this study, in that membership was by choice rather than by ascriptive membership in a social category. To become a hunter and to join a hunters' association one must be placed by one's father in the care of a skilled hunter. There are many villagers who own rifles but are not in the association but, as one chief said, a man had to love hunting to join the association. Interestingly, hunters' groups seem to operate more independently of village elders and internal village politics than do other groups. Protocol dictates that hunters inform the village chief of their activities, but he has little say in their affairs. For example, in one village, where personal animosity has resulted in the virtual secession of one *quartier* from the village and the creation of a second AV, the hunters from both sides of the divide continue to share a single association.

Leadership selection. Leadership selection is very straightforward among the hunters, and diverges from other rural associations in that age or family is not the most important criterion. The president of a hunters' association is usually the most experienced hunter, the member of the village who has been hunting the longest. In other words, a man who began hunting at a young age can become leader over an older man who began hunting at a later date. One former president of the hunters' group, who voluntarily gave up the post when he became chief, likened leadership selection to a polygamous marriage. He said that if a man takes a second wife who is older than the first she is nevertheless always the junior wife. Such seniority is the custom in leadership selection among hunters.

Decision making. In two hunters' groups, all decisions of any importance are made by the president who is the only officer. In another group, the president and his vice-president are the two most experienced hunters in the village, but they select two much younger men to lead their peers on long hunting expeditions. These four officers make decisions and then simply inform the other members without further discussion. In yet another, a frail, old, once-valiant hunter is the *tonfa*, literally, the father of the association, while a younger, more physically able hunter is president and runs the day-to-day affairs of the association. One hunter described the fond deference with which the *tonfa* is treated: "If he calls you, you go to him. It's like your father has called you. We respect him and cannot question or refuse his decisions." This is the paradox of hunters' groups—they constitute a genuinely voluntary form of association, bringing together individuals in pursuit of common interests, but they govern themselves in a more top-down manner than the ascriptive associations of their fellow villagers.

Historically, hunters and *paysans* in general have had a delicate relationship with national authorities, particularly the field staff of the national forest service (*Eaux et Forêts*). During the corrupt days of the Traoré regime, local officials often charged high taxes for firewood collection and gave no receipt, allegedly set forest fires in order to arrest chiefs and extort large 'fines' from the villages, and 'taxed' hunters heavily for killing game. This relationship greatly compromised the legitimacy of the national government in the countryside because the government officials with whom they had the most frequent contact had a reputation for rampant venality. An important role of hunters' associations during this period was to express solidarity when charges were made against a member.

Summary

The findings regarding the characteristics of the four types of organizations studied can be summarized as follows. Hunters' associations have, *prima facie*, external characteristics most similar to those of Western-style civil society, in that they are a voluntary association which has strong autonomy both from the village chief, the local representative of the national administration, and from state organs in general. However, local hunters do not express themselves and advance their interests through engagement with the state, leading one to question the role they can play in a nascent civil society. Cotton producers' associations most clearly meet the broader external and internal criteria for civil society, in that they are moderately voluntary, have moderate autonomy from the state, and actively engage in the pursuit of development objectives. This brings organizational activists into frequent interaction with state officials. Women's groups and youth groups are both ascriptive associations and both demonstrated very little autonomy and thus bear little resemblance to constituent organizations in civil society as commonly conceived.

While AV activists have frequent contact with state and parastatal officials and are loosely united under the auspices of SYCOV, the national cotton producers' union, the other three types of organizations studied have only tenuous links to the state. Both women's and youth groups were tied to national organizations under the previous regime, and a national hunters' federation is trying to unite hunters' associations to pursue their common interests, but links between these local-level associations and the nation's capital seem only tenuous at best.

Of the four types of organizations studied, all are weakly inclusive in leadership selection and only cotton producers' associations deviate from this in their decision-making procedures. One can thus only be cautiously optimistic about the prospects for AVs to contribute to the socialization of democratic values among their activists. The other organizations seem to have little potential in this regard.

These data demonstrate that local organizations in rural Africa are often very different from the idealized associations that Western democratic theorists were describing when they spoke of the role of civic organizations as classrooms of democracy. Rural associations in Mali perform vital social, economic, and cultural functions that one must comprehend in order to understand the context upon which liberal democratic institutions have been superimposed. However, researchers, and policy makers must be extremely cautious about assuming the similarity of entities which have evolved in radically different contexts.

With these reservations in mind, the next section examines the relationships between these organizational features and the political orientations of participants.

Participation and political values

This section examines several indicators of organizational participation and political attitudes, as well as several demographic control variables in order to assess systematically the effectiveness of rural organizations in political socialization.

In groups with organizational procedures that foster democratic values, higher degrees of participation (especially more devotion of time) might be expected to engender greater socialization. In other words, the more sustained the level of contact with a socializing institution, the more likely that socialization takes place. Consequently, one would expect leaders to learn more about democratic values than rank-and-file members. The weakly inclusive nature of the procedures in the organizations discussed above, however, suggests that there will be minor, if any, significant differences in attitudes between the general membership and leadership of the organizations examined here.

The two dimensions of political values discussed here are *political efficacy* and *political tolerance*. Political efficacy is arguably the dimension of political values most closely related to organizational participation since it describes feelings of competence when engaging the political system. It is therefore plausible that those engaged actively in associational life should have increased self-confidence when participating in the political system. Especially in the Malian context, where rural areas have long been marginalized by urban elites, efficacy is an important attribute.

Political tolerance seems to embody the open-mindedness required in a democratic polity since it measures a respondent's willingness to accept a political role for other social and political roles for other social and political groups.[49] It captures one's willingness to compromise with groups in spite of not sharing their points of view. In a nation-state as ethnically diverse as Mali, issues of tolerance are immediately relevant to the cohesiveness of the polity.

Four factors posited by the political socialization literature to influence the expression of political efficacy and tolerance were important to the analysis. They are:

1. *Organizational participation and organizational leadership* were included. A distinction was made between individuals who were only members of village-level cotton producers' associations, other organizations but not AVs, or both AVs and other organizations. This distinction is important given the differences seen above. Specifically, AVs tend to be more voluntary and more inclusive in decision making than other groups. For this reason, as well as because we wanted to examine the differences between single and multiple affiliations, we included these membership distinctions.

2. *Age* is important in African societies, where elders are automatically accorded great deference. For this reason, a positive relationship might be expected between age and political efficacy. On the other hand, there is no cultural or theoretical reason to expect any particular relationship between age and tolerance.

3. Since *wealth* or income is difficult to measure in parochial rural settings where people are unfamiliar with social science research and the motives of outsiders are suspect, several proxy measures were used. These included ownership of farm technology such as mechanical seeders and plows,

ownership of bicycles or mopeds, and cotton production and land holdings. These are necessarily imperfect proxies, but studies of political socialization suggest a positive association between wealth and democratic values. In any case, the various measures used allowed us to hone in on the effects of wealth on values.

4. Several measures of *education* were used, including time in formal French-language education, time in functional literacy programs employing national languages, and reading ability. A positive relationship is expected between education and democratic values such as efficacy and tolerance.

Political efficacy and tolerance

The interviews revealed no significant relationship between any combination of simple participation (that is, membership without necessarily holding an office) and political efficacy. Whether an individual belongs to a cotton producers' organization (AV), any other type of organization, or belongs to an AV *and* at least one other organization, there is no relationship with the level of political efficacy. In contrast, there is a strong positive relationship between age and efficacy. In other words, older respondents reported feelings of greater capacity to influence the political system. In a gerontocratic society, where age is respected and a certain authority comes with age, this is no surprise.

On the other hand, the strong negative relationship between wealth and political efficacy, initially puzzling, requires a more historical and structural explanation. Mali is only six years removed from an authoritarian regime dominated by an ethic of neopatrimonialism, and individuals interviewed in this study were predominantly village and organizational leaders who have traditionally served as the village-level representatives of the national administration. They have been part of and benefited from vertical patron-client networks for many years. Thus, with the advent of a new regime, there is undoubtedly continuing resistance to a new system that could greatly reduce their previous influence.

Those with higher levels of education tended to report higher feelings of political efficacy. Specifically, the 35 percent of those interviewed who identified themselves as readers were more likely to report being able to influence the opinions of others, even elected officials, and generally felt a capacity to control their own destinies. A point should be made about the relative homogeneity of the sample in terms of education: there was not a single *lycée* graduate and only very few primary school graduates in the whole sample of 252 respondents. Though not directly related to the current study, the point is unavoidable—in order to truly implicate the vast majority of Mali's people in the political system, the stark discrepancies between urban and rural access to education must be addressed. The current explosion of community schools is encouraging, but must be accompanied by a sustained effort at the national level to ensure that staffing is sufficient and curriculum adequate.[50]

No strong relationship between participation and political tolerance was found. Organizational participation does not appear to influence an attitude of political tolerance and wealth continues to be negatively related to holding democratic values. Again, village ruling families and their allies are nervous about the changes that democratization and decentralization reforms could engender at the local level. For example, in one village an elder of the village founding family told me that "democratization can only go so far—a non-Coulibaly [his family name] will never be chief. *Jamais!*"

Interestingly, organizational leaders were found to be more likely to be politically tolerant. For example, these individuals expressed more tolerance on individual expression, freedom of expression, and political compromise. It is intuitively appealing to believe that more profound levels of participation lead to greater gains in democratic values, but there are several problems. For one, internal procedures in these organizations do not automatically lead one to be sanguine about the desired socialization effects. Even ignoring this issue, there is the thorny question of self-selection. In other words, how do we know that individuals with greater levels of democratic values at the outset are not for this reason impelled to join organizations? Even if they are not more democratic upon joining, it is very plausible for organizational leaders to develop more democratic values than their rank-and-file members in organizations without democratic internal procedures. For example, organizational leaders are more likely to travel outside the village on association or village business. Regular exposure to the democratic ferment of regional capitals could plausibly have a socializing effect that their association did not.

Nevertheless, in spite of the inconclusive results on socialization effects, there is reason for optimism, particularly with respect to the fact that organizational leaders do appear to be more tolerant than rank-and-file members. When rural municipal (communal) elections finally take place, there will be a demand for promising public servants in localities throughout the land. Thousands of new elected posts as mayors or municipal councilors that have never existed before will come into being. The new councils will confront enormous challenges. For example, groups of individuals who have never held office will be making decisions on councils for which there is no precedent about brand-new systems of resource allocation. Quite probably, many of the key actors in the new councils will emerge from civil society. The inherent challenges are daunting, but will be made less so if a critical mass exists of tolerant individuals with a willingness to compromise.

Conclusion

Given the desire of many foreign assistance agencies to employ the organizations that make up civil society as building blocks of democracy, it is timely to examine the prospects of such an approach. In-depth interviews on the characteristics of local-level rural associations in southern Mali suggest that low levels of inclusivity in decision making and leadership selection in these associations will have little effect in fostering democratic values, though cotton producers' organizations (AVs) appear to have slightly higher potential than other organizations. Because of the nature of these organizations, not even more advanced levels of commitment such as leadership can be expected to foster civic values.

Based on survey results, not a single specification of simple associational membership was found to contribute significantly to civic values such as efficacy and tolerance. This includes membership in cotton producers' associations.

Interestingly, wealth and village council membership had a strong negative effect on civic values. Village ruling families and their allies are understandably worried that democratization and meaningful decentralization could result in dramatic changes in the nature and distribution of local power. These issues are particularly relevant in the context of the rural municipal elections currently planned for April 1999. (They were held in June 1999.)

While the unbridled optimism of the most ardent advocates of the socialization effects of civil society appears unwarranted in the rural Malian context, this does not mean that development strategies targeting civil society are inappropriate. On the contrary, Malian civil society is experiencing impressive growth, and the evolution of a *contre-poids* to the state could strengthen the prospects for long-term democratic consolidation. on the other hand, an explosion of growth among ascriptive, uninclusive organizations could portend chaos as plausibly as democracy.

This calls for continued emphasis on capacity-building among civil society organizations at all levels. Not-explicitly political skills such as functional literacy, numeracy, and financial bookkeeping should be taught in order to foster competence, efficacy, broader participation, and greater transparency.

On such a base could be added "applied" civic education programs emphasizing participation, oversight, accountability, and partnership in the new decentralized municipalities. In particular, in the hope that the government will follow through on promises of greater local control of the local and regional development tax (TDRL), local capacity will be needed to manage and use these funds productively.

In this vein, such capacity-building should strive to at least indirectly remedy voids of inclusiveness and autonomy. For example, every effort should be made to encourage and facilitate the participation of marginalized groups such as women, youth, and non-producers of cash crops.

The capacity-building programs should be implemented by neutral parties bearing credibility with rural people. For example, state-linked agencies that have a history of condescension and control should be kept at arms' length. Indeed, their local agents need education about the evolving system as much as rural farmers and civil society participants do.

Finally, capacity-building needs to exist at the most elementary level, literally: Mali has one of the lowest rates of primary school attendance in the world. Any program aimed at grassroots empowerment must address the low levels of both formal and non-formal literacy in rural areas, both as a needed skill in itself as well as a means of improving efficacy, participation, and ownership in the new decentralized system.

Mali's decentralization reforms portend potentially significant changes in the contours of local politics. Longstanding hereditary power could erode in the face of meaningful municipal elections and Mali's nascent civil society will likely serve as a proving ground for future local officials. Then, more than ever, it will be important to understand the forces that can foster a sense of civic community in the milieux where the vast majority of the country's citizens live.

Appendix 1

Methodology

This appendix summarizes the sampling and data collection methodologies used in this chapter. The use of both ethnographic and quantitative techniques permit a grasp of both the rich detail as well as the broad contours of organizational and individual behavior.

Given the need to evaluate the lay of the organizational landscape in the cotton zone, I chose to sample villages with different levels of organizational activity. Because independent censuses or data on organizational activity across the cotton zone do not exist, I was forced to rely on the CMDT's classification system. The CMDT promotes the creation of village-level producer associations, called *Associations Villageoises* (AVs), in order to provide a structure for the promotion of progressive growing techniques as well as the commercialization of cotton. CMDT technical assistants classify the level of organizational activity in a village as follows: A *village classique* is a village with no "modern" AV; a *village AV simple* is a village in which a formal AV exists, but where no formal links have been established with neighboring villages in order to promote development projects that are beyond the scale possible for a single village; and a *village AV/ZAER (Zone d'Animation et Expansion Rurale)* is a village that has formed formal links of cooperation with nearby villages. While recognizing the drawbacks of relying on the CMDT's classifications, we shall provisionally classify the three categories as proxies for low, medium, and high organizational activity, respectively.

CMDT records and 1987 Mali National Census village lists were employed to develop a sampling frame of over 4,000 villages and hamlets in the cotton zone. I then conducted a proportionate, multi-stage, stratified random sample to select a total of twenty-one villages for a *survey of organizational participation and political attitudes* among elders, rural organization leaders, and heads of household. I selected eight AVs/ZAER villages, seven simple AV villages, and six *villages classiques* according to their relative incidence in the sampling frame. The surveyed villages constituted a reasonable cross section of rural southern Mali. The survey was conducted over a five-week period in October and November 1995.

In each village, enumerators were instructed to compile lists of organizational officers, village elders, and heads of household not fitting into either of the first two groups. From these lists, they randomly selected four from each category for a total of twelve interviews per village. The total sample size was 252.

The survey instrument included questions on political participation and associational life, political authority, political accountability, economic and political knowledge, policy preferences, attitudes and orientations toward trust, efficacy, tolerance, materialism/post-materialism, and a broad array of demographic questions. All of the surveys were administered using Bambara, the *lingua franca* of southern Mali. Much of the survey was based on the 1993 USAID/Zambia political attitudes survey directed by Michael Bratton and Beatrice Liatto-Katundu.

The villages used for *semi-structured interviews on organizational dynamics* were chosen in order to ensure variation in terms of distance and remoteness from Bamako, organizational type, and to some degree, ethnicity. I made a purposive selection of five of the twenty-one villages surveyed and then added a Bambara cotton-producing village from the OHVN zone in which

I had done background research in 1994. These villages are described in table 1 of the main text.

I visited each of the six villages for several days during November and December 1995 accompanied by a research assistant/interpreter. Following protocol, we addressed ourselves to the village chief, proffered cola nuts, and explained the purpose of our mission. In every case, this was the second or third visit by me or my associates, and we were never refused in our request to interview village elders and associational leaders. When possible and as a minimum, we interviewed the village chief or his principal adviser, the president or secretary of the AV (where applicable), the women's group president, the youth group president, and the hunters' association president (where applicable). Occasionally, when we had more time and access, or if initial informants were not very forthcoming, we interviewed additional people. We interviewed six or seven leaders in every village. A total of forty-one in-depth village-level interviews were conducted, as well as eleven key informant interviews above the village level, for a total of fifty-two interviews. Thirty-three interviews were conducted entirely in Bambara, and many of the remainder were conducted at least partially in Bambara.

Notes

1. Cheikh Hamidou Kane, *L'aventure ambiguë*, p. 92. "Every hour that passes brings a supplement of ignition to the crucible in which the world is being fused. We have not had the same past, you and ourselves, but we shall have, strictly, the same future. The era of separate destinies has run its course."

2. This includes all direct DGSO funding, plus additional resources earmarked for civil society support in Mali's three northern regions.

3. Huntingon 1991.

4. *Democracy* is generally conceived of as describing a government which is responsive to all of its citizens. These citizens are viewed as political equals, enjoy a broad array of civil and political liberties, and participate in the change of governments through periodic, competitive elections (Dahl 1989). For a wide-reaching work on democratization in the African context, see Bratton and van de Walle 1997.

5. For a practitioner's perspective, see Strobe Talbott, "Democracy and the national interest," *Foreign Affairs* 75 (6): 47–63 (1996). For a sympathetic academic point of view, see Graham T. Allison, Jr. and Robert P. Beschel, Jr., "Can the United States promote democracy?" *Political Science Quarterly* 107(1): 81–98 (1992).

6. USAID 1994.

7. Bratton 1989, 428; Ignatieff 1995, 135.

8. Putnam 1993, 1995.

9. Hadenius and Uggla 1996.

10. Ibid., 1622.

11. Bratton 1994; Diamond 1994.

12. Fatton 1995, 72.

13. Putnam 1993, 15.

14. Holm, Molutsi, and Somolekae 1996, 43.

15. Chazan 1982.

16. Bratton 1989.

17. Monga 1995, 362.

18. Gellner 1994, 9.

19. Hyman 1959; Dennis et al. 1968; Jennings and Niemi 1981; Niemi and Hepburn 1995.

20. Almond and Verba 1980, 399–400; Verba 1965, 550–51.

21. Bermeo 1992.

22. See, for example, Hyman 1959; Campbell et al. 1960; Jennings and Niemi 1981.

23. Verba 1965, 551.

24. Putnam 1993, 1995.

25. Muller, Seligson, and Turan 1987, 29–30.

26. Diamond 1994, 12.

27. Bratton 1994, 10. As well, Bratton and Nicolas van de Walle define neopatrimonialism as a regime type in which the defining characteristic is the maintenance of authority through personal patronage rather than ideology or law: "The distinction between private and public interests is purposely blurred . . . in return for material rewards, clients mobilize political support and refer all decisions upward as a mark of deference to patrons" (Bratton and van de Walle 1994, 458).

28. Almond and Verba 1963.

29. In the African context, see, for example, Lucas 1994; Holm, Molutsi, and Somolekae 1996; Degnbol 1996; Burgess 1997; Smith 1997; and Bingen 1994 and 1998.

30. *New York Times*, 29 April 1996, 16 October 1996.

31. *New York Times*, 7 September 1997; *Jeune Afrique*, 1–7 October 1997.

32. *Jeune Afrique*, 3–9 September 1997 (author's translation).

33. In this chapter "cotton-producing zone" and "CMDT zone" are used interchangeably, even though some commercial cotton is also produced in the smaller *Opération Haute Vallée du Niger* (OHVN).

34. This is a region that overwhelmingly practices Islam, though there are some large indigenous religion enclaves. The majority ethnicity is the Bambara (Bamanan)/Malinke group, though several other groups predominate in certain areas. Much of the zone speaks Bambara (Bamanankan) as a first language, and virtually all men in the non-Bambara areas speak it as a second language, though many women do not. With an adult literacy rate of only 28.4 percent, Mali ranks fourth-from-last in the world on the United

Nations Development Program's (UNDP) educational attainment index (UNDP 1996, p. 137).

35. Fifty-two in-depth interviews were conducted with associational leaders, village elders, and various key informants from the agricultural sector. The survey instrument included questions in Bambara on political participation and associational life, political authority, political accountability, economic and political knowledge, policy preferences, attitudes and orientations toward trust, efficacy, tolerance, materialism/post-materialism, and a broad array of demographic questions. Much of the survey was based on the 1993 USAID/Zambia political attitudes survey directed by Michael Bratton and Beatrice Liatto-Katundu (Bratton and Liatto-Katundu 1994).

36. Lachenmann 1986; Buijsrogge 1989; and Ouédraogo 1990.

37. Buijsrogge 1989, 118–19.

38. Bingen 1994, 58.

39. Dioné 1989, 333–34.

40. Jones 1976; Jacquemot 1981; Belloncle 1982; and Dembélé 1987.

41. Dioné 1989, 334.

42. Belloncle 1982; Dembélé 1987.

43. Dioné 1989, 335.

44. Bingen 1994, 59–60. The CMDT is a parastatal jointly owned by a French agency and the Malian government. Rural leaders make little distinction between the CMDT and the Malian state.

45. In one village, a battle over succession to the *chefferie* and alleged corruption by the eventual victor led to intervention by local *arrondissement* government authorities which, in turn, led to the virtual secession of the rival's *quartier* from the village and the creation of a second AV by ousted officers of the original AV. Cases of this sort of village fragmentation, or *éclatement*, may reduce village chief and elder control of AVs and thereby increase AV autonomy, but at the cost of social cohesion.

46. IMRAD 1994.

47. The youth group in one village became virtually defunct a generation ago and young people simply put together *fêtes* based on individual cash contributions. Then, about five years ago, they re-activated the youth group. Why, if the social functions of the group were still being performed on an ad hoc basis, was the group necessary? The president explained that they saw active youth groups existing in other villages and wanted to demonstrate that they, too, worked well together.

48. In one village the hunters' association stated that it had existed "since long before Samory." This is a reference to Samory Touré, the great Malinké empire builder who led resistance to the French in the 1880s and 1890s and converted many of his subjects to Islam. At various times in his conquests during the period 1870–1898 he controlled parts of what are now Guinea, Mali, Ivory Coast, and Sierra Leone. Samory is often used by older Malians as a reference point for how recently a past event took place.

49. Sullivan et al. 1981.

50. Charlick et al. 1998.

Bibliography

Allison, Graham T., Jr,. and Robert P. Beschel, Jr. 1992. "Can the United States promote democracy?" *Political Science Quarterly* 107: 81–98.

Almond, Gabriel A., and Sidney Verba. 1963. *The Civic Culture: Political Attitudes and Democracy in Five Nations.* Princeton NJ: Princeton University Press.

———. 1980. *The Civic Culture Revisited.* Boston: Little, Brown.

Bazin, Jean. 1985. "A chacun son Bambara." In *Au Coeur de l'ethnie: ethnies, tribalisme et état en Afrique,* edited by Jean-Loup Amselle and Elikia M'Bokolo, 87–127. Paris: Découverte.

Belloncle, Guy. 1982. *La question paysanne en Afrique noire.* Paris: Karthala.

Bermeo, Nancy. 1992. "Democracy and the lessons of dictatorship." *Comparative Politics* 24 (3): 273.

Bingen, R. James. 1994. "Agricultural development policy and grassroots democracy in Mali: the emergence of Mali's farmer movement." *African Rural and Urban Studies* 1 (1): 57–72.

———. 1998. "Cotton, democracy, and development." *Journal of Modern African Studies* 36 (2): 265–85.

Bratton, Michael. 1989. "Beyond the state: civil society and associational life in Africa." *World Politics* 41 (3): 407–30.

———. 1994. "Civil society and political transition in Africa." *IDR Reports* 11.

Bratton, Michael, and Beatrice Liatto-Katundu. 1994. "Political culture in Zambia: a pilot survey." Political Reform in Africa working paper no. 7, Michigan State University, Department of Political Science.

Bratton, Michael, and Nicolas van de Walle. 1994. "Neopatrimonial regimes and political transitions in Africa." *World Politics* 46 (4): 453.

———. 1997. *Democratic Experiments in Africa: Regime Transitions in Comparative Perspective.* Cambridge UK: Cambridge University Press.

Buijsrogge, Piet. 1989. *Initiatives paysannes en Afrique de l'Ouest.* Paris: l'Harmattan.

Burgess, Stephen F. 1997. "Smallholder voice and rural transformation: Zimbabwe and Kenya compared." *Comparative Politics* 29 (2): 127–50.

Campbell, Angus, Philip E. Converse, Warren E. Miller, and Donald E. Stokes. 1960. *The American Voter.* New York: John Wiley and Sons.

Chambers, Robert. 1983. *Rural Development: Putting the Last First.* Essex UK: Longman.

Charlick, Robert, Susanna D. Wing, and Mariam Koné. 1998. "The political economy of educational policy reform in Mali: a stakeholder analysis." Report to USAID/Mali, 30 September 1998.

Chazan, Naomi. 1982. "The new politics of participation in tropical Africa." *Comparative Politics* 14: 169–89.

Dahl, Robert A. 1989. *Democracy and Its Critics*. New Haven: Yale University Press.

Davis, John Uniack. 1997a. "The internal dynamics of local-level rural associations in Mali: the prospects of a nascent civil society." Paper presented at the annual meeting of the Midwest Political Science Association, Chicago, April 1997.

———. 1997b. "Civil society and civic values: the case of rural organizations in southern Mali." Paper presented at the African Studies Association Annual Conference, Columbus, Ohio, 13 November 1997.

Degnbol, Tove. 1996. "The interactive approach to the study of state and society relations." *Forum for Development Studies* 2: 327–51.

Dembélé, K. 1987. "State policies on agriculture and food production in Mali," in Thandika Mkandawire and Naceur Bourenane, *The State and Agriculture in Africa*. London: Codesria Book Series.

Dennis, Jack, Leon Lindberg, Donald McCrone, and Rodney Stiefbold. 1968. "Political socialization to democratic orientations in four western systems." *Comparative Political Studies* 1: 71–101.

Diamond, Larry. 1994. "Rethinking civil society: toward democratic consolidation." *Journal of Democracy* 5 (3).

Dioné, Josué. 1989. "Informing food security policy in Mali: interactions between technology, institutions and market reforms." Unpublished Ph.D. dissertation, Department of Agricultural Economics, Michigan State University.

Direction Nationale de l'Action Coopérative (DNACOOP). 1989. *Receuil de Textes Législatifs et Réglementaires Régissant le Mouvement Coopératif en République du Mali*. Bamako: DNACOOP.

Fatton, Robert, Jr. 1995. "Africa in the age of democratization: the civic limitations of civil society." *African Studies Review* 38 (2): 67–99.

Gellner, Ernest. 1994. *Conditions of Liberty: Civil Society and its Rivals*. London: Penguin.

Hadenius, Axel, and Fredrik Uggla. 1996. "Making civil society work, promoting democratic development: what can states and donors do?" *World Development* 24 (10): 1621–39.

Holm, John D., Patrick P. Molutsi, and Gloria Somolekae. 1996. "The development of civil society in a democratic state: the Botswana model." *African Studies Review* 39 (2): 43–69.

Huntington, Samuel P. 1991. *The Third Wave: Democratization in the Late Twentieth Century.* Norman: University of Oklahoma Press.

Hyman, Herbert. 1959. *Political Socialization: A Study in the Psychology of Political Behavior.* Glencoe, Ill.: Free Press.

Ignatieff, Michael. 1995. "On civil society: why Eastern Europe's revolutions could succeed." *Foreign Affairs* 74 (2): 128.

Institut Malien de Recherches Appliquées au Développement (IMRAD). 1994. "Le mouvement paysan au Mali." Unpublished manuscript.

Inglehart Ronald. 1988. "The renaissance of political culture." *American Political Science Review* 82 (4): 1203–30.

Jacquemot, Pierre, ed. 1981. *Le Mali, le paysan, et l'état.* Paris: l'Harmattan.

Jennings, M. Kent and Richard G. Niemi. 1981. *Generations and Politics.* Princeton: Princeton University Press.

Jeune Afrique. "Mali: en attendant le procès." 3–9 September 1997: 6–7.

———. "Mali: après l'orage" (special section). 1–7 October 1997: 77–128.

Jones, William I. 1976. *Planning and Economic Policy: Socialist Mali and Her Neighbors.* Washngton, D.C.: Three Continents Press.

Kane, Cheikh Hamidou. 1961. *L'aventure ambiguë.* Paris: Julliard.

Kim, Jae-On and Charles W. Mueller. 1978a. *Introduction to Factor Analysis: What It Is and How to Do It.* Newbury Park, Calif.: Sage.

———. 1978b. *Factor Analysis: Statistical Methods and Practical Issues.* Newbury Park, Calif.: Sage.

Lachenmann, Gudrun. 1986. "Rural development in Mali: destabilisation and social organization." *Journal of International Agriculture* 25: 217–33.

Lucas, John. 1994. "The state, civil society, and regional elites: a study of three associations in Kano, Nigeria." *African Affairs* 93 (370): 21–38.

Monga, Célestin. 1995. "Civil society and democratisation in francophone Africa." *The Journal of Modern African Studies* 33 (3): 359.

Moss, Todd J. 1995. "U.S. policy and democratisation in Africa: the limits of liberal universalism." *The Journal of Modern African Studies* 33 (2): 189.

Muller, Edward N., and Mitchell A. Seligson. 1994. "Civic culture and democracy: the question of causal relationships." *American Political Science Review* 88 (3): 635–52.

Muller, Edward N., Mitchell A. Selgson, and Ilter Turan. 1987. "Education, participation, and support for democratic norms." *Comparative Politics* 20 (1): 19–34.

New York Times. "Democracy in Mali" (editorial). 29 April 1996: A10.

———. "In one poor African nation, democracy thrives." 16 October 1996: A3.

———. "Despite setbacks, democracy gains in Africa," 11 January 1997:. A3.
———. "Mali's slips reflect stumbling African democracy." 7 September 1997: A3.
Niemi, Richard G., and Mary A. Hepburn. 1995. "The rebirth of political socialization." *Perspectives on Political Science* 24: 7–22.
Ouédraogo, Bernard Lédea. 1990. *Entraide villageoise et développement: groupements paysans au Burkina Faso*. Paris: l'Harmattan.
Putnam, Robert D. 1993. *Making Democracy Work: Civic Traditions in Modern Italy*. Princeton: Princeton University Press.
———. 1995. "Bowling alone: America's declining social capital." *Journal of Democracy* 6 (1): 65–78.
Sandbrook, Richard. 1996. "Transitions without consolidation: democratization in six African cases," *Third World Quarterly* 17 (1): 69–87.
Schmitter, Phillippe C. and Terry Lynn Karl. 1991. "What democracy is . . . and is not." *Journal of Democracy* 2: 75–88.
Smith, Zeric Kay. 1997. "'From Demons to Democrats': Mali's student movement 1991–1996." *Review of African Political Economy* 72: 249–63.
Stepan, Alfred. 1988. *Rethinking Military Politics: Brazil and the Southern Cone*. Princeton: Princeton University Press.
Sullivan, John L., George E. Marcus, Stanley Feldman, and James E. Piereson. 1981. "The sources of political tolerance: a multivariate analysis." *American Political Science Review* 75: 92–106.
Sullivan, John L., James Piereson, and George E. Marcus. 1982. *Political Tolerance and American Democracy*. Chicago: University of Chicago Press.
Talbott, Strobe. 1996. "Democracy and the national interest." *Foreign Affairs* 75 (6): 47–63.
Tocqueville, Alexis de. 1945. *Democracy in America*. 1846. Reprint, New York: Vintage.
United Nations Development Program (UNDP). 1996. *Human Development Report 1996*. Oxford, UK: Oxford University Press.
Verba, Sidney. 1965. "Comparative political culture." In *Political Culture and Political Development*, edited by Lucian W. Pye and Sidney Verba. Princeton: Princeton University Press.
Witte, Robert S., and John S. Witte. 1997. *Statistics* (5th edition). Fort Worth and Orlando: Harcourt Brace.
World Bank. 1996. *World Development Report 1996*. Oxford, UK: Oxford University Press.

Young, Tom. 1993. "Elections and electoral politics in Africa." *Africa* 63 (3): 299–312.

This research was conducted while the author was a research associate at the *Institut Malien de Recherches Appliquées au Développement* (IMRAD), an institute for development policy research located in Bamako, Mali. IMRAD provided intellectual sustenance and extensive logistical support. Financial support was provided by the U.S. Agency for International Development (USAID) and the Michigan State University Graduate School, College of Social Science, and Department of Political Science. Data used in this chapter were presented in papers at the annual meetings of the Midwest Political Science Association, Chicago, 10 April 1997, and the African Studies Association, Columbus, Ohio, 12 November 1997.

Improving Women's Health in Mali: Research, Policy Review, and Recommendations

NANCY MEZEY

T his chapter discusses how a democratized Mali might address issues concerning women's health care. The chapter begins with an overview of two
approaches to understanding health care issues—a social-psychological model
and a social-structural model, which is used in more recent research of women's
health care issues.[1] Following this overview, I present the results of my own
field research in Mali concerning the gender differences in pharmaceutical use
and purchases in rural Mali. I also discuss the limited information available on
past and current health care initiatives in Mali. Finally, I discuss policies for
improving women's health in Mali and financing health care initiatives.

Studies of Health-Seeking Behavior

Policy makers and development agencies are beginning to recognize the
important connection between gender inequality within households and the
health of girls and women.[2] Most past studies have used a social-psychological model to research household decision-making and health care in Africa,
and particularly in Mali. Unlike studies based on a social-structural model,
studies using a social-psychological model fail to address unequal power relations within households that affect health-seeking behavior.

Social-psychological studies of health-seeking behavior

Social-psychological models of health-seeking behavior—the model upon
which most health-seeking behavior research in Africa has relied—use the
ideas of predisposing, enabling, and need factors to help explain the use of
health services.

Predisposing factors are seen as "givens," and include personal or cultural values, health beliefs, family composition, gender, and age. Enabling factors, on the other hand, are seen as those factors that offer people the resources to seek health services. Enabling factors include both family resources such as income, insurance, and family savings, and community resources such as the availability of services.[3]

The need factor involves the perceived severity of an illness and the response of the family or individual to that perception. For many theorists and researchers, the need factor is the most immediate cause for health service use. Researchers have noted that if the perceived severity of an illness is high or perceived as requiring immediate medical attention, then need will most likely be the determining factor for seeking health services.

The social-psychological health-seeking model is problematic for three reasons. First, research framed by the model often defines a household as a unified unit. For example, in evaluating household demand for health in Mali, Birdsall and her colleagues assumed that people in the household share an income.[4] They also assumed that household members have equal access to the resources of other household members, ignoring power differentials between women and men that can lead to differing access to resources.

Works by Guyer, Dwyer, and Bruce, however, contend that this concept of African households is inappropriate and misleading.[5] Many married African women and men do not pool their incomes or resources, nor do they share information on such resources with their spouse(s). "Enabling factors" will vary with an African household. A more systematic analysis of the social and economic position of each individual household member, such as wealth rank-ing,[6] is needed to assess a particular household member's access to and pos-session of financial and material resources that can enable access to health care.

Second, this model of health-seeking ignores unequal power relations between women and men and how unequal gender relations within households can lead to unequal access to important resources such as health care.[7] For example, in *Family Mediation of Health Care in an African Community (Mali)*, Slobin analyzes the role of African families in therapeutic activity. [8] She acknowledges how family interactions shape both the illness experience and the therapeutic process and recognizes the unequal control of resources by men. But she does not extend this observation into her analysis of women's access to health care.

Facility-based studies also do not adequately address the issue of gender inequalities in Mali. A study by Mallé et al. examined the institutional maternal mortality rate in Mali and found that approximately 200 women out of 100,000 women die in Malian health institutions from reproductive illnesses.[9] In fact, treatable problems such as hemorrhage, toxemia, and infections accounted for 80 percent of the 360 recorded maternal deaths in twenty-four health facilities between 1988 and 1992. In the Mopti region, where much of the study was conducted, the authors found that maternal deaths represented over 50 percent of all female inpatient deaths.

Despite these findings, the authors do not address issues of gender inequality either within the health system or within Malian communities and families. Instead they conclude that preventable birth complications "result in death [because of the] poor quality and maldistribution of health services, lack of transport, and late use of allopathic services."[10] They recommend, therefore, increasing the availability of cesarean sections, providing appropriate drugs and blood transfusion facilities, educating the health care staff, and improving basic hygiene practices. While these are important recommendations, they do not address larger issues of gender inequalities: Is it only at the institutional level that adequate provisions to care for pregnant women are lacking? What efforts do families and communities make to ensure good health care for pregnant women at home? If better transportation, more educated staff, and more sophisticated medical procedures were readily available, would they be used to save women's lives over the lives of male patients who could also use more advanced medical facilities? These types of empirical questions remain unanswered.

Another facility-based health-seeking study, conducted by Künzel et al., compares the efficiency of maternal and prenatal health in Mali, Togo, and Nigeria in terms of socio-economic factors, maternal age at delivery, prenatal care, management of delivery, prenatal health, and maternal health.[11] The authors found that the efficiency rates of Mali's health system with respect to obstetrical care are low. In fact, maternal mortality was "highest in Mali: 2,000 maternal deaths per 100,000 live births . . . a tragedy of women's health."[12] According to the authors, the reason for this tragedy is that women enter motherhood too early and maternal health is neglected.[13] They recommend, therefore, teaching young women "how to prevent early pregnancies and how to perform child spacing for a better social life."[14] This recommendation rests, however, on the assumption that young women, or any women for that matter, have control over their reproductive lives, ignoring the fact that many African women do not always have that luxury.[15]

The third problem with the social-psychological model of health seeking arises from its failure to recognize how gender differences are based on socially constructed differences between women and men. Instead, most studies assume that *biological* attributes and not *socially-learned* behaviors and expectations influence health seeking. The social-psychological model denies the notion that health care differences between women and men are socially constructed and not biologically determined.

Coppo et al. examined how particular variables—including how far a household is from a health center, domestic hygiene, educational levels, economic status, the type of illness and its duration, and the sex and age of the patient—affected health-seeking behavior in Mali.[16] In particular, the authors wanted to see if these variables affected patients' use of different medical resources, including self-medication, allopathic health care centers, and traditional healers. When the authors found that the illness rate was higher for women than for men, they assumed that the differences in rates of illness between women and men were biologically based and fixed or static in nature.

While the previously discussed studies of Malian health care and health-seeking behavior do not adequately address issues of women's use of and access to health care, they at least address women's health care issues. Some studies on Malian health care ignore women almost completely.[17] Furthermore, despite the problems presented by the social-psychological model of health-seeking behavior, the model offers a potentially useful tool for addressing certain aspects of health-seeking behavior. In particular, the social-psychological model is useful for gathering data on the gender differences that exist in health-seeking behavior. The model is inadequate, however, for answering *why* such differences exist.

Social-structural models of health-seeking behavior

In contrast to the social-psychological model, the social-structural model addresses why gender differences exist in health-seeking behavior of women and men. This model stipulates that individual action must be understood in terms of the structural forces and social inequalities in which it is embedded.[18] Rather than seeing gender as an individual characteristic, a social-structural model understands how gender is a fundamental organizing principle. As such, this model acknowledges that many societies are organized along lines of unequal power relations between men and women. Thus, rather than describing gender differences in health-seeking behavior, a structural model explains gender differences by looking at how men and women have different access to health care and different household decision-making power concerning health care issues.

Very few empirical studies, however, use a structural model to understand the fundamental and underlying power differences that shape gender differences in health-seeking behavior. Castle's study, *Intra-Household differentials in Women's Status: Household Function and Focus as Determinants of Children's Illness Management and Care in Rural Mali*, may be one of the few to look at how unequal power relations within households affect health-seeking behavior in Mali.[19] The premise of Castle's work is that researchers need to examine how women in the same household differ from one another, not just how they differ from men. According to Castle, differences between women have "consequences for health-seeking behavior and health outcomes,"[20] particularly for the women's children.

Additionally, Castle discusses how the household's political and social economy is based on power relationships between individuals who bargain and negotiate for household resources. Decisions concerning children's health care are the results of such bargaining.

While Castle's study does not examine women's own health-seeking behavior, her study is important because it looks at how women's household status, based on power dynamics within the household, influences mothers' health-seeking behavior when their children are sick. She examines how the status mothers have within the household influences the "types and degrees of social and financial assistance at their disposal when their children become ill . . ."[21] If power relations between mothers in the same household influence the type and quality of health care their children receive, does it not stand to reason that power relations between women and other household members will also influence the type and quality of health care the women themselves receive? This is a critical empirical question that has not been adequately addressed.

Gender Differences in the Purchasing of Pharmaceuticals in Rural Mali

My own research into the connections between government health care use and the purchasing of prescribed pharmaceuticals indicate that women and men use health care services differently and purchase pharmaceuticals for different illnesses at different rates. The research survey was conducted in 1992, just before the democratization of the current Malian government.

I conducted this research in the small urban center of Sansanding (*Sinzani*), a district (*arrondissement*) capital in the Segou region of Mali. The town of Sansanding has a population of approximately 10,000. Sansanding district includes thirty villages, has a population of nearly 30,000, and covers roughly 600 square kilometers. While some of the villages have retained their traditional religion, most villagers are Muslim. This is evidenced by the eight elaborate mosques in Sansanding. Sansanding has several ethnic groups, including Bambara, Bozo, Fulani, Maraka, and Mossi. Bambara is the predominant ethnic group and language spoken. It is also the language in which the interview team conducted the survey.

Government health care facilities

In Sansanding proper there is one dispensary and one maternity ward. They serve the entire district, although there is a second dispensary 16 kilometers away.[22] At the time of the study, the dispensary was overseen by a head nurse (*Infirmière d'Etat*) who had received three years of medical training after completing the ninth grade. Also staffing the dispensary was a certified nurse (*Infirmière Certifiée*) with a similar education and a nurse's aide (*Aide Soignant*) who had a sixth-grade education. These three health workers had similar responsibilities covering a wide range of health problems except those requiring surgery. Only the head and certified nurses were authorized to write prescriptions. All three nurses were male.

The maternity ward operated under the supervision of the head nurse at the dispensary. The head midwife (*Matrônne*) had finished fifth grade and had been working at the maternity ward for eighteen years. She was aided by a nurse/midwife (*Sage Femme*) whose education was similar to the head nurse at the dispensary. At the time of the study there was a third health worker who had finished the ninth grade and then trained with the Red Cross for six months. Finally, there was a traditional midwife who was unsalaried, had more than fifteen years of midwife experience, but had no formal education. She was the only health worker at the maternity ward who did not write prescriptions.

The ratio of government health workers to villagers was approximately 1:4,000. This was high in comparison to the national average of 1:1,350 nurses to villagers.[23]

While consultations with a health worker at a government health facility in Mali were free, patients paid for the prescribed medications in cash at one of the three local pharmacies. Pharmacies in Mali were operated by the government until the system was privatized in 1991. Two of the pharmacies were owned and staffed by the same villager and his family. The third was owned by a male villager who had hired a worker to staff the facility. The owners set the prices of the pharmaceuticals based on the price of pharmaceuticals in the capital city of Bamako plus the cost of round-trip travel and the pharmacists' profits.

Traditional healers

In addition to government health facilities, there were at least twelve traditional healers in Sansanding proper and thirty-four in the surrounding villages, a ratio of about 1:650 healers to villagers. Most healers had a specialty—pediatric, pulmonary, gastrointestinal, and orthopedic illnesses. The three healers I interviewed as expert informants stated that people commonly pay what they are able; the healers never fix a price. Payment often comes in the form of cola nuts or small change (between 50–300 FCFA, $0.16 to $1.00). Many healers were farmers or fishers by trade who had trained to be healers by family members or village elders.

Islamic healers

There were at least twenty-nine *marabouts* (Islamic healers) in Sansanding proper and thirteen in the remaining villages, a ratio of 1:715 *marabouts* to villagers. *Marabouts* in Sansanding healed many illnesses, both physical and mental. People also visited *marabouts* to resolve problems related to marriage, finances, employment, and travel. Of the twenty-nine *marabouts* in Sansanding, twenty-four treated medical illnesses. *Marabouts* study for many years to learn their trade. Clients pay for treatment with cash, through bartering, and by in-kind methods. Most *marabouts* are expensive, often requiring the client to supply sheep, chickens, cloth, and other costly items.

Tracking prescription purchases

With a team of five interviewers, I surveyed all patients seeking medical treatment at either the dispensary or maternity ward over a five-week period; this covered 469 patients of which 370 received prescriptions.[24] The pre-consultation survey instrument identified respondents' demographic characteristics, reasons for seeking medical treatment, anxiety about and perceived level of the severity of the illness, previous treatments sought to cure the illness, the costs of these treatments, and how the patient got the money to pay for the treatments. The post-consultation survey assessed the respondent's satisfaction with the visit, whether the health worker explained the nature and severity of the diagnosed illness, and if the respondent had a new level of anxiety and perceived severity of the illness based on the health worker's information.

In addition to these surveys, I interviewed villagers and expert informants in the area. The expert informants included traditional, Islamic, and government health care professionals and officials. These in-depth interviews provided insight into the scope and nature of the different medical systems and particular health care issues.

In order to frame my research, I relied on a social-psychological model of health-seeking behavior. Using this framework, I hypothesized how the need (measured by the respondents' perceived severity and anxiety), perceived efficacy of the prescribed medication, financial means, perceived nature of an illness, the respondents' occupation, education, marital status, and the patients' age would influence purchasing behavior.[25]

Purchasing patterns of women

Female patients who were unable to work during their illness episodes were more likely to purchase the medications. Because women have many household and agricultural responsibilities, it is important that they recover quickly from an illness in order to rejoin the work force.

The farther away from medical care or the longer it took to get to a clinic, the more likely a female patient was to purchase the medications. This is probably because of the poor access some female patients have to health facilities. If a patient found the time and money to travel to a health facility, she was more likely to find the means to purchase the required pharmaceuticals.

Female patients who believed they had malaria were more likely to purchase the prescribed medications. The self-diagnosis of malaria was associated with lower anxiety levels concerning the illness. The lower anxiety levels probably stem from patients' familiarity with malaria and its treatment.

Not surprisingly, female patients with more cash available were more likely to purchase the prescribed medications. However, which female patients had money varied by educational background, marital status, duration of illness, and occupation. For example, those female patients who had been educated in government-run schools had more cash available to them. Married patients and patients with longer-term illnesses and domestic or agricultural occupations had less cash available to them.

Female patients who believed they had reproductive illnesses were less likely to purchase the prescribed medications. This was because women with reproductive problems had little confidence in the efficacy of government pharmaceuticals for their illness. They also had less cash available with which to purchase the medications.

Purchasing patterns of men

As with female patients, significant patterns of pharmaceutical use emerged among the male patients.

Men with self-diagnosed musculoskeletal ailments, such as broken bones, were less likely to purchase the prescribed medications. This was true despite higher levels of perceived severity and anxiety about their illness and an inability to work due to their illness. Key informants discussed how many patients preferred to go to traditional healers for musculoskeletal ailments, particularly for broken bones. Traditional healers have a much better reputation for a quick cure than do government health care workers.

Unlike women, men with self-diagnosed malaria were less likely to purchase the prescribed medications. This was true despite higher levels of confidence in government pharmaceuticals for curing malaria and a guaranteed funding source.

Similar to female patients, male patients who had more cash available were more likely to purchase the medications. Men with more cash available tended to be married and to work in occupations that offer a steady source of income.

Not surprisingly, male patients who did not earn a wage were less likely to purchase the prescribed medications. These patients had less guaranteed financial means.

Implications of prescription-purchase study

This study clearly indicates the need to focus on distinct populations, such as women and men, instead of the aggregate group. The findings show that male and female patients have different health-seeking and purchasing behaviors. For female patients, my research supports the notion that women's health issues, particularly reproductive health issues, cannot effectively be addressed if they are not separated from the health needs of the larger population. Malian culture emphasizes women's roles as biological reproducers. Men can marry multiple wives in order to increase their wealth of children. A woman unable to bear children often perceives herself as inadequate to meet her societal and familial responsibilities.

Women were found to have high levels of anxiety and perceived severity associated with reproductive illness. However, they did not purchase the prescribed medications because they had little confidence that the medicine would help cure their illnesses. In addition, key informants discussed how women often perceive reproductive problems to be associated with supernatural causes and therefore seek help from marabouts and traditional healers.

In talking with key informants I found that female patients were also less willing to discuss their illnesses, whether reproductive or not, with male health care workers. However, the head of the dispensary, who oversaw all of the government health facilities in the district, required the health workers in the maternity ward to direct any non-pregnancy related issues to the dispensary where only men worked. The maternity health workers often disregarded this mandate by meeting with their patients at home or after business hours. However, some women probably never sought help either for fear of having to visit a male health worker or because they did not think the maternity workers would be able to help them. These findings point to the need for Malian health services to more adequately address issues concerning women's health involving both reproductive and non-reproductive illnesses.

Women's Health Care in the Era of Democracy and Decentralization

To date, the empirical research on health-seeking primarily in Mali has largely ignored issues specific to women's health. This section reviews how a social-structural analysis helps our understanding of the main causes of women's unique health problems, key health needs of Malian women and of the general population, past and current initiatives that the Malian government is taking to improve health care, additional initiatives that target women's health issues, and several ways to finance new programs to promote women's health.

Underlying causes of health problems of women

While there is limited research to indicate that unequal gender relations embedded both within Malian social structures and within Malian households affect women's morbidity, mortality, and access to health care, evidence from other industrializing nations supports this observation.[26] Based on this evidence and on my own research and experience in Mali, it is possible to identify how gender inequality, particularly inequality in social institutions such as the economy, education, and households, is the main cause of many women's health problems.

Separating gender discrimination within larger society and within households is difficult because they are closely linked. Women around the world are largely in charge of maintaining households, food preparation, and other non-paid labor. Because women's time is occupied by unpaid tasks, they have little time to work in the paid labor market. Women's blocked access to paid labor and education directly influences their health status.[27] As discussed earlier, research indicates that women's lack of income reduces their decision-making power within households, including the power to make decisions concerning who in the household gains access to health care. Furthermore, because women's time is heavily occupied with household chores, most girls are denied access to formal education. Research shows that lower levels of education for women affect the nutritional and health status of girls.[28] Thus, gender discrimination that denies women access to paid labor and education directly affects the health status of females of all ages.

The inaccessibility to paid labor also places women in a disadvantaged social position. In addition to working long hours for no wages, women are denied access to land and inheritance rights. This further lowers women's social status and creates an excuse for men to value boys over girls. Furthermore, lower social and economic status of women is manifested through less access to nutritious food, as well as greater exposure to physical, sexual, and mental abuse.[29] Thus, gender discrimination both within households and throughout larger society not only denies women access to adequate health care, but actually increases women's health risks and creates health problems specific to women.

Identifying health needs of Malian women

It is important to identify both women's low social and economic status as the underlying cause of many female health problems and to identify particular illnesses that result from gender discrimination. Gender discrimination affects women of all ages differently. Worldwide, girls are born with inherent biological advantages that allow them to survive harsh conditions more readily than boys. But discrimination against girls such as poorer nutrition, less immediate health attention than boys, and female genital mutilation can negate those inherent advantages. Similarly, during adolescence girls face a variety of health risks that boys do not face. These include exposure to sexually transmitted diseases (STDs), including HIV/AIDS, through forced sexual relations with older men, undernutrition and micronutrient deficiency, and early childbearing.[30] In Mali, for example, by the age of eighteen, more the 40 percent of adolescent females have already given birth.[31]

Adult women also face unwanted pregnancies and unsafe abortions, pregnancy complications, malnutrition, exposure to STDs and HIV/AIDS, as well as sexual, mental, and physical violence.[32] In addition to maternal mortality, another serious problem that African women face is gendered violence. Issues of domestic violence, rape, and sexual assault are beginning to receive more attention in discussions on African women's health.[33] Such discussions are important given the prevalence of violence against women in Africa. A study conducted in Kenya, for example, found that 42 percent of women were "beaten regularly."[34] Similar studies need to be conducted in Mali to determine the extent of violence against women and how it taxes women, their families, and health care resources.

Finally, women who are in their postreproductive years face health problems such as cardiovascular diseases, gynecological cancers, osteoporosis, osteoarthritis, and diabetes. While these illnesses are caused by biological changes, social factors that have taxed women throughout their lives, such as nutritional deprivation, hazardous and heavy work, perpetual childbearing, and low self-esteem, leave many older women physically and mentally weak. Furthermore, abandonment and widowhood often leave older women in even poorer conditions.[35] How older women in Mali are affected by gender discrimination and poor access to health care is an empirical question in need of research.

General health concerns

In addition to health concerns specific to women, there are several general health concerns that affect both women and men. These general health concerns include a poor infrastructure, lack of safe water and proper sanitation, and lack of affordable and available pharmaceuticals.

Poor infrastructure includes a lack of paved roads for easy travel—particularly during the rainy season, inadequate routine and emergency transportation, and a lack of well-staffed and well-located rural health facilities. In addition, the expense of local transportation prohibits many rural inhabitants from traveling at all.[36] Long distances to health facilities are particularly salient for women. Because women work longer hours for less pay than men, finding time and money to travel long distances to health facilities presents a larger obstacle for women than for men.[37]

Even if villagers make it to a rural health facility, there is no emergency transport system to take patients to better-equipped urban health facilities. Lack of emergency transport is particularly problematic for pregnancy- and labor-related emergencies. For example, many women traveled from surrounding villages to the maternity ward in Sansanding to deliver their babies. But when there were complications with the delivery, there was no formal or affordable means to transport women to the better-equipped and better-staffed hospital in Markala, 20 kilometers away.

The fact that rural health facilities are poorly equipped and the staff poorly trained to address emergency situations and complications is also a major problem associated with poor infrastructure in Mali (and other African nations). In Mali in 1990, there were 19,450 inhabitants per physician and 1,890 inhabitants per nurse.[38] In addition, the few health workers who practice in more rural health facilities are poorly trained. For example, in 1987, only 32 percent of pregnant Malian women had deliveries by trained attendants.[39] The lack of well-trained health workers in rural health facilities is a problem that plagues most of Mali.

Unsafe water and a lack of sanitation also pose major health risks to Malians. Water contaminated with diseases such as Guinea worm, giardia, amoebas, and schistosomiasis, to name a few, cause major health problems. Despite these health threats, only about 53 percent of the urban population and 38 percent of the rural population in Mali had access to uncontaminated water supplies in 1991.[40]

In addition to contaminated water, a lack of covered latrines and unprotected food sources leads to greater fecal-oral transmission of diseases.[41] However, in Mali in 1990, while 81 percent of the urban population had "reasonable access to sanitary means of excreta and waste disposal," only 10 percent of the rural population had such access.[42] Women who care for sick household members are doubly burdened, both with poor health themselves and with caring for other sick household members.[43]

A final general concern that affects the entire population is the lack of available and affordable pharmaceuticals. A study conducted by the World Health Organization (WHO) estimated that approximately 60 percent of sub-Saharan Africans have no regular access to the pharmaceuticals they need. The lack of regular access is caused by poor infrastructure to transport pharmaceuticals to rural areas, by management and logistical problems, and by financial constraints. Financial problems occur largely because over 90 percent of all pharmaceuticals in sub-Saharan Africa are imported.[44]

The lack of accessible pharmaceuticals in Mali was apparent during my research; empty shelves in the pharmacies were common. Pharmaceuticals that were available often cost more than most villagers, particularly women, could afford. For example, the average woman with a reproductive illness arrived at the maternity ward with 900 CFAF ($3.00 at the time of the research). But the average price of drugs at any of the three private pharmacies in town was 1,834 CFAF. My findings are similar to other studies conducted in Mali.[45] Thus, while visits to the dispensary or maternity ward are generally free, patients are unable to complete their treatment because of costly or unavailable pharmaceuticals. These findings indicate a need to re-evaluate so-called "free" health services when pharmaceuticals are not included in the health care package.

Recommendations for Improving Women's Health Care in Democratic Mali

The problems of women's health and health care are complex and cannot be solved by short-term or simple solutions. In order to provide a comprehensive package to improve women's health care, solutions must target gender discrimination, address women's specific health issues, and concentrate on general health issues that affect women, men, and children. Before suggesting recommendations for improving women's health in Mali, it is useful to look at some current Malian health initiatives. Comprehensive research needs to be conducted to establish what new innovations would work in specific, localized areas of Mali, particularly given the country's ethnic and religious diversity.

Malian health initiatives

In 1987, several sub-Saharan African nations, including Mali, participated in the "Bamako Initiative." Sponsored by WHO and UNICEF, the Bamako Initiative called for the "decentralization of public health systems and strengthening community participation in health."[46] This initiative included suggestions for cost recovery programs at the community level, such as user fees for services and essential drugs and revolving drug funds. Despite its good intentions, the Bamako Initiative was "not formulated as a comprehensive strategy for the health sector" and its effects have been limited.[47]

In December 1990, the Malian government built on the Bamako Initiative by implementing the Community-Managed Health Care Program (CMHCP). This new program aimed "at improving the health status of Mali's population, particularly women and children, by increasing the coverage and quality of health services, integrating family planning in primary health care services, and providing access to safe drinking water."[48] These goals were operationalized through a decentralized system of community health centers (CHC) where local villagers participated in "mapping health facilities and their areas of coverage, defining operation and cost recovery rules, and setting up management mechanisms run by elected committees."[49] CHCs were implemented in thirty-six districts in five regions of Mali. Since its inception and through its use of CHCs, the CMHCP has improved the Malian health care system. During the first five years of implementation, vaccination coverage, contraceptive use, and pre-natal consultations increased. Furthermore, "following the introduction of essential drugs, the average cost of a prescription" dropped to between

600 and 1200 CFAF, which is below current national averages and within the financial reach of many more people.[50]

Building upon the CMHCP and in a renewed effort to improve its health care system, in December 1998 Mali announced a new health care initiative. With the help of the World Bank, WHO, UNICEF, the African Development Bank, the Islamic Development Bank, and other donors, the Malian Ministry of Health is undertaking a $400 million project called the Integrated Health Sector Development Program (IHSDP). The IHSDP aims at "meeting the health needs of the underserved segments of the population and accelerate the country's demographic transition toward slower population growth."[51]

The IHSDP recognizes several key problems in addressing Malian health, including infectious and parasitic diseases such as malaria, measles, tetanus, respiratory infections, and diarrhea. In addition, the Malian government has recognized the country's high rates of infant and maternal mortality, as well high fertility rates. Given these health issues, the project will focus on three major components: (1) expanding access to basic health care, including preventative, curative, and reproductive health services; (2) strengthening health system management schemes; and (3) "developing sustainable financing schemes for health sector development with safety nets for the poor."[52]

These three components will be implemented using a decentralized strategy. Offices at the national level will provide policy guidance, monitor the overall program, and coordinate donors. Also on the national level, the Directorate of Public Health will "be responsible for technical support and specific program monitoring and evaluation."[53] The Directorate of Administration and Finance will be responsible for budget-related and financial matters. At the regional level, Regional Health Directorates will be in charge of implementing "programs of good quality, affordable care, and services" through the use of community-managed health care facilities.[54]

It is difficult to discern how much attention the IHSDP pays to women's health. The World Bank notes the need for targeting reproductive health and for including women in community management of local health facilities. Furthermore, the Bank recognizes that the problem of high fertility rates are the result of ". . . low school enrollment of girls, and difficulties in overcoming gender-based constraints to the integration of women in the economy."[55] While the Bank acknowledges the need to target gender discrimination when addressing women's health, there are no apparent strategies built into the IHSDP that directly aim at ending gender discrimination. The following subsections suggest ways to combat gender discrimination and to reduce women's health risks in Mali, with the understanding that Malian women must be integrally involved in determining how to develop and implement any of these suggestions.

Gender discrimination

As discussed earlier, gender discrimination is the underlying cause of women's specific health problems in Africa. Gender discrimination results in women's low social and economic status and is caused by women's lack of access to the paid labor market; overburdening non-paid household chores; lack of access to education, land tenure rights, and nutritious foods; and frequent exposure to physical, sexual, and emotional abuse. Because gender discrimination is a complex and long-standing historical aspect of Malian life, long-term solutions are needed. First, the Malian government needs to show a strong commitment to enacting more equitable laws. For example, if women are to gain access to the labor market, new labor market policies and employment laws should be implemented.

New family laws could be enacted to help prevent gender discrimination in households. Family laws could prohibit domestic violence and penalize offenders, allow divorce without financial penalties for women, and allow women to claim custody of their children after divorce rather than forcing women to leave their children with their ex-husbands. Finally, laws could be developed to ensure equal access to land and property, particularly in the case of inheritance laws and economic projects that allocate land to project participants. For example, gardening, agricultural, and small business projects should ensure that women have equal access to land and property.

In addition to new laws, the educational needs of girls and women should be addressed. Families could be given incentives to send their daughters to school. Furthermore, schools could be encouraged to support female education at all levels and teachers could be penalized for discriminating against female students.

Finally, men should also be targeted in public education programs aiming to end gender discrimination because men make most of the decisions about how resources (including health care) are distributed and what work women may or may not do. Men's involvement will help men recognize that women's improved economic and social status not only contributes to improved women's health, but also to the improved physical and economic health of Malian households and Malian society at large.

Solutions for women's specific health needs

In addition to longer-term solutions to end gender discrimination, more immediate solutions should target women's specific health needs. Many of the health needs of young girls and adolescents could be met by their adult caretakers. Adults need to understand the importance of good nutrition for both girls and boys and the importance of girls' participation in formal education. Community and educational efforts should target adolescents themselves to educate girls and boys on having safe sex, using contraceptives to avoid unwanted pregnancies, and the legal and social implications of violence against women. In addition, girls should be offered some alternatives in unwanted pregnancies other than being banished or facing unsafe or illegal abortions.

Greater attention to women in their child-bearing years would address the major health issues specific to women. Specific approaches could include improved maternal and prenatal care, such as improved family planning and pregnancy services. Furthermore, in making use of local resources, it is important to train traditional birth attendants in current practices and encourage them to work with government and private health care workers. In addition, the number of female physicians and nurses could be increased, thereby offering women the option to visit health care facilities staffed by female health care providers. Clustering services for women and children would help optimize women's time spent at health care facilities as well.

The health needs of older Malian women must also be met. Some diseases associated with old age in women, such as gynecological cancers, may have cost-prohibitive treatments. But families should be encouraged to promote the health of elderly women by supplying nutritious meals, not forcing elderly women (or men) to participate in hazardous or heavy work, and insuring that widowed women are materially and emotionally cared for.

General health concerns

In addition to the recommendations specific to gender discrimination and women's health, other improvements can ensure a stronger infrastructure, safe water and sanitation, and make affordable pharmaceuticals available. Paving roads in more rural and remote areas in Mali would facilitate travel to health centers. Furthermore, the use of mobile clinics could help compensate for the lack of health facilities and the expense of travel. Mobile clinics could run immunization programs and health education programs in more remote areas of Mali. But while mobile clinics can provide more preventative and routine services, a formal system of emergency transport needs to be provided between rural health posts and urban hospitals. How the emergency needs can best be met in different regions of Mali should be determined through focused research efforts.

In addition to mobile clinics and emergency services, increasing the number of health facilities staffed with competent, trained health workers would save villagers time in transportation. In addition, better-trained staff would save villagers the frustration of leaving a health clinic with no better understanding of their illnesses than before they arrived. Health workers could also be trained in the benefits of traditional and religious healing in order to help patients determine their best course of treatment.

One of the most important areas of improving the health of Mali's general population, including women, is improving drug availability and affordability. While I discuss how to fund such efforts in the following section, pharmaceuticals should be provided as part of government health care packages not through expensive and separate, private pharmacies. Furthermore, more of an effort should be made to manufacture generic drugs in Mali, rather than using expensive imports.

Financing Malian Health Initiatives

The recommendations above may seem overwhelming in number, but implementing interventions to reduce female morbidity and mortality is cost-effective. The health of women is crucial to the health of Mali and Africa in general.

> . . .Women form the backbone of African economies. They produce most of the food necessary for a household, cook for the family, fetch water, clean the house and care for the children, the sick and the elderly at home. The death of a woman results in both economic and social hardship for the family and community.[56]

Financing health programs that aim at improving women's health, therefore, not only improves women's health, but also improves the health of men and children, as well as the social and economic health of Malian society. Furthermore, health programs that target women are more cost-effective than programs targeting men. In fact, ". . . highly cost-effective interventions— those costing less than $100 per disability saved—can benefit more females than males between the ages of five and forty-four."[57] Thus, implementing many of the interventions discussed above are worth the money spent. However, the question remains as to the most cost-effective way of paying for such interventions.

Past and current health care initiatives have been partially financed by the Malian government and by external donors. But despite public and foreign subsidies, 75 percent of recurrent health care charges have been financed by Malian households.[58] It is clear that many Malians, particularly women, do not have the means to cover health care costs. Yet both the Bamako Initiative and newer health initiatives have incorporated cost recovery plans in the form of user fees to recuperate health care costs. While user fees may be necessary, other means of covering health costs include an alternative method of user fees, a localized method of insurance, and bartering that may help reduce costs for those people, including women, who cannot currently afford public health care.

An alternative method of user fees

Cost recovery schemes such as user fees (fee-for-service) have been implemented throughout Africa to recuperate health care costs. Fees for visiting health facilities and obtaining pharmaceuticals have been incorporated into national health care plans. Critics of such schemes claim that user fees in Africa create even greater barriers to health care access for specific groups of people, particularly women and poor people.[59] Critics also argue that programs attempting to raise funds for primary health care at the community level, such as the Bamako Initiative, have been too hasty and not based on large enough studies. Components such as efficacy, empathy, geographical accessibility, and availability must also be factored into cost recovery schemes.[60]

In an attempt to further study the effect of user fees on accessibility to health care, Diop and colleagues conducted a study in Niger. Health care in Niger is similar to Malian health care in that visits to public health facilities are free, but patients purchase drugs from private pharmacies or street vendors. To conduct their study, the researchers selected three districts. One district served as a control where no changes in user fees or health services were introduced. In the second, a fee-for-episode of illness scheme where patients paid a fixed amount was used. In the third, the researchers used a lower fee-for-episode but charged a small annual tax to district taxpayers.[61] The revenues in the three districts were handled by local and district-level committees and were mostly used to finance pharmaceuticals. In all three districts, initial stocks of generic drugs were supplied to improve drug availability, and health workers were given additional training in diagnosis and treatment protocols, as well as in financial management.

The findings of this study show several key factors that favor the tax + fee scheme. First, in the tax + fee district, usage of health services increased dramatically, much more so than in the fee-for-episode district or in the control district. Furthermore, the tax + fee district showed a significant improvement in the utilization of public health facilities among children and women, as well as a double in the utilization rate of the poorest 25 percent of the population.[62] The increased usage of public health services in the other districts was attributed to quality improvements such as drug availability. However, pre-paying for health care in the form of taxes, coupled with a lower per-visit fee attracted more people than to the higher fee-per-episode (but no pre-paid tax) district.

The second important finding is that while utilization rates dropped for people living more than one hour away from the facility in the control district, in the other two districts utilization increased for people living between one and three hours away from the facilities. This finding shows that "once drugs were more readily available at public health facilities, people perceived that the marginal benefits from using the services were higher than the marginal costs of the long travel time."[63]

The third important finding is that the use of *preventive* services increased in the tax + fee district, particularly in the use of prenatal care for women. While there were no significant changes in the control district or in the fee-for-service district, there was a significant increase in the use of prenatal services in the tax + fee district. Thus, not only did the tax + fee scheme increase women's general use of public health care, it also increased women's use of preventative services.

The fourth important finding supporting the implementation of tax + fee schemes for health care is that this scheme proved more cost-effective than the fee-for-service scheme. For example, in the control district, the average illness-related expenditure remained at its original amount. The average illness-related expenditure in the fee-for-service district declined, saving patients about 40 percent on health care usage. In the tax + fee district, the average illness-related expenditure declined even further, although the villagers had already paid additional money. When the taxes were averaged into the cost per visit, patients saved about 36 percent on health care usage in the tax + fee district.

Despite the lower savings in the tax + fee district, villagers preferred this system of payment. Interviews showed that 85 percent of the patients strongly preferred the tax + fee scheme because "it is easier to finance the cost of illness when part of the cost is prepaid."[64] Not only is the tax + fee scheme preferred by patients, but it also generates greater revenue to maintain itself.

These findings indicate that there are cost recovery programs that recoup most of the cost of health care and that can actually increase usage of public health facilities by the general population as well as by women and poorer people. By increasing drug availability, pre-paying some of the costs through taxes, and improving technical and management skills, innovative cost recovery schemes can pay for health care. Research similar to that conducted in Niger should be conducted in Mali to determine how much people are willing to pay through a combination of taxes and fees-per-episode, and how much will need to be collected to cover the cost of an ameliorated health and pharmaceutical program.

Additional financing schemes

In addition to this type of user fee scheme, two additional ways to help poorer populations, including women, pay for health care emerged during my research in Mali. These two schemes incorporate existing local efforts of Malian women and men to take control of their financial needs, rather than looking to government or development agencies for help.

The first is a localized "insurance" program in the form of a revolving fund. While formal health insurance programs exist in Mali for public sector employees, only about 3 percent of that population is insured.[65] Because most public employees are men, women are unlikely to be insured at all. Several African communities, including some in Mali, have tried to incorporate revolving funds to purchase pharmaceuticals. These communities started by accruing an initial stock of drugs purchased by the government, community members, or an outside donor. Then the drugs were sold to community members to recover the cost of the drugs. Unfortunately, these revolving funds have run into problems, including mismanagement of funds and sharp increases of drug prices.[66] In addition, women do not always have access to these funds if they are regulated by men.

While national insurance plans and community-run revolving drug funds have not worked in the past in Mali, combining and adjusting both of these strategies, along with ensuring that women maintain control of their own money, may prove more effective in helping women cover health care costs. The women whom I interviewed in Mali during my study stated that they use a revolving fund system (*pari wari*) to access lump sums of money to make larger investments or purchases. Several women contribute a specified amount of money during a specified time period and then rotate who gets to access the total sum of money each month. For example, ten women may contribute 100 CFAF ($0.33) every two weeks to their revolving fund. Every month, a different woman can pull the sum of money (in this case 2,000 CFAF) to pay for whatever she pleases. Using this example, 2,000 CFAF is more than enough to pay for public health care fees. Currently, however, this system of revolving funds is not used specifically to cover health care costs. Perhaps a modified version of this revolving fund can be instituted using small groups of women, whereby each woman pays a certain amount of money toward future health care, thus creating a form of localized insurance. Each woman can pull out money as needed per illness episode.

The women in Sansanding offered another suggestion for paying for public health care. As noted earlier, payment for traditional healers is often small change or cola nuts, whatever the patient can afford. Payment for marabouts is often in the form of barter. Patients barter expensive items such as sheep, chickens, or cloth for the service of marabouts. Despite the high cost of marabouts, Malian women and men frequent these healers regularly. Women suggested that their ability to barter for services, rather than pay cash, facilitated the use of marabouts. While the economics of bartering can be complicated, particularly on the large scale of public health facilities, this form of payment may help women who have less cash access public health care. Further research needs to be conducted to evaluate whether revolving funds for health insurance and bartering for health in Mali are feasible and efficient.

Conclusion

This chapter presented and critiqued current research on and policies concerning women's health care in Mali and suggested alternative research and policy agendas to target the root causes of women's unique health problems and general health concerns. The research conducted to date is based primarily on social-psychological models of health seeking behavior. While this research can be used to detect certain gender differences in both usage patterns and illness episodes, it does not address larger social-structural issues such as institutionalized and household-level gender discrimination that not only prevent women from gaining access to adequate health care, but actually are the root causes of many women-specific ailments. Thus, new research initiatives are needed to examine how gender discrimination in Mali affects the health of women. This research must aim at local groups of women by region, ethnicity, religion, and age, in order to address the great diversity of women in Mali.

Similarly, policy efforts aimed at improving the health of Malian women have historically and currently acknowledged women's poorer social and economic status, but have not implemented comprehensive solutions aimed at combating gender discrimination in Mali. Thus, based on the findings of the newly proposed research initiatives, health care programs should work in collaboration with educational and economic institutions to ensure that Malian women become equal citizens with men.

Finally, innovative financing schemes should be implemented to meet the needs of localized groups of women and men. As shown by the discussion of localized insurance schemes and bartering for health services, health planners should look to local approaches before relying on top-down measures. In addition to user fee methods, localized insurance schemes and bartering can help ensure than Malian women, men, and children have better financial and physical access to high quality health care.

Notes

1. Only literature published in English is reviewed here. For examples of health research published in French, see Brunet-Jailly (1993).

2. World Bank 1995.

3. Andersen 1968.

4. Birdsall et al. 1986.

5. Guyer 1980; Dwyer and Bruce 1988.

6. Grandin 1994.

7. Vlassoff 1994; Freedman and Maine 1993.

8. Slobin 1991.

9. Mallé et al. 1994.

10. Ibid., 19.

11. Künzel et al. 1996.

12. Ibid., 14.

13. Fathalla 1994, cited in Künzel et al. 1996, 14.

14. Künzel et al. 1996, 14.

15. Merchant 1996; Turshen 1991.

16. Coppo et al. 1992.

17. See, for example, Hielscher and Sommerfeld 1985 and Kegels 1994.

18. Baca Zinn and Dill 1994; Collins 1989; Guyer 1988.

19. Castle 1993.

20. Ibid., 137.

21. Ibid., 155.

22. Only facilities in Sansanding were included in the study.

23. U.S. Department of State 1993.

24. While this facility-based approach was useful in conducting my research, it was limited in that it excluded people who sought help exclusively at traditional or Islamic healers or who did not seek any medical treatment.

25. I used multiple regression to analyze the data, disaggregating the sample by gender and looking at specific differences between female and male purchasing behavior. Different patterns in purchasing behavior emerged.

26. Daly et al. 1999; Freedman and Maine 1993; Vlassoff 1994.

27. Daly et al. 1999.

28. Merchant and Kurz 1993.

29. Ibid.

30. Merchant 1996; Merchant and Kurz 1993.

31. Senderwitz 1993 and Population Reference Bureau 1992, as cited in Daly et al. 1999.

32. Daly et al. 1999; Merchant 1996.

33. Africa Recovery 1998, 12.

34. Raikes 1990.

35. Koblinsky et al. 1993; Merchant and Kurz 1993.

36. Diop et al. 1995.

37. Gertler and van der Gaag 1990.

38. World Bank 1993, 292.

39. Center for International Health Information 1996, 1.

40. Ibid.

41. World Bank 1994a.

42. Center for International Health Information 1996, 1, 12.

43. World Bank 1994b.

44. World Bank 1994a.

45. Coulibaly and Kéita 1996; Diop et al. 1995.

46. Diop et al. 1995, 223.

47. Nolan and Turbat 1995, 4.

48. CIESIN/World Bank 1998.

49. World Bank 1998.

50. Ibid.

51. World Bank 1999.

52. Ibid.

53. Ibid.

54. Ibid.

55. Ibid.

56. Koenig et al. 1988, as cited in Daly et al. 1999.

57. World Bank 1994b, 9.

58. Coulibaly and Kéita 1996, 355.

59. Diop et al. 1995, 231; Waddington and Enyimayew 1989.

60. Unger et al. 1990.

61. Diop et al. 1995, 226.

62. Ibid., 229.

63. Ibid., 230.

64. Ibid., 234.

65. Nolan and Turbat 1995, 40.

66. World Bank 1994a.

Bibliography

Africa Recovery. 1998. "Women and social services." *Africa Recovery Briefing Paper* April (11): 10–12.

Andersen, Margaret L. 1997. *Thinking about Women: Sociological Perspectives on Sex and Gender*, 4th ed. Boston: Allyn & Bacon.

Andersen, Ronald. 1968. *A Behavioral Model of Families' Use of Health Services*. Chicago: Center for Health Administration Studies, University of Chicago.

Baca Zinn, Maxine, and Bonnie Thornton Dill (eds.). 1994. *Women of Color in U.S. Society*. Philadelphia: Temple University Press.

Birdsall, Nancy, François Orivel, Martha Ainsworth, and Punam Chuhan. 1986. "Paying for health and schooling services in rural Africa: a Mali case study." Population, Health, and Nutrition Department, World Bank.

Brunet-Jailly, Joseph (ed.) 1993. *Se Soigner au Mali*. Paris: Karthala and ORSTOM.

Castle, Sarah E. 1993. "Intra-household differentials in women's status: household function and focus as determinants of children's illness management and care in rural Mali." *Health Transition Review* 3 (2): 137–57.

Center for International Health Information. 1996. "Health statistics report/ Mali."

CIESIN/World Bank. 1998. "Community-managed health care programs in Mali." In World Bank [online]. Available: <http://www.ciesin.org> or <http://www.worldbank.org/html/extdr/hnp/hddflash/hcnote/hrn029.html> [January 1999].

Collins, Patricia Hill. 1989. *Toward a New Vision: Race, Class and Gender as Categories of Analysis and Connection*. Memphis: The Research Clearinghouse and Curriculum Integration Project Center for Research on Women, Memphis State University.

Coppo, P., L. Pisani, and A. Kéita. 1992. "Perceived morbidity and health behavior in a Dogon community." *Social Science and Medicine* 34 (11): 1227–35.

Coulibaly, Seydou O., and Moussa Kéita. 1996. "Économie de la Santé au Mali." *Cahiers Santé*, 353–59.

Daly, Patricia, Michael Azefor, and Boniface Nasah. 1999. "Safe motherhood in Francophone Africa: Some improvements but not enough." In World Bank [online]. Available <http://www.worldbank.org/html/extdr/hnp/hddflash/hcwp/hrwp001.html> [January 1999].

Diop, François, Abdo Yazbeck, and Ricardo Bitrán. 1995. "The impact of alternative cost recovery schemes on access and equity in Niger." *Health Policy and Planning* 10 (3): 223–40.

Dwyer, Daisy, and Judith Bruce, eds., 1988. *A Home Divided: Women and Income in the Third World.* Stanford: Stanford University Press.

Freedman, Lynn P., and Deborah Maine. 1993. "Women's mortality: a legacy of neglect." In *The Health of Women: A Global Perspective*, edited by Marge Koblinsky, Judith Timyan, and Jill Gay. Boulder: Westview Press, 147–70.

Gertler, Paul, and Jacques van der Gaag. 1990. *The Willingness to Pay for Medical Care: Evidence from Two Developing Countries.* Baltimore: Johns Hopkins University Press.

Grandin, Barbara E. 1994. "Wealth ranking." In *Tools for the Field: Methodologies Handbook for Gender Analysis in Agriculture*, edited by Hilary Sims Feldstein and Janice Jiggins. West Hartford: Kumarian Press.

Guyer, Jane. 1980. "Household budgets and women's incomes." In *Symposium on Women in the Work Force at the American Anthropological Association Meetings*, Working Paper No. 28. Boston University, Brookline, Mass.: African Studies Center.

Guyer, Jane. 1988. "Dynamic approaches to domestic budgeting: cases and methods from Africa." In *A Home Divided: Women and Income in the Third World*, edited by Daisy Dwyer and Judith Bruce. Stanford: Stanford University Press.

Hielscher, Sibylle, and Johannes Sommerfeld. 1985. "Concepts of illness and the utilization of health-care services in a rural Malian village." *Social Science and Medicine* 21 (4): 469–81.

Kegels, G. 1994. "Paying for health care instead of buying drugs: an experience from western Mali." *Ann. Soc. Belge Med. Trop.* (74) 149–60.

Künzel, W., J. Herrero, P. Onwuhafua, T. Staub, and C. Hornung. 1996. "Maternal and perinatal health in Mali, Togo, and Nigeria." *European Journal of Obstetrics & Gynecology* (69) 11–17.

Mallé, D., D. A. Ross, O. M. R. Campbell, and S. R. A. Huttly. 1994. "Institutional maternal mortality in Mali." *International Journal of Gynecology & Obstetrics* (46) 19–26.

Merchant, Kathleen M. 1996. "Women's health and development." In *The Gendered New World Order: Militarism, Development, and the Environment*, edited by Jennifer Turpin and Lois Ann Loarentzen. New York: Routledge.

Merchant, Kathleen M., and Kathleen M. Kurz. 1993. "Women's nutrition through the life cycle: social and biological vulnerabilities." In *The Health of Women: A Global Perspective*, edited by Marge Koblinsky, Judith Timyan, and Jill Gay. Boulder: Westview Press.

Nolan, Brian, and Vincent Turbat. 1995. *Cost Recovery in Public Health Services in Sub-Saharan Africa*. Washington, D.C.: The World Bank.

Raikes, Alanagh. 1990. *Pregnancy, Birthing, and Family Planning in Kenya: Changing Patterns of Behavior. A Health Service Utilization Study in Kisii District*. Copenhagen: Centre for Development Research.

Slobin, Kathleen Overin. 1991. "Family mediation of health care in an African community (Mali)." Ph.D. dissertation. University of California, San Francisco.

Turshen, Meredeth. 1991. "Gender and health in Africa." In *Women and Health in Africa*, edited by Meredeth Turshen. Trenton: Africa World Press, Inc., 107–23.

Unger, Jean-Pierre, Amadou Mbaye, and Moussa Diao. 1990. "From Bamako to Kolda: A case study of medicines and the financing of district health services." *Health Planning and Policy* 5 (4): 367–77.

U.S. Department of State. 1993. "Background notes: Mali." *U.S. Department of State, Bureau of Public Affairs* 6 (April) (3). Washington, D.C.

Waddington, Catriona J. and K. A. Enyimayew. 1989. "A price to pay: The impact of user charges in Ashanti-Akim district, Ghana." *International Journal of Health Planning and Management* 4 (1): 17–47.

Vlassoff, Carol. 1994. "Gender inequalities in health in the Third World: Uncharted ground." *Social Science and Medicine* 39: 1249–59.

World Bank. 1993. *World Development Report 1993: Investing in Health*. New York: Oxford University Press.

———. 1994a. *Better Health in Africa: Experiences and Lessons Learned*. Washington, D.C.: The World Bank.

———. 1994b. *A New Agenda for Women's Health and Nutrition*. Washington, D.C.: The World Bank.

————. 1995. *Toward Gender Equality: The Role of Public Policy.* Washington, D.C.: The World Bank.

————. 1998. "News release." In The World Bank Group [online]. Available: <http://www.worldbank.org/html/extdr/extme/2051.html> [January 1999].

————. 1999. "Mali—Integrated Health Sector Development Project." In the World Bank [online]. <http://www.worldbank.org/pics/pid/ml40652.txt> [January 1999].

Prospects for Development and Democracy in West Africa: Agrarian Politics in Mali

R. James Bingen

Introduction

In the course of an exploratory research activity in southern Mali during 1992, I witnessed an especially heated confrontation between an older farmer and a representative from one of the country's parastatal crop production agencies. The farmer was one of the local leaders for the new union of cotton farmers, the Malian Union of Cotton and Food Crop Producers (SYCOV).[1] Over the next three years, I had the opportunity to learn more and write about this union and its role in agricultural policy making and research.[2]

Most of this work focused on the relationship between key organizational features and SYCOV's effectiveness in agricultural policy and program implementation.[3] Internal administrative and management issues continue to loom large for SYCOV and are being addressed, in part, through a long-term program of organizational development with CIRAD.[4]

The political issues confronting Malian cotton farmers can be assessed in terms of two closely related themes: (1) the international political economy of cotton, and (2) the emergence of, and relationships, between various Malian agricultural and rural interest groups. A recently published article begins to address this first topic by examining international corporate and public capital and the process of democratization and development in Mali.[5] This chapter focuses on the second theme and explores how an understanding of the politics of agricultural interest groups in Mali might contribute to the study of democratization and development in sub-Saharan Africa.

These groups remain absent from international press reports that tend to concentrate on the more readily observable contributions of a lively press and vibrant multiparty politics to democratization in Mali.[6] This discovery of the

Malian democratic experiment under the Third Republic may signal a place for Mali on the still-emerging global strategic, economic, and political agendas of the post-Cold War era. Malian agricultural and rural interests may never play much of a publicly recognized role on these agendas, but they will be key actors in Malian development and deserve our critical attention.

Historical Overview

Historical reviews of Malian politics give little notice to the role of agricultural interest groups and unions in the colonial politics of the Soudan.[7] Archival references, however, help us to identify three historically important policy continuities since the colonial era that help improve our understanding of contemporary agricultural interest groups in Mali. These include governmental preference to protect commodity processing and marketing interests over producer interests, a governmental-corporate understanding concerning the 'division of investments' in agriculture, and a governmental interest in promoting agricultural groups as the means for carrying out rural development programs.

Colonial cotton politics

A brief and incompletely documented exchange of correspondence among some French settlers in Kayes, colonial administrators, and the Deputy for the Soudan and Upper Volta offers some evidence of the colonial government's preference to protect processing and marketing interests over those of either French settler or African producers. Shortly after the end of World War I, a small group of French agriculturalists formed the first agricultural union, the *Syndicat des Agriculteurs du Soudan Français,* in order to lobby for a subsidy to grow cotton in the region around the town of Kayes. Their appeal, launched perhaps in the hope that France's continuing 'cotton crisis' might reverse the colonial government's bias against settler agriculture, was unsuccessful.[8] The governor-general argued that governmental support for cotton production would only favor a small number of European producers and that the government's priorities instead should be in infrastructure development and the *"vulgarisation de nos méthodes agricoles chez les indigènes."*

This decision reinforced a related policy preference for a system of direct subsidies to the French textile industry for processing and marketing through the Colonial Cotton Association (*Association Cotonnière Coloniale* and what would eventually become the CFDT [*Compagnie Francaise pour le Développement des Fibres Textiles*]) plus the *corvée* on peasant farmers to produce cotton for the textile firms.[9] In other words, the request from the Kayes *Syndicat* directly contradicted colonial policy to subsidize the textile industry and to invest in agricultural research for the development of new cotton varieties that would be more attractive on the European market.

Finally, undaunted by the immense problems raised by the government-imposed Indigenous Provident Societies, colonial administrators in the Soudan were committed to creating village-level groups to implement various development activities, especially those involving the expansion of irrigated agriculture.[10] Just prior to World War II, for example, colonial administrators appeared ready to launch *syndicats agricoles indigènes* to help organize the settlement of irrigated production areas and to serve as production and equipment supply cooperatives. As discussed during the early 1930s, these *syndicats* appear remarkable similar to the *associations villageoises* or village associations that are central to most of the country's current production programs.

Very little is known about the first Malian (Soudanise) farmers union, the *Syndicat des Paysans du Soudan Français*, that was established at the end of 1946 and became the *Syndicat des Agriculteurs du Soudan* in 1957. This group was initially affiliated with the *Union Territoriale des Travailleurs du Soudan (UTTS)*, part of the *Union Générale des Travailleurs d'Afrique Noire (UGTAN)*, and it also had contacts with the International Union of Agriculturalists in Rome.[11] It is not known why the union separated from the UTTS in 1959, but the history of the RDA and the trade union movement continued to be closely intertwined.[12]

While the union was concerned with agricultural (primarily peanut) prices, its program covered a broad social and economic agenda. The union called for several agricultural policy changes, including the conversion of registered forest areas into crop land, the allocation of land around towns for vegetable production, improved availability of equipment and supplies, and more animal traction. In addition, the union brought attention to crop damage by elephants and hippopotamus, rural illiteracy, poor roads, and arbitrary administrative practices in rural areas. Finally, the union asked to be consulted during the discussions of the *loi-cadre*, and it called for the establishment of a *Chambre d'Agriculture au Soudan*.

These historical elements are sketchy and incomplete, but they do suggest the need to focus less on how colonial rule might have blocked ". . . much of the social space within which a society might become civil . . ." and more on how various interests responded to the ". . . radical reordering of political space imposed by the colonial partition. . . ."[13]

Early independence

Mali's political leaders have regularly stated their commitment to villages and village-level organizations as the basis for building the country's rural economy. The Kéita government idealized the Malian village as a model of socialist organization and saw the state as a key actor in revitalizing the productive forces of the traditional village economy. As a former member of this government noted, however, the government's 1968 report, the *Summary Report on the Seminar on Cooperation in the Rural Environment,* recognized that socialism had not penetrated into the countryside during the seven-eight years of the Kéita regime.[14]

The Traoré regime did not bring any significant changes in the overall approach to rural organization. Villages were given the opportunity to establish *Tons Villageois* or village-level cooperatives, and party officials sought everyone's adherence to the UDPM. Similar to what Robinson found in Burkina Faso and Niger, the Traoré regime used the ethos of grassroots participation primarily to legitimize a corporatist form of political representation.[15]

By the end of the Traoré regime in early 1991, thirty years of repeated, government-led assaults on political expression in the countryside had generated two types of responses among peasant farmers: the creation or reinforcement of their own types of organization; or—more generally—an approach of no objection, but also no acceptance, in response to mostly government-led efforts to organize villagers.[16] As the following discussion indicates, however, neither the more highly capitalized farmers nor the peasant farmers had exited from political life.

Agricultural Interest Groups

Chamber of Agriculture

Following the initiation of a long-term and continuing program of Cereals Market Policy Reform (PRMC) in 1981, the government negotiated a broader Agricultural Sector Adjustment Plan (PASA) with the World Bank in 1985 to liberalize the rural economy. In addition to cereals market liberalization and specific pricing policies, this plan involved closing five of the country's rural development organizations (*opérations*) and the negotiation of three performance agreements with the cereals marketing agency (OPAM), the cotton production agency (CMDT), and the *Office du Niger.*

While international attention focused on the contribution of cereals marketing and price policy reform to the revitalization of small-scale agriculture, the PASA reforms also generated a much broader *crise sociale* among broad and diverse *groupes socio-professionels* in the agricultural sector. Their interests threatened, and feeling 'disconnected' from the PASA decision-making process, these groups organized what they called a *grande consultation populaire* with the president to request representation on a par with the Chamber of Commerce and the National Federation of Employers.

Representatives of these mostly highly capitalized farmers and farm groups were specifically interested in measures for 'liberalizing' the importation and sale of agricultural equipment and supplies. Based on this interest, they asked the government in 1986 to establish an ad hoc committee to examine the establishment of a Chamber of Agriculture similar to the Chambers of Agriculture in France, Côte d'Ivoire, Morocco, Cameroon, and Togo. The political influence of the groups pressing for a Chamber encouraged the government to respond quite rapidly. A Malian Chamber of Agriculture became law by April 1988[17] and established its headquarters, the *Maison du Paysan*, a block away from the Ministry of Agriculture in downtown Bamako.

During the 1991 National Conference that followed the overthrow of the Traoré government, the Chamber of Agriculture played a key role in the discussions of the Rural Sub-Commission that called for the convening of a Rural Estates-General by the end of the year. The Rural Estates-General was indeed a unique political affair in Malian political history and it did present the new (transitional) government with a challenging agenda for the post-Traoré era. The demands emanating from this first national forum, however, largely reflected the special interests of those closely affiliated with the Chamber of Agriculture. In fact, the Chamber 'captured' the Estates-General at the expense of hearing directly from the numerous, emerging groups of peasant farmers (see discussion of SPCK below).[18]

Despite their earlier success in securing a place in government decision-making circles concerning structural adjustment measures that directly affected more capital-intensive agricultural production activities, the leadership of the Chamber admits that the events of March 1991 revealed the extent to which they had become out of step with most of rural society and with other government policies related to decentralization and the *responsabilisation* of rural communities. In response, the Chamber saw the Estates-General as a means to take a 'new' and revitalized leadership role as the consular institution responsible for promoting the professionalization of the agricultural sector and for encouraging a greater dialogue and *concentration* on the full range of rural issues.

In this position, the Chamber conceives of a dramatic change in the structure of Malian agriculture. For the Chamber, the future of Malian agricultural development lies in replacing the *exploitation traditionnelle* and traditional, peasant-farmer management practices with a more professional agriculture based on more "rational methods" commonly found in commercial and industrial enterprises.[19] Consistent with this position, the Chamber backs selected measures of the agenda outlined in the government's *Schéma Directeur du Développement Rural*. These measures would encourage the development of a more capitalized agriculture through (1) the *responsabilisation* or greater rural participation in management of rural development activities; (2) *décentralisation* or the establishment of decentralized territorial collectivities; and (3) the *désengagement de l'Etat*, or those policies that encourage the privatization of production, marketing, and strengthening of the private sector in agriculture.

With support from the FAO, and in an effort to ride the crest of the government's decentralization wave, the Chamber of Agriculture has recently reorganized around nine regional, decentralized Chambers of Agriculture that are 'coordinated' by the Bamako-based Permanent Assembly of Chambers of Agriculture of Mali (*Assemblée Permanente des Chambres d'Agriculture du Mali, APCAM*).[20] The new formula is intended to assure broad representation of all rural sectors through regional assemblies that will act in an advisory capacity to regional administrators and facilitate information and communication between professional rural groups and the regional administrators. In sum, the new APCAM describes itself as multi-sectoral (horizontal) or a type of intermediate body (*corps intermédiaire*) whose mission is to operate in the general interest of the rural population and to serve the professionalization of agriculture through communication, training, and information.

The new Chamber outlined its Five Year Plan (1994–1998) at its official opening meeting at the end of November 1994. The overall objectives of the new Chamber include direct involvement in policy making to assure the representation of professional interests and to promote the professionalization of agriculture. For the Chamber, this role does not specifically involve support for other farm groups, even though it provided office space for SYCOV in Bamako. Instead, it reflects an interest in linking with capitalized agricultural interests around the world through the International Federation of Agricultural Producers (IFAP) and in addressing issues that are of direct and immediate concern to more capitalized agricultural interests in Mali. Some of these issues include natural resource management, agricultural processing, studies related to horticultural production and agricultural input supply, and the preparation of a statute that would give farmers juridical standing. According to the Chamber, a statute that offers farmers legal and financial standing similar to that of a commercial or industrial enterprise will encourage greater capital investment in the country's rural development.

Syndicat des Paysans du Cercle de Kita (SPCK)

Among Kita peasant farmers, agricultural unionism enjoys a long and revered history. Many still willingly and ardently recall their militant days with the US-RDA and the events surrounding the arbitrary suppression of the *Syndicat des Agriculteurs* in the final days of colonial rule. With high expectations for their cause in the new, independent US-RDA Mali, they also remember their profound disappointment with the Kéita regime's demand for the farmers to affiliate with the National Union of Workers (UNTM) as part of the new government's policy of "responsible participation."

The economic opportunities, improved conditions, and services that accompanied the peanut boom of the late 1960s and 1970s undoubtedly dampened but did not extinguish the spark of union enthusiasm. The government's response to the collapse of peanuts and the start of the broader economic decline in the early 1980s did little more than remind the Kita farmers of the need to wait a little longer for their day. Just as they had refused earlier to align with the UNTM, the Kita farmers in the 1980s saw the proposals for a Chamber of Agriculture as a means to employ retired government administrators friendly to the Traoré regime and to 'capture' peasant farmers.

The events of March 1991 appeared to offer the day for which union leaders were waiting and they took their request to (re)-establish a union to the regional administrative officer, the *Commandant de Cercle*. The commandant refused to acknowledge legal standing for such a group, arguing that the (regional) Chamber of Agriculture represented the concerns of area farmers. The underlying and unspoken rationale appears to have been based on two fears. First, approval of the proposed union would amount to a public (and official) acknowledgment of what everyone already knew about the corporatist nature of the Chamber and would thereby further undermine its credibility as a representative for peasant-farmers. Second, given that the request came of old militants of the US-RDA, approval might pave the way for those interested in re-creating 'Modibo's Mali.'

Rebuffed as well at the *Maison du Paysan* in Bamako, the militants turned to their next closest available ally in the National Workers Union. Inspired by their recent participation in an international conference that specifically had called upon worker unions to help in establishing farmer unions, the UNTM leadership warmly received the farmers and recommended that they set-up their union as a section of SYNAPRO (*Syndicat National de la Production*). With no other available option, the Kita farmers reluctantly accepted this proposal, fully aware of their paradoxical partnership with a union that represented their sometime local adversaries in the government's agricultural extension, livestock, and forestry services.

National-level approval, however, was meaningless back in Kita. The Minister of Territorial Administration personally intervened the day before the union's planned organizational meeting to secure the begrudging approval of the commandant and the regional Chamber of Agriculture officers for the new union's right to organize and to meet publicly. The animosity between these players was so great, in fact, that many members of the union had to be dissuaded from physically attacking the Chamber of Agriculture officers. During the transition period from the downfall of the Traoré regime to the establishment of the Third Republic, this type of "total blockage" between various groups of citizens and local administrative officials appears to have been fairly common throughout the country.[21]

Because of the deep-seated nature of this conflict, a national UNTM representative had to solicit the reluctant agreement of the SPCK to participate in planning for the Rural Estates-General. Despite public recognition and reconciliation with the new Chamber, the SPCK leadership still feels quite strongly that the Rural Estates-General was an "affair" of the Chamber of Agriculture in which the concerns and interests of the SPCK played no role.

With the assignment of a new commandant to Kita, the SPCK agreed to participate in joint union-administrative visits to each *arrondissement* in order to deal with the farmers' outstanding debts (and taxes), to inform villagers about the new union, and to identify local problems. These visits lasted from May through early July 1992 and the results were used as the basis for a popular (and unprecedented) farmer-financed Development Conference for the Kita Cercle on 30 June–1 July 1993. Attended by representatives from the newly established Cotton Farmers' Union, SYCOV, as well as representatives from every governmental agency, nongovernmental organization, and political party with an office in Kita, the conference prepared a list of development priorities based on their discussion of the results of the 1992 visits to the *arrondissements*. The development priorities included requests for an investment in cotton production; improved availability of agricultural equipment and supplies, including special attention to women's needs; marketing outlets and improved roads; and the rehabilitation of the local peanut oil processing plant. The union presented these demands to the minister of Rural Development and the president's Office, but got little concrete response.

At the same time, the SPCK appears to share a series of 'organizational development' problems with other peasant farmer-based interest groups in Mali: potential members remember an era of empty promises from the regional Chamber of Agriculture and remain skeptical that the SPCK represents a really different organization of, and for, them. SPCK's relations with the area development service (ODIMO) are also, at best, strained. The SPCK threatens the lucrative agricultural equipment and supply resale 'business' of some ODIMO agents and challenges the adequacy of ODIMO's technical services. In response, and as found in the CMDT zone, local-level agricultural agents either try to sabotage or slander the union. Clearly, the SPCK will continue to confront numerous challenges to its legitimacy and efficacy in the countryside.

Syndicat des Producteurs de Coton et Vivriers (SYCOV)

In response to farmers' complaints against dishonest cotton grading and weighing practices, the newly nationalized Malian Company for Textile Development (*Compagnie Malienne pour le Développement des Fibres Textiles,* CMDT) in 1974 gradually began to transfer responsibility for cotton grading and weighing, equipment and supply orders, and credit management to designated village groups. After several years of fairly informal agreements with these groups, the CMDT formalized the relationship through the establishment of Village Associations (*Associations Villageoises,* AVs). In collaboration with the government, the CMDT also secured World Bank financing to support functional literacy training that would give AV members the literacy and numeracy skills required to fulfill credit and marketing tasks and the preparation of account books in the Bambara language.

Over the years, many of the AV leaders who had been selected as CMDT 'pilot farmers' developed both a sense of partnership with the CMDT and of federation among themselves through their participation in various types of special training or consultative sessions sponsored by the CMDT and other development agencies. Consequently, in 1989 when the CMDT decided to implement a new credit policy that would increase producers' risk and liability, these new leaders felt confident in their 'right' to complain and to seek a negotiated settlement with the CMDT.

Their success in reversing the CMDT policy revealed the power of joint, organized action, and a small group decided to hold regular information meetings and to establish an informal coordinating committee (*Comité de Coordination des AV et Tons*). In the course of their coordination meetings, the AV leaders discovered their shared feeling that cotton production was becoming less and less profitable. The meetings also accelerated the circulation of various rumors, of which two were especially bothersome. First, cotton producers understood that for many years the CMDT village extension agents, in response to their own declining purchasing power, often sacrificed extension time to moonlight for extra income from other activities. Thus, when the news circulated about possible pay hikes for these agents, alongside increases in equipment and supply costs for growers, coordinating committee members wanted to know why price adjustments were not being made to increase the purchase price of cotton. Second, cotton producers historically had been able to purchase adequate supplies of animal feed made from cotton meal for their work oxen. Starting in 1989–1990, however, cotton meal supplies dwindled and the producers couldn't get clear answers to their questions about what the CMDT had done with "their" cotton for their animals.

With the overthrow of the Traoré regime, cotton producers encouraged the coordinating committee to go public with their growing frustrations. Based largely on their earlier success in 1989, the coordinating committee formulated the producers' demands into twelve grievances (*doléances*). These dealt with long-standing pricing and marketing issues, including the apparent shortages of, and high prices for animal (cotton cake) feed on the open market and the CMDT's decision to use an industrial rather than village classification system for purchasing cotton. While the political conditions during the first months of the transition government allowed producers a measure of previously unavailable political freedom, they were also the source of considerable political apprehension and uncertainty. It wasn't altogether clear to regional CMDT and government officials, for example, that the producers' demands were not a vanguard, grassroots effort by Traoré sympathizers to reinstall the previous regime.[22] Thus, when the director of the regional CMDT office in Koutiala refused on purely legalistic grounds to accept the producers' grievances, the producers felt justified in calling a cotton strike just as planting was to begin.

After considerable deliberation, the minister of Rural Development intervened personally in order to reach a negotiated settlement between the producers and the CMDT. Many within the CMDT criticized the minister's personal intervention for unnecessarily politicizing the affair and legitimizing the (future) SYCOV. Her involvement and the representation of the transition government, however, helped defuse the conflict and pave the way for the

CMDT to initiate a series of steps designed to restore a spirit of trust and certainty with cotton farmers.

The CMDT agreed to the minister's request to accept the coordination committee as a legitimate representative body for cotton farmers and to arrive at a negotiated settlement. In addition, the CMDT took several steps designed to help re-establish a 'family' relationship with cotton farmers. With support from the World Bank, the CMDT/CFDT organized a training and information program on the international cotton market (*filière*) and ran a survey of the producers' cotton marketing problems and concerns. In addition, the CMDT/CFDT financed two additional training and information activities: a 'study trip' of the cotton marketing chain from Bamako to Paris and Le Havre, and information-discussion sessions in Bambara that described CMDT's performance agreement (*Contrat-Plan*) with the government and its rural development program for producers.

Finally, in September 1991, the CMDT hosted a public roundtable discussion of cotton issues with the Ministry of Rural Development, donor agencies (including representatives from the French Ministry of Cooperation, the *Caisse Française du Développement*, the European Development Fund and the World Bank), the producers, and the CMDT. The roundtable approved the establishment of a representative cotton producer organization that would collaborate closely with the CMDT, the Chamber of Agriculture, the government administration, and other technical services to guarantee the widest possible diffusion of information to all cotton producers. Specifically, the roundtable recommended the incorporation of this organization as a signatory to the CMDT performance agreement as well as its representation in several CMDT-Government policy-making units, (the CMDT Management Board [*Conseil d'Administration*] and the Stabilization Fund Management Committee), including the option of becoming a shareholder in the CMDT. Based largely on the recommendations of this roundtable, SYCOV became a full partner with the CMDT in the 1994 re-negotiations of the CMDT performance agreement (*contrat plan*). With this, Malian cotton producers, for the first time Malian history, had a direct voice in influencing agricultural policy.

African Agrarian Politics and Political Development

The above observations on the history of the agrarian politics of three quite different agricultural interest groups in Mali offer evidence that could help in elaborating a political theory for development. Following the careers of such groups can tell us much about the permeability and openness of African political regimes.[23] More specifically, a focus on these kinds of groups could help improve our understanding of the complementary relationships between democratic participation, constitutional liberty, social pluralism, and economic position.[24] The Chamber, SPCK, and SYCOV occupy significantly different places in Mali's political economy. As such, their political histories help us to identify how new political groups or movements contribute to developing democracy as they make claims and confront governmental agencies, as well as fend off efforts at co-optation, and balance various types of international support.

The concept of political opportunities may offer one approach to a comparative analysis. Outlined by Jenkins and Klandermans, political opportunities for groups like those discussed in this chapter are created by the organization of the state; arrangements among political elites and administrators; the structure, ideology, and composition of political parties; and various types of international arrangements. As the case studies illustrate, states and various international actors shape the conflict and alliance systems that help shape the emergence and development of political groups. But these groups are also their own agents of change; they act upon these opportunities and their actions help to generate new opportunities in an increasingly global arena.[25]

Moreover, the case studies illustrate the importance of specifying two additional features of political opportunities. First, access to state institutions will vary by type of territorial centralization. In general, the greater the degree of governmental decentralization, the greater will be the degree of formal access. In addition, the functional concentration of state power, the coherence of public administration (for example, level of professionalism, or fragmentation and lack of internal coordination), as well as the institutionalization of direct democratic procedures will affect a group's opportunities at any one point in time. In short, we need sharpened analytic tools that allow us to move beyond the conceptual construct of the state as a monolithic entity. In its place we need to work toward a more empirically based concept that helps us capture the 'state' as a contradictory, disunified set of structures, processes, and discourses, in which different actors and agencies often act at cross purposes. For example, the events surrounding the re-emergence of the SPCK illustrate the discontinuities among state agencies.

Similarly, we need to improve our analytic ability to discern the role of and relationships with the 'new' political parties. Farmers and agricultural interest groups in Mali publicly shun partisan politics. Like rank-and-file workers elsewhere, Malian farmers resist both the affiliation of political parties with their groups (unions) and the imposition of any political ideology.[26] At the same time, some close observers of Malian politics have expressed considerable concern that partisan politics may even be anti-developmental in the villages.[27]

Second, it is useful to distinguish between various types of success. Procedural success, or the formal recognition of groups as legitimate representatives of demands, varies significantly from substantive success in which a policy change occurs, or structural success in which there is a transformation of the political opportunity structure.[28]

Finally, a focus on political opportunities may offer new insights on the "globalization" of agrarian politics in sub-Saharan Africa. Emerging transnational institutions and the capacity for cross-national communication provide new political opportunities and expanded resources that can turn previously local groups into significant national and sometimes regional actors. As McAdam and others remind us, global economic integration and communication facilitates political exchange among allied actors.[29]

Attention to these types of structural and institutional issues of political action, with appropriate attention to historical evidence, may offer a viable and theoretically rich, analytic alternative to the concept of political culture in the study of democratization and development. Such an approach frees us from assumptions about the importance of the shared nature of traditions of political action or reciprocity in explaining political action. In addition, the political histories presented in this chapter confirm that our understanding of Mali's continuing political struggles requires a perspective sensitive to the on-going negotiation, re-interpretation, and mediation among a range of national and international interests. Finally, attention to structural and institutional factors promises to offer a more concrete and directly political means for evaluating proposals designed to improve the contribution of rural and agricultural interest groups in democratization and development.

Next Steps and Conclusion

SYCOV and SPCK have recently been joined by the *Syndicat des Paysans de Mali Ouest* (SYPAMO) as well as the *Syndicat des Paysans de Kita* (SYPROKA) and the *Syndicat des Exploitants Agricoles de l'Office du Niger* (SEXAGON). Other groups have been formed around potatoes and mangoes, and an *Association des Organisations Professionnelles Paysannes* (AOPP) has been established. In short, it appears that agrarian politics is alive and more vibrant than it ever has been in contemporary Malian history.

This level of political activity also attracts significant foreign interest and support. Since its emergence, for example, SYCOV has been carefully courted by several independent French organizations (*Fondation pour le Progrès de l'Homme, Centre Français de Solidarité Internationale, CIEPAC, SOLA-*

GRAL), as well as French consulting firms like IRAM and independent government agencies like CIRAD, to establish its credentials as a professional association. With financing from the Ministry of Cooperation, the French farmers' group (Association Française de Développement International, AFDI) lends its weight to this argument through its program of support for African Farmers' Organizations (Appui aux Organisations Paysannes Africaines, AOPA). With its focus on farmer-to-farmer exchange and its encouragement of regional networking among West African farmers, SYCOV's leaders find AFDI's program especially inviting and easily accessible with their regional office in Bamako. SYCOV's participation in the Africa-wide farmers' network (Agricultures, Paysannes et Modernisation, APM) financed largely by the FPH also offers special opportunities to discover how other farm leaders confront similar problems, and to begin developing a possible basis for international solidarity. This network has devoted considerable effort to informing SYCOV's leaders, as well as the leaders of several other West African cotton farmer unions, how they fit into and gain from the CFDT-led world market strategy and position.

The short life of a Malian-initiated and -led organization, the Association for Safeguard and Reinforcement of Democracy (Association pour la Sauvegarde et le Renforcement de la Démocratie, ASARED), however, reminds us of the fragility of agrarian politics. In the mid-1990s, ASARED tried to launch a politically based, collaborative effort to establish and strengthen the dialogue among a wide variety of rural and agricultural groups and national and local governmental agencies and representatives. In June 1994, ASARED (with financial assistance from Canada) took the bold step of convening representatives from almost twenty farmer organizations to plan a national seminar on agricultural unionism and democracy. This effort was not a conspicuous success; only one or two regional preparatory seminars were held. Despite the political openness in the Third Republic for the expression of new agrarian interests, the opportunities for a more collaborative agrarian coalition may still need to be created.

At this point the condition of agrarian unionism and democracy in Mali is ambiguous at best. Several producer strikes in the cotton sector have been averted, but the cost to the independence of Malian farmers is not yet clear. The issues raised in this chapter may help to clarify our understanding of these types of political ambiguities on the road to democratization and help to focus attention on those conditions and processes that allow Malian farmers to move beyond the art of the possible to the art of creating new possibilities.

Notes

1. SYCOV—*Syndicat des Producteurs de Coton et Vivriers.*

2. Bingen et al. 1993; Josserand and Bingen 1995; Bingen et al. 1995.

3. Bingen 1996; cf. also Bratton 1990.

4. CIRAD—*Centre de Coopération Internationale en Recherche Agronomique pour le Développement.* See Mercoiret et al. 1996.

5. Bingen 1998.

6. See *New York Times*, 29 April 1996 and 16 October 1996; *The Courrier* 159 (September-October 1996).

7. Hodgkin and Morgenthau 1964; Morgenthau 1964.

8. Roberts 1996.

9. See Young 1994.

10. Bingen 1985.

11. Docking 1999.

12. Morgenthau 1964.

13. Young 1994.

14. From an interview with Amadou Seydou Traoré, USRDA spokesman, reported in *The Courrier* 159 (September–October 1996), 22–23; also see Bingen 1985. This suggests that it may be necessary to revise the common interpretation of this era as one of state engagement in society; see, for example, Bratton 1994.

15. Robinson 1992.

16. Also see Brown 1987.

17. *Loi* 88-56/AN-RM of 5 April 1988 *Portant Création de la Chambre d'Agriculture du Mali* as a public, professional organization (*à caractère professionnel*). See Keeler 1987 for an analysis of the corporatist role of the Chamber of Agriculture in France.

18. This represents a significant re-interpretation of an earlier assessment of the Estates-General; see Bingen 1994.

19. The 'professionalization' of African agriculture has been widely discussed in French governmental and nongovernmental circles for several years.

20. *Loi* 93–044 of 4 August 1993 and *décret* 93–295/PG-RM of 18 August 1993.

21. See Tag 1994; Bingen 1994; Bingen et al. 1993.

22. Many of the most active and vocal members of the coordinating committee belonged to a village association and cooperative *(Ton)* that had received a special visit from the former president and that the previous regime had widely publicized as a model of village cooperation.

23. Gamson 1990.

24. Sklar 1987.

25. Jenkins 1995, 14–35; Jenkins and Klandermans 1995, 3–13.

26. Sklar 1994.

27. Soké 1993 (9–22 Août).

28. Kriesi 1995, 167–98.

29. McAdam et al. 1996.

Bibliography

Bingen, R. James. 1985. *Food Production and Rural Development in the Sahel. Lessons from Mali's Opération Riz-Ségou.* Boulder: Westview Press.

———. 1994. "Agricultural development policy and grassroots democracy in Mali: the emergence of Mali's farmer movement." *African Rural and Urban Studies* 1 (1): 57–72.

———. 1996. "Leaders, leadership and democratization in West Africa: observations from the cotton farmers movement in Mali." *Agriculture and Human Values* 13 (2): 24–32.

———. 1998. "Cotton, democracy and development in Mali." *The Journal of Modern African Studies* 36 (2): 265–85.

Bingen, R. James, D. Carney, and E. Dembélé. 1995. *The Malian Union of Cotton and Food Crop Producers: The Current and Potential Role in Technology Development and Transfer.* London: ODI Research and Extension Network.

Bingen, R. James, Brent Simpson, and Adama Berthé. 1993. *Analysis of Service Delivery Systems to Farmers and Village Associations in the Zone of the Office de la Haute Vallée du Niger.* East Lansing: Dept. of Resource Development, Michigan State University.

Bratton, Michael. 1990. "Non-governmental organizations in Africa: can they influence public policy?" *Development and Change* 21: 87–118.

———. 1994. "Peasant-state relations in postcolonial Africa: patterns of engagement and disengagement." In *State Power and Social Forces. Domination and Transformation in the Third World,* edited by J. S. Migdal, A. Kohli and V. Shue. Cambridge: Cambridge University Press.

Brown, C. 1987. "Rural local institutions for agricultural development in Botswana: no objection but no acceptance." In *Sustainable Agriculture in Africa,* edited by E. A. McDougall. Trenton: Africa World Press.

Docking, T. W. 1999. International influence on civil society in Mali: the case of the cotton farmers' union, SYCOV. Unpublished Ph.D. dissertation, Boston University, Boston, Massachusetts.

Gamson, William. 1990. *The Strategy of Social Protest* (2nd edition). Belmont, Calif.: Wadsworth Publishing Co.

Hodgkin, Thomas, and Ruth S. Morgenthau. 1964. "Mali." In *Political Parties and National Integration in Tropical Africa*, edited by C. G. Rosberg and J. S. Coleman. Princeton: Princeton University Press.

Jenkins, J. C. 1995. "Social movements, political representation, and the state: an agenda and comparative framework." In *The Politics of Social Protest: Comparative Perspectives on States and Social Movements*, edited by J. C. Jenkins and B. Klandermans. Minneapolis: University of Minnesota Press.

Jenkins, J. C., and B. Klandermans, B. 1995. "The politics of social protest." In *The Politics of Social Protest: Comparative Perspectives on States and Social Movements*, edited by J. C. Jenkins and B. Klandermans. Minneapolis: University of Minnesota Press.

Josserand, Henri, and R. James Bingen. 1995. *Economic Management in the Sahe—A Study of Policy Advocacy in Mali*. Burlington, VT: US Agency for International Development, Decentralization: Finance and Management Project.

Keeler, John T. S. 1987. *The Politics of Neocorporatism in France. Farmers, the State, and Agricultural Policy-making in the Fifth Republic*. New York: Oxford.

Kriesi, H. 1995. "The political opportunity structure of new social movements: its impact on their mobilization." In *The Politics of Social Protest: Comparative Perspectives on States and Social Movements*, edited by J. C. Jenkins and B. Klandermans. Minneapolis: University of Minnesota Press.

McAdam, D., S. Tarrow, and C. Tilly. 1996. "To map contentious politics." *Mobilization: An International Journal* 1 (1): 17–34.

Mercoiret, M. R., P. M. Bosc, and B. Losch. 1996. *Organisations Paysannes et Innovation. Les Organisations Paysannes face au Désengagement de l'Etat*. Montpellier: CIRAD-SAR U.R. ISAA.

Morgenthau, Ruth S. 1964. *Political Parties in French-Speaking West Africa*. Oxford: Clarendon Press.

Roberts, R. L. 1996. *Two Worlds of Cotton. Colonialism and the Regional Economy in the French Soudan, 1800–1946*. Stanford: Stanford University Press.

Robinson, Pearl T. 1992. "Grassroots legitimation of military governance in Burkina Faso and Niger: the core contradictions in Africa." In *Governance and Politics in Africa*, edited by G. Hyden and M. Bratton. Boulder: Lynne Rienner.

Sklar, Richard L. 1987. "Developmental democracy." *Comparative Studies in Society and History* 29 (4): 686–714.

Sklar, Richard L. 1994. "Social class and political action in Africa: the bourgeoisie and the proletariat." In *Political Development and the New Realism in Sub-Saharan Africa*, edited by D. E. Apter and C. G. Rosberg. Charlottesville: University Press of Virginia.

Soké, Gongoloma. 1993. "Multipartisme et développement local: l'impasse." *Cauris*, 9–22 Août, 2.

Tag, Sylvia. 1994. *Paysans, Etat et Démocratisation au Mali: Enquête en Milieu Rural, Hamburg African Studies*. Hamburg: Institute for African Affairs.

Young, Crawford. 1994. "In search of civil society." In *Civil Society and the State in Africa*, edited by J. W. Harbeson, D. Rothchild, and N. Chazan. Boulder: Lynne Rienner.

Epilogue

Malian Democracy: A Continuing Process for the Quest of Perfection

CHEICK OUMAR DIARRAH

translated by *Cheikh Anta Mbacke Babou*

The Third Malian Republic[1] is based on a commitment by the country's political leaders to build a dynamic democracy grounded on the rule of law and respect for human rights. The choice of these leaders to promote a democratic and pluralist society stems from their belief in the values of democracy, and their conviction that only effective participation of the population in the management of the country can help the development process.

Mali's democratic movement was born out of a unique confluence of economic, political, and social crises. Efforts were made during the Second Republic to work with the World Bank and the International Monetary Fund to address the country's deteriorating economic and social conditions through a structural adjustment program. As the government became increasingly autocratic, the Malian people responded with waves of protests and demonstrations that finally swept away the government.

Aware of the people's pending demands and expectations, as well as the country's meager resources, the leaders of the Third Republic were convinced that their actions needed to be based on the following principles. First, they sought to develop a pluralist democracy based on the rule of law and the personal responsibility of all citizens. Second, they recognized the importance of creating the conditions for a strong national consensus through effective and wide public participation in all decision making. Third, they sought to re-build channels of communication between the government and the citizens to assure that government could learn about the needs of the people and take adequate measures to respond to those needs.

This chapter briefly reviews the recent political history of the Third Republic as a reminder of the difficulties that arose on the way to building a pluralist and participatory democracy in Mali, and indicates some of the continuing challenges confronting the Malian people.

Governments of the Third Republic

Well before his election as president of Mali in June 1992, Alpha Oumar Konaré expressed his conviction that the government of the new republic must embody diverse political creeds. This belief has been the basis for continuing efforts throughout the Konaré presidency to encourage the participation of opposition parties in all the governments that have been formed since his election.

The first government of the Third Republic—Implementation of the Republican Pact[2]

The goal of the first government of the Third Republic was to implement the commitment to a broad-based, multi-party Republican Pact. But the president's party, ADEMA/PASJ, dominated the government.[3]

Besides Prime Minister Younoussi Touré, the first government of the Third Republic had a secretary of state and twenty-three ministries. The ADEMA/PASJ and its allies (US/RDA, PDP) held four state ministries. ADEMA/PASJ members also held eleven ministries. The parties that endorsed the Republican Pact were given five ministries. Two other ministries were held by individuals people with no party affiliation, and the *Mouvements et Fronts Unifiés de l'Azawad* (MFUA) held one ministry.

This government was in charge of laying the foundation for three long-term efforts: change, improved governmental management, and a revitalized communication with citizens. As the government was formed, President Konaré declared, "We are engaged in the path of change—change that will put the well-being of our society at the forefront of our preoccupation, change that will better the life of the Malians."[4] He recognized, however, that change would occur only when the government could assure the following conditions: "the re-enforcement of the fundamental democratic values, national cohesion, restoration of the credibility of the state, encouragement of a citizenry founded on the active participation of the population in the management of the country, and renewed trust in the institutions."

President Konaré added that the concerted management of the institutions "does not mean the repugnant sharing of the so-called republican cake or the constitution of a political clientele through the distribution of prebends and sinecures. Instead, it acknowledges the existence of forces favorable to change and the necessity to unite all people to contribute to the well-being of the nation, regardless of political differences."

Finally, communication was to be a critical dimension of the political action for the first government and President Konaré stated, ". . . the democratic system of government, as well as our will to create a social dialogue and popular participation, require us to maintain a permanent channel of communication with the people and the necessity to continuously explain our decisions and actions."

The second government—Broadening the political base

Despite the best efforts to establish an inclusive government, on 9 April 1993, President Konaré accepted the collective resignation of the government led by Prime Minister Younoussi Touré. The following Monday, Abdoulaye Sékou Sow was appointed prime minister of the second government of the Third Republic.

The new team was expected to realize the continuing commitment to a broad based government. To do so, ADEMA/PASJ initiated a series of negotiations with the *Congrés National d'Initiative Démocratique-Faso Yiriwa Ton* (CNID-FYT) and with the *Rassemblement pour la Démocratie et le Progrès* (RDP). On 14 April 1993, these two parties agreed to participate in the new government.

In the second government, nineteen ministerial positions were divided among seven parties: (ADEMA/PASJ–nine; CNID-FYT–three; US/RDA and RDP–two each; and one each for PDP, MFUA, and RDT). The uniqueness of this government was demonstrated by the involvement of the CNID-FYT, which had been very active in opposition to the first government of Younoussi Touré. By early 1993, however, it appeared that CNID-FYT recognized the fragility of Malian democratic institutions and thus decided to participate in the struggle to protect and defend democracy and the rule of law.

The main task assigned to this government was the achievement of social peace through efforts to guarantee human rights and restore the authority of the state and confidence in the government through a permanent dialogue between the government, citizens, and the political parties. In particular the new government was charged to deal with many specific and pressing problems related to the school system, health care, the National Pact,[5] the army, decentralization, foreign policy, and the environment.

Moreover, the government confronted a wide range of long-term development issues including the creation of an investor-friendly environment and the development of the private sector; a sustained program for agricultural development; industrial and natural resources development; and improved governmental administration, management, and service.

This challenging agenda created tremendous political controversy and, almost nine months after his appointment, Prime Minister Abdoulaye Sékou Sow resigned. His resignation was followed by the withdrawal of the RDP and the CNID-FYT from the coalition government. The political crisis heightened in February 1994 when the Union of Malian Students erected barricades in Bamako and other major cities and demonstrated to show their disapproval and discontent with the policies of the second government. Continuing uncertainty created by the devaluation of the CFA franc further complicated and exacerbated the popular discontent.

The third government—Restoration of authority and renewal of political debate

Ibrahima Boubacar Kéita was appointed prime minister on 4 February 1994. He faced a difficult and complex situation. The CNID-FYT and the RDP decided not to join the third government. Thus, the new prime minister had to look primarily to the ADEMA/PASJ to assemble a government.

The formation of this new government took place in a context of deep political crisis, perhaps the deepest that the country had faced since 1992. The students adopted a type of nocturnal urban guerilla warfare that created generalized insecurity in several cities throughout the country. In addition, the political parties regrouped into two coalitions outside of government. The first was composed of the BDIA, PLD, PMD, PRDT, PSP, *Front National*, UDD, UFDP, PUDP-UNDP, and RDP, and was led by CNID-FYT. The second coalition, called the Forum for National Sensibility, was led by the US/RDA. Both tried to fashion a new redistribution of the political forces in the country. Continuing rebellion in the northern part of the country added to the political tension.

Social issues continued to be determining factors in the political evolution of the country. After a series of negotiations, the dialogue between the government and the students broke down over disagreements regarding the attribution of financial aid. The students rioted and the government responded by closing the schools. Student leaders who openly acknowledged their involvement in the rioting and looting were arrested.

From mid-February to the end of March 1994, the political turmoil in the country peaked. Opposition parties and all sorts of associations organized meetings and demonstrations to pressure the government. These actions were capped at the end of March by *opération ville morte*.[6]

The prime minister, however, managed to overcome the partisan politics that were deadlocking the country and restore the authority and credibility of the state. Succeeding where his predecessors had failed, he progressively projected an image of a courageous, hard-working, and frank prime minister whose deeds spoke louder than his words.

Regional Consultations

The failure of the *opération ville morte* made the opposition parties aware that they had a limited capacity to mobilize the public against the government. However, as the political crisis receded, the population fell into a sort of apathy and indifference. Consequently, a major task of the government was to re-mobilize the public opinion and to redirect the energy of the population. In response, President Konaré organized a series of "Regional Consultations" throughout the country in order to achieve four goals.

The first goal was to disseminate information about governmental policy and the nature of the problems that confronted the nation. The government hoped that this type of discussion would end the diffusion of rumors and false information that polluted the political atmosphere in the country.

Second, the government wished to initiate an open debate about the major challenges that faced the country. This discussion aimed at developing and deepening the pluralist democracy. By listening to the citizens, the government expected to improve democratic governance.

Third, the regional consultations aimed to achieve national reconciliation and reframe the political debates around issues that really mattered to the Malian people. This was necessary because there was no consensus about what ought to be done in order to overcome the country's social crises.

Fourth, it was necessary to work out a new political and social program based on the governmental agenda and supplemented by concrete proposals and inputs from the society as a whole.

Over a period of two weeks, these regional consultations regrouped representatives from political parties, nongovernmental associations, and the civil service for three days in each region of the country. They discussed issues related to the unrest in the north, the school system crisis, insecurity, the problems of democracy, structural adjustment and the consequences of the devaluation of the CFA franc, foreign policy, and African integration. Following the consultations, a national meeting was convened to prepare a synthesis and elaboration of the conclusions of the regional discussions.

Despite their initial refusal to participate, the opposition parties responded to the popular endorsement of the consultations and decided to participate in all of the discussions. Thus, these consultations can be seen as a contribution to democratic development by allowing direct interaction between government and citizens. At a minimum, they provided an opportunity to gauge the mood of the nation and to discuss responses to the society's needs.

Moreover, the regional consultations facilitated the renewal of a dialogue between government and citizens, between political actors, between political and civil society and between people belonging to the same party. They helped to find appropriate solutions to the difficult problems that had divided the nation for months. Finally, they favored the re-establishment of a peaceful and sane political climate.

In particular, the regional consultations helped the government to deal with one critical issue—insecurity in the north of Mali, and to lay the foundation for a framework of dialogue between the government and human rights organizations.

The northern problem

Despite the fact that both the government and the MFUA had signed the National Pact in April 1992, insecurity persisted in the northern regions of Mali. This situation stemmed from profound divisions within the MFUA, the difficulties of the national security forces to achieve control of the situation, and foreign intervention. By 1994, insecurity reached an intolerable level and the people were compelled to organize their own defense. Armed groups from both sides clashed. The political basis of the peace achieved through the National Pact was fragile, certainly in large part because influential actors such as nomad and agriculturalist leaders, as well as representatives from groups in the civil society in the north, had not been involved in the peace negotiations.

By allowing a direct dialogue between the different components of the society, the regional consultations helped to overcome the political deadlock. Because this dialogue took into account the genuine preoccupations of the population in the north, it has achieved a stable peace. Refugees have started to come home from neighboring countries and fighters have agreed to lay down their weapons and to re-start a productive civilian life. The government was able to achieve these results through the grass roots involvement of the people.

L'Espace d'Interpellation Democratique—EID

EID was instituted by the Malian government in December 1994. This is a forum in which members of human rights organizations, humanitarian agencies, and other nongovernmental organizations can question members of the government about their actions. An honorary jury composed of respected and independent personalities moderate a meeting during which questions pertaining to human rights, the situation in the state prisons, freedom of the press, etc., are raised and debated. After the meeting the jurors make recommendations to the government.

A Continuing Process

Since March 1991, the twin issues of economic development and pluralist democracy continue to challenge Mali's new democratic experiment. It would seem that a new perspective is needed on almost everything—the role of government and how it operates, the role of political parties and new political institutions, and the life of citizens, as well as a whole series of problems related to economic, social, and cultural well-being and relations. How can a democracy be nourished and flourish when its people are eroded by extreme poverty and illiteracy? What role should the media play in shaping the public debate?

The African political project in the coming decades must allow the people to realize their profound aspirations for a society of moral and material well-being with a life lived in liberty and dignity. This will require nothing less than a social transformation, but one that is grounded in an understanding of Africa's actual historical situation. To help bring about such a transformation, African states and Africa's political leaders must rediscover and recognize their role in service to their people as citizens. It is only on this condition that Africa will be able to participate with confidence in building our civilization for the twenty-first century.

In 1997, the government organized its second set of elections that resulted in the victory of Alpha Oumar Konaré and the ADEMA/PASJ. The organization of this election has shown the maturity of the Malian democracy. However, this democracy is still fragile because of the economic and ecological constraints on the country and the lack of a deep-rooted democratic culture among a largely illiterate population. Clearly, the Malian people must continue to confront numerous challenges for the consolidation and perfection of their new democracy.

Notes

1. When Alpha Oumar Konaré was elected president of the Third Republic on 8 June 1992, he became the fourth Malian head of state since political independence in 1960,

and followed Modibo Kéita (First Republic, 1960–68), Moussa Traoré (Second Republic, 1968–91), and Amadou Toumani Touré (president of the *Comité de Transition pour le Salut du Peuple, CTSP* [Transition Committee for National Safety], 1991–92).

The political forces that led to popular insurrection and the downfall of the Second Republic in March 1991 continued to create a turbulent political environment during the first two years of the Third Republic. Younoussi Touré, who formed the first government of the Third Republic in June 1992, was forced to resign less than a year later (in April 1993) because of the "school crisis." The successor government of Abdoulaye Sekou Sow lasted until February 1994, but with the accession of Ibrahim Boubacar Kéita, the government stabilized.

2. The Republican Pact was a political document intended to bring together the country's democratic political forces around a set of political principles that would guide governmental policies and programs in the new pluralist democracy. All the political parties of the parliamentary majority of the first government signed the document stating their acceptance of these principles.

3. The following initialisms are used in the text:

ADEMA/PASJ *Alliance pour la Démocratie au Mali/Parti Africain pour la Solidarité et la Justice*
BDIA   *Bloc Démocratique pour l'Intégration en Afrique*
CNID-FYT   *Congrès National d'Initiative Démocratique–Faso Yiriwa Ton*
MFUA   *Mouvements et Fronts Unifiés de l'Azawad*
PDP   *Parti Démocratique pour la Justice*
PLD   *Parti Libéral Démocrate*
PMD   *Parti Malien pour le Développement*
PRDT   *Parti du Renouveau Démocratique et du Travail*
PSP   *Parti Progressiste Soudanais*
PUDP   *Parti pour l'Unité, la Démocratie, et le Progrès*
RDP   *Rassemblement pour la Démocratie et le Progrès*
RDT   *Rassemblement pour la Démocratie et le Travail*
UDD   *Union pour la Démocratie et le Développement*
UFDP   *Union des Forces Démocratiques pour le Progrès*
UNDP   *Union Nationale pour la Démocratie et le Progrès*
US/RDA   *Union Soudanaise Rassemblement Démocratique Africain*

4. The quotations in this paragraph and the next two are taken from recorded speeches of President Alpha Konaré.

5. The National Pact was the agreement signed between MFUA – *Mouvements et Fronts Unifiés de l'Azawad* (United Front Movement of Azawad) and the Toumani Touré transition government (CTSP). Based on a series of intense negotiations between MFUA and CTSP mediated by Algeria, the pact was intended to serve as the basis for ending the northern rebellion.

6. As an extra-parliamentary way to show the extent of its popular support, the political opposition launched *opération ville morte* to shut down all economic activity (businesses, transportation) in Bamako and the regional capitals.

About the Contributors

R. James Bingen (Ph.D., Political Science, UCLA) is professor in the Department of Resource Development, Michigan State University. He lived in Ségou with his family in 1975–76 where he studied *Opération Riz-Ségou* with a grant from the Ford Foundation Foreign Area Fellowship Program. His publications on Mali include *Food Production and Rural Development in the Sahel: The Case of Opération Riz-Ségou*, a chapter on the OHVN in *Technology Transfer and Public Policy*, and numerous monographs and journal articles.

Andrew F. Clark (Ph.D., History, MSU) is associate professor of African and global history at the University of North Carolina at Wilmington. He has lived, traveled, and researched extensively in Senegambia, Guinea, and Mali. A revised version of Clark's dissertation, *From Frontier to Backwater: Economy and Society in the Upper Senegal Valley (West Africa), 1850–1920,* was published by the University Press of America. He is co-author of the *Historical Dictionary of Senegal* (2nd edition) and has written numerous journal articles on Senegambian and Malian history and society.

John Uniack Davis (Ph.D., Political Science, MSU) has spent more than five years living and working in West Africa. He is currently based in Niger, working as a consultant in the fields of democratic governance, monitoring, and evaluation. Davis's research and dissertation focused on local organizations and democracy in Mali.

Niama Nango Dembélé (Ph.D., Agricultural Economics, MSU) is visiting assistant professor of agricultural economics at MSU, based in Bamako, Mali. He directs MSU's USAID-funded program on strengthening agricultural market information and food policy analysis in Mali.

Salifou B. Diarra (M.S., Agricultural Economics, MSU) is director of Mali's agricultural market information system, the *Observatoire du Marche Agricole* (OMA). He has directed OMA, and its predecessor, the *Systeme d'Information sur le Marche* (SIM), since SIM's inception in 1989.

Cheick Oumar Diarrah (Doctorate, Political Science, University of Bordeaux) has been the ambassador from the Republic of Mali to the United States since 1995. Earlier he served as advisor to the Malian prime minister and chief of staff to the minister of National Education. His most recent publications include *Le défi démocratique au Mali* (Mali's Democratic Challenge) and *Vers la IIIème République du Mali* (Toward Mali's Third Republic), both published by Editions L'Harmattan, Paris.

Georges Dimithè (Ph.D., Agricultural Economics, MSU) was a visiting assistant professor in the Department of Agricultural Economics, MSU, after receiving his degree. He is currently an economist for the International Fertilizer Development Center, Muscle Shoals, Alabama, where he is helping to design a strategic framework for promoting the emergence and development of sustainable agricultural input supply systems in sub-Saharan Africa.

Josué Dioné (Ph.D., Agricultural Economics, MSU) is principal policy economist with the African Development Bank in Abidjan, Côte d'Ivoire, where he directs food security policy analysis. Dioné, who has held the rank of visiting associate professor of agricultural economics at MSU, is widely regarded as the leading West African expert on food security policy analysis.

Maria Grosz-Ngaté (Ph.D., Anthropology, MSU) is assistant director at the Center for African Studies, University of Florida (Gainesville). Her research has focused on social and cultural transformation in the Ségou region of Mali.

John Hanson (Ph.D., History, MSU) is associate professor of history at Indiana University, Bloomington. His publications include *Migration, Jihad and Muslim Authority in West Africa: the Fukane Colonies in Karta*, and *After the Jihad: the Reign of Ahmad al-Kabir in the Western Sudan*, edited, translated, and annotated with David Robinson. His current research includes work on Mande peoples living in Ghana.

Ghislaine Lydon is a Ph.D. candidate in history at Michigan State University. She recently spent twenty months doing research in West Africa (Mali,

Mauritania, and Senegal) and is now writing a dissertation on trans-Saharan trading networks in western Africa.

Nancy Mezey is a doctoral student in sociology at Michigan State University. Her areas of interest are families, sexualities, and African studies. As a Peace Corps Volunteer she lived in the Ségou region of Mali from 1988–90 and worked on agricultural and health/nutrition projects. Mezey returned to Mali in 1992 and in 1994 to conduct her master's research on health-seeking behavior in Sansanding. She is currently completing her dissertation.

David Rawson (Ph.D., Political Science, American University) was U.S. ambassador to the Republic of Mali from 1996 through 1999. He has held numerous posts in Africa since joining the U.S. Foreign Service in 1971, including U.S. ambassador to Rwanda. His publications include studies on foreign assistance, military governance, and trends in U.S. policy toward Africa. He is currently Distinguished Visiting Professor of Political Science, Hillsdale College.

David Robinson (Ph.D., History, Columbia) conducted research in Mali in 1976 and 1979, under the auspices of then-Minister of Culture Alpha Oumar Konaré, which culminated in his important study of an Islamic empire in Mali—*The Holy War of Umar Tal* (published in French as *La Guerre Sainte d'Umar Tal*). Robinson, in collaboration with Louis Brenner, also developed an inventory of a seminal Arabic library that was taken from Mali in 1890 by the conquering French, *La Bibliotheque Umarienne de Ségou*, which has been an invaluable resource for scholars.

John M. Staatz (Ph.D., Agricultural Economics, MSU) is professor of agricultural economics at Michigan State University. Since 1985 he has worked with other faculty, students, and Malian colleagues on issues related to food security research, outreach, and education in Mali and the Sahel region of West Africa; he is co-director of the USAID-MSU Food Security Cooperative Agreement. In addition to numerous articles and monographs on food security, Staatz is a co-editor of *International Agricultural Development*.

James F. Tefft (M.S., Agricultural Economics, MSU) works for MSU's Agricultural Economics Food Security Cooperative Agreement in Mali, first as technical assistant to the Cereal Market Information System, then in the *Institut du Sahel*'s food security unit. He currently works on the Food Security

II project, based in East Lansing, managing a research project on the links between agricultural productivity and nutrition in Mali.